PIGSKIN
NATION

SPORT AND SOCIETY

Series Editors
Randy Roberts
Aram Goudsouzian

Founding Editors
Benjamin G. Rader
Randy Roberts

A list of books in the series appears at the end of this book.

PIGSKIN NATION

How the NFL Remade AMERICAN POLITICS

JESSE BERRETT

UNIVERSITY OF
ILLINOIS PRESS
Urbana, Chicago, and Springfield

© 2018 by the Board of Trustees
of the University of Illinois
All rights reserved
1 2 3 4 5 C P 5 4 3 2 1
∞ This book is printed on acid-free paper.

Library of Congress Cataloging-in-Publication Data
Names: Berrett, Jesse Isaac, author.
Title: Pigskin nation : how the NFL remade American
    politics / Jesse Berrett.
Description: urbana : University of Illinois Press, 2018.
    | Series: Sport and society | Includes bibliographical
    references and index.
Identifiers: LCCN 2017048958| ISBN 9780252041709
    (hardback : alk. paper) | ISBN 9780252083327
    (paperback : alk. paper)
Subjects: LCSH: National Football League—History—
    United States—20th century. | Football—United
    States—History—20th century. | Football—Political
    aspects—United States. | Political culture—United
    States—History—20th century. | BISAC: SPORTS &
    RECREATION / Football. | HISTORY / United States /
    20th Century. | POLITICAL SCIENCE / Government /
    National.
Classification: LCC GV955.5.N35 B45 2018 | DDC
    796.332/64—dc23
LC record available at https://lccn.loc.gov/2017048958

E-book ISBN 978-0-252-05037-4

For Susan

For Dave + Kathy,

In appreciation.

Enjoy the acknowledgement!

Thanks again for all of your help.

With love and gratitude.

Contents

Acknowledgments

    One of my professors in college, Gerald Linderman, began the acknowledgments for his book on the experience of soldiers in the Civil War with the wonderfully concise phrase, "I owe much to many." I've always wanted to borrow that.

    I owe much to many. My thanks for initial help and encouragement from Christopher Loomis, Peter Olney, Michael Oriard, and David Wiggins. I especially appreciate Michael very generously *not* telling me not to bother, as his work had covered all of the bases, so to speak, after I sent him an extraordinarily vague exploratory email on this subject.

    Thanks to the archivists and curators whose expert help steered me through mazes of material. In roughly chronological order, my thanks to Tab Lewis at the National Archives; John O'Connell at the Ford Library; Cate Mayfield at the Mill Valley Library local history room; Melissa Bowman, Mary O'Leary, and Jonah Steinhart at Tam High; Peter Waack, Mike Rempter, Mary O'Brien, and Ed Galvin at Syracuse; Joe Smith and Charles Lamb at the Notre Dame archives; Kevin Haire and Michelle Drobik at Ohio State; Nancy Dewald at Penn State; Sheon Montgomery at the Texas Tech Vietnam Archive; David McCartney at the University of Iowa libraries; Jane LaBarbara and Kevin Fredette at the West Virginia and Regional History Center; Liz Novara at the University of Maryland; the staff of the Richard Nixon Library for helping me eventually fill out those forms more or less correctly; William Baehr at the FDR Library; Jim Rutter and

Alan George at Stanford; Lee Grady at the Wisconsin Historical Society; Lauren Leeman at the Missouri State Historical Society; Sean Benjamin at Tulane; Pam Eisenberg at the Nixon papers; Cliff Hight at Kansas State; Jane Klain at the Paley Center; and Carole Parnes at CBS. The interlibrary-loan staff at the San Francisco Public Library, which got to know me quite well, has repeatedly and generously dealt with my endless Link+ and ILL requests; finally, my local Presidio branch has always been a source of generosity and help.

Thanks to everyone whose precision and creativity taught me how much more I had to learn about research, particularly Peggy Ann Brown for her astonishing expertise in and around every archive and database in Washington, D.C.; Eric Wright for excellent assistance in the *Fairmont Times;* David Williams at the Wisconsin Historical Society; Mick Caouette in Minnesota; Mira Kohl at Tulane; Jared Lucky at Yale; and Scott Russell at the Nixon papers.

Thanks also to those who took the time to answer a question or five from someone they'd never heard of or met: Alex Belth and John Schulian for their inexhaustible well of knowledge about sportswriters and sportswriting; Saul Austerlitz for a random question about Chip Oliver; Peter Richardson for *Ramparts*; H. Bruce Franklin for pointing me to *Hearts and Minds*; Dan Daly for book suggestions; Liz Grady for explaining some of the ins and outs of photograph rights; Travis Vogan for his suggestions about screenshots; John Campbell McMillian for his encouragement and useful suggestions about where to look in the alternative press and whom to talk to; John Fortunato for his thoughts and comments on branding; Professor Emeritus Jerry Lewis, Alan Canfora, and especially Tom Grace, who went far above and beyond while putting the finishing touches on his own book, at and about Kent State. Thanks also to Richard Zitrin for sharing his often-painful memories of Kent State and Woody Hayes, and to George Solomon for his thoughts about sports journalism in the period. Thanks to Eric Miller for some thought-provoking suggestions about Christopher Lasch; Tom Dowling for his vivid and funny memories of crossing lances with Spiro Agnew and George Allen; Meredith Lair and Michael Kramer for explaining how USO tours worked and why I should not try to use unit newspapers; Phil Hetu at the Polynesian Football Hall of Fame for putting me in touch with Ray Schoenke; Ray Schoenke, for his memories and photographs of the McGovern campaign and 1970s Washington; Craig Fifer and Anna Leider in Virginia. It goes without saying that any remaining errors are my own.

At the University of Illinois Press, thanks to Danny Nasset for shepherding this project, and Danny and the anonymous readers for the press for helping me shape something out of the five-hundred-page monstrosity I originally attempted to inflict on readers. Thanks also to Kevin Cunningham, Tad Ringo, and Walt Evans for their expertise in getting the book ready for production. My gratitude to Susan Storch for indexing.

Among people I could impose on personally, thanks to Gale Jesi for explaining photographic techniques and to Marissa Rosenberg-Carlson for quick research assistance that saved me a trip. I'll get you that sundae someday. Charlene Li for helping me figure out how to get the book started; my colleague Sudie Sides for wisdom as a reader and human being that has taught me so much for so many years (and also for making me get rid of all those parentheses); Aram Goudsouzian for his generosity, support, and encouragement; Dave and Kathy Rosenberg-Wohl for reading over the manuscript and continually forcing me to rethink what I was doing and why I was doing it; my colleagues in the History Department at UHS past and present—Carolyn McNulty, Jenny Kline, Chris Martin, Ezra Davidson, Chuck Witschorik, David Roth, Justin Morgan Johnson—for getting me through the day with laughs and hot sauce. Thanks to everyone else who lent a sympathetic ear and especially Michael Holt and Scott Laughlin, who commiserated about how hard it is to write, let alone write well.

But my biggest debt is to my family. My parents, Josh and Lynne, have always been the biggest champions in my corner and were unstintingly enthusiastic supporters and press agents at every stage of the process. (And Dad's getting into Michigan for graduate school fifty years ago inadvertently set the stage for this project by making me forever a UM football fan.) Though we ended up not going with the title my brother Dan and I came up with while walking around Minneapolis, I learned a lot from him about how to write something that normal people might want to read, and I treasure our yearly baseball trips. Thanks to Isaac for allowing Dad to use the computer on occasion, and for all the terrible knock-knock jokes. But my biggest debt is to my wife, Susan Etlinger, who took time out of her own busy writing and speaking schedule to check in with me from the other side of the house, read various chapters, and hear me try out ideas. She believed in me even when I didn't believe in myself, and her love and faith kept me going on this project in the most fundamental sense. Maybe someday she'll even watch a football game with me. I couldn't have finished the book, or done much of anything, really, without her. It is gratefully dedicated to her.

Finally, to all of my students over the years, from those who said, "That sounds great! I'm totally going to read that!" to those who wondered, "What were you doing again?" to Erin, who supportively asked, "Why would you want to do *that*?!" (You just wait for my response to *your* first book!), my gratitude for encouraging and challenging me every day, and for making me love my job. A bunch of you promised to buy the book and have me autograph it. Guys, here's your chance.

INTRODUCTION
Football's Taking Over

"Poverty may make a comeback," [I said]. "Perhaps
it won't be called poverty, but they'll call it something else." "Maybe they could call it pro football,"
McAlister said. "Americans don't seem to lose interest in *that*." "Let's not lose our perspective," I said
angrily. "Pro football is not a joking matter."
—Art Buchwald, "Poverty Is Out"[1]

Pro football became America's game in the sixties. Everyone was
saying so. In April 1960, just as baseball season began, Roger Kahn observed a
profound cultural shift. Writing in *Sport* under the headline "Football's Taking
Over," Kahn saw "tremendous vitality" in the sport that had overtaken baseball. "[N]ations, like individuals, tire of certain games," he wrote. "The noise
is coming from the football fields." As if to punctuate the point, in December
1961 Redskins owner George Marshall bragged that his team was powering
a financial dynamo. Football was "more important to the nation's economy"
than baseball, he claimed, because it boasted "sex appeal."

Kahn's hypothesis quickly took on an aura of received truth inside the
Time-Life imperium. *Time* celebrated football's rise throughout the decade. Its
1962 cover story on Vince Lombardi ran a banner acclaiming "the sport of the
'60s": "no other sport offers so much to so many." Herbert Warren Wind wrote
in the *New Yorker* that month that Lombardi had shaped pro football "into a
game so precise, so tactically fascinating and deeply enthralling that today,
in the judgment of many observers, it has supplanted major-league baseball."

Two years after it dismissed college football as "a losing business," *Fortune*'s 1964 study of professional football's finances called the sport "wonderfully attuned to the pace and style of American life in the 1960s." By 1970, a *Time* editorialist relished "a mystique, an obsession, and a secular religion" that he shared with millions.

This argument was so trendy that Marshall McLuhan made it, observing in his 1964 book *Understanding Media* that "when cultures change, so do games" and using professional football to prove the proposition. In 1970, a Giants' game program asserted that "in Fall, football is the American way of life." Radicals agreed. Lefty Millman wrote in *Liberation News Service* that "the kind of sport that fits into today's America . . . incorporate[s] lots of bodily contact and a sophisticated use of strategy. . . . This is exactly what's happening [in] football." In 1965, a Harris poll documented that football had surpassed baseball in popularity, while Gallup delayed this recognition until 1972. When Richard Nixon told a crowd in Green Bay that "the 1960s will be described as the decade when football became the No. 1 sport," the number-one fan was merely adding a presidential signature to what a broad popular referendum had universally decreed.[2]

The NFL did not settle for its product's innate appeal. The league's print and visual arms spent the 1960s persuading readers and viewers that its brand was quintessentially American and perfectly in tune with the contemporary world. Clearly hoping for tangible evidence that this labor had borne fruit, the league commissioned Gallup's 1972 poll for $38,000. By any measure, NFL merchandisers were doing land-office business. One journalist counted 10,400 officially licensed items for sale in 1974. Why so many? Because football is "what makes this country great," an executive with one of the many official vendors explained. The league's burgeoning visual spectacles pushed that claim further, associating the NFL with patriotism, the military in Vietnam, even the Bicentennial. In a remark that cultural critics have cited repeatedly ever since, *Washington Star* columnist Mary McGrory summed up the consensus in 1975: "baseball is what we were, football is what we have become." No one who trots out this oft-recycled remark, however, addresses the context in which McGrory wrote it: she was responding to a much-mocked NFL essay contest, officially tied to the next summer's Bicentennial celebrations, that explicitly asked its teenage entrants to explore the league's role in American history. So McGrory's one-liner, offered in a tone of weary acceptance, attests just as much to the overtness of the NFL's unceasing efforts to promote its importance as to the mainstream success those efforts met.[3]

While it may seem strange to take the National Football League seriously as a purveyor of culture, treating the music, art, and movies of the 1960s as keys to popular feeling seems obvious by this point. Why not similarly credit the country's most popular sport as an equally important component of the period's mass-cultural environment—particularly when the NFL retained its own publishing house, movie studio, and lobbyists, and when those creators of culture consistently turned out work far more substantial and intellectually ambitious than it had any need to be? The league's promotional efforts—down to that essay contest—repeatedly argued that its brand of football was meaningful, provoking journalists, academics, and social critics to consider seriously the place of the sport in contemporary society, even if not all were ready to award it significance at the time. Nixon became a cog in the NFL's marketing machine just as much as he and his staff put it to their own uses. "We imagine pro football as a power grid, pulsating and popularly rooted," the president of NFL Properties told a reporter. "If it's a good product, everybody benefits." That's exactly what we expect to hear from a PR flack, but that doesn't mean he was wrong.[4]

The popular rootedness of pro football having been accepted as fact, it necessarily became a cultural factor. Masses and classes loved it, producing think pieces wrangling over why the sport resonated so widely. In 1967, radical journalist and future Students for a Democratic Society historian Kirkpatrick Sale penned a lengthy celebration of the middle linebacker for the *New York Times Magazine* adorned with quotations from, among others, Clausewitz, Eugene McCarthy, and Dick Butkus. William Phillips's 1969 essay in *Commentary* identified "the real thing, pro ball," as a "secret vice . . . the opiate of the intellectuals." The next year, the *New York Times* called it "the new obsession . . . a prime source of American literature." Even advertising and television danced to football's tune, with nationally famous players pushing light beer and car-rental agencies, and evening news remade by an aesthetic Roone Arledge had birthed on college football telecasts and honed on *Monday Night Football*.

Similar processes were taking place just then in political campaigning. Football and politics shared stylistic affinities, each merging spectacle and content. A new and influential band of campaign consultants compared their pastime to football, meaning not that it was brutal and violent but that it was dynamic, popular, hard-fought, and visually appealing. Their multipronged promotional efforts echoed those of the NFL by sending candidates to football games, encouraging players and coaches to endorse candidates and run for office, and stage-managing party conventions that conveyed competence and confidence through what were in essence scripted plays designed to create effective television. Gary Hart, George McGovern's campaign manager, called it "the Kennedy/Lombardi school": football became both a metaphor for American achievement and an effective means of reaching voters.[5]

The politics collectively created by the league and aspiring politicians absolutely sold appearance. But it is worth considering the substantive aspects of football's importance in American life as well. NFL football provided the field on which political players fought for dominance. These politics addressed and invigorated new audiences. So-called Middle Americans might be induced to vote for candidates who liked the game. Politically centrist players could act as engaged democratic citizens rather than merely hawk products. Traditionalist coaches and radical athletes like Dave Meggyesy, both inspired by what they considered the fundamental bloodthirstiness of American culture, found themselves gifted with megaphones through which to defend order or criticize the Vietnam War. Joe Kapp seized the opportunity to speak up for striking farmworkers.

That field definitely tilted right. Football readily lent itself to conservative political causes. Football players had broken strikes since the first Red Scare and were still sometimes called out to quell campus riots, and a White House memo urged the president to let a friendly journalist accompany him to a game because "the *Pro Football Annual* people are our voters." Chuck Benedict, the magazine's publisher, boasted that he was an "irrevocable, lifetime Nixonite" and vowed, "If there's any way I can assist in the next campaign, please try me!" Publicly and privately, the Nixon administration constantly invoked football. In his notorious 1971 memo delineating precisely "how we can use the available federal machinery to screw our political enemies," John Dean explained, "we do not need an elaborate mechanism or *game plan*." Noting the Republican habit of appropriating football's language and imagery, one sportswriter objected that "the right wing is replacing the single wing and the double wing."

Aggressive, violent, and rife with militaristic lingo, football seemed precisely the kind of institution any right-thinking lefty would disdain—"the cause of everything from unemployment to cancer," conservative Colts' line-backer Mike Curtis protested. "I never see that many short-haired people except pigs at a demonstration," a writer for the *Berkeley Tribe* sneered at the crowd cheering on Curtis's team. Meggyesy told dissenting GIs that "in exchange for this doubtful honor men do insane things like letting themselves get beat senseless each day on the gridiron or getting their shit blown away in Vietnam." In his campaign for governor of California, Timothy Leary promised to de-emphasize the game. Writers from the alternative press consistently reiterated the vision that football, as Austin's *The Rag* explained, was "not that far removed in its style and rhetoric from President Nixon justifying the violence in SE Asia." Distaste for such ties had seeped so deeply into the mainstream that the crowd booed when the Secretary of Defense ceremonially inducted eighty-eight young men, all of them wearing Packers booster hats, into the navy as part of pregame entertainment in 1973. "It was a sick scene," one journalist thought.[6]

But politicians like Robert Kennedy, Hubert Humphrey, and George McGovern eagerly sought endorsements, had pro players campaign on their behalf, and saw no contradiction between loving the sport and standing for civil rights and racial equality. When they weren't tying football to the war, alternative weeklies staged football games, *The Rag* inviting "hairy freaks" to join "a number of long-haired teams, and even hav[e] league competition." Asked to evaluate Meggyesy's criticisms, McGovern snapped, "That's a bunch of baloney."[7]

This interweaving of football and politics does not reflect a dumbing-down of American politics or merely replicate the standard narrative of post-'60s conservative realignment. Rather, we see a vigorous, and inconclusive, scrimmage among corporations, national politicians, and heretofore-obscure athletes in which no single participant—neither the NFL nor Richard Nixon nor a radical like Dave Meggyesy—succeeded in cementing a dominant political meaning for the nation's most popular sport. As with much of '70s culture, a huge array of actors inspired or horrified by upheavals inherited from the '60s fought directly and openly over the meaning of America. Was it a field of play where, as neoconservative intellectuals held, merit invariably won? Was it late-imperial Rome, a festival of bloodlust before the inevitable fall? Or perhaps a postmodern condition in which discourse trumped reality? Football's popularity less simplified this conversation than provided a new language that fomented broad debate. And the NFL, profit-minded entity that it was, officially endorsed multiple readings of its product by supporting each of these positions at various times.

Pigskin Nation focuses on the period between 1966 and 1974, during which football, politics, and culture entwined themselves in ever more complex ways. At the beginning of 1966, the NFL became the first professional league to send players to Vietnam as goodwill ambassadors. In October, congressional blessing of the AFL/NFL merger made the first Super Bowl possible, but only after a Louisiana delegation determined to wrangle a team for its home state outmaneuvered a Brooklyn congressman dubious about the merger's economic benefits for players. In November, Richard Nixon, the crucial political figure of the next decade, made his comeback by quarterbacking the Republicans to significant gains in the midterm elections. The next month, the NFL came in for wide public criticism for its players' magical ability to avoid active service in the war. By 1974, the United States had pulled its forces from Vietnam, Nixon had resigned, and even the *New Yorker* was mocking the Super Bowl as empty spectacle. But by then the notion that professional football was America's game, and thus indicated something significant about the country, had become conventional wisdom.

This book's first half follows the NFL's efforts to explain pro football's popularity to America at large, along with its attempts to steer the debate through print, television, and patriotic pageantry. Chapter 1 explores how league publications encouraged and attempted to manage a range of interpretations of professional football. These books set out a playing field and opened it for discussion. Even as liberal social observers worried about pro football's rising appeal, conservatives celebrated its meritocratic traditionalism, radicals found it terrifying, and journalists increasingly made fun of its pretentions to gravitas, David Boss's books conveyed the broad notion that football *mattered*. Chapter 2 discusses the impact of the 1960 CBS documentary *The Violent World of Sam Huff,* which treated professional football as a painful workplace, and NFL Films' subsequent reshaping of that story to celebrate the sport's spectacular aspects, ignore its physical toll, and mute individual players' ability to capitalize on their images. By 1967, thanks to NFL Films, football looked and sounded different on television than it had in 1957, and it meant different things. Chapter 3 then considers how the league created and shaped a mythology that served its cultural and political desires, an increasingly pressing need as the AFL and NFL engaged in various forms of anti-competitive behavior that would be much easier to accomplish if friendly officials could be persuaded that professional football had civic value and that there was benefit in doing favors for the NFL. By 1976, the league's vision of itself had been ratified by multiple governmental organs and officially sanctioned by the organization administering the Bicentennial.

As the NFL went about accumulating cultural capital, a broad array of political actors simultaneously strove to convert that capital into votes. The book's second half considers the variety of efforts these actors made to capitalize on professional football's popularity. Chapter 4 explores a range of responses to the notion of professional football as a cultural force. Campaign consultants compared their efforts to playing the game and tallied their won-lost records; politicians referred offhandedly to game plans and fourth quarters; journalists pondered what socially engaged sportswriting should cover and how they might critique or resist the cultural/political dynamo that the NFL had become. Chapter 5 delves specifically into Richard Nixon's notoriously passionate feelings about the sport, examining the ways in which it was at once an authentic, deeply meaningful experience for him and an inherently political means of polarizing the American public. Nixon and his staff invoked football and attendance at football games at strategic junctures throughout 1969 and 1970 to build a lasting political coalition, isolate the left, and cement Republican gains in Congress. Though Nixon's team grew increasingly adroit at positioning football in opposition to everything disordered and un-American, this strategy ultimately fell short of putting a new coalition in place. Chapter 6 discusses the rising prominence of athletes in political campaigns after 1960, culminating with a wave of football players who served as endorsers and proxy campaigners across the spectrum in the 1968 and 1972 presidential elections. Though in some cases athletes simply bolstered the candidate's regular-guy credentials, players like Ray Schoenke and Ed Podolak became deeply and authentically committed. Sam Huff and Jack Kemp, who stumped for presidential candidates and worked on political campaigns before entering races of their own, discovered the benefits and the limits of the celebrity that football had brought them.

The last three chapters point us toward the future. Chapter 7 traces the course of radical athletes who dropped out of professional football in hopes of finding their ways to a better world. Dave Meggyesy, most famously, became pro football's first public intellectual after writing a best-selling book chronicling the opening of his mind to the sport's violent authoritarianism. Publications boasting serious mainstream cachet reviewed these books and considered their implications for America more broadly. But none of these radical gestures, well-intentioned though they were, brought about the revolution. Instead, figures like Meggyesy revealed how this new political culture enabled figures on the left as well as the right to capitalize on celebrity and chart new modes of being. Similarly, chapter 8 considers the football coaches who became political figures in this period, to a degree far beyond any had before. Both Vince Lombardi and George Allen struck observers as appealing candidates, Lombardi in particular drawing interest from both left and right. But neither ever ran for office or had any real interest in doing so; instead, Lombardi predicted a different future entwining of sports and politics, in which both coaches and elected officials aspired to CEO status.

The epilogue traces the rise of Ronald Reagan, the politician best equipped to synthesize a new language from these materials. In 1980, his repeated appeals to "win one for the Gipper" returned the nation to earlier ways of thinking about what football, and therefore America, meant. He represented one possible result of this struggle, not its necessary conclusion. Reagan picked and chose unpredictably. He had played and broadcast football, but unlike Nixon, Reagan did not attempt to leverage those experiences into a tie to the common man. Nor did he celebrate football's vivid contemporaneity, or accent its authoritarian response to social problems. Instead, Reagan piled myth on myth, his (con)fusion with the role of George Gipp in the 1940 biopic *Knute Rockne, All American,* the role that made his career, underpinning a hazy nostalgia that placed football deep in the nation's past. In his hands, football stood for a simpler, more primal, almost pre-capitalist America. Yet Reagan's imagery, built as it was on his role in a movie, blurred commerce, reality, and fantasy every bit as much as did the ideas of his predecessors. The argument was by no means over, but for the time being he had settled these debates and revealed how the sport of the '60s could remain relevant well into the '80s.

PART I

MAKING FOOTBALL IMPORTANT

1

No Football Fans, Just Football Intellectuals

Football is unique among American sports . . . and as played by professionals in the past decade, it has replaced baseball as our national sport. We may be trying to tell ourselves something.
—Thomas Morgan, "The American War Game"[1]

In the 1950s, serious people didn't pay attention to professional football. Only four of the more than 150 articles in the *New York Times'* massive collection of sports pieces from its first century, published in 1951, concerned the NFL, and Allison Danzig's 1956 *History of American Football* described only the college variety. The nonfan majority dismissed it as little more than barely regulated mayhem. What Steelers' coach Chuck Noll labeled a "criminal element" in the 1970s, a charge that landed him in court on charges of slander and libel, ruled the field. Forty-niners linebacker Hardy Brown, a notorious "black hat," knocked out twenty-one opponents in twelve games in 1951. *Life* depicted "Savagery on Sunday" in 1955—so insultingly that two members of the Eagles won libel suits against the magazine. The trial offered this inspiring example of self-defense from Bucko Kilroy, who had been ejected from a game in 1948 for kneeing the opposing center in the groin: "It is all according to what you mean by kicking." Fans did their part to live up to this reputation: a riot in San Francisco after a 1958 Colts–49ers tilt required eighteen radio cars, twenty motorcycle policemen, and eight patrol wagons to put down.

Forty-niners' owner Vic Morabito, alarmed by rumors that fans intended to "get him," summoned a police escort to get home safely.[2]

Within fifteen years, these terms changed drastically. By 1970, to a surprising number of intellectual admirers, professional football served as a resonant image of precise, disciplined application of force. What one magazine admiringly termed "complex violence" made pro football worth thinking about, and worth thinking with. Formerly eminent college-football writers suddenly found themselves "having to apologize for their existence," wrote one observer. The sport's literature exploded in the 1960s, general-interest magazines giving it heavy coverage and specialty magazines catering to the devoted fan. Books poured from the presses, and prestigious cultural critics turned their eyes to the pro game, even if they often did not like what they saw. This vigorous and highly varied production posed significant challenges for the NFL's promotional apparatus.

David Boss, an idiosyncratic visionary who imprinted his personal stamp on what could well have been mere boilerplate, oversaw the league's publishing arm, the Creative Services Division. His products aimed for a hip, plugged-in readership. Without intending anything as complex as Pop Art's simultaneous critique and embodiment of mass-mediated fabrications, his productions aspired to and gestured in that direction. Boss's work was corporate propaganda—a Coke can rather than Warhol's paintings of Coke cans—but corporate propaganda that often boasted unexpected intellectual heft.[3]

NFL Creative did not just produce but actively solicited interpretations; it was in the business of getting outsiders to think seriously about NFL football. This created a challenge: intellectuals and journalists uninvested in the league's bottom line often ascribed enormously different, and often unflattering, meanings to the same events. All of these perspectives abstracted from players' experiences of the game, approaching the game as spectacle or drama far more often than as lived experience. The league had no problem with this—it just wanted to limit what those abstractions were. In an intermittently successful attempt to wrest control of the narrative, the NFL spent the '60s working out how to assert its historical importance and cultural value with enough clarity to blunt intellectuals' worst criticisms, yet retain enough vagueness to avoid tying itself to any particular political persuasion.

By the early 1970s, its print productions aggressively defined the relation between NFL football and American culture by gathering up frequently diametrically opposed arguments and asserting a larger claim: professional football was vigorous, heroic, fair, painful, but necessary—*the* essential expression of a complex and multifarious America. The NFL attracted serious consideration of its product, but its lack of control over the means of intellectual production meant that quite a few of those considering the significance of professional football came to conclusions that the league would have preferred they not reach.

Savagery to Science

Michael Oriard, who has read more journalistic coverage of the sport than anyone, notices "a dramatic shift" in visions of the NFL late in the 1950s. In part this came about because pro football actually *was* less violent, for PR and practical reasons: the reign of the "Black Hats" ended, spurred by increased public awareness of their brutality (especially the *Life* pictorial) and by the precision of Vince Lombardi's offenses, which remorselessly punished headhunters who failed to fill their assigned lanes on defense. College football did its part by enduring its most trying days yet. "Is college football destroying itself?" *Readers Digest* wondered in 1959. The scandals pocking the decade provoked broad recognition of the gaping disparities between the ideal of amateurism and the reality of multiple student-athletes' cheating, boosters' amassing slush funds to pay players, and coaches' eviscerating their schools' academic requirements nationwide—a repeated, and repeatedly transient, theme since the 1880s. The breadth of such wrongdoing impelled mainstream media outlets to discover a renewed appetite for critical coverage. "Too Much Football" might induce a "Football Headache," prompting exasperated onlookers to contemplate "The Hypocrisy of College Football." Hugh McElhenny, whom the University of Washington had enriched to the tune of $30,000 and three cars, admitted, "Hell, I can't afford to graduate." His 49ers teammates joked that he took a pay cut to join them—a one-liner that painted professional players as, ironically, both more upstanding and less well-compensated than their collegiate counterparts.[4]

That avalanche of hypocrisy impelled journalists to suddenly discern redemptive qualities in the pro game's "flowering of violence and exactitude," as *Life* put it. And not a moment too soon. Judging from books like *The Decline of the American Male* (1958) and films like *Rebel Without a Cause* (1955), the average American man was a pathetic shrimp dominated by women and frightened of even the meekest assertion of autonomy. But professional football was here to save the day. The *New York Times* wrote that "the magnificence of the spectacle, the artistry of the performances and the savagery of the play" in the championship game "could not help but make converts of any who had not previously seen the light." Modern celebrity professionals date to this period: Johnny Unitas was the first pro football player to be more famous than any college player. *Time*'s November 1959 cover story, "A Man's Game," featured the granite face of Giants middle linebacker Sam Huff, only the second NFL player to appear there, and exclaimed over the exotic mammals on the field: "mountains of muscle" manning the defensive line; linebackers, "agile as jungle cats"; "lean, whippet-fast" defensive backs; "magnificently muscled" Jim Brown. Pro football, argued the magazine, was "a game of precise and powerful virtuosity." Huff passed on less virtuosic counsel to the young people of America: "Play as hard and vicious as you can" to avoid injury. Though the "unspoken code" is that "there is no deliberate intent to maim," noted *Time*, "even at its cleanest, pro football is a game of awesome violence."[5]

Popular-magazine editors felt a particular fondness for the notion of pro football as a manly yet highly technical profession ("a school of violence," the *New York Times* had it), repeatedly publishing more or less the same article over the next decade and usually teasing the story on the cover. The same month that *Time* profiled Huff, the *Saturday Evening Post* ran a piece in which hardbitten Steeler quarterback Bobby Layne warned, "This is no game for kids. You have to be a man and be treated like one." *Life* ran five minimally different stories between 1960 and 1972, with topics as similar as "Battle Cry: Get the Quarterback!" (1961) and "Suicide Squad: Pro Football's Most Violent Men" (1971), illustrating the latter feature with a photo spread showing players getting walloped in gruesome detail. The October 1966 cover story in *Life* extolled linemen's "delicate violence, using skills as precise as they are brutal and blunt." Perian Conerly even joked in 1963 that she should title her journal of life as the wife of the Giants quarterback *Massacre on Sunday: A Searing Indictment of Pro Football*. The bad old days were now fodder for winking nostalgia.[6]

Suddenly, professional football was popular. (Mary McGrory called it a cult.) But why? The quantity of arguments *for* its exploding appeal was surpassed only by explanations *of* that appeal. In the late '60s, coverage changed again: now football was not just violent and technical but also interesting. "There are no football *fans* anymore," one journalist wrote in 1971, just "football intellectuals." While that was obviously not the case, a wave of thinkers began to wax sociological about the game's appeal, pointing to the consolations of the lonely crowd, the need for clarity, the development of a new consciousness, or some atavistic desire for pleasures the modern world denied.

This marked a significant change. College football, with its national profile, array of scandals, and cultural cachet, had attracted serious attention from social critics, muckrakers, celebrity correspondents, and activists since the 1880s. Professional football had drawn sporadic interest, most notably from the communist and African American journalists who forced the newly relocated Los Angeles Rams, and eventually the entire NFL, to reintegrate from the late 1940s onward. But in general it was a newspaper backwater, the toy department's toy department. Frank Gifford ruefully recalled that when he joined the Giants, not a single one of New York's eight dailies bothered to assign a reporter to the team, relegating coverage to a collection of "second-stringers moonlighting between baseball seasons." Don Weiss, the NFL's head of Super Bowl promotion, noted that when Rozelle took over, many papers simply ran league press releases verbatim, a phenomenon journalist Leonard Shecter found easy to explain: "Sports editors were content to put their weakest men on pro football . . . [and] suddenly found themselves with out-of-fashion writers covering an in-fashion sport." Lest this read as Shecter's habitual cynicism, Weiss himself agreed that at the time the "least experienced, least talented" writers walked the NFL beat. In Peter Gent's satirical *North Dallas Forty*, the local paper's pro football reporter "usually stumble[d] into the press box about midway through the third quarter, pick[ed] up the play-by-play sheet, and beg[a]n to write his story. That year he won three national awards for outstanding sports journalism."[7]

The resulting critical awakening produced a broad and diverse range of writing. *Sports Illustrated* was the first to upgrade its coverage to match the NFL's improved output. The magazine devoted extensive space after 1960 to what its editor had "a strong hunch . . . is our sport. We have grown with it, and each of us is a phenomenon of the times." Pro football books of the '60s capitalized on the phenomenon with lush technocratic productions, even coffee-table volumes like Joe Namath's *A Matter of Style* bursting with page upon page of detailed play diagrams that it was assumed would make sense to the reader. A number of think pieces by intellectuals pondered what exactly the game meant for a changing America. Adversarial journalists took heed of pro football's exploding popularity and warned darkly of its dangerous consequences.

It remained unclear exactly who read these pieces. The football audience was presumed to be the best and the brightest: sophisticated, powerful, in the know, comfortable with intricacy. At the same time, political analysts were calling sport the preferred pastime of the middle American, catharsis for lumpen, violent masses whose appreciation demanded no deeper reflection than did, say, demolition derby. (This proved a particularly tricky paradox for player/politicians like Sam Huff and Jack Kemp to negotiate.) "Lower middle-class virtues" undoubtedly "play a part in whatever orderliness there is in daily American life," one social critic wrote. "They help make football a high-salience issue and foreign affairs a low-salience issue." Defending the rights and pride of "unmeltable ethnics" against a wave of WASP condescension, Michael Novak found the sport "a metaphor for the gap between intellectuals and ethnic peoples." Could it serve the classes *and* the masses? These perspectives most clearly conflicted after Super Bowl V, which experts uniformly mocked for its inept play and ardent fans loved for its exciting last-second finish. "What do you want: good drama or good form?" one journalist asked. Most of the time, these two groups talked past one another.[8]

The NFL had to figure out whom its products should address—intellectuals? Middle Americans? Both, somehow? But first it had to construct the apparatus that would turn out that product. NFL Enterprises, the first modern promotional organization, was incorporated in October 1959 at the behest of someone outside the organization, an executive for Roy Rogers. The ascension to power of Pete Rozelle, the first commissioner who had neither played football nor owned a team, set the league on course toward mainstream popularity. "He is a child czar," John Lardner wrote, but "he thinks quickly and moves smoothly."

Coming from the world of public relations, Rozelle saw the league's primary challenge as one of managing perception—an insight so revolutionary in this context that journalist Jerry Izenberg compares him "as a visionary" to P. T. Barnum, "but he always sold reality, not illusion." Rozelle's vision fundamentally held that "anything that caused people to connect with pro football, and created positive associations with the sport, could only help in the long run." One media and communications scholar calls him "instrumental in defining the current sports brand" for the NFL. (A few years later, consultants and image managers began to bring the same modes of thinking to the political sphere.) An intuitive promoter, Rozelle modeled his efforts in each area on those of Walt Disney, who had expanded a single product into a multimedia empire. But Izenberg got it slightly wrong: Rozelle adroitly created a particular vision of the league that, while hardly illusory, strategically advanced not reality but rather the story the NFL wanted to be told. He also, as Travis Vogan points out, fundamentally changed the notion of who the NFL commissioner was and what he should do.[9]

He instituted immediate changes, both symbolic and practical, to start producing those stories. On the night in 1960 that he was chosen after an exhausting twenty-three ballots, Rozelle's first official move was a vow to relocate the league office and its staff of seven from the back room of a bank in Bala Cynwyd, a Philadelphia suburb chosen for no better reason than that it was a six-minute drive from previous commissioner Bert Bell's house, to Rockefeller Center in New York, close by networks and advertising agencies. The rival AFL made the same move in 1963. The endgame was to supplant baseball as the national pastime. Rozelle "very consciously and privately" uncorked a bottle of champagne at the end of every baseball season and had a single promotional goal in mind for the first Super Bowl: "for people to wind up believing how much better this game experience was than the World Series." Within a decade, he had achieved his goal.

He began by controlling impressions. In the spring of 1961, Rozelle convinced Jim Kensil of the Associated Press to cross over and become the NFL's first PR director. By the start of the season, Kensil ("the most underrated, most forgotten sports executive in the history of this country," according to Ernie Accorsi, who spent three decades in and around NFL front offices) was tutoring the print media in how to tell stories the NFL way. Rozelle's ulterior motive, a longtime associate explained, was less to control coverage than to induce favorable reporting through good will: helping writers do their jobs would make them fans who were "less inclined to go out of their way to criticize us." Replacing the modest mimeographed weekly summaries Bell's office had sent to papers in NFL cities, which one journalist dismissed as "about an exciting as an evening watching a fly crawl up a drape," Kensil steered the reporters' narrative of the game's significance by using Teletype to issue centralized pregame reports to outlets across the nation that contained up-to-date statistics, notable stories about the teams involved, records of their previous meetings, and keys to the game.

These pregame reports became standard travel equipment—so much so that late-'60s dossiers for President Nixon and Vice President Agnew contain copies of these reports for whichever game they were attending. Players on USO tours of Vietnam, and the league they represented, were similarly heralded. Rozelle relied so heavily on Kensil, who phoned him more than ten times a night at the beginning of their collaboration, that he called him "my offensive and defensive coordinator." Kensil was one of many Rozelle hires who were adept at selling the sport. At one point in the '60s, every league official with policy-making authority had previous experience in public relations. And these measures worked: reporters who covered the NFL in the 1960s and early '70s regularly celebrated the "greatest PR staff . . . any sports general ever had" for establishing "the smoothest operation in the world of sports." More recently, a business-school professor has agreed, lionizing the NFL leadership's exemplary "continuity, purpose, and diligence," its "open and forthright manner" of choosing its leaders, and its "laserlike focus on fan experience."[10]

Rozelle's "ability to put his fingers on an idea whose time had come was uncanny," Frank Gifford recalled. In 1963, he created NFL Properties to regulate usage of the league's name and avoid diluting its appeal. "It occurred to me," Rozelle told a confidant, "that someday I would walk into a supermarket and see NFL toilet paper or into a drug store and find an NFL jock-itch remedy. Enough was enough." In that year the Pro Football Hall of Fame opened in Canton, Ohio, giving the game an official narrative of its history and a pilgrimage site. Rozelle simultaneously faced down a gambling scandal by suspending stars Paul Hornung and Alex Karras, a measure *Sports Illustrated* honored by naming him Sportsman of the Year in early 1964 for salvaging the credibility of "the sporting phenomenon of our time."

Behind the scenes, Rozelle began to amass cultural and political capital by sending players to Vietnam, distributing NFL Films to influential institutions throughout the world, and building connections in Washington and on Wall Street. In 1961 he ("as skillful a politician as I have seen in my life," according to Jack Kent Cooke) began enforcing the notion of "League Think," inducing the owners to follow the AFL's example and sign a collective TV contract evening out the enormous gaps between markets as disparate as Green Bay and New York; equally important, he successfully lobbied Congress to allow the NFL to perpetrate revenue sharing, a clear antitrust violation that did much to ensure competitive balance. He later said that "borrowing" the AFL's policy represented "the most important thing that I have done as commissioner." Rozelle then faced down the most obstreperous owners, Washington's George Marshall and Chicago's George Halas, cementing his unquestioned authority. Five years later, similar legerdemain, and granting of a franchise to New Orleans, smoothed the similarly anticompetitive AFL-NFL merger. Jerry Izenberg recalled how effectively Rozelle controlled the story, preventing leaks by promising him "every single thing that happened, inside stuff" if he just held off for a few days: "I would've been an idiot to write it. So I didn't."[11]

The groundwork had been laid. But at the time, outsiders were still defining what the NFL was and which audiences it served. By the mid-'60s, the consensus was clear: football was a game for highbrows and social climbers. "How many working stiffs can afford season tickets?" wondered *TV Guide*. The sport's complexity, and by extension elitist appeal, was taken for granted. Football writer Bob Curran complained about the "cult of football snobs . . . that has given pro football a language that reads like a code and has enveloped the game in a mystique that has made the players shadowy mechanical figures." Another journalist wrote in 1968 that baseball was "a game for kids, cab-drivers pulling long night shifts and the old Jewish men who stand on Flatbush Avenue outside Garfield's Cafeteria. It's a beer drinker's game." Football, on the other hand, had "snob appeal . . . everyone uses war game parlance as if they were bastard sons of Robert McNamara. . . . The season ticket holders are the ad boys with their plaid-covered flasks." Jerry Izenberg dismissed "the fraudulent mystique of a brotherhood . . . which operates on the theory that only a brain surgeon can understand the 'real game.'" Frederick Exley's *A Fan's Notes* centers on his worship of the Giants of the early 1960s, "my delight, my folly, my anodyne, my intellectual stimulation," whom he watched every week while issuing "an unceasing, pedantic commentary . . . on the character of the game."

Was the NFL leaving Main Street for Wall Street? Hunter S. Thompson mourned that the pleasure that had seduced him a decade before, "a very hip and private vice to be into," was ruined. He loved squeezing into ramshackle neighborhood Kezar Stadium to cheer for the 49ers alongside 30,000 "extremely heavy drinkers," at least 10,000 of whom "were out there for no reason except to get involved in serious violence." In far-off Candlestick Park, he suffered the same upper-middle-class stuffed shirts he'd endured recently in Oakland: "a sort of half-rich mob of nervous doctors, lawyers, and bank officers who would sit through a whole game without ever making a sound." Sportswriters scorned the Cowboys' luxurious Texas Stadium, opened in 1971, as "the House of Greed" and goggled at "people mill[ing] about with their cocktails" in the halls, "as if they were at a convention in a hotel." In 1973, *New York* pointed out that Wall Street had been going "bananas over sports" since the mid-60s, with Merrill Lynch discovering that its biggest producers shared a "strong interest in spectator sports, especially football."[12]

A Violent Answer to Dullness

Some intellectuals now found pro football worth consideration. Every generation of thinkers has its fads; in the '50s, the little magazines in New York were preoccupied by what "mass culture" was, how and if it might be sliced into better and worse varieties, whether or not vigilant policing could counteract its dangers. While it would be ludicrous to argue that football replaced mass culture as the subject of predominant intellectual interest, there are enough of these pieces to suggest serious intellectual engagement with the topic. The terms changed as the concerns of the day developed, but the fundamental sense that football posed a cultural problem that needed to be diagnosed—or celebrated, or pathologized, or some combination of both—ran through these pieces.

The other major change was that intellectuals began to write as fans, first hesitantly and then proudly, rather than disinterested students of social formations; halfway or so through the piece would come the claim to authority attained through actually watching football games *for fun* rather than as a matter of intellectual responsibility. Writing about football as an intellectual demanded that you, at some point, turn off your brain and just *feel*. "As a fan, I can only sneer at someone who wants to turn a great football game into listening to Mozart," one critic wrote. In multiple ways, we see further proof of pro football's strengthened hold on the popular imagination, along with its ability to convince fans to blunt their own critical faculties, but also the alarming prospect for the NFL that such a wide variety of thinkers could well imagine things the league would rather they not consider.[13]

The most popular arguments struggled to value precisely the cathartic and expressive truths that the NFL expressed. Thomas Morgan's "The Wham in Pro Football," which ran in *Esquire* in 1959, extolled the "controlled violence" and "brutal rhythm" that provided "a violent answer to dullness" for spineless organization men who "ought to get away from" their families and renew their sense of self, a difficult feat in big cities. Football—whether watched or played—represented one of the last bastions of manly independence in a pallid, conformist America. Yet Morgan did not seem wholly sold on the game's beneficial qualities, concluding that "whether we should also be hearing the clang of doom and cries of Christians in the arena is any man's guess."

Richard Schickel's 1969 piece in *Commentary* similarly understood it as satisfying "some psychological needs of post-industrial man that may not be assuaged unless he should carelessly manage to turn himself into post-civilized man." Football provided "clear-cut resolution," a release from "the tensions of ambiguity" through indulgence of "traditional, untrammeled American virtues" that seemed especially necessary in the harsh conditions of the upper Midwest, where life was "graceless and effortful," just like the region's most popular game, a game invented and still fundamentally owned there. It was Frederick Jackson Turner's frontier thesis, outfitted in cleats and a helmet. William Phillips's piece in the same magazine later that year agreed, locating pro football's popularity in "the fact that it makes respectable the most primitive feelings about violence, patriotism, manhood. The similarity to war is unmistakable. . . . There is even a general draft." Both men consciously wrote as fans as well as cultural critics; Schickel calls the Packers "the only part of my heritage that I care very much about anymore," and Phillips went on to simultaneously boast of and mourn his attachment to the consistently mediocre Giants: "It is hard to invest your competitive feelings in a team that's a success when it wins more than it loses. . . . But the Giants are all I have."[14]

Rather than adding new elements to this mix, intellectual appreciations of pro football over the decade after Morgan's article mixed the same ingredients in different proportions. Given the changing tenor of the wider culture, it is no surprise that in the late '60s Maileresque meditations on the redemptive possibilities of violence came more and more to the fore. James Toback's new-journalistic hagiography of Jim Brown theorized that "baseball had become slow and dull. . . . Basketball was fast, but promised more than it finally yielded, legally repressing the violence it suggested at every turn. . . . Only football constituted a full and satisfactory transformation of energy." Radicals frequently found this horrifying. "That football has replaced baseball as our national pastime indicates only that our increased metabolism has ruptured our sensibility," one wrote. Even determinedly centrist pieces like Champ Clark's 1970 appreciation in *Time*, which relished football's ruggedly American democracy of outcome—"this game is no stacked deck, like the stabbing to death of a wounded bull"—recognized "love of violence, including the spillage of blood" as central to the sport's mystique, something that appealed to both sexes.[15]

Thomas Edwards's "The Sporting Gripe," published in *Partisan Review* in 1971, presented the most unusual perspective (hardly a surprise in this most resolutely independent of little magazines), and one that also appeared, oddly enough, in NFL Creative productions. Edwards thought that the majority of sociopolitical claims being made about the sport were overblown. Football was not war or politics or anything besides itself: to see politics "at the expense of the particular and obvious qualities of the object observed . . . is dangerous, impoverishing nonsense." He saw sport as just as much "a form of art" as of war, assuming that one defined art not through "lingering elitist resonances" but in the fullest Pop sense—to any broadminded spectator, "good journalism, pop music, film, commercial design, advertising and so forth" were just as fulfilling aesthetically as a great football game. He held that "to make sport directly represent American life is not a very good way of understanding what's wrong with that life." Instead, Edwards argued, sport represented at its core a pure expression of intent, "an idea of terribly difficult perfection that can't be named in words."[16]

The 1975 essay contest on the NFL's role in American history, part of the league's attempt to hitch a ride on the Bicentennial, attracted widespread mockery. But this entirely fair question, even if clumsily put, provoked at least one response of lasting value. The *Washington Star* garnered responses from "recognized and eminent scholars of American history," several of whom (historian of the South C. Vann Woodward, colonial historian Bernard Bailyn, political historian James MacGregor Burns) did not feel qualified to answer. "Why would an historian necessarily know anything about the National Football League?" Burns wondered. But intellectual historian Christopher Lasch, who had stopped watching because he thought the NFL tedious and predictable, found the question fascinating: "God, you could do a lovely piece on the professionalization of sports. You could show how it grew as an industry. . . . I wouldn't want to dismiss it as trivial, because it really is big business, and you can never dismiss the importance of big business." His thinking stimulated by the question—and possibly piqued, suggests Lasch's biographer, by its easy dismissal by nearly all of the other panelists (among whom was his father-in-law, Henry Steele Commager)—Lasch continued his answer in the 1979 bestseller *The Culture of Narcissism,* which devoted an entire chapter to the "degradation of sport" over previous decades.[17]

The kind of modesty Thomas Edwards suggested tended not to appeal to most critics of the game, who of course wanted to show off their acumen at establishing a particular significance for professional football. Observers loved football, hated football, thought it signified a great deal, denied that it meant anything. To the extent that a consensus existed, it was that football was violent, and that said violence reflected cultural truths that were ennobling, troubling, or both at once. There was plenty for the NFL to work with.

A Game for Our Time

All of these perspectives so obviously demanded acknowledgment that Don DeLillo's 1972 novel *End Zone* split the difference, parodying liberal and conservative perspectives yet endorsing the fundamental truth that football means ... something. Before embarking on a play-by-play summary of the climactic contest between undefeated powerhouses Logos College and West Centrex Biotechnical, the author breaks the fourth wall: "The spectator, at this point, is certain to wonder whether he must now endure a football game in print—the author's way of adding his own neat quarter-notch to the scarred bluesteel of combat writing. The game, after all, is known for its assault-technology motif, and numerous commentators have been willing to risk death by analogy in their public discussions of the resemblance between football and war."

DeLillo explains that "this sort of thing is of little interest," quoting one of the novel's characters, who later remarks that "we don't need substitutes because we've got the real thing." Instead, he says, "sport is a benign illusion, the illusion that order is possible. It's a form of society that is rat-free and without harm to the unborn," before circling back around, in the most basic sense, to the notion that "here is not just order but civilization": that football's jargon and line calls fulfill the spectator's need for meaning, a sense (false though it may be) that the world is fundamentally intelligible. DeLillo's book, oversupplied with symbols of militarization and violence, makes every contemporary interpretation of football's significance into a joke, but in doing so he endorses the meaning-making that they represent.[18]

Ironically, this satire best captures the spirit in which the league itself approached the notion of football's significance. David Boss, director of NFL Creative and the league's point man on these issues, responded cannily to divided and contradictory interpretations of what the NFL meant. "More than any single person," Boss is responsible for "changing the state of sports graphics in this country," a colleague recalled. When the NFL Hall of Fame presented him with its Daniel F. Reeves Pioneer Award in 1992, the citation emphasized his creation of "an Image-Enhancing Concept New to Professional Sports." His productions granted some truth to almost every proposition above. This falls within limits, of course: Boss was hardly in the business of supporting anyone who assailed football's underpinnings as fascist; the NFL was just as invested as were conservative critics and politicians in drawing lines between acceptable and unacceptable. But many of his books admit that the quantity of aggression demanded and celebrated in football suggests something troubling about American culture. Boss took what could easily have amounted to dross turned out in bulk to sell the pro game and produced a series of substantive and complex books that reflect a surprisingly fluid adjustment to quickly changing cultural norms.

In the attempt to cater to a new, clued-in demographic, Boss's efforts bear crucial similarities to the changes sweeping commercial culture at the time. Columbia Records' notoriously ham-fisted "The Man can't bust our music" 1968 ads represent the low point of a major corporation's attempt to masquerade as the voice of the people, but the period's most innovative advertisers compellingly offered the public "authenticity, individuality, difference, and rebellion" through products like the Volkswagen Beetle. Many of those advertisers hired on for political campaigns; in 1968, Hubert Humphrey retained Doyle Dane Bernbach, whose accounts included Volkswagen and Avis. Campaign consultant Joe Napolitan told Mike Wallace on a special episode of *60 Minutes* in 1970 that he "didn't know anything about government." "Electing candidates, that's my business," he boasted, and he would tell people what they needed to hear without tipping into pure pandering. Boss pulled off an equally tricky balancing act, overseeing unapologetically mass-produced productions that sold an institution as obviously unrevolutionary as the NFL while offering up subversive and resistant notions of America at the same time. They too retailed the sport as "American" in almost any way you chose to define the term.[19]

In 1969, Boss oversaw *The First 50 Years: The Story of the National Football League*, a handsome oversized history dedicated to "the American spirit, which has reflected this most courageous, complex and creative game to reflect and challenge itself." The book opens with a flourish—seven Pop-arty full-page spreads, ranging from close-ups of players' faces to solarized shots of linemen clashing to receivers high-stepping into the end zone to blurry attempts to capture the sensation of being tackled—that convey just how now and with-it football is. Inside, a colorful infographic presents a timeline of NFL history, detailed and complex play and formation diagrams explain the evolution of tactics, a capsule narrative goes decade-by-decade, full-color spreads introduce us to sixteen great players and ten important games, and more. The book aims to locate football firmly in respectable culture, to impress the visitor with the owner's taste and intelligence, dignifying and elevating the purchase of a sports book. One reviewer called it "positively breath-taking" in parts.[20]

A comparison to the non-Rozelle world highlights just how effectively official NFL productions sold particular notions of professional football. Once the league entered public consciousness, histories began to appear in profusion: Tex Maule and Robert Riger's *The Pros: A Documentary of Professional Football in America* in 1960, Robert Smith's *Pro Football: The History of the Game and the Great Players* and Spike Claassen's *History of Professional Football* in 1963. Yet another of these volumes, Maule's 1963 book *The Game*, also abundantly illustrated, superficially resembles Boss's productions. It begins with twenty-five pages of full-color photographs, adds black-and-white shots on nearly every page inside, and covers team and league histories and the development of formations. Without being asked, Maule sanitizes less-appealing aspects of NFL history. He does not touch on the issue of segregation when discussing the Rams and Browns, who broke the color barrier in the NFL and AAFC, and even seems to sympathize with Redskins owner and unrepentant segregationist George Marshall, who "was criticized for not drafting Negro football players. He defended himself by saying that if the proper Negro player were available, he would draft him. Strong pressure put on him by various groups solidified his resentment." But unlike Boss's books, Maule has no larger project beyond the assertion that "professional football has become America's national sport." He defends the NFL's reputation without reaching outside the game for significance: pro football started out small and got bigger. That's the story.[21]

Boss, in contrast, puts across the party line, as much verbally as visually. An introductory section expands on what the opening photos have already taught us: in many ways, professional football is "a game for our time." More precisely, these opening pages try out any available theory to explain the sport's appeal—historical, religious, cultural, political, anthropological. The sheer number of ideas the book throws at the reader suggests not desperation, but the expectation that something, it doesn't especially matter what, will stick in a useful way. We see here a deft repurposing of nearly every interpretation offered up by intellectuals over the previous decade. Just as the Romans admired gladiators and the British revered their knights, America has football, "her own vicarious warfare, nurtured by the technology which is this land's hallmark and tuned to the needs of this people's spirit." Older concerns about football's brutality are now markers of its existential value:

"The very difficulty of the game is a call to excellence, an invitation for a man to express himself violently and powerfully." Football also amounts to a collective religious/psychological ritual, with "resounding congregations of the American people" celebrating "flashing, brutal magnificence" that occupies "an important position in the psyche of an unsettled and generous nation."

And yet NFL football does not simply celebrate retrograde values. Instead, it's one of the only things left uniting a country riven by racial and political turmoil, on which the book sounds surprisingly leftish: "Crowded into increasingly unmanageable cities, governed by a seemingly unreachable bureaucracy, given an unwanted war in Asia and the upheavals of racial and educational factions at home . . . the nation fell into a period of introspection its leaders could not assuage. In such a mood, the people turned gratefully to a sport whose driving excitement not only filled certain needs more felt than acknowledged, but did so in patterns well suited to this complex, scientific society." Hinting at both left-wing and right-wing visions of "the Sixties," Boss ended up not in the middle but on all sides at once.[22]

What *are* those "certain needs more felt than acknowledged"? Football could be all things to all people. For conservatives, football embodied unstinting meritocracy, "a game of physical dominance; the weak are punished unmercifully and the unskilled are run off the field. . . . Moral overtones pervade the entire field of football strategy." For new leftists, forced "to search for challenges in a Saran-Wrapped existence," football incarnated the authentic self. Modern man could meet and overcome obstacles to self-realization on the field. For aesthetes, football was Pop fun: "Culture in the world today is commercial art forms developed by genius. It is this which . . . draws the line between legitimacy and promotion. It is this which makes the Beatles accredited and Truffaut, Mailer, and Dylan the interpreters of our life style." Further exploiting this line of argument, a subsequent NFL-Creative effort, *More Than a Game,* enlisted Marvel Comics to depict players as "the superheroes' superheroes." Dallas linebacker Lee Roy Jordan, photographed pursuing a ball carrier in a pose echoed by a drawing of the newly revived Captain America, was a "marvel of the 1970s, living it up after a decade of cataclysmic combat."

Lest this parade of assertions come across as mere puffery, a section titled "The Football Experience" explored the topic from multiple angles but added, "It is not possible to present a simple and complete picture because the reality is complex, contradictory and without end." This was followed by quotations from players and theories from psychologists, anthropologists, doctors, and, the times being what they were, the mandatory contribution from Marshall McLuhan, on peak experience, violence, fear, catharsis, and love. We can also see the book subtly sanitizing the league's history: in 1946, the NFL breaks a color barrier it is never acknowledged as imposing. In 1963, its widely lambasted choice to play two days after the Kennedy assassination never happened. And Chuck Bednarik's hit on Frank Gifford in 1960, perhaps the result of "the heavy masculinity" that weighted everything he ever did, "backfired into public disapproval." Even his game-saving heroics in the championship-game win over Green Bay "would not blot out the demonic image of that nightmarish moment." Football is violent, but not sadistic. An assured merging of the self-exploration sold by *The Whole Earth Catalogue,* the conceptual heavy lifting pulled off in *Esquire,* and inside dope from *Sports Illustrated,* the book is an astonishingly intelligent and modern production years ahead of its time in clarity of explanation and aesthetic sophistication. Rozelle even brought an autographed copy to Brian Piccolo as he lay stricken in the hospital, as if the power of football could heal.[23]

In 1973, Boss put out *The Pro Football Experience,* his "magnum opus," in the words of one NFL historian. A reviewer in the *National Observer* raved about the book, calling it "sensational . . . a whiz-bang and oversized document with astonishing photographs. . . . Here we have a truly creative exhibition of how to reproduce a picture and get it on a page with grace." This lavishly illustrated coffee-table volume was published by Harry Abrams, which typically issued fine-art books, and printed on heavy-coated paper stock, with an introduction by Roger Kahn. Kahn had just enjoyed enormous success with *The Boys of Summer,* making him the pre-eminent lyricist of baseball. Choosing him to celebrate pro football in essence officially endorsed the argument that *it* had now climbed to the top of the spectator-sports heap.

Casting his eyes backward, Kahn believed that football expressed modernity: "The country acquired a new sophistication after World War II. . . . The surge of football, as we feel it, could only really begin when the sport joined baseball, theology and law and relied on its professionals." He rehearsed common complaints against the game—brutality, self-seriousness, lack of humor—only to excuse them as products of a fallen world: "The game, like society, like life, is flawed." The NFL's solicitude for female fans remaining decades in the future; he then added that "the sport of football, with its excitement, violence, danger, courage, pain, touches the maleness of things. . . . [T]hat, I think, is the secret source of its success." As in the previous volume, football clarified the truths of (male) personal and national identity in valuable ways.[24]

Here, too, text and image merged seamlessly, presenting an anthropology of a day at the game, or every game, from players getting stretched and taped to fans tailgating and streaming into the stadium to the empty locker room and grandstand at game's end. If the NFL Films classic *They Call It Pro Football* were a book, this is what it would be. In addition to beautifully composed action shots, we see the halftime show, fans' headgear, John Madden thrusting his arms skyward in victory. This is an industry so confident of its social and cultural prominence that the book repurposes voices and prose styles in best Pop fashion. Some descriptions are impressionistic: "Coals grow in braziers, champagne corks pop, ice clinks in glasses and a buzz of voices carries across the morning. Inside, in the depths of the stadium, a more somber assemblage is occurring."

At other times, the book channels Hemingway: the game starts, and we're inside the huddle, where "there is precision and order and it is everywhere." Sometimes, it's melodrama: "The value of a professional athlete is directly attributable to the health of his body. And each play, each game, each year, robs him of his gifts. Twelve minutes can be a very long time." And finally, there's What It All Means, which reiterates the ideas offered in *The First Fifty Years* but adds the kinds of qualifiers suggested by Thomas Edwards's *Partisan Review* piece: "Professional football is a game, not a war. It is for Sunday afternoon, not forever. It is for win or loss, not life or death. But right now, the season is at stake. . . . Sense the electricity in the air as a nation sits joined together." There's more assurance than in *The First Fifty Years,* less anxious need to justify football with quotations from a team of experts. This is a book without a case to make. Boss let the pictures do the talking, and they document football's place in the national consciousness beyond a doubt.[25]

It took effort, and some imagination, for professional football to make itself culturally important enough to use for political gain. David Boss could hardly drown out the voices of those who found football worth mocking. But he did not need to do so. Nor did he need to offer an interpretation of his own. What he did, quite successfully, was endorse the idea that the NFL was absolutely worthy of serious intellectual consideration, then present so many possible interpretations that no single one could dominate. Unless you utterly rejected

American culture's fundamental assumptions, Boss had something to offer you, someplace to grab hold of pro football: it was expansive enough to include multiple, contradictory meanings. And his notion of the NFL's kaleidoscope of significances fed directly into the widely varied uses that political actors on both left and right would make of it in the early '70s. By committing the league to a broad but unspecific notion of significance, Boss offered radicals and conservatives alike a podium. Rozelle intuited that any sort of "positive association with the sport" was beneficial. Boss translated that adage into print, aiding and abetting the vigorous and sometimes angry debates that ensued.

2

Search and Destroy

For sheer, cliff-hanging entertainment nothing
quite approaches pro football as it is played today.
Each Sunday a growing army of fans happily
immerse themselves in real-life episodes rivaling
Tailspin Tommy and *The Perils of Pauline*.
—"Fans Go Ga-Ga Over Pro Football"[1]

After three highly praised seasons, *The Twentieth Century*
was getting stale. Documenting "the men and women who have shaped our
times"—its first episode profiled the "Man of the Century," Winston Churchill,
and others considered Mussolini, the Windsors, and Gandhi—the "finely
crafted" programs of this "paragon of the genre" had already won multiple
awards. In the summer of 1960, a survey of documentary programming praised
it as "on the whole the outstanding educational program in network television." But executive producer Burton Benjamin wanted to catch "the wave of
the future" by getting his cameras out into the world and telling "meaningful
stories about people," even though "in some circles this is considered a television heresy. . . . Better to have a man tell the story to a camera for 10 minutes."
Riding the New Haven line home from Manhattan every evening, Benjamin
learned what the surrounding businessmen found meaningful: "world affairs,
politics, even professional football." And so season four of *The Twentieth Century* kicked off in late October 1960 with *The Violent World of Sam Huff*.[2]

Football is always refracted to audiences through a medium. Newspapers
made the college game a national obsession in the Gilded Age; television did

the same for the professionals. From the beginning, the association advanced the interests of both parties. Television made pro football popular, and pro football made television relevant. For both the forty-five million viewers who watched the 1958 "greatest game ever played" between the Colts and Giants and those within the league itself, Alan Ameche tumbling into the end zone in overtime was the Shot Heard 'Round the World. Colts receiver Raymond Berry remembered seeing Commissioner Bert Bell crying in the back of the locker room after the game: "I think he knew what we didn't—yet. That this was a watershed." An Iowa columnist wrote the next day that "Professional football (thanks to television) has made a terrific impact. . . . On every hand you could hear fans replaying the exciting sudden-death game." Within a year, *New York Times TV* columnist Jack Gould was praising "the best spectator sport on television . . . an athletic tour de force."

Viewers around the country came to similar realizations. Roone Arledge, a young stage manager at New York City's WRCA, resolved that "we'd better change, too, or we'd get left behind. And the place to begin . . . was seeing the game as a story we were uniquely equipped to tell." Watching in his Houston hotel room, multimillionaire oilman Lamar Hunt decided to toss a bit of his bankroll at football—"this sport really has everything. And it televises well." Denied an NFL franchise despite repeated attempts to buy into the league, Hunt organized the AFL, which added all sorts of fan-friendly wrinkles: southern teams, players' last names on their jerseys, two-point conversions, a visible game clock. These innovations pushed the older league to respond in kind, sometimes immediately (as when it awarded new franchises to Dallas and Minnesota by 1961) and sometimes much more slowly (players' names on their jerseys, two-point conversions). Most important for the future of the industry, Hunt convinced AFL owners to share revenue from the league's contract with ABC, something Bell had been unable to sell on his end. "Pool the TV money," Bell had advised the Broncos' owner. "This is a very important thing."[3]

What to show was just as important. From the beginning, even before the ascension of the image-conscious Pete Rozelle, the NFL was acutely aware of what went over the airwaves. In testimony before Congress in 1957, Bell defended censorship as "in the best interests of the public and professional football and the players." That year *TV Guide* ran an editorial urging whichever network won the league's next TV contract to "strike a blow for freedom" by actually showing what was happening on the field rather than knuckling under to Bell's "usual ukase on how cameramen mustn't show players fighting" and flipping to the crowd instead. Three years later the magazine was still on the case, demanding that television "cover the story. If a fight erupts during the contest, it is distinctly part of the story." (The new commissioner had admitted that televising fights set "the wrong kind of example for youngsters.") In the *Times,* Jack Gould mocked the networks' "sissy" coverage as "childish nonsense." Yet while the AFL let its broadcast partner televise fights and arguments, the NFL continued to ban depictions of violence per se. Even in the first Super Bowl, Gould complained, the league's "iron-clad control" mandated that the announcers mention the thirty thousand unsold tickets "as briefly as possible."[4]

The NFL had to learn subtlety. Television was key to the league's exploding popularity, but it needed careful handling to transmit the messages that Rozelle preferred. Rather than continuing the coercion that so affronted critics on TV broadcasts, the league's house artists mastered the new medium, influencing and defining the league's image. Far more successfully than David Boss had in print, NFL Films' cultivation of a compelling aesthetic convinced large numbers of viewers that professional football was exactly what the league said it was—a spectacular, vivid, and heroic showcase for passionate excellence rather than a violent and often damaging workplace.

I Always Feel Real Good Whenever I Hit Someone

Sam Huff's appearance on the cover of *Time* in the fall of 1959 had made him famous, the satisfying onomatopoeia of the name "Huff" adding to his appeal. So from Burton Benjamin's perspective, the professional player to profile was obvious. "There's no place for nice guys," Huff informs the viewer at the outset of *The Violent World*. "I always feel real good whenever I hit someone. It's kill or be killed." CBS advertised the half-hour documentary in precisely the terms then coming into vogue, promising to reveal "how professional football has become an exacting science, with hours of classroom work as well as body conditioning, scrimmages, and bone-crunching play." "Today you will play pro football, riding on Sam Huff's broad back," Walter Cronkite promised. During training camp, practice, and an exhibition game, CBS wired him with a ten-ounce box "about the size of two packs of cigarettes" that cost $600; doing so during the regular season was "out of the question," Benjamin recalled, though Steelers' middle linebacker Bill Saul became the first player officially wired during a real game only seven years later.

The documentary forecasts HBO's *Hard Knocks* and the "Mic'd Up" segments on today's NFL telecasts—and, in those portions clearly arranged for the camera, it anticipates in primitive form the "authenticity" crafted for maximum entertainment on reality TV. It is also a marker of the NFL's unfocused and defensive attitude toward media promotion. Benjamin remembered the Giants and the league office "wrestl[ing] with it. . . . [F]inally, without enthusiasm, they said go ahead." The head of CBS Sports responded with equal horror to Huff's opening remarks: "My God, Rozelle . . . hates the word 'violence' and he isn't wild about 'kill' either."[5]

Given that Rozelle adored these qualities when NFL Films celebrated them, perhaps the greatest sin of *The Violent World* was that it did not depict NFL-quality ferociousness aesthetically. Football was simply an accumulation of large men doing their jobs by deliberately colliding at speed, over and over—so many collisions that Huff broke six microphones during filming. Contemporary reviewers did not consider pro football glamorous, and they focused less on science than on pain. The documentary's unvarnished realism had something to teach everyone about what the sport was really like. ("Just as violent as it always was," according to *New York Times* sportswriter Arthur Daley.) Those who feared the game had become soft should see it; those "who are aware, or believe they are, of the ruggedness of the sport, must see the masterful film . . . to find out how little anyone who hasn't suffered, slaved and slugged with the [players] knows," one critic wrote admiringly. Most reviewers celebrated how viscerally Benjamin's microphones brought home the "smashing body contact," the "crunch of flesh and bone," and the "literally bone crushing quality . . . of a jarring, exciting sport," as *Variety* called it. Less than a month later, Eagles linebacker Chuck Bednarik's devastation of Frank Gifford—"the hardest tackle I ever made," he said—brought home the truth of these descriptions. "It's so realistic," Huff said after a screening, "it even scares me."[6]

Despite the reviewers' focus, *The Violent World of Sam Huff* actually delivered something more complex than the celebration of ferocity that the title promised: one man's life and work in "the exacting science that professional football has become," a phrase one reviewer lifted straight from the publicity material, treated as a subject of serious interest. Game footage occupied less than one-fifth of the twenty-five minutes of airtime. Instead, viewers heard a good deal more conversation than one would expect in a film about football, including an interview with Huff's wife about their courtship and her expectation of his family responsibilities; segments with his parents and high-school coach were cut from the final version. As with every episode of *The Twentieth Century,* the segment came complete with a "Television Teaching Aid," courtesy of sponsor Prudential, that listed recommended reading and suggested classroom activities, and it could be borrowed free of charge.

True to his show's vision, Benjamin mounted a social-realist justification of Huff's potentially crippling career choice: a "violent world" enveloped him years before he put on pads. Huff grew up in Farmington, West Virginia, without running water or indoor plumbing in a house rented from the company for $8 a month, at the northern end of what Michael Harrington's *The Other America* seared into the national conscience two years later as "a belt of misery." It's a town where, as Huff matter-of-factly remarks while standing in front of the mine where his father went to work at thirteen, the football field had no stands and almost no grass. Coal was all he knew as a youngster, but "it's a very dangerous operation. . . . As long as I can play football, I'm going to stay out of there."

His campaign for Congress in the spring of 1970 emphasized Huff's lifelong connection to and compassion for miners, as well as his luck in escaping poverty for the bright lights and endorsement deals of New York. But he remained so money-conscious that, in an autobiography published thirty years after filming, he gratefully recalled the $500 and free rental car CBS had provided him. In the film, Huff explains that his scholarship to West Virginia University made college possible and that, though he had gone to Morgantown to play football, he realized that he should take his education and marriage seriously, and so he graduated on time.[7]

At training camp in Vermont, the film emphasizes the social and athletic ordeals facing rookies hoping to crack the roster and spotlights the intellectual challenge of playing for the Giants. Numerous features at the time highlighted the complexity of the team's defense, still parsing former coordinator Tom Landry's conceptual innovations after his jump to Dallas. One journalist described the "big, leather-bound, loose-leaf notebook" every defensive player received as "not only his most important single piece of equipment but the focal point of his professional life." Viewers see Huff's teammates pore diligently over these playbooks like enormous third-graders, after which coordinator Harland Svare quizzes them about their responsibilities on every play. (Svare subsequently called the meeting place "a powder room . . . [with] little folding chairs—the kind they used to have at Sunday school.") There's

Sam Huff (at right) joins a singalong with Rosey Grier and Dick Modzelewski during training camp. Note Huff wearing one of Andy Robustelli's striped shirts.

time for fun, too. The defense joins cheerfully in an obviously staged but nonetheless charming folk song about kielbasa, led in Polish by defensive tackle Dick Modzelewski, as Rosey Grier beams and strums his guitar.

The actual game has no story on offer—unlike the epic clashes that NFL Films would sculpt from footage just a few years later, the sound is natural and the on-field events are given no narrative arc. Moreover, the fighting that made Rozelle so skittish cropped up far more often than he could have wanted. Football was unusual, but still just a workplace. Cronkite's narration repeatedly emphasizes that this is work, not play, describing adhesive tape as "the club's first-line defense of its investment" and the NFL as "big business." The film never gestures toward any larger import; football is not notably patriotic or American, certainly not a significant indicator of national spirit. The ultimate image of the sport resembled what George Plimpton conveyed in *Paper Lion* three years later—a painful and exacting job, played by a band of endearing, gigantic, but fundamentally normal people. In the closing shot, Huff totters out of the locker room in a suit, so sore that his wife might have to help him out of bed the next morning, but proud of an honest day's toil. As he concludes, "It's a rough game. . . . But I've got no complaints. Pro football's been real good to me."[8]

Even at this early stage of the romance between television and pro football, the benefits of mass exposure, and the impulse to perform, were clear to players, far more quickly than to the league itself. One complained to a journalist in 1959 that "people on the street don't know one football player from another. They never get a close-up of us." *The Violent World* offered them a chance. Before the game, George Halas reminded members of his team that hitting Huff would win them airtime. Several of them tried. In an anecdote that Huff endlessly retold, end Harlon Hill crashed into him long after the whistle had blown. "Now, what'd you do that for, Harlon?" Huff demanded. "You never hit anyone in your life." "Oh, I was just trying to get on TV," Hill replied sheepishly.

Hill's impromptu audition did not earn him a turn in the spotlight, but Willard Dewveall hit paydirt by cheap-shotting Huff with a forearm under the chin. Huff yelped, "You do that one more time, 88, and I'm gonna sock you one." That made the cut. Huff later explained that he had grasped the ground rules: he didn't want Dewveall to hear his name spoken on television and instead referred to him only by number. End Andy Robustelli, who "was in so many businesses you couldn't keep up with him," also understood what was now possible. He had gotten into clothing that year, and so Huff's star turn represented a marketing opportunity for him: in several scenes Huff and his friends model the striped shirts Robustelli was currently selling. What Huff did not mention was the subsequent change in his own play. Frank Gifford, who had taken acting classes himself, affectionately recalled the "great dramatic flair" with which his teammate continued performing, chattering on the field and adding the "theatrical trick" of an extra roll on the ground to dramatize and underline every open-field tackle.[9]

"Because of his prominence in the telecast, Huff may face some taunts," an early review accurately predicted. The notion that he was showing off for the cameras dogged Huff long after his playing days. "If it weren't for the movie," Packers assistant coach Tom Fears sneered three years later, "he'd be just another linebacker fighting to hold on to his job." Huff complained in his autobiography that after winning defensive MVP in 1959, he was not even named All-Pro in 1960 despite having a better year, which he ascribed to "resentment for all the attention I was getting." He may have been on to

Huff (#70) at work, organizing the defense.

something. A 1970 history of pro football's early days called him only the third-best linebacker in the league and attributed his celebrity to playing in New York. In his 1971 exposé *They Call It a Game,* Bernie Parrish accused Huff of "piling on a lot" to win himself more "dollars and cents TV exposure" and getting "away with it because of his press buildup." Just before getting fired from the *Washington Daily News* that summer, Jack Mann explained that "people at football games in this town do not really understand what is going on because they are not the fans," a proposition he supported by adding that Redskins' ticket-holders were the kind of idiots who cheered the recently retired Huff "for putting the coup de grace on a gang tackle." Huff blamed still-lingering bitterness that he had been oversold by the media two decades before for the delay in his induction to the Hall of Fame. A sportswriter for the *Washington Post* agreed, writing upon Huff's election that "some may have thought that the extraordinarily graphic film . . . raised Huff's fame to heights disproportionate to his ability."

Huff was simultaneously an unsung pioneer in using media coverage to capitalize on an image that paid off for him on and off the field and an early victim of the notion that there was something untoward about his doing so.

He was "no more than a TV creation from a Madison Avenue imagination . . . less a football player than a cigarette advertisement," sneered a syndicated columnist in 1963. But within a decade, players straightforwardly admitted the benefits of mass exposure. As the Colts' Mike Curtis put it in 1972, "every little bit of recognition, every mention of your name on TV, helps you at contract time. It helps determine the amount of the fee you draw for personal appearances and endorsements. Recognition is the key to everything." Joe Kapp prided himself on *not* diversifying his portfolio: "I'm not interested in all those side issues: Brodie and his golf, Namath and his nightclubs, Kramer and his books. . . . I'm a pro football player, and that's enough." In 1976, Fran Tarkenton, no stranger to self-promotion, dismissed "*The Violent World of Sam Huff* business and all of that. Partly for that reason it got to be fashionable to call Sam an overrated football player. I'm sure he never was."[10]

As with critics' response to *The Violent World,* the most renowned photographic images from these years suggest popular belief in football's savagery much more than in its expertise. They depict mortal men in pain, not superheroes. Gifford had winced and said "I quit" when shown the Huff film. A month later, John Zimmerman's photograph unblinkingly contemplated Bednarik rejoicing over his unconscious body. Gifford suffered a spinal concussion and did not return to the field for eighteen months. "I thought Gifford was dead. But that didn't take away from the beauty of the hit," Huff recalled. Bednarik, who always maintained that he was celebrating the Eagles' recovery of the football and not his devastation of Gifford, resembles a mythic hero from the Trojan War relishing his downed foe. Today that image of violent triumph remains so significant that a large-scale print hangs in the halls of *Sports Illustrated.*

Combat photographer Morris Berman's 1964 shot captured a haggard Y. A. Tittle slumped on the ground, a warrior so comprehensively crushed that even the rivulets of blood sprinkling his scalp lie exhausted. Tittle had just been blindsided by Pittsburgh defensive end John Baker, a hit that shattered cartilage in his ribs, cracked his sternum, and gave him a concussion. "Hell of a way to get famous!" he wrote later. Berman's second most famous image depicted the strung-up corpses of Benito Mussolini and his mistress. Tittle's collapse is one of only three photographs displayed at the National Press Photographers Association headquarters, alongside the flag-raising at Iwo Jima and the explosion of the *Hindenburg,* a tribute to how completely it captures the entire complex of ideas orbiting early '60s pro football. Detached from their specific context, both photographs have become iconic images of what *The Wide World of Sports* would memorably call "the agony of defeat"; in their time, both vividly illustrated what many took to be the fundamental appeal, *and* the fundamental problem, posed by professional football. And both celebrate the last generation of pre–NFL Films players on something closer to their own terms. When it took control of the film-making process, the NFL made sure that professional football itself, rather than any individual player, was the product on display.[11]

George Plimpton found a way to bring these themes home. Rather than hearing Sam Huff blast into running backs, Plimpton's readers could get into the huddle themselves. The experience was both exhilarating and terrifying. He distilled several wide-eyed weeks in the summer of 1963 as the Detroit Lions' third-string quarterback into *Paper Lion,* which spent months on the best-seller lists and in book-club advertisements; one journalist called it "the year's runaway gift" for the 1966 holiday season. By 1970, his first three forays into participatory sports journalism, *Out of My League* (baseball), *Paper Lion* (football), and *The Bogey Man* (golf), had sold a combined two million copies. In 1968 *Paper Lion* became a movie, with Alan Alda as Plimpton and Vince Lombardi making a cameo as Vince Lombardi.

In most of the ways that we measure these things, *Paper Lion* is by far the single most popular piece of writing on football from the 1960s and '70s. As in *Violent World,* Plimpton depicts training camp as a grand adventure of male bonding and storytelling sporadically interrupted by football. But in setting and conception, *Paper Lion* is essentially pastoral. Literally so: camp takes place on a bucolic prep-school campus, with Episcopalian bishops flitting past in the dusk. The author is enraptured by the players (enormous boys with whom he plays pranks), dazzled by the complexity of the game plan, entertained by the coaches' byplay, and repeatedly astounded by the technique attendant on what appear to be the simplest actions. Tackling proves a formidable task. "If you wrapped your arms around the tackling dummy, and hung on and tried to wrestle it down," he discovers, "the bag turned over and one sagged ignominiously to the sawdust pit, the bag on top."[12]

But Plimpton endows his story with an additional layer of meaning. While retaining *The Violent World*'s emphasis on the mental and physical skill this painful game demands, Plimpton adds the notion of testing one's mettle. The players readily indulge the author's need to register his own experience: when he survives his first snap, "I had gone through something that made me, if tenuously, one of them; they stood around for a while watching me savor it." In light of where football writing would venture over the next decade, what's interesting is the things Plimpton feels little call to explore—the social and political ramifications of the sport, the authoritarian power structure its coaches constantly reinforce, the emotional and spiritual toll it exerts on players. Instead, he constantly emphasizes how professionalism organizes and disciplines violence; he marvels at the "infinitely melancholy gasps of violent effort" erupting from the notorious nutcracker (or "Oklahoma") drill, a brutal close-quarters battle for dominance between offensive and defensive linemen, and wonders that more fights do not erupt. "It was hard to keep one's equanimity banging into someone else . . . and finally the tempers could not be contained," he learns, but "there'd be none of it on the field."

For Plimpton, these are the registers that matter; football requires precise execution, and his failure under pressure (he runs five plays in a scrimmage, fails to get three of them off at all, and loses twenty-nine yards) reflects both the enormous challenge of succeeding at the game and the value of Plimpton's courageous attempt to make it. He does complete a pass while in street clothes just before leaving training camp, atoning at least somewhat for his previous failure. What suffuses the book most of all is an ache of longing—to be so young and strong and vividly alive, to be that adept at such a demanding profession, and most of all, to be one of and with *them*.[13]

They Call It Pro Football

The NFL's house artists, Ed and Steve Sabol, remixed and reshaped these ingredients. Most were already present by 1960. Popular commentators found pro football spectacularly violent, emotionally meaningful, exciting, and highly technical ("precise and bruising," *Life* said), all themes that NFL Films would highlight. Sometimes it rewrote these articles nearly literally. A 1960 *Sports Illustrated* cover story, "The Violent Face of Pro Football," celebrated line play with almost exactly the blood-and-iron elegies that John Facenda would deliver with legendary gravitas in NFL Films' mid-'60s productions: "In the ruck of the line the huge men fight their most savage (and least noticed) wars. The rules are their own, and almost the only law the linemen know is survival." From Plimpton the Sabols took the notion that self-expression and existential assertion accounted for the sport's newfound popularity.

Then they made two crucial, and paradoxical, changes that rendered this language glorious and heroic: first, they removed words like "kill." Through their eyes, football's violence became impersonal, a matter of technique. Huff's clear-eyed vision of desperate scrabbling for dominance was abstracted and disconnected from individual players through sound design and stirring visual imagery. The closer viewers got to the action, the less they could link it to any one player. Second, the focus on skill and expertise muted the notion of football as a job. NFL Films implied that players trained and suffered out of sheer aesthetic joy rather than for a paycheck; it never referred to them as investments. Instead, adroit deployment of different linguistic registers and musical cues dramatized the varieties of experience possible within "the sport of our time," a vivid choreography of pain precisely executed by "eleven trained men on the field of play, each man a specialist," as NFL Films' essential production, *They Call It Pro Football,* put it.[14]

NFL Films did not become the definitive visual presenter of professional football overnight. Tel-Ra Productions, run by Bert Bell's friend Wally Orr, had broadcast NFL championship games from 1946 onward, from a distance— "press box views of big plays, presented in chronological order, accompanied by marching-band music and the cloying, alliterative voice-overs so common at the time," in one historian's words. Ed Sabol would later parody this style of narration: "Milt Plum pegs a peach of a pass to become the apple of coach George Wilson's eye." In 1962, in a story that NFL Films has consciously fashioned into legend, Sabol, an incorrigible self-promoter whose Blair Motion Pictures had exactly one release to its credit—a "creative and financial disaster" called *To Catch a Whale*—approached Rozelle and offered to double Tel-Ra's $1,500 bid for rights to the league championship, a bargain whose price quickly ascended to $10,000 in 1963 and $20,000 in 1964. He promised to capture the action from every angle with a lavish eight-camera setup (Tel-Ra had used four the previous year, and most televised sports productions made do with two) and to lend high drama to what had previously been simple news features. "We are not journalists but romantics," his son Steve liked to say.

Ed and Steve Sabol, whose firm the league brought in-house in 1965 by having every franchise put up $20,000 and renamed NFL Films, revolutionized the structure and intent of football films. Now they told stories, often from unexpectedly intimate angles, with unprecedented closeness and ferocity. NFL Films "has made a dramatic game more dramatic, a fast and violent sport faster and more violent . . . something slightly surrealistic, infinitely modern, genuinely artistic and captivating," a journalist rhapsodized in 1967. The Sabols added an element of conscious postmodernism, dangling references to Kurosawa, Eisenstein, Fellini, military lingo, any musical genre that seemed appropriate (from classical to acid rock), even *The Joy of Sex*. Audrey Sabol, Ed's wife and Steve's mother, ran an art gallery and befriended Pop artists like Wayne Thiebaud and Roy Lichtenstein, her aesthetic sophistication lending the firm a deeper range of reference. But the Sabols' respect for the institutions that had previously taught Americans to understand football was key to their success: they honored the tradition of embellishment by taking over Grantland Rice's role as bestower of Homeric epithets on the legends they made, most famously "America's Team" for the Cowboys, and much of their narration appropriated mainstream magazines' manly-yet-skilled praise of the NFL.

Matching its romantic message, NFL Films' reach stretched well beyond the confines of the football season: in addition to specialty highlight films, there was *NFL Game of the Week, This Is the NFL,* the summertime show *NFL Action,* and highlight packages for *The Tonight Show*. If you couldn't catch these shows, NFL Films would bring the national pastime to you, seeding professional football throughout the culture (and the world) at large. Showings were held, at very reasonable rates, at Playboy Clubs, banks (who received versions "made exclusively for bank sponsorship"), and YMCAs; sales meetings and booster-club luncheons; on transcontinental flights; at the Continental Hotel in Paris, where homesick Americans could enjoy a weekly taste of their native land by watching highlights while chomping hot dogs; on U.S. Navy submarines, as morale-builders; even in Saudi Arabia, where oil companies exhibited films to "American workers far from home."

Football was America's most popular sport overseas, which was fitting in that only the army used more Kodak film stock than did NFL Films. General Creighton Abrams observed in a 1971 conversation with Defense Secretary Melvin Laird that "the men are most interested in [it]. It's not because it's the football season. . . . These films are important to them." That November, Laird publicly pledged "a two-minute bureaucratic drill" to ensure that the Armed Forces network immediately provided more televised football to servicemen. Secretary of State William Rogers brought a supply of NFL Films' productions with him when he toured the Far East. Air Force One flew a film to Lyndon Johnson's ranch in Texas so he could entertain his guests, and Richard Nixon ordered a big-hits special for the White House.[15]

NFL Films was never meant to be a profit center, nor was it. Ed Sabol once joked that the league made more on concessions and parking than from its films, and that organization has never produced more than 0.5 percent of league revenue. (Rozelle asked merely that it not lose money.) Nor was it meant simply to move product. Rozelle resisted demands that it be brought to New York and made part of a centralized promotional apparatus. He wanted it to retain its independence and its unique vision. But its house style—epic, martial, backed by original orchestral scores, with announcer John Facenda, "the Voice of God," adding portentous narration—did more than anything to make the league's desired cluster of associations tangible, breathable, visceral. Every big play was historic, every collision stupefyingly fast yet without long-term consequence, every player part of a seamless whole. Race did not matter; dissent, political or cultural, was nonexistent or, at worst, just added color to what happened on the field. Despite Rozelle's fear of Sam Huff's "violent world," NFL Films also made comedy out of violence: its big-hit features included *Bellringers* and *The Nutcracker Suite* in the '60s alone, the titles suggesting just how cheerfully they celebrated repeated depictions of men getting concussed.

The Sabols' hunger to romanticize dovetailed perfectly with Rozelle's utilitarianism and with NFL owners' financial goals. "He understood even better than we did how we were remaking the game of football," Steve Sabol recalled. The filmmakers minimized onscreen coverage of players who had not signed contracts and even edited "the classiest spectators it could find" into Bears highlights, no matter which team they supported or where the game had been played, to satisfy demanding owner George Halas. "Where would Paul Revere be without Longfellow's poems?" Steve Sabol asked. NFL Films taught viewers how to watch and understand football; they made it intelligible, narrative, packed it with cultural and political import—so effectively that a Japanese crowd at a 1976 exhibition grew unruly when the game on the field proved less relentlessly exciting than the films had led them to expect. Equally important, they did so in service of a broader imperative to sell the whole industry and to control what these representations showed. Players of Huff's generation briefly enjoyed the chance to capitalize on their own images. But now institutional imperatives dominated: NFL Films always sold the sport as greater than any individual player.[16]

Citizen Kane in Shoulder Pads

NFL Films' first production, *Pro Football's Longest Day,* depicted the 1962 championship between the Giants and Packers in ways much closer to the Tel-Ra past than the Sabols might have hoped. The rigid storytelling and Chris Schenkel's cornball narration uncomfortably recalled the precursors Ed Sabol mocked: "The fans have come prepared. They're keyed for a great game, a game of football's fundamentals—the hard block, the rugged tackle, the tough runner who stays on his feet, the quarterback whose passes ride the wind to a receiver whose hands survive the bitter cold." "Del Shofner walks upfield with catlike grace. Whose eyes are always upon him? The eyes of Tittle, Y. A., the take-charge guy." The lack of natural sound and pervasive rah-rah band music disconnected the viewer from the action, and the earlier film's focus on individuality (putting a microphone on Huff to let his twang come through unadulterated, for instance) was replaced by a distanced vision of a collective that the metaphor of team-as-army underscored. We have moved, if anything, backward from *The Violent World of Sam Huff.*

The end product did take significant steps forward technologically. Rozelle considered it the best football film he'd ever seen. Presenting the action almost literally play-by-play rather than abstracting the most vivid moments, the Sabols' eight cameras got the viewer much closer to the field, including just outside the huddle or on the sideline on some plays; the viewer felt the speed and power of pro football infinitely more powerfully than he or she could in footage from, say, the legendary 1958 game. Occasional slow-motion replays— a technology so advanced that when CBS used it during the Army–Navy game the next year, the announcer broke in to clarify that "this is a videotape. They did not score again"—explained the design and structure of important plays to the viewer with clarity, so football became intelligible, not just a fog of bodies.

But NFL Films had not yet threaded its preferred mythology through its productions to heighten their meaning. The title explored later productions' customary militaristic register with its reference to the wide-screen D-Day epic *The Longest Day,* released earlier that fall; Ed Sabol had landed at Normandy himself on June 16, 1944. But the narrative frame the Sabols would perfect was more aspiration than reality at this point. After initial footage framed the clash as between humble, nose-to-the-grindstone Green Bay, "the last of the town teams," and bustling, ruthless New York—problematic from the league's perspective in that it highlighted possible moral and financial

Pro Football's Longest Day: two steps forward, one step back.

disparities rather than celebrating the institution as a whole—the remainder entirely ignored that framing. Schenkel's closing narration told us merely that "to Coach Vince Lombardi, this may have been the greatest game ever played. He can't be sure. But one thing is certain: this was football's longest day." The film does not proclaim football's cultural significance, nor does it make claims for the sport's beauty or aesthetic qualities; it is too timid to do more than reiterate that the game was hard-fought. Particularly when compared to the sagas NFL Films would subsequently fashion, *Pro Football's Longest Day* is dramatically inert.[17]

Five years later, NFL Films had learned how to sell the stories it wanted. Steve Sabol dubbed *They Call It Pro Football* "the *Citizen Kane* of football films. Everything after that was influenced and affected by that film"; it now resides in the Library of Congress' National Film Registry alongside the actual *Citizen Kane*. Rozelle summoned the Sabols to the league office the week after its premiere at Toots Shor's to tell them how pleased he was. The filmmakers' romantic conception touched on every major theme he wanted to present:

football is now, today, popular; football is endlessly exciting and epic; football is a ritualized performance by experts that we should watch in a state of awed rapture that the film models for us. At a press preview in the spring of 1967, the assembled sportswriters broke "into wild cheers, whistles, and handclaps." "We got carried away like everyone else," one attendee recalled. "I've never seen its equal for excitement, thrills, and drama." Reviewers had received *The Violent World of Sam Huff* within the framework of pro football as a brutal but technically demanding profession, with particular stress on its brutality. Seven years later, this film ratified their personal and professional investment in the notion that NFL football was beautiful and significant, not job but spectacle. NFL Films' web site proudly boasts that the film has become scripture: "Every filmmaking motif for which our work is recognized can be traced to that watershed production, which is required viewing for every Films intern class the day it arrives."[18]

It is not too much to call *They Call It Pro Football* a work of mass-media genius. Fifty years after its production, the film's symphonic arrangement of groans, crashes, and arcing passes adroitly harmonizes football's visceral, percussive aspects and its flashes of grace and delicacy. It marked the first assembly of the classic NFL Films ingredients: close-quarters combat camerawork, Facenda's booming narration of Steve Sabol's text (influenced by Kipling and Poe, he said), and the flourishes of composer Sam Spence, who would turn Ed Sabol's hummed fragments into complete scores.

The film begins with a recitation of the honors it has received and an assertion that it "speaks an international language—the beauty and violence of professional football." It is art rather than commerce. We then behold several minutes of fast-cut pregame pageantry even before the credits—fans blow trumpets, drums boom, cymbals clash (showcasing the precision displays of several historically black colleges' marching bands and presaging the artful violence to follow on the field), balloons and birds take to the sky, a man in a jet pack blasts off. Facenda's first words set out the league's mythopoetic ideal: "It starts with a whistle and ends with a gun. Sixty minutes of close-in action from kickoff [which we watch as he says the words] to touchdown." We head to training camp to grasp the effort disciplined professionalism demands: these men train punishingly for excellence, heralded by a shot of a center's sweating forearm (an unusual and original choice of focus and a Steve Sabol trademark). Filmed from below, giants blast into blocking sleds or each other, grunting viciously, pads exploding like gunshots: Plimpton's epiphanies made audible. Recall the previous film's throwing up of its hands at what it all means. Was the 1962 championship "the greatest game ever played"? Vince Lombardi did not know. Neither did the filmmakers. This film tells us, and tells us, and tells us.[19]

NFL Films' aesthetic, and its sense of the story it wanted to tell, had advanced remarkably. Here all the elements harmonize perfectly. Spence's wittily deployed music gives what's on the screen dramatic heft and hip cachet, evoking spaghetti westerns, Bernard Herrmann's Hitchcock scores, spy-movie jazz. A kickoff floating through the air gets a riff that hints at "Flight of the Bumblebee." They are put in service of a brief but complete course in football aesthetics. The film expertly instructs the viewer how different the world looks, feels, and sounds to each of these highly-trained specialists. As Plimpton had intuited, quarterbacks, men directing the action, earn an authoritative pop-Hemingway terseness: "The quarterback lives in a world of pressure. How well he lives with it, and reacts to it, determines how good he is." Johnny Unitas is "a classic quarterback, whose timing and control is cool, swift, precise." An abundance of NFL Films' signature shot, the perfectly framed, in-focus football spiraling from the passer into his receiver's hands, is the filmmakers' own version of grace under pressure, demonstrating both the beauty of the game and the technical expertise the Sabols' cameramen had gained. We stay in the backfield, with jazzy flourishes for "racehorse halfbacks" like Gale Sayers and pounding drums for "locomotive fullbacks" as they run over and through tacklers.[20]

Then the film changes its tune, literally, in its exaltation of the game's fundamental aggression: we start with a football lying innocent and untroubled on torn turf. Facenda explains that we are now beholding no man's land, where games are won and lost. The score rumbles menacingly, heavy on brass and martial drumbeats, as we behold linemen's taped, scarred and broken fists in close-up. "The hands of combat, the hands of pros," Facenda intones. "This is the part of the game rarely seen by the spectator: the shattering impact of a block. The mountainous size of an onrushing defender. The splintering force of a forearm shiver [Unitas goes flying]. One ton of muscle with a one-track mind [Bill Brown of the Vikings collapses under an avalanche of Colts]." Then it's on to the ravages of the middle linebacker, as Facenda repeatedly growls "search and destroy," a term that bore far more contemporary relevance than did D-Day, having migrated into general usage from army terminology only a year or so before. In September 1966, influential columnist Joseph Alsop wrote that this game plan was "clearly beginning to produce major results" in Vietnam and that the war "is progressing considerably more hopefully than almost anyone supposes at home." The film manages to eat its cake and have it, depicting players being submarined and dropped on their heads while celebrating the professionalism and grit of everyone involved.

Contemporary Hollywood films like *Bonnie and Clyde* and *The Wild Bunch* used the same tools to critique the American thirst for violence, at home and in the world; both movies conclude in fusillades of bullets that jerk their charismatic antiheroes in horrific slow-motion ballets. But for NFL Films, this isn't "savagery on Sunday," and the military phrasing bears no troublesome associations. "Search and destroy" is not quite "kill," though it's not far away, either. We are watching poetry, jazz, modern dance deepened and emboldened by manly, disciplined ferocity. These cultural and rhetorical links underscore the insight of columnist Robert Lipsyte, who accurately termed such productions "splendid little wars," evoking the historic association of media manipulation with the Spanish-American War, and by extension accusing the NFL of complicity in conflicts from Vietnam to the Persian Gulf. Network coverage of the actual war distressed viewers with footage of Marines casually setting fire to hutches with their Zippo lighters, but here violence is savored, appreciated, and disconnected from its aftermath. The film occasionally gestures at the game's cost, describing receivers as boasting "the hands, the moves, the grace . . . and a willing disregard for the consequences." But we never see, nor are we prompted to imagine, any of these players' needing help getting out of bed the next day. They exist entirely on the field.[21]

The conclusion of *They Call It Pro Football* measures its distance from *Pro Football's Longest Day* with special clarity. The previous film more or less stumbled to an end, but here Facenda recites a hard-boiled hymn of praise to the game's physical, aesthetic, and spiritual excellences, as well as a celebration of the millions of Americans who love what they all add up to: "A call. The ball is snapped and the play continues. A drama of man on man in a race against the clock. It's precision, persistence, power. The unleashed speed of the kickoff. The whistling feet of a great runner. The reckless fury of a goal-line stand. The crowning glory of a winning touchdown. The swelling roar of the crowd. It's called pro football." The narration ends, the music clashes triumphantly, the crowd rushes the field, the owners' box goes nuts, and we exit with a closing shot of the NFL shield, a fully harmonized fusion of product, image,

From *They Call It Pro Football*: one ton of muscle with a one-track mind.

and message. Reviewers agreed, extolling the "action-packed display of the beauty and violence of the game—and its impact on the entire country."

Once this style had been perfected, the NFL's house organs could deploy it to countermand threats to the official story. Arch-dissident Dave Meggyesy accused football of being fascistic and dehumanizing while George Sauer charged it of complicity in racism and militarism from the start. Both stopped playing the sport. NFL Films rendered such critiques just part of the game's wonderfully American multiplicity by tuning in to radical players' insurgent energies, turning on a hip soundtrack, and dropping out the politics. *The New Breed* (1971) celebrated "a new breed of athlete [who] has arrived with a new look, a new lifestyle . . . but the same old commitment and zest for the sport." The new breed apparently did not include Meggyesy, Sauer, Chip Oliver, Johnny Sample, Bernie Parrish, or any of the other players who attacked the sport. Instead, it showcased Tim Rossovich, "the first football hero of the Aquarius generation," a former USC linebacker who lived on the beach, played vigorous volleyball matches, built driftwood sculptures—and also informed us that his favorite film was *Patton*, who "would have made a great football coach." He wanted to show "the youth of today . . . that a person with long hair doesn't have to be associated with something bad," which the film proved by associating him with something good: Rossovich angrily paced the sidelines and barked at his teammates to play harder and better.

The other player featured, Dickie Post, co-owned a fashion boutique catering to "sunshine people" in California and was depicted in a brief psychedelic interlude embarking on what seemed very clearly to be a drug-enhanced bicycle ride while garbed in a black hat and fantastically patterned pants. Post remarked that "I can't find anything more satisfying, to me, for six months of the year than playing football," an assertion of self that the film echoed with footage of his slithering runs backed by chiming country-folk guitar and trippy alliteration:

> He comes at a defense shrouded by his blockers, with all his power locked in his legs, legs that are short, snake-dancing stumps, loose and limber legs, built on four-speed swivels, that slipstream him past the howl and havoc of the hunters. Post is past master at running into the hurricane's eye, and emerging untouched at touchdown's door. . . . 190 pounds of Silly Putty, oozing in all directions at once.

Thirty years later, when the danger had passed, NFL Films got around to Meggyesy, producing a short segment called "Rebel with a Cause" that treated him respectfully and gave airtime to Harry Edwards as well. It admitted that no forum for dissent existed at the time (without mentioning NFL Films' own refusal to tell dissenters' stories when they mattered), but still framed even this story as one about the sport's inherent excellence: "Bottom line?" it has Meggyesy concluding. "It's a great game."

In later years football-as-war tropes became so ubiquitous that Lipsyte would criticize Facenda's "Dunkirk voice" for devaluing words like "courage, heroism, and tragedy." We can see the extent to which *The Violent World of Sam Huff* represented a road not taken, for television as a whole, for televised sports, and for the players whose pain and excellence was being so adroitly capitalized. That road led to frank acknowledgment of the game's violent culture (all those on-field fights), the off-field costs of football as actually played, and fuller compassion for the identities and histories of those who "suffered, slaved, and slugged" on the field, as the reviewer put it. It treated football as an exotic job, but still a job, rather than an epic and mythological clash. Lacking an overarching corporate vision, it allowed an individual player to put his personality on display and shape the story. Huff did so quite literally, repeatedly showing the film on the campaign trail in 1970 to publicize his candidacy and attest to his working-class bona fides in a hardscrabble region of West Virginia. It might well have raised questions about how well players were paid, and how long their careers typically lasted.

But even though this version constituted "television heresy," as Benjamin described it, in 1960, it lacked narrative drive. It lacked spectacle. It did not stir the blood so much as awaken a sense of pained empathy. It would doubtless have enticed many fewer corporations to buy advertising spots. It was educational rather than promotional. As almost goes without saying, it would not have been anywhere near as popular as the NFL's or major networks' television programming. It clashed with the emerging world of spectacle and self-advertising where political candidates had to promote themselves to an electorate learning to consume campaigns as increasingly indistinguishable from any other consumer good. Worst of all, it contravened Rozelle's fundamental vision of the game. Understanding professional football as "more business than sport," he explained, "can only hurt the game." Instead, "we sell an experience."

They Call It Pro Football did everything its makers wanted. "It is inconceivable that anything could approach this," raved an astonished sportswriter. The film was not tied to a specific team, season, or game, so it was infinitely reusable. It extolled NFL football's meaning, glory, excitement, and passion and backed up these claims with a multimedia assault on the viewer, whose ideal state would be stupefied wonder. Here, pain was made aesthetic, visually appealing—and irrelevant. Watching NFL Films' defining productions, violence seems abundant but curiously depersonalized, happening to large bodies whose connection to normal life is at best notional. These are gods, not beings who suffer, and certainly not workers. Such productions rendered football as a succession of sensational high points suitable for selling (highlights were literally grouped into "packages"), a pseudo-event rather than a continuous and sometimes dull experience.[22]

As such, this visual language made football particularly amenable to the new world of politics, with its quick-hitting commercials and adroit use of media to sell. Given the cost and difficulty of making competing films, it quickly became the *only* available visual language, teaching viewers how football looked and sounded in an ideal world. Every famous highlight, from that point on, was *NFL Films'* famous highlight. And the film culminated with a shot of the NFL shield, a direct reminder of exactly who had put all of this wonderment in front of you. No wonder Rozelle loved *They Call It Pro Football* the moment he saw it. Institutionally, the NFL had worked out the cultural and intellectual dimensions of the visual story it chose to tell. It had so comprehensively told that story that fans and critics alike had little choice but to call pro football exactly what Pete Rozelle wanted them to call it.

3

The NFL's Role in American History (Somebody's Gotta Be Kidding)

In a very real way, the National Football League
is American history. I believe this is why we as a
nation must look to the future, when, God willing,
this sort of thing will never happen again.
—Lois Gould, "The Road Ahead"[1]

David Boss aimed to land his books on the coffee tables and in the minds of educated, affluent readers. The Sabols' films sold pro football as spectacle to devoted and casual fans around the world. A third audience required the conversion of this cultural capital into political capital. As the NFL grew to prominence, it increasingly ran into obstructions that friendly local and national office-holders could remove. Convincing politicians to do the league's bidding, or at least look more positively on its endeavors, entailed not merely that the NFL make itself sufficiently important to be worth favors; it also needed the construction and sale of an appealing and convincing mythology. This process happened piecemeal rather than intentionally, but the results were the same: by the mid-'70s, the federal government had assured the NFL that its place was secure.

Baseball aroused warm feelings in legislators' hearts. In 1922, the Supreme Court awarded the major leagues full immunity from antitrust law because baseball games did not constitute interstate commerce; they were, in Oliver Wendell Holmes's phrasing, "personal effort, not related to production." Given multiple opportunities to revise this decision over the next half-century, the Court resorted instead to myth. In the 1972 decision *Kuhn v. Flood,* Harry Blackmun denied free agency to players by first invoking not legal principle but the "colorful days" of the nineteenth-century-game and then enumerating "the many names . . . that have sparked the diamond and its environs and that have provided tinder for recaptured thrills, for reminiscence and comparisons, and for conversation and anticipation in-season and off-season." Baseball's mythic resonances, not its actual economic structure, were what mattered.

During wartime, baseball provided a public service. In January 1942, Franklin Roosevelt implored commissioner Kenesaw Mountain Landis to keep the national pastime going. Professional baseball players, he argued, "are a definite recreational asset to at least 20,000,000 of their fellow citizens." He did not extend that consideration to professional football players. In June, Roosevelt wrote Congressman John McCormack that "there have been a number of inquiries lately about the football season. . . . Obviously high school and college football should be encouraged in times like this." Again, the NFL did not merit mention as a "recreational asset." Its "biggest fan" in Washington was a Democratic congressman from Pittsburgh who moonlighted as an NFL referee. As a result, even though it underlined its patriotism by playing the national anthem and ceremonially honoring the armed forces, the league "teetered on the brink of shutting down" nearly every season through 1945.[2]

As the 1960s began, professional football knew that it could not rely on romantic indulgence from politicians and judges. Politicians looking to make a point could and did use college football to do so. Governor Ross Barnett chose an Ole Miss home game, emboldened by an atmosphere of menacing hysteria that onlookers likened to a Nazi rally, to publicly defy James Meredith's attempt to register for classes at the university in 1962. John F. Kennedy responded by mobilizing the same resource, "a tradition of honor and courage won on the field of battle and on the gridiron," to inspire the school to live up to its highest principles. Worse, when the NFL attempted to provide solace to the nation by playing its full slate two days after Kennedy's assassination (which consultations with the family encouraged it to do) and adding flag ceremonies and moments of silence to games, observers blasted it for insensitivity. Fans in Cleveland that Sunday were so enraged by the sight of the Cowboys that Bob Lilly wondered "whether we were going to get shot." One ex-fan wrote that "I have had no use for the National Football League since November 24th" because it had played its schedule, then demanded payment from CBS, which had not televised any games. "In my view," he added, "such greedy moneygrubbers should have the book thrown at them."[3]

Yet within just a few years, professional football had become the Establishment's sport. Washington was "a male town, and football is its game . . . the right metaphor for its politics," journalist Hedrick Smith wrote. All three local papers (the *Post,* the *Star,* and the *Daily News*) subjected the Redskins' machinations to serious scrutiny that made the city's two pastimes nearly indistinguishable. "Not to possess Redskins season tickets spells a fatal absence of status," observed Mary McGrory, an astute observer of local mores. Cars sported bumper stickers demanding, "Redskins—Love Them or Leave Town." Out of both calculation and love, all manner of local figures brought football into their day jobs. *Time* described Henry Kissinger as analyzing the game, which the president had taught him to appreciate, "as if it were a parable of war and peace." Widely syndicated *Post* humor columnist Art Buchwald, who endlessly twitted Richard Nixon's love of the sport, sat in owner Edward Bennett Williams's box at every game, fretting that the president might show up and kick him out. The capital's sportswriters, *The Washingtonian* charged, "obsessed as they are with power, winning, and being a front-runner, wouldn't touch [a loser] with a ten-foot pole." Another writer suggested that football "subconsciously caught up" fans in the city's deepest preoccupations, sex and politics. "If the Washington world, personal and political, were only as open and airy as baseball," he lamented. "Alas, it is like the Redskins."[4]

How did this change come about? As we've seen, the league insistently brandished its patriotic credentials throughout the 1960s. But self-promotion on its own was hardly enough. Instead, in a positive feedback loop, as the NFL repeatedly boasted that it was America's most popular sport, federal officials became increasingly invested in doing the league's bidding—particularly if doing so produced a franchise, but often just because they counted themselves as football fans. During debate over the AFL-NFL merger, multiple congressmen supported the measure because it would ultimately benefit their local teams. Lawrence O'Brien, Lyndon Johnson's special assistant for congressional relations, ascribed this power to the NFL's increasingly effective application of leverage, noting that the upper house proved notably hospitable. He recalled "inordinate efforts on behalf of the NFL in the Senate" by Senators in "constant quest . . . for a franchise location in their state." Public interest, "fanned by media," he added, added up to overwhelming legislative force. By 1975, "football is a game of specialists," conservative columnist George Will snorted, and Congress had become the owners' "'specialty team' specializing in defense of the indefensible."[5]

But several crucial contradictions went generally unremarked in this crusade to elevate the NFL to a bulwark of Americanism. From its image as a ruggedly capitalist enterprise (even as its commissioner and owners constantly reiterated the need for collectivization) to its sending players to Vietnam to support the war effort (while simultaneously flexing political muscle to prevent those players from actually serving) to its feverishly jingoistic public spectacles (which incurred as much mockery and criticism as mainstream support)—extending even to its misbegotten bid to win official sanction as part of the Bicentennial—the NFL's patriotic efforts were at once its most contested and its most emblematic. In this deeply politicized sphere of the wider culture, where the NFL most insistently exerted its soft power, we most clearly see the smaller failures and broader successes of its attempts to insinuate itself into larger conversations.

Fat-Cat Republicans Who Vote Socialist

It's one of the great ironies of the period that leftish critics who shuddered at football's fascistic on-field politics missed fundamental ways in which, from the beginning, off the field the NFL endorsed a political vision very much in line with cooperative hopes and dreams. Despite its advertising itself as the embodiment of all-American capitalism—and despite donations heavily slanted toward Republican politicians, especially in recent years—the league's founders compiled a consistent track record of collectivist behavior, with the most powerful members explicitly calling for communal allocation of resources. "We are a bunch of fat cat Republicans who vote socialist on football," Cleveland owner Art Modell once said. An economist studying the NFL's means of maintaining competitive balance posed them "in stark contrast to American capitalism." Or as the libertarian magazine *Reason* pointed out in an attack on the college draft's affront to the invisible hand, "the NFL shield has stood resolutely against labor freedom since 1935."[6]

The Bears, Packers, and Giants dominated pro football's early years, and that success enabled them to sign the best players, who were free to sell their talents on the open market. Thirty teams folded in the NFL's first decade. Responding to systemic inequities, in May 1935 the owners of the most powerful franchises agreed to institute a college draft that gave to each according to its need rather than allowing what league president Joe Carr termed "pro-miscuous scrambling" for players. (The sub-headline on the *New York Times* story read "Football League Aims to Strengthen Weaker Clubs.") At almost the same time, the Du Pont family and its allies met in New York to found the American Liberty League and oppose the New Deal. The array of businessmen who ran the NFL, however, made a very different argument. "We could give them [fans] competition only if the teams had some sort of equality," found-ing father George Halas explained. Yet the draft did not immediately create a level playing field—the same three teams appeared in ten of the first eleven championship games in the draft era. "Every year, the rich get richer and the poor get poorer," Commissioner Bert Bell worried. The league continued its search for a way to better equalize the resources available to its franchises.[7]

Television revenue provided a far more effective means of sustaining com-petitive balance; without it, only the Giants and Redskins would have turned a profit in 1952. But television also made vastly divergent resources available. In 1953, the Rams enjoyed a $100,000 contract with Los Angeles' Admiral Television, while the Packers made do with a mere $5,000. The need to keep the Packers competitive with their big-city opponents consistently motivated league-wide decisions and paid off handsomely with the team's dominance in the early and mid-60s. In testimony before Congress, Rozelle championed the measures taken to ensure that Green Bay, which had produced "one of the finest football teams in the history of professional football," could compete with New York, Los Angeles, and Chicago. Even in the early '50s, Federal Judge Allan Grim accepted such arguments, ruling that the NFL could restrict televi-sion conflicts with home games because "professional football is a unique type of business. . . . It is not necessary and indeed it is unwise for all the teams to compete as hard as they can against each other."

As the 1960s began, NFL broadcasts remained a patchwork of NBC, CBS, and Cleveland's Sports Network. The Giants' radio-TV rights brought in $370,000 in 1961, the Packers' $120,000. The upstart AFL, which "couldn't possibly have competed" without TV, as Commissioner Joe Foss said repeat-edly, shared its ABC revenues equally, the Raiders making merely $24,000 less than the Oilers. As part of his cultivation of "league think," Rozelle cajoled NFL owners into copying this plan, once more choosing competitive balance over a purely free market. Again, they did so explicitly in the common inter-est, the Giants' Wellington Mara remarking, "We should all share, I guess. Or we're going to lose some of the smaller teams down the line."[8]

But the older league remained nervous about its room for maneuver, a worry that was soon justified. The NFL submitted its prospective $9 million deal with CBS to Judge Grim in the summer of 1961 to make sure it passed muster, but Grim ruled that the contract constituted an unreasonable violation of the Sherman Act, a decision that would also invalidate the AFL's arrangement. After executives from both leagues testified to Congress that, as Foss put it, "it is necessary to prevent too great disparity in . . . television income," which "requires the pooling of revenues," House Judiciary Committee chair Emanuel Celler introduced the Sports Broadcasting Act to sanction both arrangements. The Act parroted the long-standing argument that collectivist behavior was necessary to ensure professional football's long-term survival, allowing these contracts as long as "such agreement increases rather than decreases the number of professional football clubs so operating." In one of the multiple ironies that accompanied these maneuvers, in 1950, as Republican candidate for governor of South Dakota, Foss had charged his Democratic opponent, future Dolphins owner Joe Robbie, with endorsing "every socialistic plan that has come to the Senate floor." Times had changed.[9]

Each league's viability having been assured, the NFL immediately schemed to keep the best college players from its rival by colluding to draft them so they could play where they preferred. But a free market in salaries promoted often-ruinous competition. When they could not hide collegians from the other league (tales of skullduggery by "babysitters" are legion in this period), teams had to bid competitively for the best talent, most notoriously producing Joe Namath's shocking $427,000 contract with the Jets, and were accordingly spending themselves into oblivion. Without a merger, "weak teams like Denver and Boston as well, perhaps, as Kansas City, Pittsburgh and Miami could not long survive a protracted money war," an NFL spokesman admitted. In a series of secret meetings, Tex Schramm of the Cowboys and Lamar Hunt of the Chiefs hammered out an agreement to unite the competing enterprises without moving or folding a single franchise. In the summer of 1966, a bill permitting the AFL and NFL to merge, play a title game, and institute a common draft made its way through the Senate.

Rozelle had not particularly desired a merger, but once it became a fait accompli, he spent four months lobbying for as much congressional latitude as he could get. He gave up on a Senate measure that awarded pro football baseball's blanket antitrust exemption and settled for extension of the 1961 provisions, testifying that "substantially the same basis of economic opportunity" and a common draft would foster greater parity among teams and slow runaway salaries produced by interleague bidding wars; he produced more than four single-spaced pages of statements from players and newspapers nationwide in support of this proposition.[10]

Celler, still in charge of the House Subcommittee on Anti-Trust and Monopoly, single-handedly stalled the merger. The bill had passed without public hearing, and Celler suspected that the new entity, which enjoyed "virtually unlimited power over a group of employees," would benefit neither league's workforce. Because pro football was "now one of the most important spectator sports in the United States," he bore the responsibility of ensuring that its growth "is not arrested by precipitous legislation." His colleague, Robert Kastenmeier of Wisconsin, agreed, noting the irony that "these football owners engage in an activity that is intrinsically competitive but feel that they cannot compete . . . as other businesses or enterprises do. So they want the rules changed." Celler drew support from citizens who saw the issue as pitting big business against ordinary citizens, one correspondent wishing him "every success if it is your intention to try to protect the individual against the monied self-interest group" and another agreeing that "pro football, with its national attention and interest, certainly should not be able to do things that businesses, etc. cannot."

But powerful forces were lining up behind the NFL. Most of Celler's committee supported the bill, and twenty-five similar measures had been introduced in the House. Democrats and Republicans agreed: failure to pass one of these bills would disappoint "millions of sports followers," as New Jersey's Peter Rodino warned. Colorado's Byron Rogers noted that the Broncos had won just one game that season but could "compete on more even terms with other franchises" with the law's aid, and Minnesota's Clark MacGregor, a "rabid fan" of the winless Vikings, agreed that the legislation would help his favorite team. Aside from Celler and a few allies, most of Congress intuited and accepted the tenets of league think; they approached this and most subsequent questions as fans.[11]

Stuart Symington, Missouri's senior senator, proved notably obliging. Symington pushed to bring teams to the state, then keep them there, in every major sport. He helped bring the NHL Blues, fought Charles Finley's attempt to move the A's to Oakland, and even threatened the Bidwills with congressional action if the NFL Cardinals left town. After Lamar Hunt invited the senator and his wife to a Chiefs' game in 1965, Symington sent Hunt a thank-you note offering assistance: "If there is any way that I could be of possible service to you for bringing that fine team to Missouri, I am sure you know what a privilege that would be." The next summer, Hunt called in the marker. "We need some help to get the Sports Bill or some other type of related anti-trust clearance," he wrote, adding, "will appreciate any help you can give" and enclosing a memo rehearsing the league's talking points. Symington was as good as his word, directing aides to follow the process of the legislation in the House and sending Celler multiple letters on the topic. Even before receiving Hunt's note, he passed along a telegram from the Bidwills, "prominent constituents and my good friends," asking that Celler hold hearings as soon as possible. Two months later, he sent Celler a *Kansas City Star* editorial supporting the merger with a note hoping "we can work this one out, because professional football now means a very great deal to St. Louis as well as Kansas City. Anything you could do to expedite this legislation would be deeply appreciated by every Missourian."

Rozelle exerted his own form of pressure, warning that delay imperiled "the super game," as AFL commissioner Milt Woodard dubbed it, to be played next January, and that denying the combined entity legal protection would open it up to endless litigation. Cowboys' President Tex Schramm, one of the architects of the merger, added that Celler failed to grasp how pro football worked: "The nature of our business makes it essential that we maintain a competitive balance between the teams, not destroy yourself by destroying the competitive balance." The vast majority of citizens who wrote Celler agreed. "Since this fine sport is enjoyed by so many and epitomizes our wonderful America almost more than anything I know," a man from Dallas begged, he hoped the chairman would reconsider. A former "ardent supporter" claimed that he had surveyed 845 people, 796 of whom favored the merger. He might never again support the congressman because "WE, THE PEOPLE that elected you WANT THIS MEASURE PASSED."[12]

One columnist defined the fundamental issue from the owners' perspective: "If the brakes are not applied [to runaway salaries], athletes will keep their bargaining power but will have no place to use it" because multiple franchises, or one league, or both, might bankrupt themselves. Jack Kemp, then heading the AFL Players' Association, defended the merger as therefore "in the best interest" of everyone involved. Many of his colleagues disagreed. The Browns and Oilers voted unanimously to oppose the merger, and House majority whip Hale Boggs's files contain desperate telegrams from players on the Browns,

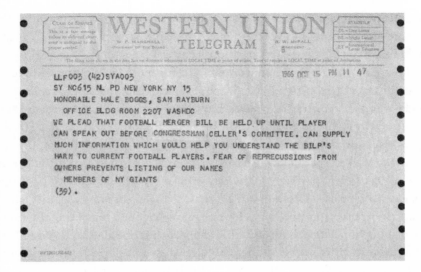

Telegram from New York Giants players to Hale Boggs. (Folder 15, Box 56, Hale and Lindy Boggs Papers, Louisiana Research Collection, Tulane University)

Giants ("fear of repercussions from owners prevents listing of our names"), Raiders ("players should be heard"), Chargers ("we know it seriously [h]its at our rights"), Eagles, Redskins ("kills opportunity of players to voice their opinion"), the president of the NFL Players' Association, the Association's legal counsel, and the AFL Players' Association's general counsel. None got the chance to speak. Taking the players' side, Celler pointed out to the NFL's counsel that "you are trying to prevent . . . these players asking what in your estimation are exorbitant salaries or wages. . . . [Y]ou want to be sure that you can cut them down." He was absolutely right: within five years, the salaries commanded by new players had dropped, by one measure, by one-third to one-half.[13]

Instead, "Pete found a way, as usual," one team owner marveled. As Lawrence O'Brien recalled, the NFL effectively, and repeatedly, "played off expansion against legislation." In exchange for a franchise in New Orleans, Boggs (a native of the city) and his fellow Louisianan, Senate majority whip Russell Long, made what journalists could not resist calling an end-run around Celler by attaching the measure to a budget bill favored by the Johnson administration, assuring that it would pass through the Ways and Means Committee and be ratified before players could testify against it. Boggs's son later confirmed that it was "definitely a quid pro quo": multiple accounts recount Boggs's holding up the bill's passage until Rozelle guaranteed a franchise.

Both Long and Boggs had worked hard for more than a year with local booster David Dixon to procure a team. Competition between the leagues had produced expansion franchises, but Dixon worried that the present allotment of teams slotted perfectly into six divisions of four teams each, leaving New Orleans out in the cold should the two leagues become one. As such, he aimed to stall merger talks until New Orleans was assured that it could join. (After that, he was perfectly fine with cutting off further competition.) Boggs repeatedly promised Dixon that "I am anxious to help in every way that I can," and Dixon in turn praised Boggs for remaining "right on top of the situation," furnishing him with talking points and urging him to call Rozelle directly to "express an attitude of helpfulness." Boggs wrote Rozelle in April to attest to the "highest quality and integrity" of Dixon and his associates and the "unlimited future" of metropolitan New Orleans, statements he repeated to the NFL's meeting on expansion in May and again before the House committee, adding that it was simply a matter of justice: because "professional football has many aspects, some of which are very much associated with the growth of our communities," it would constitute "gross discrimination against our community in not being able to have a franchise. . . . It is what New Orleans and Louisiana wants. It is what the South wants. . . . We have come of age and we deserve a team."[14]

Celler, whose last request for a delay was shouted down, denounced "a shameful thing to do to any group of employees," and later disgustedly told Bernie Parrish that "pro football provides the circus for the hordes." Ever alert to the probability of future entanglements, Rozelle, according to one biographer, subsequently sent Celler a handwritten note apologizing for the maneuver, with the excuse that the enormous pressure exerted by millions of fans had left him no choice. (No such note appears in Celler's files, however.) Just two weeks after Dixon wrote him pressing for speedy confirmation of the franchise in order to ensure passage of the amendment enabling construction of the Superdome, Rozelle duly made the announcement. Boggs hailed this "public service" as "one of the truly historic days" for the city because now "we are on a par, sports-wise, with the other great centers of the United States."[15]

In 1972, the league's policy of blacking out televised games on every station within seventy-five miles of the game, even when the stadium was sold out, prevented Richard Nixon from watching his friend George Allen's Redskins face the Packers in the playoffs from inside the White House. As the *New York Times* noted in passing, the Redskins' improved play moved this question onto the national agenda; the fact that "the team has been in the playoffs the past two years was a factor in the pressure." Infuriated, Nixon threatened to sue. "Get the whole country riled up," he instructed the attorney general. In this case, the president was hardly the only fan with political power at his disposal: bills banning blackouts and threatening the league's anti-trust exemption had been introduced in the House every year since 1969. In 1971, a Florida circuit-court judge lambasted "a transgression and usurpation of the airwaves and the people who own them" when the policy denied 2.5 million South Floridians the opportunity to watch Super Bowl V because it was played in Miami's Orange Bowl.

Rather than enacting any of these bills, the House Interstate Commerce subcommittee acted with "uncommon speed" and "rammed through" without debate an NFL-backed measure preserving blackout rights for games that had not sold out seventy-two hours before their scheduled start, leaving the anti-trust exemption entirely untouched. It passed the House 336–37, and then 76–6 by voice vote in the always-obliging Senate. An irritated Jack Kemp, who had wanted no change at all, protested, "I think the Gulf of Tonkin resolution was the last one to move this fast." "It's not true that Congress is divided, paralyzed, and unable to act with decision and leadership," Nicholas von Hoffman acidly commented. "The pro football fans of America will be able to see their teams' home games this year on television."[16]

Politicians, Pete Rozelle, and team owners repeatedly argued both that professional football's rise to prominence not just encouraged but demanded communal behavior and that their enterprise represented capitalist individualism at its finest. From time to time, sportswriters pointed out this fundamental contradiction. As the merger was taking shape, Dick Young wrote that "the football fellows . . . are offering to put on a great big wonderful championship game . . . and all they ask in return is immunity from lawsuits, which isn't really asking for much. Just a license to steal." In 1971, Jerry Izenberg added that "Professional football is not a business. We know this because all businesses are subject to anti-trust legislation, and apparently professional football is not." Three years later, George Will acerbically noted that, "Like other businessmen begging government to spare them the agony of competition, the [owners] say competition would destroy their industry. . . . What rot."[17]

Yet political invocations of the sport determinedly ignored these off-field machinations. From this perspective, everything that mattered took place on the field, where football tutored spectators in the Protestant ethic and the spirit of capitalism. Conservative Baltimore linebacker Mike Curtis explained that "The American people do not want socialism. Not in their government, and certainly not in their sports." Spiro Agnew, a rabid Colts fan (one of the team's first fifty season-ticket holders, he boasted that he had missed only two home games in twenty years before the 1968 campaign forced him to skip the season opener), repeatedly extolled the "arduous route" to success that sports exemplified. He explained that "it is the spirit of competition that has made our economic system the envy of the world." In 1973, Lamar Hunt wrote Stuart Symington to oppose the TV bill, which he termed "offensive to the concepts of free enterprise," and later passed on "an especially significant" letter from a constituent complaining that the proposal "must be part of a bad dream or else I suddenly find myself in Russia." "I am worried about this," Symington responded three days later. "All I want to do is what is right."[18]

This disparity presents such cognitive dissonance that Kemp, a longtime free-market advocate, felt called upon to deny its very existence in the preface to a book replete with examples of NFL owners' collaborative behavior. "Nothing could be further from the truth" that the league is collective in any way, Kemp wrote. "How has the NFL accomplished all this? By competing with other sports franchises—not itself—and winning in a free market of ideas." In what we might fairly term moving the goalposts, Kemp defined the league's consistent policy of "not competing with itself" as highly individualistic, fully in keeping with its fundamentally conservative public image. In a 1977 symposium on government regulation of pro sports at the libertarian American Enterprise Institute, however, he straightforwardly admitted, "when the Buffalo Bills play the New York Jets, they are not out to wipe each other off the economic field or to wipe each other out financially." Pro football, he stated simply, "is not economic competition." In reality, the league's survival, and then its prosperity, are very much "a tribute to the power of collaborative advantage," as one Harvard business professor put it: a firm, and almost unrivaled, tradition of the richest looking out for the poorest. "Few industry associations have been able to do this as effectively," she added.[19]

With Nixon stumbling reluctantly toward resignation and the capital in a fever about whose secrets would tumble out next, surely the summer of

1974 offered a golden moment to depict the league as a monopolistic cartel restricting its employees' freedom while selling itself as the embodiment of all-American self-reliance. But the players' strike, which began in July, reveals instead how thoroughly most Americans had bought the line that owners were small businessmen just trying to make an honest buck and players cosseted snobs too lazy to get real jobs. "These popinjays are no blue-collar workers," one journalist wrote indignantly in 1970, and attitudes had hardened since. NFL Films had helped to erase the ideas enunciated in *The Violent World of Sam Huff*.[20]

The fundamental issues were inarguable. Players demanded liberties granted to most laborers during the New Deal: the right to movement without undue restriction from one job to another when their contracts were done (substantially hampered by the "Rozelle Rule," which allowed the commissioner to award whatever compensation he deemed appropriate to a team losing a free agent) and cessation of "fines, curfews, and silly rules," including $1,000 for wearing socks to breakfast in New Orleans or for making derogatory remarks about the team in Atlanta. They cast their cause in a contemporary idiom ("no freedom, no football," strikers' T-shirts read), and columnists had written sympathetically about exactly these issues. "19 moves out of 6,000 contracts [in a five-year period] . . . suggests that the 'inhibiting effect' of the 'option plus compensation' arrangement is every bit as severe as the players claim," one concluded. A congressman from California agreed, noting that "we're supposed to be believers in free competitive enterprise, but some of these [owners] want no competition at all."

Unfortunately, the demands of athletes did not register as an urgent matter of social justice. This period marked a low point in popular conception of workers and workers' rights; historian Jefferson Cowie calls it a sense that "it was not simply that specific groups of workers were defeated at specific places, but that the very *idea* of workers in civic and popular discourse was defeated." Thus, "for the first time in the entire history of professional football, the fans are against the players and for the owners." The Giants' Wellington Mara claimed that his mail was running forty- or fifty-to-one in favor of management. The *Miami Herald* noticed "a staggering difference in verbal firepower": NFL owners rhapsodized over the game's traditions and warned of the looming threat of "anarchy" that unionization posed, while NFLPA press releases "written out of an all-night delicatessen" near union headquarters at the Squire Midtown Hotel treated football as a cartel stifling workers' rights. Rozelle's guidance to the league in this area constituted "the deciding factor" in the strike, in one biographer's estimation.[21]

Under these circumstances, it is hardly shocking how few observers took the players' side. Michael Oriard studied columnists from twenty-six papers, only two of whom questioned the dishonest financial figures (understating individual team profits by fully 80 percent) that the owners used to make their case. Bernie Parrish had convincingly debunked such claims in *They Call It a Game* but obscured the justice of his arguments with a farrago of other accusations, so three years later they were apparently forgotten. Only four papers, Oriard notes, "consistently sided with the players." The *Milwaukee Journal* surveyed readers in July and found that 89 percent supported the owners over "denim-clad Bolsheviks" who should "come out into the work world and punch a time clock every day." Even William Barry Furlong of the *Washington Post,* who thought halfway through the strike that "the tactical and public relations edge belongs to the players," predicted that the owners' "clear, dramatic and specific examples" and reliance on passionate appeals to imaginary notions of the NFL would win out. Popular discussion applauded the "independence" of players who crossed picket lines and warned of the threat posed to fans' enjoyment by, apparently, only the remaining strikers, rather than noting the NFL's monopolistic labor relations. By the second week of August, the owners not having budged on a single issue, everyone was back in camp.[22]

Magical Immunities

In Vietnam, too, the league's rhetoric masked a much more politically complicated reality. Both the NCAA and the NFL organized player tours, the colleges somewhat more successfully than the pros. NCAA Executive Director Walter Byers consciously aligned his organization with the establishment at the height of public controversy, running advertisements defending Nixon's conduct of the war to counteract protests inside stadiums, and later extolling Agnew's stalwartness. Despite having made a clear choice, in the summer of 1970 he hypocritically worried that the *Left* would distort and misuse football's nonpartisan essence by tying it to contemporary issues: "The politicizing process . . . carried on by a relatively small number of young people who really are not very serious students . . . will focus on the dedication and discipline necessary to achieve athletic success. . . . It is not unlikely that those playful SDS-types might like to test the administration's courage by interrupting a football game or two." His organization was just then collaborating with the Defense Department to send eight student-athletes, six of them football players, on two-and-a-half week visits to Vietnam and military hospitals in the Pacific.[23]

Though the players do not seem to have been given explicit guidance, the clear presumption was that such tours would further emphasize the NCAA's support for the war—as well as, "through some kind of celebrity magic," render the soldiers' experience more bearable. Both parties in this transaction were busily promoting their preferred visions. The Defense Department's PR expenditures exploded in these years, one estimate in early 1971 guessing that they reached $190 million, exceeding the combined news budget of all three commercial networks by $44 million. Defense hired newsmen and actors to narrate its documentaries and produced feature films that undermined dissent and argued for continued prosecution of the war. "It seems ironic, that while our finest men are fighting halfway across the world, other young men and women safe at home openly advocate abandonment of Vietnam to communism," *Dragnet* star Jack Webb intoned in *A Day in Vietnam*. "Perhaps they really don't know what this war is about."

The biggest celebrities played only the largest and most secure bases—so many so that soldiers there grew bored when second-rank entertainers came by—but players made a habit of visiting smaller and more out-of-the-way outposts. They met servicemen, screened highlight films, handed out pennants and decals, and encouraged every enlisted man to make use of the GI Bill after discharge. An Air Force pilot remembered such visits with gratitude, noting that protests back home "didn't affect us. What we wanted to hear were the replays of the football games."[24]

Officially, the collegians' first visit was a success. After the players' departure, a lieutenant colonel wrote appreciatively that they "had brought a very cherished part of America with them. . . . We were particularly grateful to have had the opportunity of meeting and talking with the stars of a game most of us consider our national pastime." After-action reports sketched the same picture, noting that "handshake-type tours" like this one tended to fare much better out in the bush. Younger players proved "particularly appealing to a greater number of GIs" because they came across as equals; this group was "very personable and well-received." The players occasionally wandered off on their own, and their minder, the NCAA's assistant executive director, "said they were all grown men and he did not intend to treat them like children." Fortunately, a quick refresher on the importance of staying together reminded them to follow orders.

In the end, the athletes "did a remarkably fine job of raising the morale of the troops." The Defense Department was "even more enthusiastic" about the program, sending another four football players and New Mexico's coach to visit servicemen over the Christmas holiday. Though on this trip their escort had to remove women from two players' shared room after midnight, on the whole he too found that, "with the exception of a few rare occasions, the players were accepted by the men with a tremendous amount of success." The entertainment coordinator thought the players' youth and honesty made it "the best handshake tour I've had."[25]

Yet the things they carried back doubtless disappointed Walter Byers. Jim Plunkett, who visited a hotel in Japan and did not get to Vietnam, reported that "It was so sad. It made me wonder why it had to happen." In his autobiography, he remembered that "I might have led an anti-war rally" after the trip. Texas linebacker Scott Henderson "saw a combination of bad mistakes" and now viewed South Vietnam as "a satellite of the United States" rather than an independent nation. Notre Dame guard and co-captain Larry DiNardo wrote a troubled essay discussing his experiences that the school printed in the program for its first home game of the 1970 season. He was gratified to sit down with each soldier and talk rather than merely wandering through—"it gave me a sense of doing something more worthwhile, accomplishing more than just a passing handshake." But television had not prepared him for "the depravity, the heartache, indeed, the obscenity of the war, its devastations, paradoxes and frustrations." DiNardo found Saigon "appalling . . . if you have any feeling for humanity" and returned with the "foremost" impression that the war was "a total waste."[26]

DiNardo later told the school newspaper that "My political views changed entirely after that trip. You have to be there and see the look on those soldiers' faces." But most players refused to take sides. DiNardo refused to appear at political rallies or endorse candidates in a larger cause: "I don't want to be a hero of the New Left. I mean, who's not against this war?" Opinion polls showed that two-thirds of respondents considered the war a mistake, and Gallup didn't even bother asking the question after May 1971. More than half those surveyed supported immediate American withdrawal, regardless of the outcome. In November 1970, the captain of Army's football team earned headlines by making the same point, promising that of course he would do his duty if he was sent overseas, but "football players are the most liberal-thinking cadets in the whole academy. . . . If you polled the team and asked everybody about Vietnam, I think the feeling would be overwhelmingly in favor of our getting out of there."[27]

Even if college players spoke out after their tours much more openly than did the pros, college tours mostly succeeded from a PR standpoint. The players were the soldiers' age, eager to interact as equals, and prone to forgivable mistakes any young men on their own might well make. Professional players' tours, in contrast, inevitably highlighted the paradox that middle Americans' favorite sport was played by pampered professionals who did not adjust easily to the rigors and restrictions of a combat zone. Pete Rozelle had made the NFL the first major league to send players to Vietnam; the initial cohort, which included Johnny Unitas, Sam Huff, and Frank Gifford, departed in January 1966 for a somewhat ramshackle affair that Gifford described in his diary as "a jock *Dr. Strangelove*." The propaganda purposes were clear here: the league's press releases, no doubt written under the direction of Jim Kensil, reiterated football's popularity and consequent civic value. The handout accompanying one 1969 tour, for instance, boasted that "no spectator sport in the history of the United States has enjoyed the sudden growth in popularity that has been accorded to professional football. . . . The NFL and AFL teams have grown in stature along with the major cities of the United States that they represent."

Later excursions—two in 1969, three in 1971 that spent a combined fifty-one days paying visits, three more in 1972—were more tightly organized than the first but ran into more difficulties. Unitas refused to go back in 1969 when Defense refused to underwrite his $1 million insurance policy. Escorts complained that professional players expected pampering that accorded with their celebrity status, getting "grumpy" when filling out forms in a poorly air-conditioned lounge and protesting when their days began at 0730. ("Players had been used to a lot of sleep.") Sometimes their freshly pressed clothing affronted sweat-soaked soldiers digging ditches. Fortunately, at least in this case, the Cowboys' Dan Reeves picked up a shovel and pitched in. "Little individual acts like this . . . brought the players close to the American fighting man."

Still, the pros wandered off during periods assigned for relaxation, then whined about lack of rest. "If they choose, lacking proper guidance, to forego assigned sleep time for personal pleasures—then they should be mature

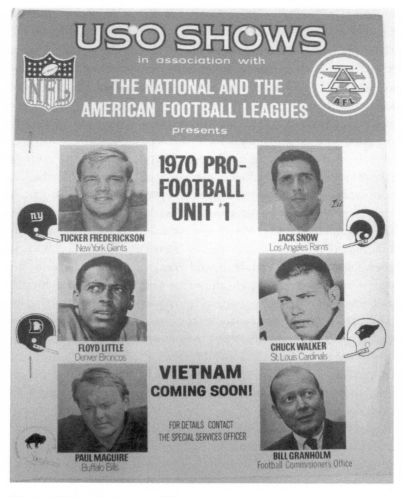

Flier for USO tour in Vietnam, 1970. (National Archives)

enough to assign the responsibility for excessive irritation where it belongs," one escort acerbically pointed out in early 1969. "Because many of these people are understandably not capable of this responsibility, it would appear to be the escort officer's job to remind them, as tactfully as possible, of the very generous nature of their visit with us." Sometimes their celebrity opened doors the military preferred to remain closed. In what was "most certainly an error in judgment," one escort brought the players by the disreputable local motel that served as the Da Nang Press Center ("something like a 1925 auto court, the Long Branch Saloon in Dodge City . . . and a Mexican gambling den," one reporter wrote), among other things, and began extolling "in lavish detail the treasures that lay beyond the guarded gates . . . at least twenty or thirty round-eyes" waiting there every night. Perhaps, the captain intimated, he could get them a discount with the women inside. The players, who "were very enthusiastic, naturally," became "disappointed and disgruntled" when turned away and spent the remainder of the night drinking.[28]

None of these efforts to establish the NFL's concern for the American fighting man dispelled the stench of special privilege that clung to the league when it came time to change uniforms. In late July 1970, Lt. Bob Kalsu, formerly of the Buffalo Bills, became the only active player to give his life in Vietnam when his unit came under mortar fire. In World War II, draft boards did the NFL no favors. The league had done its part and more: despite there being only 330 total roster spots, 638 players served (some, admittedly, as stars of service teams), and in the spring of 1943 several franchises merged when they nearly ran out of 4-F players; the Steelers were down to six.

Late in 1966, a sudden onslaught of articles made clear that professional football players faced far fewer hazards than even other college-educated men of their age, who comprised merely 2 percent of draftees. The league had already become so entrenched that politicians and the military bent over backward to cater to its needs. *Life* acidly noted "pro football's magical immunity" to call-ups: 27 percent of those classified 1-A between the ages of eighteen and thirty-five were drafted, yet somehow only two NFL players out of 960 got the call. The league's soft power lent its franchises the clout to stash draft-eligible men in the National Guard and reserves almost at will despite a 100,000-man waiting list for Guard postings in 1968—"such a dodge," one critic wrote, "that if there had been a call-up there scarcely would have been a football season."[29] A sergeant in Maryland, photographed by *Life* striking a football pose in his very own Colts uniform, openly admitted to "an arrangement" with the team. In Green Bay, all it took was a phone call: "How would you like a couple of Packers in your outfit?" The FBI investigated two army recruiters, one a Korean War veteran who had won three battle stars and a Purple Heart, and their contact inside the Guard, all of whom conspired to guarantee a Jets player a local reserve spot for $200.[30]

Lucien Nedzi, a Democratic representative from Michigan who had seen combat in both World War II and Korea, was so incensed by *Life*'s revelations that he demanded an accounting from the Defense Department. Two weeks later, an embarrassed Defense Secretary Robert McNamara offered the excuse that "procedures being followed in reserve enlistment programs may have resulted in showing preference to those individuals who have the highest mental and physical qualifications, thus bypassing other earlier applicants," and ordered that by February all reserve organizations fill vacancies on a first-come, first-served basis. A preliminary report released the next April found 360 athletes still stationed in military-reserve units, nearly two hundred of them football players. NFL franchises quizzed on this topic displayed great solicitude for privacy, explaining that they either had no idea of their players' status or could not release it. "Their respect for that confidence is so ethical that it exceeds that of the Selective Service System," the reporter asking the questions noted. Ultimately, the army slightly lowered its standards to permit drafting of more athletes and required that all such cases undergo review by the army surgeon general.[31]

Players now began to do their service when called. After multiple postponements, Cardinals' starting quarterback Charley Johnson had to fulfill a two-year obligation just as training camp was getting underway in 1967, as did Giants' kicker Pete Gogolak, three rejections and nine months after his initial physical. He got weekends off to kick, then missed the entirety of the 1968 season when posted to Germany. Yet such anecdotal evidence, along with the changes in Defense Department policy, did not dent widespread public skepticism. A June 1967 poll revealed that 78 percent of respondents thought that "a lot" of draft-dodging was taking place, with 64 percent believing that "prominent athletes and other celebrities" received special treatment.

Perhaps for good reason: the several-month sequence that, despite the Steelers' best efforts, eventually got Rocky Bleier to the front in 1969, where he won a Purple Heart and a Bronze Star, revealed just how many strings professional teams could pull. When Bleier received notice that his student deferment had expired, the team assured him that "we'll get this taken care of," but its pet congressman had lost his bid for reelection and its friendly army general had died, leaving him to the mercies of his hometown draft board, which ordered him to take a physical. When a spot opened in a local National Guard unit, the team's business manager told Bleier, "Even if you have to lie [about having been called up elsewhere], just get into it." When the hometown board responded by inducting him, the team sent him to a colonel in the Marine Reserve who also worked as a "longtime football and basketball official" and was a friend of the Rooney family. When the colonel could not guarantee Bleier a spot for the next fall's class, nor did Bleier feel right in rigging up an injury sufficiently damaging to delay induction and get him into Marine Officer Candidate School instead, then, and only then, did he have to appear.

An outraged Art Rooney Jr. later wrote without irony that, "What Bleier had done at Notre Dame, and what he might possibly do for the Pittsburgh Steelers, made no difference whatever" to the woman who ran the board. Still, the battlefield heroics of Bleier and Bill Carpenter, famous a decade before as Army's "lonesome end," were far more the exception than the rule. "The drudgery and the dying are being done, as usual, by nonentities," Jack Mann wrote. A mere six NFL players ended up serving in the war.[32]

Political Exploitation at Its Best

It was testimony to the success of its marketing efforts that few observers at the time connected these dots, which would certainly have complicated the NFL's attempts to tie itself to the most patriotic American emblems. In contrast, pregame and halftime shows, which combined marketing with a broader tradition of public pageantry, staked hyper-patriotic claims that some critics did find troubling. Rozelle proudly described "a conscious effort on our part to bring the element of patriotism into the Super Bowl." Between 1968 and 1974, the NFL frantically waved the flag through pregame flyovers, chest-thumping halftime shows, and appearances by astronauts.

It began with symbols that bore little partisan ballast. Ten astronauts were given VIP passes for Super Bowl I, and the halftime show featured a band playing the theme from *The Sound of Music*, then forming the shootout at the OK Corral, the Liberty Bell, and a map of the country. The crew of Apollo 8 led the Pledge of Allegiance at Super Bowl III in 1969.[33] In a spot of free advertising that must have made the NFL's day, two months later, fifteen-year-old Eddie Borman told his father, "that trip around the moon was well worth it." Rozelle was more honest about who needed whom, remarking that the astronauts "were thanking me over and over, when I was grateful to *them* for coming." The NFL found this convergence of images so congenial that it invited the crew of Apollo 11 to do the same honors in 1970 and that of Apollo 17 in 1973.

In an apposite symmetry of spectacle, in 1979 NASA returned the favor by hiring NFL Films to commemorate the tenth anniversary of Apollo 11, which it treated as more or less narratively indistinguishable from a football game. One sportswriter had fantasized about that possibility in 1971, suggesting that public disinterest in Apollo 14 might best be remedied by an interview between Howard Cosell and Alan Shepard, "an astronaut who truly glides across the surface of the moon with the grace of a deer." "People can relate to the Super Bowl easier," Shepard remarked. "The space program is a continual selling job." Buzz Aldrin later wistfully commented that if NFL Films had promoted NASA full-time, the government would never have cut the agency's budget.[34]

Overheated celebrations in January quickly became a cliché, and by the early 1970s they read as more openly Republican. The 1970 Super Bowl pregame show featured the New Christy Minstrels, "young Americans who demonstrate—with guitars." Halftime "employed 20,000 balloons, 50 American flags, 3,000 pigeons, [and] 37 muskets" in celebration of the Battle of New Orleans. In theory, at least: according to one sportswriter, "contrary to the history books, the British were winning easily." *TV Guide* called it "mind-boggling," and not in a good way. Critics began to charge that the NFL was taking sides while pretending not to.

Radicals had already pictured professional football games as potential Nuremberg rallies. "The time immediately following the end of the first half of the Green Bay football game has been designated as the official hour of thanksgiving" for "5 years of LBJ, the armed forces, hydrogen bombs, J. Edgar Hoover, the CIA, Richard Nixon, and Spiro Agnew," *The Rag* imagined in 1968. "A uniform time will allow people to note dissenting individuals and report them." Now more mainstream sportswriters joined them. "Never in the history of this country, with the exception of V-J Night, has 'God Bless America' been played as many times as it has been played on televised football games," Jerry Izenberg wrote in the fall of 1970. "This came at a time when the President and his people were out hitting hard. If you opposed the war, you opposed America. Now, translate that to, if you opposed America (which you didn't in the first place) you opposed football, and if you opposed football, well, my God, where will it all lead?" The networks did their part to associate football with pro-war sentiment, NBC and CBS arguing that televising a flyover by military jets in missing-man formation after the Super Bowl was apolitical "because it was hard not to sympathize with the prisoners." One troubled sportswriter called it "political exploitation at its best—or worst—depending on your politics."

After the 1971 Super Bowl, Izenberg protested the "non-stop half-time marathon of 'America the Beautiful' and 'The Battle Hymn of the Republic' played against a backdrop of two million trombones, a half-million baton slingers, and enough patriotic floats to repel the British invasion of Washington." Hunter S. Thompson went further, predicting a dangerous level of compensation after America's inevitable departure from Vietnam: "all kinds of madness—bizarre halftime shows with much more violence and sex than they have now. People flogging each other . . . cockfights or gladiator matches. We wiped out the Indians. We tried to move into Indochina but it didn't work. That aggression will have to be expressed in another form."[35]

Dan Jenkins memorably skewered such would-be sacraments in his 1972 novel *Semi-Tough,* piling patriotic signifiers atop one another in a multiplatform assault on the senses until symbolic delirium results. At the Super Bowl, Billy Clyde Puckett's coach warns him and the rest of the Giants to prepare themselves for patriotic pregame onslaughts from every direction and in every genre:

> We might have a long time to lay around the dressing room after we warmed up because the National Football League had a fairly lavish pregame show planned. . . .
>
> Several hundred birds—all painted red, white and blue—would be released from cages somewhere and they would fly over the coliseum in the formation of an American flag.
>
> As the red, white and blue birds flew over, Boke Kellum, the Western TV star, would recite the Declaration of Independence.
>
> Next would be somebody dressed up like Mickey Mouse and somebody else dressed up like Donald Duck joining the actress Camille Virl in singing "God Bless America."
>
> And right in the middle of the singing, here would come this Air Force cargo plane to let loose fifty sky divers who would come dropping into the coliseum.
>
> Each sky diver would be dressed up in the regional costume of a state, and he would land in the coliseum in the order in which his state became a United State. . . .
>
> Finally . . . the teams would be introduced and two thousand crippled and maimed soldiers on crutches and in wheel chairs and on stretchers would render the "Star-Spangled Banner."[36]

His parody reveals just how widespread suspicion already was of Super Bowl ceremonies' will to power.

Rag Days

All of this overkill, comparatively rudimentary as it was, helps explain the nostalgia that cropped up just as halftimes started to bloat. "Professional football is an enterprise that tends to ignore its past," one journalist wrote in 1970. "The emphasis is always on the onward and upward." Bob Curran's *Pro Football's Rag Days* (1969), Myron Cope's *The Game That Was* (1970), and Gerald Eskenazi's *There Were Giants in Those Days* (1976) partook in the gush of warm feelings for the past that brought forth *American Graffiti* and *The Way We Were* (both released in 1973) and a spate of enormously popular baseball books, like Roger Kahn's gauzy *The Boys of Summer* (1972). None of them relished an atavistic age of head-knocking that the modern game had repudiated in a concession to weak-kneed modern sensibilities. (This perspective rendered invisible those "savagery on Sunday" articles from the 1950s.) Instead, these books reflected a new sense that the NFL had a history worth telling, though they preferred to idealize an allegedly simpler, apolitical, and less commercially saturated past.

Once upon a time, from this perspective, men wore crewcuts, heroes were worth worshipping, and sports mirrored a society in harmony. All of these books dissented from the aura of spectacle and self-importance that permeated the contemporary NFL—and that the various NFL enterprises had been striving mightily to imprint on every reader or viewer's brain—looking back warmly to an endearingly ramshackle collective endeavor where players earned a princely $100 per game and a franchise could sell for a dollar. The scarcity of money formed a major theme in each book; George Halas told Cope that the Bears had earned a cumulative profit of $71.63 in 1921, a resoundingly untrue fable he had peddled for years. Never averse to selling to the zeitgeist, NFL Creative turned out its own versions, Mickey Herskowitz's *The Golden Age of Pro Football* and the edited collection *More Than a Game,* in 1974.[37]

According to *They Call It Pro Football,* which opened with grainy 1920s footage of "22 nameless men grappling in the mud," or NFL Productions' *The First Fifty Years,* society and league had evolved together from colonies to world power: "The pioneers worked hard and played hard to build a dream which has manifested in the last third of the twentieth century. . . . As these modern warriors flash through their patterned movements, with high-speed precision and a fierceness borne of the near perfection of the human physique, it is hard to connect them with the beleaguered men who pioneered their game fifty years ago. . . . Yet they are tied by inheritance and spirit."[38] These books voyaged back to that less commercial world, where football was untainted by the modern promotional apparatus, most especially television.

For these writers, the past was harsher yet truer, its meanings plainer and more real than they were today. Curran's "rag days" end with the ascension of Rozelle, the start of the "riches era." Eskenazi celebrates the '50s Giants as "relief on Sundays from the ever-present reality of the real world." Cope limits his scope to players from the game's beginnings to the early 1950s, "when television money began to come into the game in a meaningful way." He takes readers to a time when "there were no offers to endorse shaving cream" and "an America we shall never see again" expressed itself in all its vigor. Many of the players he interviewed agreed. As Red Grange put it, these days football was "important, and there isn't anything very funny in it. . . . The fate of the nation did not depend on whether you won or lost." Professional football once had the freedom *not* to matter.

Yet there never was a time when "there were no offers to endorse shaving cream." Multiple players boasted endorsement deals in the 1930s: Cliff Montgomery of the Dodgers advertised Camel cigarettes and Sid Luckman had a radio program. In 1937, Benny Friedman and Bronko Nagurski became the first football players to appear on Wheaties boxes. Eskenazi's Giants had been Madison Avenue darlings, with Frank Gifford and Charlie Conerly, one of the first Marlboro Men, especially attractive to advertisers. The photogenic Gifford endorsed Rapid Shave cream, Mennen aftershave, Vitalis hair tonic, Dry Sack sherry, Wilson sporting goods, Lucky Strike cigarettes, Planters nuts, Willard batteries, Jantzen sportswear, and Westinghouse appliances. In 1959, Sam Huff did PR for a cigarette company and went down into a mine, reluctantly, to celebrate being named "Coal Athlete of the Year" by the National Coal Policy Conference. *The Violent World* got him an offseason job, and then a second career, with the textile firm J.P. Stevens, which hired "a pro football hero with his own brand name" and made him into "a hard-driving promotional spokesman . . . just as handy with an attaché case as he is with a football." Nonetheless, the mythic appeal of olden days, and the refusal to admit the reality that football had never wanted to free itself of mass-media taint—had in fact always been a robustly commercialized proposition—hints at lingering fantasies of escape from what the NFL was becoming.[39]

An American Institution

By the mid-'70s, the NFL's commemoration of its product's significance, its underlining and capitalization of MEANING, had spurred far more derision for canapés and plastic helmets than celebration of anything about the game. These jokes only grew louder when the league clamored for official acknowledgment of its importance. For obvious reasons, the NFL hoped very much to stitch itself into the Bicentennial, but it had not figured out how to do so. By no means was this effort unusual. "All large commercial ventures want to play," Mary McGrory wrote. Gulf Oil sponsored a wagon-train pilgrimage to Valley Forge. The Smithsonian relied on American Airlines and General Foods to help fund its observances. In the absence of official outreach, in March 1975 American Revolution Bicentennial Administration (ARBA) head John Warner thanked the conspicuously patriotic George Allen for offering to fill a "void within the world of sport. Sports are one of the most vital elements of our daily existence and indeed our national heritage." Even so, the ARBA did not expect the NFL's approach two months later; its proposal for a role in the Bicentennial occasioned surprise. "There is nothing wrong with your eyes, the attached brief sheet is real," one staff member wrote Warner's deputy at the end of May.[40]

Public-relations director Don Weiss proposed a three-part commemoration: the Hall of Fame game in August, an essay contest for the fall, and "incorporation of the Bicentennial theme" into halftime at next January's Super Bowl. The ARBA staff seconded the application in terms that would have made the league's promotional apparatus glow: "The NFL is an exceptional organization and has a history which emphasizes public service and cooperation with government agencies." The brief approvingly mentioned the league's public-safety spots on conservation and energy and its work with the Drug Enforcement Administration, the Defense Department, the United Way, and the Office of Minority Business Enterprise. The NFL's program was national, feasible, and linked to the Bicentennial. More than that, "The NFL is not just a professional sports organization, it is an American Institution [capitalization in original]. Needless to say, this program provides a unique opportunity."

At the end of June, Warner approved the initiative, noting that the ARBA "considers it a privilege to recognize those programs which emphasize the ideas associated with the evolution of this nation, particularly those which have been so important in strengthening our posture domestically and internationally. The NFL has indeed contributed to this process." The work done in public relations, films and books, and visits to Vietnam had paid off handsomely with governmental ratification of the NFL's claims for its significance, and in nearly the exact terms that the league had been pushing on the public for a decade.[41]

Had the process stopped there, everything would have been fine. In August 1975, the NFL proudly publicized its status as "the first professional sports organization to receive official recognition for its contributions to the nation's 200th anniversary celebration." The Bengals and Redskins affixed official Bicentennial emblems to the shoulders of their jerseys at their exhibition in Canton, and that game and the Super Bowl became certified Bicentennial events. Rozelle also announced the essay contest for high-school students, with a deadline of November 15. The essays, on the topic of "the NFL's Role in American History," should run 500–750 words and be sent to a post-office box in Minnesota. The winner would receive a $10,000 college scholarship, a substantial sum. Conservative outlets like the *Wall Street Journal* welcomed a correction in perspective: "The fever that led some people to perceive the NFL as a budding Panzer division has subsided. Nevertheless, a little revisionism . . . might help balance the scales" by reminding Americans at large of the great contributions the league had made to the nation's spirit.[42]

That opinion was not widely shared. One newspaper described reactions ranging from "derisiveness to hysterical laughter. . . . The NFL essay contest may become a first-rate example of freedom of expression by showing that Americans can say anything—no matter how silly." Russell Baker bestowed "this month's Utter Nonsense Award" on the league and turned in a mocking entry claiming that "for 300 years, this miserable collection of colonialists eked out their dreary existence on that brutal soil with nothing to do on Sunday afternoons after church but go to church again. Fortunately . . . if the colonies became a nation . . . the long-sought National Football League could become a reality." Columnists, Mary McGrory most notably, delighted in publishing studiedly ponderous entries.

The Sporting News derided the NFL's "delusions of grandeur": "its place in American history? You'll need a microscope to find it." A month later, the magazine reiterated that the NFL "wouldn't wince a bit if any of its contest entrants compared the building of the nation with the building of a football dynasty." (As we've seen, this is a fair reading of some of David Boss's productions.) *New York* magazine titled its summit, "The NFL's Role in American

The NFL/Bicentennial essay contest is open to all American citizens between the ages of 14 and 18 who are not already registered at a college or university. The deadline is November 15, 1975. Prizes total $25,000, including a $10,000 college scholarship and trip to the Super Bowl as first prize. The essay topic is: "The NFL's Role in American History." All entries, which must contain 500 to 750 words, should be mailed to NFL/Bicentennial Scholarship, P.O. Box 867, Winona, Minnesota 55987. Contest rules available by writing to the NFL Office.

The NFL announces its misbegotten Bicentennial-essay contest, October 1975.

History (Somebody's Gotta Be Kidding)." In late December, the *Los Angeles Times* included the contest as one of the NFL season's lowlights. "We had the purest of motives," Don Weiss pleaded. He then said the whole thing had been the government's idea.[43]

But the quantity of ridicule of this particular stab for significance should not obscure the larger point. The essay contest attests to the league's success rather than its failure. As the supporting memo pointed out, many different government agencies happily cooperated with the NFL. The winning essay depicted football as a colorblind meritocracy ("one's ability as a football player counts, not one's race or religion. Influential friends or family cannot win a player a position") that exemplified *e pluribus unum*: teams cemented communal, municipal, and sometimes even regional identities for Virginians, Texans, and New Yorkers. Only three years later, NFL Films' anointing of the Cowboys as "America's team" in its 1978 highlight reel was a runaway success.[44] Even as cooperation underwrote the league's success, onlookers applauded its competitive, individualist bona fides. Even as it strove to keep its players off the front lines, the NFL promoted itself as the most visibly patriotic institution in the country. The league's unquestioned cultural and political power by the mid-70s was an organic, collective creation, equally a product of its soft power and of awareness of its popularity that induced government bureaucrats at all levels to hurry to its aid: truly, a national pastime.

PART II

MAKING FOOTBALL POLITICAL

4

The Kennedy/Lombardi School

You are not following the game plan.
—White House investigator John Caulfield to
captured Watergate burglar James McCord[1]

In 1925, when Calvin Coolidge met Red Grange, then playing
for the Bears, he had no idea he was in the presence of greatness. "I've always
liked animal acts," Coolidge said. "That sort of remark today," the *Wall Street
Journal* editorialized, "would be grounds for impeachment." Every candidate
in the 1970 California gubernatorial election took a position on football,
rising star (and sitting governor) Ronald Reagan and challenger Jesse Un-
ruh dropping in at Rams practices and third-party candidate Timothy Leary
pledging to use the power of the office to de-emphasize that "speed and booze
game" in favor of baseball, "a gentle marijuana game." At year's end, noting
that the victorious Reagan had called to congratulate the Raider who caught
the game-clinching touchdown pass against the Dolphins in the playoffs,
one journalist thought that the gesture hinted at a White House run. In the
future, he predicted, game programs might list "not only a player's name . . .
but also his political affiliation." The Raider in question, Rod Sherman, was in
fact a Republican who served as an alternate convention delegate (in Miami,
coincidentally) in 1972.[2]

It was not simply that presidents now had to identify famous football players on sight. Nor did they merely need to refer to last night's game, or pay
attention to the NFL's legislative desires. The similarities and obligations ran

deeper. By the early 1970s, to many observers talking politics meant talking football. The two grew increasingly hard to distinguish: the same players, the same turns of phrase, the same behaviors. Consultants and image manufacturers constantly likened it to their craft, and football *itself* became a way of conducting these politics. Noting that the Defense Department had bought Redskins tickets for Northrup executives, Mary McGrory acidly noted, "It does seem that it should have been the other way around, but that is a whole other question." Former quarterback Jack Kemp, a political "No. 1 draft choice, a bonus baby," as a *Sports Illustrated* reporter following his campaign put it, led a wave of player-politicians. "One wishes," a journalist wrote, "that flankerbacks . . . would confine their exploits to the playing field and keep away from board rooms [and] political campaigns."

Instead, at the 1972 Republican convention, the Packers' Bart Starr introduced Gerald Ford and Kemp gave an "electrifying" speech seconding the nomination of Spiro Agnew—a clue, many thought, that he was being showcased for the Senate in 1974 or vice presidency in 1976. Nixon and Agnew made statements by going to games and applauding and criticizing particular players. Football "reflects our politics, our economic system, our college-board examinations, and, in short, our whole way of life," Jerry Izenberg wrote. If you understood pro football, you understood politics, and vice versa.[3]

These repeated crossovers in turn provoked sportswriters and readers to debate what constituted news. When the *Washington Post* detailed its prizewinning political columnist David Broder to cover a Redskins' *preseason* game, what was the proper ambit of the sports pages? Some found the whole enterprise suspect. This period marked the heyday of the anti-sports sports book, authors feverishly denouncing a complex repressive pathology that they variously labeled a "sports syndrome," "jockocracy," or "SportsWorld," as Robert Lipsyte subtitled his 1975 attack on "An American Dreamland." Leonard Shecter concluded *The Jocks,* the most outraged of these books, with the plea that "there are shadows on our land, shadows of hate and war and poverty and despair. So we get caught up in games. There must be better ways to spend our time." Others strove to untangle cause and effect. "We all ran out to buy tickets," Dave Kindred remembered, "hooked forever when instant replay let us see the violence repeated. Vietnam and Kent State, the Democrats in Chicago, Medgar Evers shot in Mississippi, JFK and Bobby and Martin Luther King . . . violence in reality and in shoulder pads." Still others decided to resist this spectacle by mocking the Super Bowl, the ultimate political-athletic spectacle.[4]

The interconnections and affinities between football and politics provoked a huge and not always coherent range of attempts to grapple with the contours of this new culture. This new language did not simply pit left against right, nor was it just another theater of engagement for paralyzing contemporary cultural and social conflicts. Instead, the kinds of spectacle embodied in the new politics and football moved in multiple directions, empowering a variety of contestants to make themselves heard.

I'll Take My Candidate and Beat Yours

The first campaign consultants plied their trade in the 1930s, and Vance Packard's best-selling *The Hidden Persuaders* warned about their machinations in 1957. By the mid-'60s the trend had gained unmistakable national momentum. Twenty-five House races were professionally managed in 1960; by 1968, 125 were. Senate candidates availing themselves of complete campaign-management services rose 722 percent from the mid-'50s to the late-'60s, those contending for the House 842 percent. Republicans embraced such tactics especially eagerly, their spending on electronic media in presidential elections alone exploding from $2 million in 1952 to $12.6 million in 1968, with Democrats' jumping from $1.5 million to $6.1 million over the same period.[5]

The experts handling these contests, wielding job titles like campaign management consultant, PR counselor, advertising agent, marketing researcher, and media advance person, repeatedly invoked the politics-as-football analogy. Vic Gold, one of the trade's most unabashed practitioners, followed his tribulations in what Nixon called "the toughest job in the country"—Spiro Agnew's press secretary—by becoming an avid fan of the art of "putting points on the board during the network evening news show." "Like Don Meredith in his cherry-picker announcer's booth," he wrote in his mordant color commentary on the heavily stage-managed 1976 election, "the Retired Flack kibitzes the candidates, their Game Plans and their Teams, Wednesday morning quarterbacking the Thrill of Victory, the Agony of Defeat." American politics, he thought, were indistinguishable in nature and process from football: "I'll take my candidate and beat yours or, if the coin flip comes up otherwise, your candidate and beat mine [a remark generally ascribed to Oiler coach Bum Phillips].[6] It's X's and O's on a media blackboard, mousetraps and blitzes and crackback blocks and penalties and desire and execution and fumbles and breaks."[7]

Gold was hardly alone. Many practitioners of this art were quite literally keeping score, "and as they count them the records are phenomenally and uniformly successful," one scholar discovered after interviewing a large cross-section of campaign managers. A major consultant requested anonymity before confessing, "There were two long-shot races last year that I just didn't want to take because I didn't want the losses on my record." The scholar added that "it is not their business to calculate the possible impact of what they do in an election on future policy or governmental actions any more than it is the professional football player's problem to worry about the impact of football on people's attitudes toward violence and aggression. . . . They are getting paid to play a game they like." In the wake of the consultant-dominated 1970 elections, the *Washington Post* ran a box score comparing the various experts' winning percentages. "I sometimes think it's what fighting a war or playing a pro football game is like," renowned Democratic advance man Jerry Bruno wrote. What insiders contemplated with a jaundiced eye distressed onlookers, whom we might as well call spectators. A political scientist complained in 1975 about "the corruption of the discourse of politics," which at times threatened to be "completely absorbed by the language of sports." Curmudgeonly linguist Edwin Newman agreed completely, writing in 1974 that he welcomed the end of football season because of his "protective interest in the English language."[8]

The ideal candidate in these circumstances, according to the president of the Broadcast Placement Company, should convey heroism in its most telegenic form: "It is the man we are looking at and not so much his message." It did not matter what the figure in question had done, the president of one agency remarked. "You're looking at some basic qualities . . . : believability, glamour, supply and demand." Football players and coaches were prototypical new-politics figures, readymade celebrities with mainstream cachet who were already comfortable in the spotlight. Many of them openly embraced such a conception. "There are no sports stories in New York, only sagas, epics, and legends," Fran Tarkenton remarked. "You have to be aware of this before you can understand the impact of New York on a professional athlete." Both parties tried to induce Tarkenton, who had incorporated himself by the time he was thirty, to run for lieutenant governor of Georgia. Gerald Ford called players like Kemp and Tarkenton "highly qualified [as politicians] . . . because they understand the problems you face with the second guesser, the people who never caught or threw a pass."[9]

Believability and glamour played especially well when condensed into highlights. "Television has changed the whole conception of American politics," one consultant explained in a front-page *Washington Post* story in the spring of 1970. A raft of popular and scholarly books prophesied that "the expanding technology of political manipulation" through TV would lead inevitably to domination of "image candidates" equipped to win "the election game."[10] The astonished student who remarked that, after a famously surreal late-night run-in with Richard Nixon at the Lincoln Memorial just after Kent State, "you hoped it was an actor, goofing," was more right than she knew. Nixon delivered all of his most ideologically crucial addresses in these years on television, including the Silent Majority speech in 1969 and his Kansas State speech the next fall setting out the administration's agenda. "We're moving into a period where a man is going to be merchandised on television more and more. It upsets you and me, maybe, but we're not typical Americans," the top assistant to his campaign filmmaker told a reporter.

The 1970 election, the same fall as *Monday Night Football*'s first season, marked a watershed. By its end, the requirement of performance, and the notion that the success of political parties themselves depended on mastery of stagecraft, were simply taken for granted. The Republican National Committee recruited challengers for shaky Democratic seats with explicit promises of professional management. Stories abounded of a growing roster of consultants offering these candidates ever more intrusive grooming advice (a young Roger Ailes told one client to lose twenty-five pounds and grow his hair) and inventing news designed to cater to network appetites. In Indiana, Richard Roudebush's people were caught retaining eight longhairs at $75 per hippie to illustrate youth malfeasance by drinking, smoking, and littering on cue.[11]

Colleges pushing candidates for the Heisman Trophy similarly blurred the lines. "Outstanding football ability isn't enough anymore," the *Los Angeles Times* mourned. "It takes quite an advertising campaign, too." Election season started earlier and earlier. Over the summer of 1970, the University of Mississippi sent out "gorgeous posters" extolling Archie Manning as "Heroic, Exciting, Illusive [sic], Surpassing, Magic, Aeronautic, Nonpareil, Navigator, Incomparable, Nimble, Great." It later printed up bumper stickers, dolls, and buttons ("Archie's No. 1"), and even promoted a local hit, "The Ballad of Archie Who." Before the college season kicked off, someone congratulated

Mississippi's publicist on his winning campaign. (Manning finished third.) Notre Dame's sports information director changed the pronunciation of Joe Theismann's name from "Theesman" to "Thighsman" to subliminally remind voters that he deserved the award. (He finished second.) Purdue's former sports information director told an inquisitive columnist that rumors he had been fired for not delivering the school a Heisman winner were "not true. Well, not entirely true."

Stanford's unusually sophisticated campaign opened in mid-August with Sports Information Director Bob Murphy's preemptive pledge that, unlike his counterpart in Mississippi, he would absolutely *never* attempt to garner the award for Jim Plunkett "in the publicity office," which he followed with three pages "raving on and on about Plunkett's credentials . . . winning, or about to win, everything in sight" and pleading that voters "resist the 'band wagon' approach and wait." School-issued propaganda sheets "would have us believe his given names are Heisman Trophy Candidate," *Sports Illustrated* observed. In October, the school put out a four-page color booklet, purely as "a service to the media," boosting Plunkett as gifted on the field, devoted in the classroom (he boasted a B average in political science), and socially committed ("of Mexican descent," he "has withstood tremendous pressure off the football field as well as on")—"the greatest thing since cohabitation," according to one wag. He won.

A local columnist facetiously bestowed "flack-of-the-year" honors on the director for overcoming "the bloc of Southern voters" to pull off this feat. Murphy's victory announcement could just as well have heralded a winning politician. He took care to emphasize that "Plunkett won in *all five regions* of the country . . . and that includes the South, where the Archie Manning votes were most heavily located." ("The Ballad of Archie Who" had in fact encouraged "Archie Super Manning" to run for president.) There was even a campaign-finance scandal, Stanford standing accused of spending $25,000 to procure Plunkett's victory. The school retorted, perhaps not entirely truthfully, that it had spent less than $320. A disgruntled sportswriter wrote in 1971 of Heisman voting that, "by comparison, our political conventions are a model of democracy at work."[12]

To cement that impression in voters' minds, both parties strove mightily to present tighter programming for the 1972 season. Only one of them suc-ceeded. In the aftermath of the chaotic 1968 convention, the DNC established a Rules Commission tasked with establishing "a set of procedures and a format

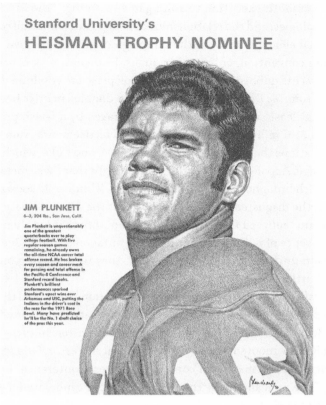

Stanford University's
HEISMAN TROPHY NOMINEE

JIM PLUNKETT
6–3, 204 lbs., San Jose, Calif.

Jim Plunkett is unquestionably one of the greatest quarterbacks ever to play college football. With five regular season games remaining, he already owns the all-time NCAA career total offense record. He has broken every season and career mark for passing and total offense in the Pacific-8 Conference and Stanford record books. Plunkett's brilliant performances sparked Stanford's upset wins over Arkansas and USC, putting the Indians in the driver's seat in the race for the 1971 Rose Bowl. Many have predicted he'll be the No. 1 draft choice of the pros this year.

Stanford's promotional brochure for Jim Plunkett's Heisman candidacy. (Courtesy of Stanford Athletics)

. . . that strikes the average voter . . . as *sensible*," the communications chair wrote. "What takes place inside the convention hall should communicate, at least in some measure, that the political party has some notion of where it is going." Yet George McGovern's decision to accept the nomination at 3:00 A.M. revealed a continuing inability to effectively control and deliver these messages. "We lost the election at Miami," the rules chair remarked. "It was all over right then and there."

The Nixon campaign made sure this would not happen. It endured only passing scandal when its meticulously crafted convention script, with every "spontaneous" demonstration scheduled down to the minute, was inadvertently leaked to the BBC. The head of Nixon's advertising agency chalked up his team's smooth execution to solid game planning: "The President likes football analogies, and the relationships of field position and ball control were the essential elements of what the campaign organization tried to do." The Republican convention, enhanced by luaus, brunches, rock concerts, and a flotilla of yachts dubbed "Nixon's Navy," took place on a podium designed by an expert from *The Dating Game*. It more than doubled in price between 1968 and 1972, at least some of that expense defrayed by a lavish program that brought in $1.6 million from 160 pages of advertisements from more than 180 corporations that included Pepsi, Ford, IBM, and Coke, which purchased the back page. Appalled by the patterns of thought that these metaphors suggested, which brought a landslide victory in 1972 but would soon destroy the president, the disgusted liberal Republicans at the Ripon Society wrote that Nixon's team "suffered from a game plan mentality that led them to believe that the essence of politics was outpointing antagonists and adversaries. . . . It was often unclear whether they thought they were playing on a football field or a battlefield."[13]

Nixon called football "perhaps my second vocation" and noted that he would happily exchange his job for Pete Rozelle's. He repeatedly remarked that, were he to do it all over again, he'd have been a sportswriter. In turn, journalists covering Rozelle mooted him as Nixon's natural successor. One sportswriter, beholding Rozelle's masterful conduct of a press conference, immediately thought, "The man should be the next Republican candidate for President." Another noted that "his power is astonishing. . . . He might just be asking himself if there are any more worlds to conquer in football." The comparison made perfect sense: both chief executives stocked their administrations with men whose experience came primarily in public relations and advertising, and both administrations diligently sold their respective products to the public.[14]

The period between 1969 and 1972 marked the high point of media buys; given the advantages of incumbency, the Nixon administration cut back significantly on its expenditures the second time around. But the changes were permanent. James Reston praised sports as "not only America's diversion and illusion but its hope. . . . They have more pageantry and even dignity than most mass occasions in American life; more teamwork, more unity." The Watergate hearings, and their political consequences, simply sustained this trend. One critic noted that testimony in the hearings revealed "the extent to which . . . language drawn from football . . . has come to permeate the day-to-day operations of the American executive branch." George Will agreed, writing that fall that, given "the patois of contrived complexity and faked sophistication" that football and politics shared, it seemed "oddly reasonable that [Howard] Cosell is thinking of running for the Senate."

When numerous commentators blamed Watergate on the baneful influence of Vince Lombardi, no one dismissed the idea as absurd. Sportswriter Leonard Koppett noted that convicted burglar Bernard Barker said that he "wasn't paid to think" of his role in the break-in. "Where, if not in sports, do young men (and women) learn the lesson that in our culture that victory 'at any cost' is an acceptable goal?" Koppett wondered. "How many athletes, especially football players, could make the same heartfelt statement [as Barker] after years of indoctrination by coaches? How many sportswriters and commentators have completely accepted, and helped disseminate, that philosophy?" "The Winning Is Everything Syndrome which is the basis of the Watergate affair originated in sports," Glenn Dickey added. The Committee to Re-Elect the President was a prototypical new-politics organism, devoted solely to Nixon's prospects, entirely independent of the Republican Party, and staffed by professionals in many of these new fields. It did its part to prove the point with the slightly rewritten version of the slogan popularly attributed to Lombardi posted in its war room: "WINNING IN POLITICS ISN'T EVERYTHING, IT'S THE ONLY THING."[15]

By 1976, this was simply how you played "the sport of politics and the politics of sport." The first official Bicentennial observance took place at the Super Bowl in January, and in the fall both campaigns buffed their merchandise to a shine. Jimmy Carter's media advisor stressed that debate preparation worked on sharpening and accentuating his "naturalness," and his PR man awarded every applause line a letter grade, dropping anything that earned less than a B. "It's a 30-second world," Gerald Ford's ad buyer remarked. The *New York Times*'s political-media critic, watching the election coverage live and then on instant replay to make sure he caught all the action, found the complexities of the campaign reduced to a football game: "Television obviously believes, in the spirit of the late Vince Lombardi, that for the politician—*every* politician—'winning isn't everything, it's the only thing.'" TV was remaking everything in its own distorted image, he concluded, "transform[ing] a window into a screen."[16]

War in Microcosm

This brand of politics is certainly problematic. Its gendered rhetoric struck preemptively against feminist inroads into male domain—as Mariah Burton Nelson put it, "the stronger women get, the more men love football." In December 1970, *TV Guide* ran what may be the first article describing a man cave, celebrating the $3,000 addition, luxuriously outfitted with ash paneling, walnut trim, and two TV sets, that an insurance man from Long Beach had annexed to his garage so he could relish Sundays "undisturbed by his wife and children." One journalist, bemused by the clubby atmosphere at a meeting of Washington's Touchdown Club, compared the ambience to "the charge up San Juan Hill." Pioneering football writer Elinor Kaine, who had to sue to be allowed merely to enter the press box at the Yale Bowl for an exhibition game, was belittled in stories like "Who's the Broad in Pro Football's Huddle?", which bemoaned the "emergence of a Hedda Hopper" to sissify the sport. The normative new-politics candidate's qualities (authority, power, manly vigor), too, were uniformly coded as male.

Further, images and metaphors from football often implied unthinking regard for traditional American notions of regeneration through violence. Dan Jenkins's sketch of "another nightmare for the year ahead" for the 1970 college season from the coaches' perspective adroitly summarized the sexism, racism, and homophobia of this understanding of national identity. Criticism of football sapped the potency of manly American nationalism: "The goalposts are decorated with draft cards, the cheerleaders wear granny dresses and they give the locomotive for Ho Chi Minh. . . . When everybody rises for the National Anthem the band plays 'Me and Bobby McGee.' Finally, on what is supposed to be the opening kickoff, the two teams jog casually toward one another, hug and kiss, light up strange cigarettes and romp off the field as one group, unfurling a huge banner that says: THE END ZONE IS WHITEY'S TURF." Several years later, a socialist English professor teaching a class on spectator sports similarly enumerated "the issues one needs to discuss about football: violence; spectator fanaticism; sexism; racism; football as a business venture . . ." The radical feminists of Iowa City's *Ain't I a Woman?* analyzed "the aggregates usually called 'teams'" that male chauvinist pigs built and concluded that "each team has its own field, yet is not content and, in true pig style, teams fight on their own and others' fields; but nothing is ever resolved."[17]

Football's values could support more egalitarian visions. Hubert Humphrey and George McGovern courted athletes and athletic endorsements with as much avidity as did Nixon and Agnew. Jack Kemp, who had famously "showered with more African-Americans than most Republicans had ever met," consistently spoke out against the Republican Party's cultivation of the white-racist vote and extolled the way that "differences of race, creed, and class were dissolved in the common struggle for the end zone." The NFL, "in particular," he rejoiced, had been "a vanguard of racial equality." "All the serious political freaks in my campaign in Aspen bet on the pro football games," Hunter S. Thompson recalled. "Gradually, sports and the freaks have come a little closer together." Football could appeal to activists every bit as much as to self-proclaimed patriots.[18]

But for most analysts on the left, the sport reeked dangerously of bread and circuses. It was generally agreed that, as Leonard Koppett put it, "football is war in microcosm." Jerry Kramer's best-selling diary, *Instant Replay,* gave each section a military title: basic training, armed combat, war's end. From a left perspective, the dots were easy to connect. "Football reflects a lot of what's wrong with America," said Atlanta's *Great Speckled Bird.* It mimicked war personally and collectively. "Body shattering is the very point of football, as killing and maiming are of war . . . [but] there is little or no protest against football." Nobody blamed Vietnam on basketball or accused even the most imperious baseball manager of complicity in atrocities. The war "had always been supported by the football mentality," wrote Paul Gardner. "Indeed, in a very real sense [it] had been *caused*" by "the idea of slugging it out with the Commies."

In one of its signature ironic juxtapositions, the anti–Vietnam War documentary *Hearts and Minds* drew the same connections, cutting directly from a grinning Col. George Patton III describing his men as "a bloody good bunch of killers" to a bloodthirsty sermon that illustrates the induction of young men by way of football. "When you go forth to war against your enemies," a clergyman exhorts Ohio high school players before a football game, "you shall not be afraid. . . . This is serious business that we're involved in. And that's religious, and God *cares!*" Football and war—each explained the other. What could you expect from a people poisoned by such propaganda but atrocities?

George Carlin's famous routine, first recorded on the 1975 album *An Evening with Wally Londo,* most indelibly presents this interpretation. When Carlin talks about baseball, he does so with a sing-song, happy-faced lilt. When he turns to football, his whole body tightens, and his speech goes clipped, hard-minded: "Baseball is a 19th century pastoral game; football is a 20th-century technological struggle. . . . Football begins in the fall, when everything is dying." The routine climaxes with a delirious, accelerating barrage of military metaphors in which the sport becomes indistinguishable from World War II: "In football, the object is for the quarterback—otherwise known as the field general—to be on target with his aerial assault, riddling the defense by hitting his receivers with deadly accuracy, in spite of the blitz, even if he has to use the shotgun. With short bullet passes and long bombs, he marches his troops into enemy territory, balancing this aerial assault with a sustained ground attack which punches holes in the forward wall of the enemy's defensive line. In baseball, the object is to go home . . . and to be safe."

Parodists turned these assumptions about football's violent essence into barbed jokes about America's foreign entanglements. Going "into Monday" might make the network president a one-term executive, one wag wrote of the daring new *Monday Night Football,* but surely that was better than "seeing ABC be a third-rate power." Jack Mann imagined Nixon frantically striving to convince fans that the Redskins' famous 73–0 destruction at the hands of the Bears in the 1940 championship represented merely "an orderly withdrawal from the field. . . . We had a plan, and it has been implemented[:] . . . to render Chicago's North Side forces incapable of carrying out a major offensive before the rainy season." The *Berkeley Barb* half-joked that Nixon's "ultimate trip" would be his own red, white, and blue coach's pullover with "Staff" on the left breast: "to hell with Congress. . . . This is his team . . . er, country, and he knows best. Vince knew what was best for the Packers, didn't he?"[19]

Conservatives split on such questions. For some, football represented application of force under law, not the chaos, cruelty, and uncontrolled aggression that terrified and angered radicals. Michael Novak bemoaned the "overwrought, disproportionate" rage against sports, noting that football in particular dramatized the rules of bourgeois social discipline. Vince Lombardi, alleged "fascist strongman," in reality spoke up for the virtues of order and hard work. Novak thought that there were thus obvious reasons for the 49ers' crowd, full of doctors, lawyers, and bank officers, that had appalled Hunter S. Thompson: "Not only are they the only ones who can afford tickets. It's their life being dramatized." William Bennett thought that left-wing assaults merely repeated radicals' fundamental misconception. Every functioning society required justice and order backed by rules and, if need be, violence. Sports rationalized that necessary force: "Many things go on at and in games that should not be seen by children and do not deserve to be imitated by anyone. None of this, however, is consistent with the *nature* of sports. . . . [U]nnecessary roughness, unsportsmanlike conduct, is not a part of the game."

For writers like Bennett, sports remained what Grantland Rice had deemed them in the mythmaking 1920s: a moral beacon directing us to better times and better selves, "an activity in which excellence can be seen and reached for and approximated each day . . . relatively unaffected by the general erosion of standards in the culture at large." Fortunately, he noted, citing the ascendant New Right (which similarly venerated 1920s' economic notions), authentic American ideals were rendering radical arguments moot: "The revolution has not done and cannot do what its progenitors argued it must do—replace the values of winning and competition with other and better non-competitive values. . . . [I]f anything, Americans seem to be resisting the tendencies toward leveling in sports." Sports, the most strictly meritocratic of enterprises, were the most American. Conservative athletes parroted the party line: Jack Kemp celebrated football as "democratic capitalism" in action; Fran Tarkenton called it "part of our free enterprise system."[20]

Others saw in the sports pages an escape from lives fraught minute-to-minute with importance. Herb Klein, Nixon's longtime press secretary and communications director and Kemp's mentor, covered sports at USC and mourned at the conclusion of his career that "I have been a newspaper correspondent, reporter, and editor, a television executive and consultant, and a press secretary and communications director, but (sometimes to my dismay) never a sports writer." Victor Gold eulogized Vince Lombardi for *National Review* and profiled Joe Theismann, now quarterbacking the Redskins, for *The Washingtonian*. Even Spiro Agnew, a dedicated foe of the media, mused that "I've considered the idea of writing a column some day. I'd be very interested in doing something in the electronic medium."[21]

When conservatives were not celebrating football's capitalistic underpinnings, they were holding that it was just a game. George Will mocked the chain of inferences: "Football brings out the sociologist that lurks in some otherwise respectable American citizens. They say football is a metaphor for America's sinfulness. You know: the violent seizure of real estate, sublimated Manifest Destiny, oh! bury my heart in the end zone." ("Sociologist" was the rote insult for any sportswriter daring to trespass the discipline's traditional limits.) But just a year before, Will had indulged his own inner sociologist, predicting that the Green Bay Packers' religion of efficiency would spell doom for the Nixon administration. No matter the political persuasion, football remained an alluring medium for advancing one's preferred interpretation of contemporary America.[22]

A Bunch of Crap Which I Consider Un-American

Quite a few leftish sportswriters wished, often vociferously, that it *were* just a game. Former *Daily Kent Stater* sports editor Rich Zitrin, whose last college memory was a Guardsman leveling a bayonet at him, remembered that sports suddenly struck him as a "a cocoon, a fantasy world. I wanted to blow up buildings." At the Democratic convention in 1968, Jerry Izenberg fled phalanxes of Richard Daley's cops, gagged on tear gas, and suffered a broken wrist in the convention hall when a policeman smashed it with his nightstick. Izenberg had never before covered anything beyond the playing field, and at first he tried jaunty athletic metaphors: "The cops are out to set a mid-America record for reporters beaten all the way into the emergency wards." But with the whole world watching, sports felt trivial; the convention "seemed to pinpoint for me just how meaningless that other world in which I was grinding out roughly 1,000 words a day, five times a week, really was." When Izenberg came home, he recalled much later, he begged his editor "to let me out of my limited world of sports to write a general column. He said no. I was angry, then depressed, then I wanted to quit. But I stuck it out, mostly because I needed the job."[23]

Journalism programs were exploding in popularity, and sportswriting was coming to terms with the modern world. Over the next few years, more and more sports journalists earnestly, often angrily, widened their job descriptions to respond to the politicization of sports, a choice that incurred equally indignant responses and the occasional death threat. "No one, no place is free of tragedy," one columnist put it two weeks after Kent State. "It can be stated as a law," Red Smith wrote in describing the consensus in 1975, "that the sportswriter whose horizons are no wider than the outfield fences is a bad sportswriter, because he has no sense of proportion and no awareness of the real world around him." "I begrudge no one entertainment, only oblivion,"

Robert Lipsyte wrote; being an informed fan now *required* that you pay attention to the world.

The changes were both personal and institutional. *Newsday* and the *Miami Herald* considered hiring investigative sports reporters; the *Washington Post* and the *Detroit News* probed the ecosystem of recruiting. The *San Francisco Examiner*'s regular "Sports Focus" offered "stories in depth and with impact about problems, personalities, and trends in sports," even publishing dispatches from exotic Columbus, where a former staffer had transferred to Ohio State "to see what life was like in America's Midwest." The biggest changes took place at the staid *Washington Star,* where Hunter S. Thompson approvingly noted that new sports editor Dave Burgin, whose hiring was announced in the fall of 1971, "is staffing his whole section with freaks." In pursuit of Burgin's dream of building "the world's finest sports section," the *Star* promoted Tom Dowling's column with the promise, or threat, that "his independent views are bound to make you react . . . one way or another." (By himself, the Harvard-educated Dowling, who had been posted to Pakistan and Iran before walking away from a promising Foreign Service career to write a bestseller about Vince Lombardi, condensed the changes occurring in sportswriting.) Burgin's jazzed-up pages, with their shouting headlines, framed boxes rather than traditional columns, and huge photographs, were "trying to duplicate in print what the television medium achieves," wrote one critic.[24]

These liberalized—radicalized would be too strong a word—sections broadened the ambit of the sports page enormously. A *Washingtonian* article in early 1971 lambasted local news outlets unwilling "to walk a city block" to cover "a minor event. They're not interested in off-beat pockets of delight." Now papers seemed to specialize in off-beat delights. The *Washington Daily News* ran long articles on the "Silent Minority" that explored how Washington's Latino community, forced to cope with constant racism and the specter of deportation, was hesitantly building its own opportunities and recreations in the shadows. Writer Tom Quinn gave radical advocacy groups like Latinos United space to explain, without a filter, that "Roman arenas, ego, competition, that's where sports is at in the United States, man . . . [but] there are many things that concern us more than sports right now": Vietnam, police brutality, race relations, and every other issue of interest. Jack Mann spent three days approvingly describing the rise of ecological consciousness and championed bicycling.

The *Times* encouraged Robert Lipsyte's assault on clichés and received wisdom. Tom Dowling interviewed the woman who babysat for the Lions' stars and coaches. The *Star*'s Kiki Levathes dismantled taboos on pregame sex, ultimately wishing for a revolution in football, spearheaded by Joe Namath's "frank discussion of sex" and Vince Lombardi's disinterest in this aspect of his players' lives, that would "open a wedge of logic and reason that will finally liberate the sport sexually." Her five-part series on "Sports and the Intellectual" included interviews with a philosopher, a painter, the director of the National Gallery, and Hunter S. Thompson himself. Magazine writers asked pointedly why there were no black quarterbacks or head coaches. In a profile of defensive back/provocateur Johnny Sample, Leonard Shecter sneaked in the fact that, when not wreaking havoc on opposing receivers, Sample earned his college degree, along with a teaching certificate in math, in four years: "He has a nimble brain." Even the *Wall Street Journal* got into the act, advocating the moral benefits of direct democracy for football players: "No matter what the system, half of the teams basically will still walk away from their games in defeat. The players themselves may become better individuals if they've participated in the decision-making process."[25]

Political journalists flagellated themselves over their alienation from "the people." Just after Chicago, the hugely influential Joseph Kraft admitted that because "most of us in the communications field are not rooted in the great mass of ordinary Americans," journalists should "exercise a certain caution, a prudent restraint . . . [and make] a special effort to understand Middle America." Some sportswriters made a mockery of that enterprise, engaging readers in sustained public battles over what their sections could properly cover and how it should be covered. "I have a problem with sports: I can't always take them seriously," Glenn Dickey wrote in the *San Francisco Chronicle*. When readers rebelled, he doubled down a week later, comparing his critics to the love-it-or-leave-it "idiot fringe" and protesting mushrooming salaries, the rat race of college recruiting, and "the way athletes are canonized." Too often, he thought, sports were "treated as seriously as war. Whose fault is that? Look in the mirror."

Rather than making a special effort to understand middle America, these writers ridiculed it at every turn. Hal Lebovitz of the *Cleveland Plain Dealer* published a lengthy apology after the resignation of Browns coach Blanton Collier regretting every harsh word he had put to paper: "Each time I wrote critically of Collier and looked in the mirror afterward, I was not pleased with

myself." Jack Mann was having none of it. "Maybe the fact that the journalists in places like Cleveland are 'community-minded' is one of the reasons
there are places like Cleveland," he snorted in the *Washington Daily News*. He
similarly dismissed the "alleged newspapers" in Detroit, which "wouldn't run
any racial stories for years." Ira Berkow, who wrote a column syndicated by
the Newspaper Enterprise Association, cherished a note scribbled by a Florida
sports editor cancelling his paper's subscription to "a bunch of crap which I
consider un-American. . . . It seems as though it's been months since Berkow
wrote anything we had any use for whatsoever."[26]

Readers and writers clashed. "Times have changed," one angry reader wrote
the *Washington Post*. "Nowadays what's the score seems less important than
who is the scorekeeper. . . . What we are told is what is [a player's] salary,
who is his agent, what are his politics, did he pay his union dues, and does he
use grass?" Another wrote in protest of a Mann column dismissing Redskins
season-ticket holders as "carriage-trade people . . . not the fans" that "the
average fan, even if he is considerably involved in catering to society's ills,
doesn't really give a damn about . . . social consciousness. . . . To a considerable
extent sports is a flight from a world of pollution, poverty, racial tension,
hunger, narcotics, and all of the other blemishes of our society." Mann had
created the template for the modern sports section at *Newsday* in the early
1960s. In a bristling memo, he pushed his staff to write in English rather than
"the lexicon of sports gibberish. . . . Maybe it isn't possible to put out a sports
section without this kind of drivel. Certainly it hasn't ever been done. But
let's try it, anyway." His great skill, though, was antagonizing management;
Newsday, Sports Illustrated, the *Detroit Free Press,* and the *Miami Herald* all
fired him. An obituary fondly remembered him as "famously obnoxious." He
provided a prime demonstration of his talent in this instance.

"There will be some kind of answer. Has to be," Mann promised. He began
by lambasting the writer as singing "the silent anthem of all that wonderful
majority that gave us Spiro Agnew," went on to mock his treatment of pollution and racial tension as mere "blemishes," and bitterly demanded, "when's
the last time one of you higher-income dolts (your expression, let the record
show) stood on the corner flipping the quarter, making the value judgment
between using it for bus fare or having that thin hamburger and walking
home?" Surely the reader could not be serious. "But the damned trouble is
you can be, and you are, you are. You and your whole loud-mouthed Silent
Majority." Mann promised even more vitriol the next day. "Do we have to

care?" he pleaded. "Is that all there is for you . . . really?" He accused the writer of demanding that "all of us . . . use spectator sports in the way people use tranquilizers, booze, pot, and acid, and as some of the subcultures in our history have rationalized brick-throwing, church-burning and rapes: as a crutch, a release, a cop-out." The *Daily News* killed the column, and Mann quit. Two days later, Ken Denlinger of the *Post* ran the best parts of what Mann had written, in solidarity.[27]

Fear and Loathing at the Super Bowl

For critical journalists, declarations of antipathy were especially important. The targets were obvious in baseball. One could write a book about the endemic disillusionment among reporters covering the early '60s Yankees, whose four-decade-old dynasty was collapsing while Mickey Mantle's body furnished a convenient objective correlative by falling to pieces. "You don't go to the zoo because you love the lion," Mann wrote of the team. The Yankees "were an arrogant, humorless organization," Stan Isaacs recalled, "which let reporters know that it was a privilege just to be covering them. Some of us didn't see it that way." Shecter called Yogi Berra "a narrow, suspicious man, jealous of the man other people supposed him to be and which he knew he was not." Instead, columnists turned their lonely eyes to Queens, rooting semi-ironically for the hapless Mets, especially inept first baseman Marv Throneberry, in the closest sportswriting has come to camp. Being a Met fan, Lipsyte theorized, was a romantic gesture that symbolized "defiance of authority": "the Metophile is a dreamer."[28]

Aside from calling Vince Lombardi a fascist, there was nothing so canonical against which to declare one's sympathies in pro football. Hence the usefulness of the Super Bowl. Paradoxically enough, sportswriters' constant sniping at the game's spectacle endorsed the NFL's notion of its importance. On the eve of the first, Edwin Pope snorted that "it's getting to be a sort of parlor game, this Super Business. . . . No less than nine press agents are scurrying around representing both the National and American leagues. They are not superfluous. . . . The only thing they won't have is a Super crowd." Jerry Izenberg derided the hubris of inflating a "monumental propaganda-spawned paper-tiger championship" into a "supercalifragilistic Punic War. . . . The proximity to Disneyland somehow seemed appropriate to whatever sane portion of the world still remained. . . . Where else did a thing like this belong?" But much coverage of the first few games emphasized primarily how disappointing they were. *New York Times* TV critic Jack Gould likened Super Bowl I to a typical Hollywood drama: "The advance build-up was more impressive than the show, and the script fell apart in the second act." Lipsyte mourned that "the millions spent to televise the game, the thousands to promote it, and the enormous emotion and work spent preparing for it, were not rewarded by either sustained drama or even moments of great excitement."[29]

By the early '70s, reporters had gotten angry; given the NFL's new cultural prominence, dissenting from the game felt like a valuable act of political and cultural resistance. In 1971, Marty Ralbovsky argued that its runaway popularity "tells as much about the state of the country as it does about the state of the game." To wit, "to seek the illusion of violence had become an acceptable, if not desirable, means of temporary escape from the very real violence of a throbbing world that threatened to shimmy itself off its own axis." "The NFL is so acutely conscious of its own grandeur that Super Bowls are designated with Roman numerals," snipped Michael Roberts, "like Popes and Lincoln Continentals." In 1973, the *Times* covered the real Silent Majority, the 172 million Americans *not* watching the Super Bowl; the next year's report began with "the sounds of jingling cash registers" and interviewed a porn vendor in Times Square who hoped that business would pick up when the game ended. The game's aura of decadent gluttony led to dark thoughts about spectacle and grandiosity, as well as an imperial-decline thesis if one inclined that way. But it had undoubtedly become a super business.

That same year, Lipsyte, always leery of popular wisdom, cocked a skeptical eye at the "mass national seminars" now convened every January. "It is just possible that the Super Bowl is much too big," Wells Twombly wrote. "It is the culmination of so many Sunday television shows that the eyelids fairly ache at the thought." In the fall of 1972, the country's most prominent fan was offered the chance to weigh in, but the White House denied posterity the possibility of a truly presidential debate over the game's cultural substance, tersely turning down an invitation from *Esquire* to have Richard Nixon cover next January's game: "There is not any interest in his doing this."[30]

By mid-decade, when it was clear that the game had to come to stay, journalists had made up their minds: the Super Bowl was the ultimate patriotic pseudo-event, a grand cacophony striving mightily to hide an essential emptiness. Leonard Koppett noted that the phenomenon had come full circle by 1974, afflicted with "universal complaints of boredom, overexposure, over-emphasis, lack of drama and anything else that could express jaded taste."

The standard move was to depict the spectacle with ironic distance while sneaking in brief game coverage. Bringing back tidings from that year's production for the *New Yorker,* Roger Angell wryly described "sports-desk lemmings," "maddened with anticipation," flinging themselves into "this newsless sea, churning up a vast froth of pregame wordage." Angell wrote warmly of the sport, "quick and difficult and forever fresh," but he had three days until actual football was played, so he manfully sat through an NFL Properties session that recounted a slogan-choked recent history through the lens of endorsement deals with politically dubious multinationals in whose company the NFL fitted all too comfortably: Chiquita, Shell, Union Carbide. He admired how expertly Pete Rozelle deflected unpleasant questions at his press conference and, later, after several "frightful parties," noted how effectively the game incarnated loneliness and alienation for "the young, active, mobile, alone American . . . who spends thirty-four percent of his year in hotel rooms and in cities that someone else has arranged for him to be in, and who loves football more and ever more . . ." After all of that buildup, Angell's two paragraphs on the Super Bowl concluded that the game had turned into the perfect emblem of post-sixties directionlessness: "The product, it turns out, isn't much good, but this should not exactly surprise us, because so many of our products . . . are not much good, either." Spectacle had drowned actual football, and the nation suffered.[31]

Hunter S. Thompson followed a short 1973 piece with the full fear-and-loathing treatment the next year. His first visit to the Super Bowl demolished the whole enterprise of sports reporting, beginning with an elegiac vision out of Grantland Rice that devolved into his trademark hallucinatory preachments: "gangs of Seconal-crazed teenagers" prowled the parking lot, sportswriters formed a "rude and brainless subculture of fascist drunks," the whole thing amounted to farce. The next year, he decided that the "sloth and moral degeneracy" of the Nixon press corps still made them "wolverines on speed" next to the dullness of "relatively elite sportswriters" detailed to the Super Bowl. On this pass at the same contest toward which Angell staggered, Thompson turned in an especially mocking mock-epic that might just answer all of his—all of *anyone's*—questions, "a crazed and futile effort to somehow explain the extremely twisted nature of my relationship with God, Nixon and the National Football League."

But despite his habitual disdain for sportswriting, Thompson's take, or at least that part of his take concerning the actual Super Bowl, steered much closer to the general tenor of coverage than he would ever admit. Just then in *TV Guide*, hardly a countercultural bastion, Al Stump was diagnosing "a case of societal near-lunacy" centered on a bore and "at times, a farce" every January. The next year, *Library Journal* got into the act, sneering at the "lackluster games" and "massive hoopla and carnival spirit" that "plagued the January football circus." For his part, Thompson quoted the same press-conference driblets that Angell had cited before rewriting last year's cliché-drugged lead by replacing "Redskins" with "Vikings." He spent all of two sentences on "one of the dullest and most predictable football games I've ever had to sit through," paying tribute to the sport by watching film with players and even celebrating the "antelope running style, twin magnets for hands . . . and eerie kind of *certainty*" of the Dolphins' Paul Warfield. For Thompson, as for most sportswriters, pro football was "over the hump." Boring, empty, and overinflated, the Super Bowl revealed that the best days were long gone.[32]

By 1976 the hurricane created by the huffing and puffing of a horde in pursuit of not much had become so powerful that the *National Observer*'s man in Miami dreamed of nothing so much as escape. Paul Hendrickson's "The Boys in the Box" covered the coverage, alluding to *The Boys on the Bus*, Timothy Crouse's famous take on the press corps' traveling circus during the 1972 election. He began with the understandable anxiety that somewhere in the mountain of sources overrunning his room—*Dallas Cowboys Weekly, Pro Quarterback, Football News, Dolphin Digest, Football News, Sport, Sports Illustrated, The Sporting News*, not to mention three daily newspapers and the daily official NFL handouts Jim Kensil had pioneered—the key to it all lay hidden: "somebody might know something I don't." The press room overwhelmed him, as did the panoply of trivia he must dignify with his presence, as did the "plenty of bull——" he was required to endure. Press groupthink produced a collective inability to recognize that "there *isn't* any good stuff, and there isn't gonna *be* any good stuff." Although prominent sportswriters he consulted disagreed with this proposition, at the game itself "I find myself listless, almost bored. The game, so far away . . . seems curiously anticlimactic." He fled the game—one that most observers found the most exciting and competitive yet—in the third quarter, journeyed through a "spookily quiet" city and headed out of town, where he could not even admit to the man next to him at the roadside café that he had been in attendance at all, much less that he was anything so debased as a sportswriter. "Enough already," pleaded *TV Guide*.[33]

In 1944, Stanley Frank's collection of "classics of sports reporting" dated "The Age of Reason" to 1931, to be succeeded by numerous subsequent discoveries of the impending arrival of intellectually vital sports journalism. Yet a 1977 study revealed that "a careful reading of the nation's major newspapers shows most sports pages to be suffering from a kind of identity crisis these days, vacillating uncertainly between the old and the new." One *New York Times* sportswriter described expectations as so low that "the higher-ups . . . just don't want us to do anything that would embarrass the paper." So it would be a mistake to argue that every sports page was suddenly bursting with robust political engagement. But sometimes, in some places, in the early '70s, the fires of the contemporary world burned in the sports section. And in doing so they revealed that we need not regard football-as-politics as simply a degradation of elevated republican discourse.

In valuable ways, football and football coverage became a vital part of what one journalist called "the new pluralistic culture emerging in this country," allowing non-elite constituencies (fans, players, sportswriters) a voice in conversations that would have entirely bypassed them only a few years before. The savviest coverage of Jack Kemp's run for Congress appeared in *Sports Illustrated*. Jack Scott wrote in to praise the piece as "must reading for anyone attempting to understand the role sport plays in contemporary American society." *TV Guide* provided substantive political reporting, tagging along with an unsuccessful 1974 Indiana House candidate desperate to make his mark in the age of television. "I'm a no no-comment man," he explained. "I'm going to be very direct with people." Readers and fans could fight over what was political and what wasn't, whose values mattered and why, where America was going, which aspects of contemporary America the playing field reflected and which it hid. Radicals and conservatives could invoke football as a symbol of everything wrong, or right, in present-day America.

Politics conducted this way, one expert remarked, "offers the potential of genuine democracy in a nation of two hundred million people." Athletes, celebrities, journalists, fans, thinkers from across the political spectrum, and politicians collectively created a complicated nest of relationships in this period. A line from a film could be every bit as "real" as sporting event, an advertising catchphrase, or a political slogan; a candidate for office could spend a decade in Congress or playing quarterback; going to a game, or watching one on TV, or making fun of one in print, might score political points. Many more things could appear, and sometimes actually be, more authentically political than they had just a few years before.[34]

5

A Real Coup with the Sports Fans

Little Dick Nixon, always the smallest punk on the
football team, has finally been sworn in as captain.
—Stew Albert, "The Dream is Dead"[1]

Richard Nixon played football, not very well, in college. To early biographers, his brief career revealed simply that even this talented, masterful politician had human failings. A 1953 profile treated the sport as one facet of a diverse record of accomplishment: At Whittier, Nixon was "a demon" debater, "always a brilliant student" in the classroom, "an enthusiastic second-stringer" on the field. A Sunday supplement published just before the 1960 election measured the candidate's humble acceptance of a "good seat on the fifty-yard line" against the luxuries cosseting his snooty opponent, who sat in a box. As Nixon put it in *In the Arena,* his final memoir, "I learned more about life sitting on the bench with Chief Newman than I did by getting A's in philosophy courses."[2]

Nixon also loved talking football. After his well-received address to the Football Writers' Association in 1959, "even some life-long Democrats were promising to vote for him," one attendee reported. He frequently employed football metaphors when talking about things that were not football. From top to bottom, his staff invoked the sport to define everything from daily planning to the course of the presidency. His cabinet commemorated the anniversary of his inaugural with a photo of a football team whose players' faces had been replaced by those of various members of the cabinet. Art Buchwald joked that the president regularly met for breakfast with the National Strategic Football Agency, "a top-secret group of men who advise him on the options he has." Early in 1972, Nixon told senior administration officials that "tonight the fourth quarter begins. . . . [T]he fourth quarter really determines the game." In an interview on *Today*, Nixon explained his reluctance to engage in media management by observing that presidents who did so "become like . . . the football teams and the rest, who become so concerned about what is written that they don't play the game well."[3]

By the early 1970s, the football career that had previously revealed indomitable drive and humble embrace of a subordinate role now disclosed disturbing pathological undertones. A wave of psychoanalytically inclined scholars remade Nixon's life into a study in frustration and failure dating back to childhood. The seed of the president's unrelenting drive hid in his response to roadblocks like not making the first string in college, one scholar opined, the subsequent rise of his prospects marking "almost a classic case of compensation for inferiority." A psychoanalyst diagnosed Nixon's "rigid posture" in one team photograph and his "serious face" in another, both tokens of the threat to his masculinity that losing a game posed.

"I have often felt that in Nixon we had a President who was living out fantasies born in the mind of a substitute football player on the Whittier College bench," McGovern's press secretary wrote. "Whatever youthful fantasies awaited fulfillment in the head of George McGovern, it was safe to say that none stemmed from the frustration, shame, envy of an intense young man who had failed to make the varsity." Philip Roth's scabrous *Our Gang* imagined Trick E. Dixon, a subject of public rage after the Cambodian invasion, playing dress-up in his hour of direst need by going on television "unbeknownst to everyone, wearing my regulation National Football League athletic supporter. I just couldn't help myself."[4]

But politics, not pathology, motivated Nixon. Sportswriters knew exactly what the president was up to. Yet against their better judgment, they nevertheless found themselves won over by the president's football talk, which they understood as simultaneously calculated and honest. Midway through a demolition of the "overhauled 1968 model," Hunter S. Thompson admitted that he'd expected Nixon didn't know the sport "from pig-hustling" and kept dropping it into conversation from time to time only because "his wizards had told him that it would make him seem like a regular guy. But I was wrong. Nixon *knows* pro football." "In an act that was contrived yet comfortable, he spoke in sports metaphors. He was obviously trying to appear friendly, pleasant and helpful, and he was, without difficulty, succeeding," Dick Schaap noted. "With each word [he] chipped away, as I had feared he would, at my preconceptions." Political journalists noted something similar. "He certainly recognizes the political usefulness of being known as a sports fan . . . but his football obsession, like his true-blue, Whittier-style patriotism, comes entirely naturally to him," Stewart Alsop wrote.

"Who could blame him for escaping into the safe sporting and political atmosphere of football" on weekends after a week immersed "in a world of ambiguities and fumbles?" asked seasoned Washington observer James Reston. At the same time, Reston could hardly miss the attendant political advantages: "He is appealing to Middle America and its values of family, community, state, and region—and football and other sports are an important part of this equation." Ironically, campaign advisors wanted him to *more directly* politicize the sport. A letter-writer in the spring of 1968 complained that Nixon had visited Green Bay without making hay from his knowledge of the Packers: "When I mention Nixon's knowledge of sports, [people] immediately seem to show a great interest in him. . . . This creates a great rapport with sports fans everywhere."[5]

In its merging of calculation and honest sentiment, these uses of football may be the quintessential Nixonian gesture, at once overt and subtle, sincere emotional response and wedge issue calculated to polarize productively. The Wallace Newman adage that the president quoted most frequently, "show me a good loser and I'll show you a loser," captures how easily athletic and political rhetoric bled into one another for him. But the sport's new popularity in this period provoked him to new heights, or depths, depending on the observer.

Nixon, that is, both loved football and used it. In 1969 and 1970, as he went to games and invoked football metaphors, Nixon began to use the sport to construct an electoral coalition that would, he hoped, sustain him into a second term and win the Republican Party the White House for a generation. Football crossed class lines, appealing to southerners and middle Americans but also to the intellectuals whose admiration Nixon at once disdained and craved. All of these audiences mattered: as a historian of his first term points out, at the time "political calculation suffused his administration with particular intensity." But even for its most famous practitioner, this politics was harder than it looked; in the long run the tactic failed to ensure the permanent cultural and electoral advantages for which the president and his staff hoped.[6]

When It Comes to Football, You Are Not Too Bright

The vote in 1968, with Nixon defeating Hubert Humphrey by merely 500,000 votes and George Wallace reaping nearly ten million, reflected what political scientists call a "critical election," one in which both major parties underwent "short, sharp reorganizations of the mass coalitional base." In 1969, the White House's major concern was simply to pull together a solid foundation for the future, and its scattershot strategy employed football as both symbol of normalcy and means of distinguishing friends from foes. Nixon aimed to build that foundation atop a newly discovered demographic. Well before the Silent Majority speech rallied this group to the president's cause in November, middle Americans had been the political find of the year. The columnist Joseph Kraft coined both the term and the most common mode of journalistic analysis in the aftermath of the Democratic convention in Chicago: Middle Americans were "the large majority of low-income whites" with whom the media had "an imperfect relation, a touch of disharmony."

Despite the enormous quantities of newsprint subsequently devoted to this topic, no one worked out exactly who middle Americans were with any greater specificity. Less a specific archetype than a menacing cloud of attitudes, middle America was often depicted, as *Newsweek* did in its cover story, as a crowd emitting a vaguely hostile buzz: "don't tread on me" soured by years at the corner bar. *U.S. News*'s November 1969 cover story on the "revolt of the middle class" included small businessmen, blue-collar workers, those sixty-five and over, white-collar workers "who somehow feel 'left out,' " and even corporate executives with the right attitudes. What *was* clear was that these people were white, not rich, sometimes afraid, and always very angry—"on the edge of open, sustained and possibly violent revolt," Pete Hamill called them in April, in an article that made a deep impression inside the White House.[7]

But they were not simply liberals who had been mugged by reality. These voters supported spending on job training, fighting pollution, and Medicare—"not a list of priorities to warm the hearts of traditional conservatives"—while demanding lower taxes and resenting black and student militancy, stances that "offered little comfort to orthodox liberals." With the group's policy preferences tangled and contradictory, taste was a surer ground on which to appeal to them. And everyone knew that middle Americans loved football.

One of the biggest hits of the fall of 1969, country singer Merle Haggard's "Okie from Muskogee," conceived as parody but received as celebration, rejoiced in the virtues of the title city, where no one took "trips on LSD," "manly footwear" meant leather boots, and football was still "the roughest thing on campus."[8] *Time* described NFL fans as "Middle America in the raw . . . the Silent Majority at its noisiest, relieving its frustrations in the visual excitement of the nation's most popular sport." Historian Arthur Schlesinger, in sneering at Spiro Agnew's middlebrow taste, inadvertently pinpointed why he became such a compelling spokesman for this group: "With his rumpus room in the basement . . . his Lawrence Welk records and his Sunday afternoons with the Baltimore Colts, Mr. Agnew was the archetype of the forgotten American who had made it."[9]

Middle Americans loved football. So did southerners. So did Richard Nixon. In October 1969, Special Counsel Harry Dent, a South Carolinian, former advisor to Strom Thurmond, and the administration's official expert on folkways below the Mason-Dixon Line (*Time* deemed him a "Southern-fried Rasputin"), found just the way for the president to capitalize on these connections. Dent forwarded to Haldeman and Chapin a clipping from that morning's *New York Times* highlighting the crucial role of football in the South: it had "probably replaced church-going as the number one social function. . . . It is more than just the favorite sport. It is now a religio-social pastime, a psychic device for the release of tensions and a vehicle for doing business." Going to a college game, Dent promised, "would be a good way to get him into a key Southern state and get to see many good people from two states, without doing anything political."

Dent's star was on the rise that summer; his office had been upgraded from the Executive Office Building to the White House in July, and he used that leverage to push the administration further right on issues of concern to southern whites, such as school desegregation. Art Buchwald, who loved football metaphors as much as Nixon did, wrote wryly that there was "some question as to who will be calling the signals against Segregation. Some say that so far Strom Thurmond has been calling them." Nixon's nomination of segregationist South Carolina judge Clement Haynsworth to the Supreme Court in August continued the theme. Football offered yet another means of outflanking George Wallace by declaring allegiance to the right people without sending explicitly racist signals. Such signals were all too overt to some: the President's unfavorability rating among African American voters skyrocketed from 17 percent in the spring of 1969 to 72 percent in the fall of 1970. Nowhere did Dent's note specify which "southerners" Nixon would meet or the skin color of those "many good people," but the implications were clear.[10]

A number of stars aligned to present what seemed like the perfect opportunity. In August, ABC Sports' Roone Arledge, soon to revolutionize TV with *Monday Night Football,* had matched what he hoped would be the top teams in the nation in a special season-ending game culminating the NCAA's 100th-anniversary festivities. The spectacle was a sop to NCAA head Walter Byers, who was loath to let Arledge profane amateur sport with advertisements for the hated professional game. The initial guess that those teams would be Arkansas and Texas, who had moved their usual October clash to early December at Arledge's behest, proved accurate. Both teams were undefeated, both all-white. And both states were in play electorally: Nixon finished second to Wallace in Arkansas in 1968 and lost Texas by a mere 39,000 votes to Humphrey.

Making his first visit to Arkansas as president, Nixon could appear before a tremendous crowd of enthusiastic white southerners and award the winner a commemorative plaque proclaiming it national champion. A regional director of the Post Office wrote his superior that local approval of the decision was broad and immediate. Attendees at a Rotary luncheon, informed that Nixon's visit had been confirmed, "expressed to me that if the President were to attend this game it would do more to enhance his acceptance by the voters of Arkansas than any type of campaigning he might do within that State. . . . This decision on the part of the President will result in terrific personal gains and acceptance for him with the important people in Arkansas."[11]

The Justice Department predicted only minor unrest that fortunately bore "no direct relation" to the president's appearance: traffic stoppages and halftime demonstrations related primarily to desegregation by an "estimated 300 negroes and an unknown number of whites." (The protest took place, mostly outside the stadium, but ABC's cameras deliberately ignored it.) Nixon visited the announcers' booth at halftime, where announcer Chris Schenkel introduced himself as "one of the many millions who are glad you won" in 1968, and the president predicted that Texas, then trailing 7–0, would do "much better offensively" in the second half if they threw the ball, which proved to be exactly right. Haldeman considered it "great stuff. . . . P gave thorough analysis of the game so far, and outlook for second half . . . proved 100% accurate. . . . A real coup with the sports fans." Presenting Texas coach Darrell Royal the #1 plaque after the game, Nixon boasted that "I've gotta brag a little" about the accuracy of his halftime predictions and promised also-undefeated Penn State a commendation of its own. Former Army coach Red Blaik wired him that "your presence and remarks . . . suggested to the country that [there] is a normalcy despite the anxieties of the time." Monsanto even sent him a commemorative square of the Astroturf on which the game had been played.[12]

But this was not great stuff to everyone. Even before the game, a "dismayed" Republican Pennsylvania Governor Raymond Shafer implored the president to "please hold judgment on Number One until after the bowl games." Republican Governor Norbert Tiemann of Nebraska complained that the decision to award Texas the national title was "shockingly premature," as did Penn State students and alumni and even the Republican caucus of the Pennsylvania House of Representatives. The university's student vice president spent a day trying to phone his objections to Press Secretary Ron Ziegler. That morning, the State College paper's front page presented a possibly overheated recounting of "the worst day in the White House pressroom since the outbreak of World War II," including three briefings in one day on the subject—"more than we've been given on the Vietnam War at any time," according to one veteran newsman.

Shirley Povich of the *Washington Post* mentioned the incident in three columns over the next three weeks, clippings of which circulated inside the White House. For the most part, Povich treated it as a tempest in a teapot, writing with tongue in cheek that "in the first place, what Mr. Nixon did Saturday was unconstitutional and a usurpation of power. . . . Nowhere in the Constitution, nor by faintest precedent, is the President authorized to go around the country awarding plaques to college football teams." At worst, Povich thought, the episode demonstrated that "he either got bad advice or took his eye off the situation momentarily."[13]

But in the eternal swing state of Pennsylvania, which Nixon had lost by nearly 170,000 votes, fans of undefeated Penn State deeply resented the perceived insult. Worse, many letter-writers explicitly identified themselves as Nixon supporters and attacked his intervention in "prejudiced polls" as an affront to democracy. "I am a member of the 'silent majority' and back you 100% in your handling of our foreign policy and our domestic problems . . . but when it comes to football, you are not too bright," one began. Patriotic Citizens of Central Pennsylvania asked, "do you follow the same policy when acting on items of greater magnitude?" A soldier warned the president to "watch your command prerogative, lest it fall off the road and into the ditch, as it appears it has in this case." "This latest blunder could cost him Pennsylvania—but good," a "fare-paying Republican" informed spokesman Ron Ziegler in yet another complaint.

Penn State Coach Joe Paterno, also a Republican and the state's most prominent football figure, repeatedly jabbed the president over this incident, telling
students after Kent State the next spring that he would not be joining their
delegation to Washington because "I can't do much good with Nixon." As
the school's graduation speaker in 1973, Paterno famously twisted the knife
again: "Who knows, I may even be the only commencement speaker this year
who doesn't give his opinion on Watergate. Although I do want to make one
comment . . . I'd like to know, how could the President know so little about
Watergate in 1973 and so much about college football in 1969?"[14]

Having learned the lesson that, like politics, college football was local, Nixon
did not venture an opinion when Ohio State beat Michigan the next November. He called to congratulate Woody Hayes but kept his own counsel on the
team's proper ranking, Hayes explaining that "I don't think he wanted to get
into that kind of politics again." In January 1971, the season having concluded
without an obvious champion, speechwriter Patrick Buchanan counseled Haldeman that the president "not get involved at all" in the issue, passing on the
1969 Povich column as "just one mark of the crap we call in on ourselves—if
we go ahead with this." All he could see were costs: doing so "would involve
us in an annual controversy."

This year in particular, ratifying the Associated Press's choice of Nebraska
over Notre Dame would lose Catholic votes and provide only incremental
advantage in a state where Nixon had rolled up nearly 60 percent of the vote
in 1968. Finally, Buchanan pointed out, recognizing Nebraska would anger
Woody Hayes, "an RN man," as well as Texas, "at least as much as last year was
an affront to Penn State." This question became a recurring joke in Nixon's
speeches over the next year, as he referred again and again to his mistake and
vowed in future merely to celebrate the excellence of whoever happened to
dominate locally. But the lesson was clear: college football was more useful
for local races than was the professional version, but also potentially far more
costly. Nobody objected when Nixon rooted for the Redskins. From now on,
he would root much more strategically.[15]

A Good Day to Watch a Football Game

Going to Arkansas helped identify Nixon's friends: the many good, important (white) people in a South turning solid red. His dealings with the
peace marches in October and November taught the White House how to deal

with foes. The two demonstrations terrified the administration, amounting to what one scholar calls "the most potent and widespread antiwar protests ever mounted in a western democracy." Despite internal warnings against just such a move, the President made the mistake of announcing three weeks before the first, the Moratorium to End the War in Vietnam, that "under no circumstances will I be affected whatever by it." He thereby came across as uninterested in the feelings of what looked increasingly like a crucial segment of the population. The remark also prompted reporters to rush to Moratorium organizers for a response, elevating them to an equality with the president that they relished. In the face of enormous public criticism, the administration backtracked, arguing that the president had merely refused to countenance distractions from his pursuit of peace. A Washington insider criticized Nixon for letting the political winds blow him where they would, "for lack of the cement of moral imperatives. . . . [He has,] in short, failed to use the Presidency."[16]

The White House emphasized that the president devoted no special attention to what was going on. Spokesman Ron Ziegler told reporters that Nixon had discussed Latin American issues in the morning and inflation in the afternoon. But his advisors were tracking events across the nation, and some met with protestors in their offices. Inside the White House it seemed clear that, in the words of urban-affairs adviser Daniel Patrick Moynihan, "the Moratorium was a success. . . . I believe the administration has been damaged." The marchers forestalled immediate escalation of the war by coming across as responsible, thoughtful, and organized rather than wild-eyed Communist dupes. Nixon wrote in his memoirs that the size of the protest destroyed whatever possibility had existed of ending the war by revealing to North Vietnam the extent of disagreement at home. But in the major ways that its organizers hoped to measure success, the Moratorium failed. They hoped to set off a tidal wave of public opinion against the war. Yet a subsequent survey of newspapers nationwide found a slight majority of columns and editorials opposing the march, and nearly 70 percent of respondents in a November poll still approved of the president's strategy in Vietnam.[17]

Nixon was nonetheless stung by the perception that he had let the protestors seize control of the narrative. Realizing that it had lost the symbolic battle, over the next month the administration tightened both its ground game and its air attack, tilting the public debate from whether or not it should listen to the voices of those in the streets to whether or not protestors had any right to speak for America. It leveled similar charges against the media.

In his autobiography, Communications Director Herb Klein admitted that 1969's press coverage was actually "better than we expected," but a week before the march, Klein sent Nixon a note promising to carry out his request to "generate some letters to the editor of *Newsweek*" for its failure to report the "tremendous ovation and reception" he had just received from Dolphins fans (making Nixon the only president ever to attend an AFL game), proof that "there is, in fact, deep enthusiasm for what you are doing."

Newsweek's profile of the president actually left off just as he flew out of Washington to Florida, so it hardly deliberately omitted what happened at the Orange Bowl. Local coverage was nothing but complimentary, pointing out that Nixon's introduction brought the fans to their feet and "set a mood for the evening." The photograph on the front page of the *Miami News* depicted a grinning Nixon autographing a Vikings pennant, absolutely relaxed and at home in the stands; the *Herald* showed him cheering alongside his confidant Bebe Rebozo. Both Nixon and Agnew attended football games that month, but in neither case did the administration attempt to score political points from their attendance.[18]

Early in November, however, Nixon's advisors began to use football as a counterpoint to the prospect of half a million protestors converging on Washington. With the Mobilization Against the War scheduled for November 15, the administration proclaimed November 10–16 "National Unity Week," to be celebrated nationwide with flag displays and "pro-administration propaganda" at college and pro football games. Alexander Butterfield suggested celebrating "united effort" at halftime: "perhaps all games could have a red, white, and blue theme or all halftimes begin with 'God Bless America' and end with 'This Land Is Your Land.' " Dwight Chapin responded that there was already a plan in hand for the next three months: "We *did* have a patriotic theme or event at the half-time of *every major college football game which was televised*. . . . We'll have [the] same for bowl games."

As always with Nixon, the Ivy League was a subject of mingled scorn and longing. A note to Haldeman pointed approvingly to an article in the *Princeton Alumni Weekly* that described the response to Princeton and Yale bands' jointly forming a peace symbol during halftime: "Many spectators booed the gesture, while a few clapped politely." A memo from Moynihan observed that Nixon supporters cheered at the right times at football games; in contrast, when Harvard played Princeton, the assembled graduates, whose net worth Moynihan estimated as "at least $10 billion," roared . . . when Harvard's band took the field, consciously mocking administration attacks on their snobbish misunderstanding of America. Nixon noted that he simply could not win over these wrong-headed "Harvard types."[19]

On the day of the march, rather than clumsily disdaining public opinion as he had in October, Nixon countered what he defined as its anti-American tone with the pro-American truths of football. The president, who usually spent his Saturdays at Camp David, devoted the morning to foreign policy and told the assembled reporters that after lunch he was going to spend Saturday afternoon the *right* way: "It was a good day to watch a football game." Characteristically, the *Post* mocked the White House's staged atmosphere of business as usual, "the theme that the administration wanted to convey. Abnormal efforts were made to get that point across." Ohio State walloped Purdue in what Nixon inaccurately predicted would be "the best college game of the year"; one journalist described the Buckeyes' dominance as so complete "you would have thought Woody had scheduled Hanoi." In a parody of Agnew's recent assault on media bias, Art Buchwald wondered why "the network in question" chose to televise violence on the field rather than "the peaceful scenes on the sidelines." Nixon's press secretary said that he did not know "how I could find out" whether or not the president had at any time mustered the will to glance out the window during the game.

To complete the theme, the next day Nixon watched the Cowboys beat the Redskins, becoming the first sitting president to attend a regular-season NFL game. Four Redskins doing National Guard service had been called up for the march but dismissed in time for kickoff; Jerry Smith complained of "spending the whole damn weekend in an open jeep, cold as hell" and admitted that while being trained to use tear gas on Saturday, he'd fumbled the canister, which hit the ground and went off. On Sunday he made it to the locker room in time to suit up and catch three touchdown passes.[20]

For critics, this "deliberate presidential cold-shoulder" to the protest emblematized Nixon's cynical, ham-fisted deployment of symbolism. The *Washington Post* raged that "for sheer piquancy, we have not heard the likes of that since Marie Antoinette." Secretary of the Interior Walter Hickel found the president's behavior troublingly anti-democratic, arguing that "there is nothing wrong with watching football. . . . But when a group of people in America wants to express an opinion, and is asking to be heard, I think it is the duty and obligation of those who are the leaders . . . to hear these people out." A year later, *The Washingtonian*'s mock 1997 obituary for "one of the most devoted sportswriters in the business" recalled an occasion, "perhaps apocryphal," in which "he sat serenely in his living room watching a football game on television despite the presence of several thousand protestors who were marching outside his house." Two years later, *Partisan Review* identified this moment as the key to what was wrong with him: "the trouble . . . isn't that he watches football but that he makes such an obvious and cheap political gesture of it, companionably winking to the Silent Majority while the Peace Freaks parade outside." Buchwald included an echo of the event in his parodic Watergate trivia quiz, question #9 asking, "President Nixon has insisted from the very beginning that he never had any knowledge of Watergate until March 21, 1973. What football games did he watch while the cover-up was going on?"[21]

From Nixon's perspective, the gesture was not obvious enough. He had learned what not to do in Arkansas: involving himself too specifically in the details could alienate football fans as well as make them into Nixon voters. In Washington he discovered that naming the right enemies was crucial. He remained eager to show himself connecting with the right audiences in the right way.

In the wake of Kent State, disconnecting Nixon from the *wrong* audiences became even more important. Peace marchers had not provided a sufficiently strong foil. Counterposing rampaging college students to football players, on the other hand, could polarize positively. Kevin Phillips's *The Emerging Republican Majority* guided the administration's tactics. Despite public denials that the president had read the book because of its controversial advocacy of racial polarization, it became "the New Testament around the Nixon White House," as Dan Rather and Gary Paul Gates wrote. Most controversially, Phillips suggested that alienating the right people made perfect political sense. Who hated whom—"that is the secret," he explained. Nixon himself remarked that he could never "win over our enemies—youth, black, Jew." Starting in the spring of 1970, football came to play an important role in his new public strategy of rallying mainstream America against the dissent, abnormality, and un-American behavior that could be linked to these groups.[22]

If There Is One Thing That Is Nonpolitical, It's Being for Bart Starr

In May 1970, administration moderates briefly strove to convince disaffected students that the system could listen. Junior staffers who fanned out to college campuses reported that most protestors had not lost faith in America: "sons and daughters of the silent majority," they wanted to feel represented rather than be dismissed as indistinguishable from the angriest radicals. Though Nixon accepted the suggestion that he create a commission to study campus unrest, the chance to further divide the electorate proved too enticing. Kent State revealed the existence of an enormous generation gap, with letters to the White House massively supporting the National Guard. Nixon publicly celebrated the hardhats who rampaged through lower Manhattan four days after the shootings, assailing a peace march and beating up anyone in the vicinity even slightly long-haired. Cultivating resentment of any and all students was easier, and played better, than suggesting that some of them might have a point. Tie opponents to "hippies, kids, Demos . . . emphasize—anti-crime, anti-demonstrations, anti-obscenity," Nixon told his staff in late July. Agnew's new coinage, "radic-libs," similarly clumped all opposition together—radicals and liberals did not deserve separate words, much less separate identities.[23]

The stakes were high. Determined to limit the typical losses for the sitting president's party, Nixon was "leading the charge" in "one of the most ambitious political efforts of any President ever in an off-year election," personally persuading strong candidates to challenge for the Senate across the country. In his memoirs Nixon described Republican losses in 1958 (thirteen seats in the Senate, forty-seven in the House) as "one of the most depressing election nights I have ever known. The statistics still make me wince." He'd smoothed the path for his own win in 1968 by traveling 127,000 miles before the 1966 midterms and visiting forty states, playing a major role in the Republicans' gain of forty-seven House seats, three Senate seats, and eight governorships (one of whom was Spiro Agnew). With twenty-five Democratic Senate seats at stake and only ten on the Republican side, the 1970 midterms offered a perfect opportunity to consolidate a new coalition; seven new Republicans would balance the Senate. Pollsters reported that voters were reluctant to commit, suspicious of politicians, hesitant to donate. They wanted someone to cater to their desires without merely mouthing platitudes.[24]

"More than one thoughtful player has wondered aloud," columnist Robert Lipsyte wrote late in the summer, "'am I playing Nixon's game?'" Indeed, the administration consciously considered how football could make itself useful. In January, the Touchdown Club of Washington had sanctioned Nixon's unofficial title as number-one fan by giving him its Mr. Sam award, which honored "a governmental figure who has contributed to and fostered sports" in especially significant ways. A week later, he called Chiefs' quarterback Len Dawson after the Super Bowl to congratulate him and to remind him that the youth of the world looked up to pro players for courage. In August, Chapin received a memo listing what Nixon's strategists, Murray Chotiner and Harry Dent, envisioned as the "target Senate races." He circulated a memo asking for "key football games . . . which we might consider for the President to attend."

The request made its way to special adviser Bud Wilkinson, the former Oklahoma coach and one-time Senate candidate. (In 1964, Nixon fought hard for Wilkinson, who had just switched parties. He lost by a mere 2.4 percent.) Wilkinson had been shuffled around the White House and assigned a series of make-work projects; his attempts at youth outreach were mocked internally as "locker-room pep talks." Now detailed to serve on a variety of task forces, he cautioned that none of the states with target races (Alaska, Connecticut, Maryland, Utah, Wyoming, New Jersey, Nevada, North Dakota) would host nationally televised games, but "any home game against a respectable opponent" would work. Among national broadcasts, he highlighted Texas at Oklahoma, Minnesota at Missouri, Notre Dame at Missouri, Tennessee at Florida, or California at USC, all in September or October. Roger Ailes, then a Republican media consultant with four candidates in hand, also urged the president to attend Notre Dame–Missouri: "I could use the help of having [Indiana Senate candidate Richard] Roudebush seated with him. . . . [T]his would also help with [Missouri Senate candidate John] Danforth." Dent plumped for Florida–Florida State as "an ideal way to strike a blow for Republicans in the State of Florida" even without television coverage. His attendance would heal rifts within the party and help candidates in northern Florida in particular. A handwritten note added that Haldeman would take up the possibility directly with the president.[25]

As it happened, Nixon had no time to attend football games. Some advisers worried that he'd missed a chance to connect with ordinary Americans; going to games created "a feeling of warmth toward the President such as comes from sharing a mutual hobby." His attendance at two games in 1969 had "made quite an impact." Perhaps he could make it to the Super Bowl? This too did not come to pass. But the president's rhetoric in his fall appearances in 1970 insistently connected these themes anyway. Campus unrest would be "the" issue, he thought. Haldeman described him as wanting to "really ram this home and make all decisions based on it. . . . Hit pornography, dope, bad kids." Over and over, Nixon contrasted "bad kids" with the good kids who played America's favorite sport.[26]

After pondering at length an invitation for the president to speak at Kansas State, the administration showed how adroitly it could convert these complex potential energies into viable political momentum, using this speech to kick off his strategic initiative for the fall. Senator Bob Dole, who had been angling for the visit for nine months, sent along a letter from school president James Mc-Cain reassuring the White House that "if past performances are any indication the President could count on an enthusiastic response." Nixon's staff remained leery of students, even those at "an agricultural school . . . [that] has had *no* disturbance," instructing Nixon to ask the senator "if he feels [Nixon] will have a good reception and any problem with student demonstrations." Even after repeated reassurances that the campus offered a safe harbor, Nixon's staffers worked hard to minimize the dangers of opposition to his speech while simultaneously celebrating the president's bravery and willingness to speak truth in the face of opposition.[27]

The school newspaper's editor called Manhattan "probably among the safest campuses in the nation, as far as presidential visits are concerned." In a less guarded moment, he admitted to an interviewer from Lawrence that Kansas State was "just like any other school—15 years ago." By way of contrast, the University of Kansas had seen race riots over the spring and summer and boasted multiple alternative weeklies and a Gay Liberation Front. The Weathermen's Demolition Squad had threatened to blow up the football stadium the previous October. None of these things were true at Kansas State. It was not entirely indifferent to political currents: the school had widely observed the Moratorium the previous October and a busload of students rode to Washington in November. The *National Catholic Reporter* even covered the dangers for Nixon of "soft-spoken dissent" cropping up in "cow town." But the left was clearly in the minority. A campus survey found that KSU seniors most often described themselves as "friendly" and "straight-laced" [sic], four times as likely as a national sample of seniors to possess "much school spirit," and very rarely as "liberal." "The overwhelming majority will greet him warmly and be flattered that he came," the director of the Office of Educational Research predicted. The school president expected "some constructive dissent," but nothing violent. Even the proprietor of a local head shop, who put up a sign about Nixon's visit to "promote comment," provoked no responses.[28]

The Kansas State band boomed out the school's fight song to kick off the speech. "Eat 'em up, eat 'em up, KSU!" the crowd roared. "I think of the fans of Wildcat football here today who have known what it is to lose—and then who have known what it is to win," the president began. "I think, too, of some of the moments of my own career: as a football player who spent most of my time on the bench, as a candidate who knew the great satisfaction of winning—and then as a candidate to learn what it is to lose." "What about the war?" yelled a heckler, briefly throwing Nixon off stride. One group of protestors sneaked a sign inside the field house. "How Many More Will You Kill?" it demanded. Warming to his theme, the president celebrated native son Alf Landon's becoming an "elder statesman" rather than wallowing in electoral defeat after his devastating loss to Franklin Roosevelt. So, too, Nixon continued, "take Kansas State and its football team."[29]

In ways both literal and symbolic, Kansas State's football team captured the Nixon spirit. The *Kansas State Collegian* raved that Coach Vince Gibson was an "immortal" who had worked miracles by taking "a sour grape and turning it into a potent purple giant." His program had recently embarked on a massive buildup of force, with an $800,000 athletic dorm (complete with swimming pool, sauna, and color TV) known locally as the Sheraton Gibson, a new stadium that seated 48,000, an expanded coaching staff, and a handsome recruiting budget. But an article on the stands in *Look* that week revealed that the program was losing money, and none of the six players drafted that spring had graduated. In a bit of foreshadowing nobody could have noted at the time, less than a month later Gibson was reprimanded for violations of NCAA ethics, eligibility, and recruiting rules and the program placed on probation for three years.[30]

The Wildcats had gone 8-60 over the seven seasons before hiring Gibson, but, just like Richard Nixon, Kansas State had not given up hope. "This pattern of playing by the rules, of losing some and winning some, of accepting the verdict and having another chance, is fundamental to the whole structure on which our liberty rests," he observed. And this was where protestors went wrong. No one could win every time in a free society, a lesson protestors would grasp if they'd ever played team sports (which, Nixon didn't even need to imply, they obviously hadn't): "Whether in a campaign, or a football game, or in debate on the great issues of the day, the answer to 'losing one' is not a rush to the barricades but a study of why." As Wallace Newman had taught him, you did not quit, no matter the score. Anti-war activists should not protest; they should think harder about why most Americans disagreed with them.

He mentioned a recent Palestinian hijacking, seguing immediately to "the same cancerous disease" of violence at home. Nixon called for an end to unrest, conclusion of the war on his terms, and continued faith in the project of America. He did not want to diminish or demean the idealism of youth, merely channel it in productive and relevant directions. Yet Agnew put the case more cogently that same day when he remarked, "it is time to discard the fiction that in a country of 200 million people, everyone is qualified to quarterback the government."[31]

The pre-speech predictions proved accurate. *Time* believed that "no Brechtian genius could have staged the audience participation better." While Governor Robert Docking and President McCain "fidgeted at the outbursts," the "anything-but-silent" crowd "went wild" and rewarded Nixon with five standing ovations in the first fifteen minutes of his speech, drowning out the forty or so dissenters, who left grumbling. "I want to apologize to the rest of the students across the country," one of them remarked. One onlooker counted twenty-nine interruptions for applause in thirty-five minutes. Nixon beamed as he left the platform and told his traveling party, "I felt we handled everything well." "He played that noisy handful . . . like an orchestra," agreed James Pearson, the state's other senator.[32]

Nixon's Kansas State visit catalyzed public distaste for radicals, reassuring the president that his course was right and, more important, popular. Middle Americans loved what he had to say. "It would be difficult to find much fault with the President's message," the *Lawrence Journal-World* editorialized. As he had with Hunter S. Thompson and Dick Schaap, Nixon talked football to smooth his way into the heart of his argument. But he also used it as substantive evidence of values on which everyone could agree; football was normal and healthy, at once nonpartisan and intensely partisan. During the speech, he ad-libbed on his prepared text, which read, "the voices of the small minority have been allowed to drown out the responsible majority." Celebrating the silent majority's confidence, he rejoiced, "that may be true in some places, but not at Kansas State!"

The crowd rewarded him with what an onlooker called a "truly deafening" roar and a "tumultuous" standing ovation. An editor of the paper protested that "we were used—exactly as planned," pointing out that Nixon had called the school "one of the great universities" in America, apparently owing entirely to its polite reception and its football team. The president promised that he "'would not for one moment call for a dull, passive conformity,'" she concluded, "but Wednesday, he found it here. . . . Trained mice couldn't have done better." The paper's radical columnist, Kansas State's resident Black Panther, bent Nixon's theme to his own ends, writing that "at the end of the first half the game was out of hand. . . . At the end of the scrimmage Country Dick had clearly defeated the K-State dissenters by a score of 15,000 to 50." If he really wanted a challenge, Nixon should schedule tougher opponents: Kent State, Jackson State, Columbia, Berkeley, Wisconsin.[33]

A few national media outlets were dubious. A columnist for the *San Francisco Chronicle* wrote angrily that "it's all well and good to radicalize the dean of men's office and that sort of thing, but let's make sure we have a winning season first." The *St. Louis Post-Dispatch* called the speech "not terribly useful for conveying a better understanding of the complicated tensions in society. . . . Students in the audience may well have wondered if Mr. Nixon were holding out a single choice, between football and radical protest, the one exemplifying the best that a youth can aspire to, the other the worst." But the vast majority of editorial responses applauded Nixon's "whopping success" and dismissed the "ranting and raving by mixed-up youth" that failed to disrupt him. "KSU's Purple Pride was showing at its best," rejoiced the *Liberal Southwest Daily Times*. From the administration's perspective, Kansas State went exactly as planned. A delighted Haldeman called it a "huge success, beyond all fondest hopes! . . . *Small* group of about 25 bad guys in the audience of 15,000, and their shouts, etc., played right into P's speech. Was really great!"

All three networks carried the speech live, and a week later Chicago insurance executive W. Clement Stone (a major Nixon contributor), *Reader's Digest,* Pepsico, and Warner-Lambert subsidized prime-time rebroadcast in nine especially important cities; the administration mailed out tens of thousands of copies; and polls revealed that 90 percent of the public found campus protests completely or mostly unjustified. President McCain thanked Nixon for his "magnificent address" and described more than a thousand "letters, telegrams, and long-distance telephone calls from persons in every state in the Union," the vast majority of which "stated that the program had given them a renewed faith in the youth of America." McCain especially celebrated Nixon's "forthright statements" about campus protest, which, he flattered the president, took "no little courage" to deliver.[34]

The Nixon team became expert in cultivating minor clashes, even inventing them when they did not occur. When the president's plane landed in Green Bay a month later, one reporter overheard a police officer ordering patrolmen manning the floodlights to "turn the lights on this bunch" of protestors as soon as the president set foot on the ramp to play up their presence. "That's what they want us to do—*now do it!*" Another news story noted mildly that even when Nixon did not face hecklers, "he sometimes acted as though they were there." Again, the teachings of Wallace Newman resounded: the point was to use football, and the values derived from playing it, to dramatize how uncivilized and marginal the forces opposing the president truly were, and how stalwart Nixon was in standing up to them.[35]

As the calendar turned to October, Nixon drove ever harder to connect with the electorate through football. Haldeman worried that "most of our candidates have a long way to go" but hoped that "if the general view that voters are really confused and seeking direction" proved true, the president's efforts would bend them his way. Wherever Nixon went, he reiterated that his conduct was above politics, even as he continually worked to cement Republican gains. At the airport in Green Bay, he'd confronted crowds of student protestors, and in town he congratulated a deeply moved Bart Starr (who had campaigned for Nixon in 1968 and would again in 1972) the night before Bart Starr Day. Here Nixon was in his element, in a town Starr called "a good crosscut" of America that recognized and admired "the qualities in you that have made you a winner and made you a champion."

"If there is one thing that is nonpolitical, it's being for Bart Starr," Nixon began his politicization of Bart Starr Day. He recalled the score of the game in 1956, the last time he'd been there, and remembered that Starr had not yet cracked the starting lineup. Leading a team of dignitaries that happened to include Secretary of Defense Melvin Laird and the Republican candidates for governor and senator, the president hit again on his preferred persisting-through-adversity theme. Instead of "whining" about sitting on the bench, "the common thing to do these days," Starr "kept trying hard and finally made it," the surest sign of a "No. 1 citizen." "Nixon himself might well derive some benefit" from his association with Starr, the most popular man in town now that Vince Lombardi had retired, a local political columnist thought. One writer had already conjoined the two early in 1968, crediting Nixon with experience, self-control, and poise so inspiring that he amounted to "a political Bart Starr, the polished pro, quarterbacking a young, fast-thinking team." The

Nixon congratulates Bart Starr on Bart Starr Day. (Courtesy Richard M. Nixon Library)

paper's front page showed the two leaders of men with their arms around one another, Nixon smiling at the crowd.[36]

When Vince Lombardi died in September, the president used that occasion to commemorate his great lesson: "A man can become a star when, above all else, he becomes an apostle of teamwork." Days later, Nixon extolled conservative AFL-CIO head George Meany and continued his attempt to win labor and Catholics away from the Democratic Party, comparing Meany "somewhat" to Lombardi: each was "strong, full of character, devoted to his church, devoted to his family, devoted to his country." He had invoked the teamwork metaphor in 1968 and now used it across Ohio and Wisconsin and North Dakota and Nebraska to encourage voters to see the slate of Republican candidates as a unit working together for the nation's good. A humor columnist dreamed up policies for the president's ideal antagonist: Communists and hippies on the Supreme Court, "cowardly surrender in Vietnam," "an anti-football law with teeth." Struck by his tactics, one reporter traveling with the campaign likened Nixon's approach to a recruiting visit from "the head coach from Siwash U. . . . It may be hard for some politicians to reduce a major political campaign to football terms, but not this one." A less charitable observer imagined "Assistant Coach" Agnew, whom one network executive dubbed "the Vince Lombardi of the Silent Majority," lionizing "the greatest coach in the history of political football. He plays hard and he plays dirty, and he expects nothing less from any of us. . . . You either play for Coach Dick Nixon, or you don't play at all."[37]

Even without any games to go to, mid-October was crammed with football for Nixon. Between trips, he squeezed in a worship service at the White House in the company of members of the Fellowship of Christian Athletes, including Bud Wilkinson and Ohio State quarterback Rex Kern. Two days after his visit to Green Bay, Nixon joined Kern's coach, Woody Hayes, a prominent supporter of the administration, at a rally in Columbus—a conjunction that in Ohioans' rankings rendered the president the second most prominent presence on the dais. The two remained so close that Nixon delivered the eulogy at Hayes's funeral in 1987. Nixon remembered that the last time he'd appeared in town, he had won the election and Ohio State was on the way to the Rose Bowl. "Based on what I have seen on the football fields," he predicted, "we are going to win in this year"—"we" apparently equating football fans and Republicans.

Nixon then took an impromptu half-hour trip to campus, the first sitting president to do so. The surprise visit afforded the president a chance to speak directly with students without press interference—even though the Secret Service agent in charge of Nixon's detail had "absolutely refused" to divert the presidential motorcade to an unsecured environment until directly ordered to make the detour. Things went just as smoothly as at Kansas State. The "generally friendly" crowd seemed more surprised than anything else by the president's appearance, regaling him with his trademark V-for-victory salute and shaking his hand. One of a dozen or so radicals present did get "practically nose-to-nose" with Nixon and informed him, "we don't care about Ohio State football. Just stop the war." When protestors started anti-war chants, the crowd shouted them down. Nixon boasted that the predominant warmth of the reception had "recharged" him and "renewed his faith in young America."[38]

The president seized every opportunity to get up close and personal with supporters, to emphasize the values they shared, and to denigrate opponents, all to the party's benefit. He used his football-related college visits to hammer home a narrative: with every appearance, the president used its favorite sport to endow the silent majority with confidence, make it visible, encourage it to roar. At the Ohio statehouse, he recalled journalists' predictions (and those of some Kansas State students) that Kansas State, where the crowd "stood up against violence," would prove an anomaly. But in Wisconsin, he said, a student from notably unruly Madison had informed him, "you know, there are a lot of Kansas States in this country." The moral of the story: even in the most treacherous radical strongholds, the youth of America were hopeful, clean-spoken, patriotic. Which you knew because they loved football.[39]

Traveling almost constantly as Election Day loomed, Nixon kept hitting on those themes. Tricia Nixon, too, dropped by the Pro Football Hall of Fame. Underlining his major arguments of the past year, Nixon implored every football fan to "consider what is best for America." He was not speaking in partisan terms, merely pointing out that he needed congressional help in fill-ing out his roster and executing his game plan to end the war and fight crime and inflation. He reassured listeners that the images of violent young people "engaging in activities that you disapprove of" were not typical; he'd been to Kansas State and Ohio State and could testify from personal experience that "the great majority of our young Americans today . . . want change, but they believe in peaceful change, as you do."

The important thing was to get off the couch, join the team, and vote. A "terrible bore in my living room because I give a running commentary on the game," Art Buchwald desperately needed the respite football offered: "It is wonderful, for three hours, not to worry about what Mr. Nixon is going to do . . . or what Agnew is going to say. That is a great thing these days." This was subject to change. Nixon visited twenty-three states in the final two weeks and recorded a statement to be played at halftime of pro telecasts on November 1. As in 1968, both sides made major football-game buys late in the campaign.[40] The Democrats purchased five minutes and the administration four-and-a-half on seventy-five CBS and NBC stations' game broadcasts, with four minutes for the local Senate candidate and thirty seconds for the president's plea, at a fraction of the network's customary rate. These were the only nationally televised political advertisements of the entire campaign, and they ran during football games. This, Buchwald joked, was a step too far: "The silent majority is willing to listen to anything the President of the United States has to say six days a week. But Sunday they set aside. . . . All they want to do is drink their cans of beer and watch two pro football teams kill each other."[41]

All told, the Republicans outspent the Democrats by $2 million. The returns were far better than had been the Democrats' in 1966—the president's party gained two Senate seats, lost nine in the House, and, in "a complete surprise," lost eleven governorships—but still disappointing. All of those football references had not cemented a new coalition in place. In fact, the centrist Ripon Society charged, Nixon had overdone it: "the President's decision to horn in" on Bart Starr Day "stirred up local animosity towards Republicans for trying to make political capital out of an authentic local hero." "When you mess around with their football games on Sunday," Buchwald added, "you're hitting them where it hurts." Two-thirds of the candidates for whom Nixon stumped lost. He had predicted that about that many Senate seats would change hands but hoped for more, Haldeman noted, and he'd thought only four governorships would change hands; the immediate task was to spin the results to convey Republican gains in the face of an "obvious . . . conspiracy in the press." Herb Klein informed dubious reporters that "the President had a major effect on making races closer than they were." But political columnist Tom Wicker, summarizing the candidate's play-calling in the way that seemed most appropriate, noted that two more Senate seats were "one point less than you get from a field goal. That's as good a way as any to measure Mr. Nixon's real gains."[42]

The Final Score

Still, portions of Nixon's symbolic campaign worked. Pondering the "Southernization of America," journalist John Egerton argued that "Nixon may even owe a large measure of his electoral success to his devotion to sports." He swept the South in 1972, beginning its turn from Democratic bulwark to a Republican stronghold. In combination with a judicious package of political concessions, declarations of cultural sympathy similarly induced the AFL-CIO to decline to endorse George McGovern in 1972, the first time in its history the organization had not supported the Democratic candidate. Nixon piled up record support from labor in the election and won the Catholic vote outright after garnering a mere 22 percent against Kennedy in 1960 and 33 percent in 1968. Working-class voters remained strongly Republican through the 1970s, giving Ronald Reagan 61 percent of the vote in 1980.[43]

A comparison with black voters is instructive. Nixon's trip to Arkansas marked his only racially inflected use of football. Though in 1970 he associated himself primarily with white players, the Nixon White House simultaneously made a substantive commitment to empower middle-class African Americans, with particular emphasis on "black athlete-entrepreneurs," more than a thousand of whom opened businesses with administration aid in 1969 alone. Staffers aimed to put black athletes to both PR and substantive uses in the

Richard Nixon meets with Gale Sayers, October 1972. (Courtesy Richard M. Nixon Library)

1972 campaign by lending Nixon credibility and testifying to his administration's willingness to put its money where its mouth was.

Gale Sayers, a former Paine-Webber trainee aiming to move into fast-food franchises, was an especially attractive free agent in 1972. In 1968, he had been a hot property, switching sides twice before ending up on Humphrey's team. The president would see Sayers "anytime he was available," his assistant promised, a visit the staff played up as especially meaningful—"as Sayers is a very well-known black personality, his endorsement should receive as wide dissemination as possible to bolster our black vote effort. This meeting would be the best means to effect that end." Sayers was willing to endorse the president "at the most propitious moment," the memo added. CREEP sent Ronald Reagan a note commending boxer George Foreman to his attention, with the suggestion that a declaration of support for the President "would best fall sometime after Sept. 25th." Jim Brown, a frequent guest at and client of the Office of Minority Business Enterprise, endorsed Nixon's "support of self-determination in the business world," as did Wilt Chamberlain (another beneficiary, for a string of diners in Los Angeles) and singers James Brown and Sammy Davis Jr.

But the underlying dissonance of the Southern Strategy, and the large number of unsubtle whispers to white racists, drowned out these voices. "I really don't think the Republican Party wants black people in it," complained a frustrated convention delegate. Georgia state representative Julian Bond denounced black Nixon supporters as "political prostitutes," and the Congressional Black Caucus blasted them as "fools" whose actions were "sickening and disgraceful." "Do they have the right" to endorse Nixon? wondered the more conservative *Black Business Digest*. Despite scattered celebrity goodwill, Nixon amassed merely 13 percent of the black vote, one point more than he had four years before.[44]

Long-term realignment of the electorate eluded him. "For all the good he did us, Nixon may as well have been running as a Democrat," a Republican official remarked: the landslide in 1972 was personal, not partisan. The president succeeded in using football to polarize, to attract those who found themselves horrified by long hair, pot, and profanity. He had gone to games, prayed and joked with players, invoked football teams and metaphors. Nixon convinced sportswriters and journalists that his feelings on the subject were real. Robert Lipsyte remembered that "the only time I found Nixon even vaguely sympathetic" was at a football banquet. But he had not convinced large numbers of voters that these sympathies should make them Republicans.

The problem was not that his symbolic politics were insubstantial; it was that they were incomplete. "A desire to win . . . is not an ideology," Stewart Alsop wrote. The president could not convincingly generalize his personal connections to the populace. His rhetoric did not articulate much that was positive beyond the temporary joys of being on the team. In a reflection of his own dark view of the world, Nixon consistently invoked football to explain the necessity of withstanding losses and taking punishment. He motivated voters to vote *against* rioting and dissolution without giving them a sufficiently attractive vision to vote *for*. The field remained open for a politician who could use these allusions and metaphors to attract as well as repel, who summoned something that resonated spiritually and emotionally. In 1980, Ronald Reagan found the imagery to do so.[45]

6

I Really Believed in the Man

Dear Sam: Is political football as violent as the
real thing? Yours, George.

—Fake intercepted telegram from the McGovern
campaign to Sam Huff, "Man of Violence"
and unsuccessful congressional candidate,
August 10, 1972[1]

The Kennedys "put celebrity-gathering into mass production," Victor Gold wrote, implying a certain cynicism about the authenticity of the process. Starting in 1960, both major parties cultivated endorsements from celebrities and athletes more avidly and more formally than ever before. Most accounts argue that it was Robert Kennedy's travels in the company of former Giant Rosey Grier and decathlete Rafer Johnson in the spring of 1968 that truly convinced campaign managers nationwide to more seriously consider the benefits of what one journalist was then describing as a "gimmick." Frank Mankiewicz, Kennedy's press secretary, remembered that neither athlete played an important intellectual role. The candidate would "come to parties and things like that and talk football with them . . . but I don't think he ever had any substantial conversations." But in his last speech, just after his victory in the California primary, Kennedy numbered Johnson and Grier prominently among "all my friends in the black community" for "making a major difference for me." For many athletes, Kennedy seemed a kindred spirit who intuitively understood their "energy and need for acclaim [and] their emerging sense of social responsibility and growing militancy."

Players' campaign engagements could comprise simply a headshot and a strained metaphor. The brochure from Athletes for Nixon in 1968 prominently featured Bart Starr's exhortations to support "the Number One quarterback calling signals for my team." Or it could entail speechmaking and direct engagement with voters that led to a lifetime of commitment. It might even involve a run for office. Athletes as proxy campaigners were at once celebrities and regular Joes. They were especially valuable, wrote Cy Laughter, an Ohio businessman who wrangled celebrities for Nixon, because "athlete[s] . . . cannot be bought. . . . [They are] the most respected of all celebrities." The coordinator of Athletes for McGovern agreed: "We think they do a better job than the movie stars."

Many national politicians felt deep affinities with football players, and getting involved gave the players a chance to represent their authentic selves rather than powering someone else's promotional apparatus. "We're working for McGovern as citizens and concerned people," Redskins' wide receiver Roy Jefferson explained, "not as commercial objects used to sell hair cream and razor blades." Even as players on the campaign trail further merged media, sports, and politics, they served real needs, for themselves and for their candidates. And they further underlined the truth that professional football had become, by 1972, a bulwark of American values that could be invoked and inflected across the political spectrum.[2]

The Real Voice of America

Both candidates in 1960 came by their enthusiasms honestly. The Kennedy family's legendary charisma drew an array of athletes into its orbit: bloodthirsty touch football games at Hickory Hill, Robert Kennedy's country home, involved, among others, Grier, George Plimpton, Supreme Court Justice Byron "Whizzer" White, and Frank Gifford, who ruefully recalled, "even for a guy who played twelve years with the Giants, it was dangerous." "Bobby was sour" if you wasted time chatting with your opponent or dropped one of his passes, Plimpton remembered. For Rafer Johnson, refusal to concede even in a pickup game signaled the strength of Kennedy's character: "It's important to me as an athlete. . . . to know that there are people who are willing to give 100 percent for the little guy, the black guy, the brown guy, the poor guy, the old guy, the young guy and the white guy." The virtues signaled by these competitions remain so central to the family's lasting mystique that in 1986 Jeb Bush felt impelled to claim *his* dynastic primacy by boasting, "we could probably beat the Kennedys in touch football . . . any goddam sport they want to play."[3]

The football roster of Athletes for Kennedy in 1960 included Big Daddy Lipscomb, Lenny Moore, Chuck Bednarik, Alan Ameche, Norm van Brocklin, and Johnny Unitas. African American athletes flocked to Kennedy's banner. The NAACP's *Crisis* noted in an examination of "Why Nixon Lost the Negro Vote" that "the list of Negro luminaries—artists, athletes, businessmen and professionals—helping the Democrats, signing advertisements, speaking, etc., seemed interminable." Nixon's Sports Advisory Committee, in contrast, ran to stars of the distant past, including Ty Cobb, Jesse Owens, Red Grange, Ernie Nevers, Helen Wills Roark, one of the Four Horsemen of Notre Dame, and Johnny Weissmuller along with, most prominently, Jackie Robinson, who subsequently broke with Nixon over his refusal to denounce Barry Goldwater's support for segregation.[4]

One of the organizers of his sports committee recognized in the spring of 1968 that, although Nixon had lost in 1960, athletic endorsements had helped swing California by "round[ing] up practically every All-American here at the time." "No sports committee was put together for the gubernatorial race against Brown" in 1962, he added, leading to his main point: "This particular fall is one in which sports will have a tremendous impact on the American public, especially before the election. . . . I believe Dick Nixon can create a new dimension to his image by his knowledge of sports and his ability to talk intelligently on them." Heeding this admonition, Nixon did somewhat better with contemporary stars than he had last time, picking up endorsements from Wilt Chamberlain and Jack Kemp, along with all but two living members of the Baseball Hall of Fame. By fall, his strategists had put together brochures celebrating "a group of American sportsmen and sportswomen who believe that Dick Nixon's election to the Presidency will put our country's 'first team' on the field . . . and that nothing less will do." Sports stars underscored Nixon's middle-class virtues and all-American normality— "the real voice of America," he called the sport at the convention, at which, when accepting the nomination, he thanked his "remarkable football coach" for helping him reach his potential.[5]

The activism of Harry Edwards, whose proposed Olympic boycott demanded that politicians respond to the injection of civil-rights concerns into the allegedly apolitical Games, had placed the politics of sport squarely on the table for 1968. Presidential candidates variously strove to ignore, endorse, or co-opt these energies. During the early stages of the campaign, observers considered Eugene McCarthy, not Nixon, the leader in Sportspeak, though McCarthy's football metaphors, true to form, held both sports and politics at an ironic distance. (Upon election to the Senate, he immediately disdained it as "the last primitive society in the Western World.") McCarthy dismissed Bobby Kennedy with the remark, "He plays touch football, I play football." Most famously, he pronounced that politics and football resembled one another in that "you have to be smart enough to understand the game and dumb enough to think it's important." Over the summer, as his campaign lost direction after Kennedy's assassination, McCarthy complained that the length of the process made it a Sisyphean undertaking, "as if someone gave you the football and you're running with it, but the field never ends." His Athletes' Committee announced its existence over the summer, led by the Redskins' Bill Briggs and heavy on NFL players.[6]

Drawing on the family's longstanding sports ties, the Robert Kennedy campaign organized a committee in March. Its chief recruiter weeded out the has-beens from 1960 and reenlisted the stars, often calling "out of the blue" and finding them "delighted and flattered." Sportsmen for Kennedy, a campaign memo noted, paid multiple dividends because "you are dealing with people who usually get press on their own steam." Calling on athletes to organize recreation projects, particularly in "urban ghetto neighborhoods in the most important states," would open a pathway for "a group which for the most part plays no meaningful role in campaigns." Rafer Johnson remembered that he ended up in a central position without anyone's having planned it: "I decided I'd help him because he was a friend of mine. . . . He was running, so I should be with him."

Choosing athletes with "political savvy" would be crucial, the memo added. But going on the road with a candidate could also teach formerly apolitical players about the practical realities of politics. Rosey Grier remembered an awakening that began in 1967, when Ethel Kennedy invited him to appear at a fundraiser for inner-city summer camps that afforded enticing glimpses of the "big-family ideal I had yearned for all my life" and induced him to contact Bobby the next spring with an offer to assist in his run for the White House. "He was sensitive to the needs of poor people and sensitive to the yearnings of blacks to contribute to the growth and destiny of the country." Both Grier and Johnson witnessed the campaign's tragic conclusion firsthand: guarding Ethel the night Bobby was shot, they wrestled the gun from Sirhan Sirhan, then prevented the crowd from beating Sirhan in retaliation. Grier was so devastated by Kennedy's assassination that he vowed never to capitalize on it in any way.[7]

The Nixon, Kennedy, and McCarthy campaigns' efforts paled next to those of Hubert Humphrey, whose staff pursued athletic endorsements with singular energy and focus. Five months of frenetic activity preceded official announcement of the more than two hundred names comprising Sports Stars for Humphrey-Muskie in October. Despite widespread attention to and criticism of Nixon's fandom, Humphrey loved football just as much and took a far more direct role in garnering athletic endorsements than did any other candidate. Humphrey started at guard for two years of high school. When he entered the powerhouse University of Minnesota, which won three national titles in the 1930s, "more than anything else, he would have liked to play football," the school's quarterback remembered, but such "a spindly little guy" had no chance to make the team. As chair of the President's Council on Physical Fitness, he invested in American athletic prowess. As had Nixon in the '50s, he insisted that Soviet Olympic success "is a challenge to us. . . . We are going to be humiliated as a great nation unless we buckle down to the task of giving our young people a chance to compete." Years later, the famously ebullient Humphrey still "particularly liked show business people and athletes. . . . [A]t the end of the day [he] would relish sitting down with those stars to relax and gossip," a longtime friend recalled.

In May, less than a week after announcing his candidacy, Humphrey directed the staff to sportswriters interested in helping out the campaign. In early July, he pointedly wondered "when we are going to announce our committee of athletes. . . . You may recall Jack Dempsey ["one of the Vice President's most devoted friends," another memo pointed out] is for me. . . . We should get at it." The vice president then laid out a comprehensive strategy that began with endorsements from boxers from the 1920s and moved forward to that day, staggering them for maximum impact—"what is important is to have each one be announced separately"—followed by "the top football players of recent vintage," then track, baseball, and basketball. "Let's start to move on it," he concluded. "Give me a report a week from now."[8]

In response, Bob Short, co-chair of Citizens for Humphrey and soon to become much-reviled owner of the Washington Senators, assured the candidate that "we have been working very actively on this. . . . We have a whole Italian task force, in effect . . . a Negro task force, etc." (An article that summer in *Jet* noted that the Humphrey campaign train "probably will boast the most integrated staff in history.") An executive director was appointed, and telegrams by the stack went out over the wires. Humphrey also wondered about the publication status of his *Sports Illustrated* article on the virtues of competition—a genre to which the bylines of Spiro Agnew and Gerald Ford also contributed. The magazine's publisher was "deeply interested" and had considered including the piece in its "blockbuster" late-summer series on the black athlete, which would have been a coup for the civil-rights-conscious candidate. Unfortunately, the article had languished, the staffer assigned to write it reporting that, "I did a draft, nobody much liked it, the project was passed on to the Sports Council staff . . . and for reasons of which I am unaware was never completed." Humphrey's interest in the cause nonetheless won him an appearance in Edwards's *The Revolt of the Black Athlete* the next year, where a photograph depicted him actively seeking "the support of many black athletes" amid five football players. Later in the summer, Humphrey phoned the deputy chairman to ensure that someone would "look after" Jackie Robinson, a prize from the defunct Rockefeller campaign, every step of the way in Chicago.[9]

Humphrey's people had athletes out on the trail by the end of May. Mel Farr of the Lions and Frank Ryan of the Browns, who had finished his PhD in mathematics and taught at Case Institute of Technology when not playing quarterback, visited Detroit, and Outland Trophy winner Lloyd Phillips clambered aboard the vice-presidential jet to Arkansas. The Humphrey campaign ruthlessly organized its outreach: two days after the assassination of Robert Kennedy, the deputy chair "had a good confidential talk with the Number One man in Kennedy's sports committee," Nick Rodis. "With luck, if Teddy doesn't run, we are bringing over Nick and his top recruits," he added. Rodis joined the team, as did several liberal Republicans from Athletes for Rockefeller compiled on a separate list.

There were a few missteps: a memo from early August did its best to identify some of "the biggest stars on the New York scene today," including Mickey "Mantel," Fran "Tarkington," Don "Maymard," Tom "Sever," and the especially unfortunate Yogi "Beria"; a front-page photo in the *Washington Post* showed the candidate holding a football incorrectly, something that "someone should tactfully point out to him." But Citizens for Humphrey cast its net widely, its lists covering not just athletes in every major-league sport but team owners, coaches and managers, and college-conference commissioners. Nor were less popular pastimes neglected: swimmers, golfers, and bowlers were targeted, and Humphrey went so far as informing the National Professional Soccer League's New York Generals that, regrettably, he would not have the time to attend a game in person. Even the Fellowship of Christian Athletes received several telegrams, though it graciously declined to endorse anyone.[10]

Nor were these requests anodyne pleas that the athlete simply allow use of his or her name. The Humphrey campaign treated athletes as serious citizens who could be trusted to evaluate and approve the candidate's stances. In May, standard wires urged the recipient to support a "pioneer of such great laws as Medicare, Peace Corps, Job Corps, Food for Peace, Arts Grants, Arms Control." As Humphrey's campaign clarified its message, the calls became louder. "The cause of sports, of fitness, of equal opportunity needs your help . . . [join] the sports committee for the one Presidential candidate with 24 years of achievement for human rights and peace," read a telegram sent in July. In August, the telegrams now gave sports top billing, trumpeting "24 years of achievement for sports, fitness, human dignity, progress and peace." A note sent to national co-chair Rafer Johnson, another prize from Kennedy's committee, went further, thanking him for "helping to prevent the triumph of reactionary forces this November, which might otherwise turn [the] hands of [the] clock back on Civil Rights, Anti-Poverty, Anti-Slum, and other Humanitarian Activities."[11]

Responses were enthusiastic. The campaign met the occasional rejection—Broncos owner Gerald Phipps pledged never to order his players what to do in their private capacities, but "as a lifelong Republican and one who looks with extreme disfavor on Democratic administrations during the past 35 years, I can assure you that I will not encourage anyone to support Hubert Humphrey." Yet despite the general perception of football as inherently right-wing, Max Winter, owner of Humphrey's home-state Vikings, was "completely committed and actively seeking support among other owners." He promised to sit down with Vince Lombardi and Art Modell of the Browns and had already spoken with Lou Spadia of the 49ers. The Eagles' owner signed on, along with Edward Bennett Williams of the Redskins, and several others were listed as possible.

In the AFL, Dolphins owner Joe Robbie, who had worked on Humphrey's campaigns in the past, led a list of "ardent supporters" that included the Patriots', Jets' and Chargers' owners. Robbie, formerly professor of economics and state chair of the Democratic Party in South Dakota, had run for governor in 1950 as Humphrey's protégé and regularly attended the Democratic National Convention. As an owner, he relished a proletarian assertiveness, proudly calling himself "a working stiff" shaking things up in what "always has been a rich man's plaything," so naturally he had a "strong desire" to be of help. He sent his assistant to meet with campaign staff to identify additional "personages who were sufficiently active nationally, personable and articulate to lead a drive to recruit national figures and even raise money." Robbie promised to lobby Carroll Rosenbloom of Baltimore, Ralph Wilson of Buffalo, and former Jet owner Sonny Werblin, though Werblin in particular should be handled with kid gloves, as he was a notorious media hog with a regrettable "tendency to run the show." In some measure, Robbie had barely switched careers. If putting together a good team in Miami did not "seem a political accomplishment," one biographer noted, "it is only due to a lack of appreciation for what the business of professional football is all about."[12]

Players were equally enthusiastic. Chargers Lance Alworth, Speedy Duncan, and John Hadl (whose former training-camp roommate, Nixon man Jack Kemp, was soon to join the RNC and kick off his own political career) pronounced themselves "pleased and honored" to become founding members: "Any help we can give is readily available." Chiefs quarterback Len Dawson was "proud to accept" his appointment. Jim Crowley, one of the Four Horsemen and Vince Lombardi's college coach, was particularly welcome, as "he can recruit for us many other great ex-Notre Dame All-Americans." As Crowley had played a prominent role in Pennsylvania state politics since his navy service during the war, both Nixon and Rockefeller had already made approaches, but Crowley contacted the Humphrey campaign and offered his service. A flurry of memos followed, the campaign hastening to wring maximum advantage from his "vast talents and abilities."[13]

Citizens for Humphrey had no qualms about putting athletes to work. Its standard letter enumerated opportunities to travel on the campaign plane, "make TV and radio spots, or handshake tours or, if you are so inclined, speeches." It then requested each athlete's itinerary through Labor Day and instructed the recipient to appeal to five fellow athletes, sweetening the pitch with quotations from the included booklet, and then pass on the names, addresses and telephone numbers of those who showed interest to the central office. Hand-written notes laid out the schedules of the Chicago teams during the Democratic convention (unfortunately, only the White Sox would be anywhere near the city) and noted that former Packers great Jim Taylor was in Houston but might be enticed to the press conference announcing Humphrey's sports committee. The campaign wrote the Packers, hoping that new head coach Phil Bengtson would allow Willie Wood and Bob Jeter, both founding members of the committee, to flee training camp and attend the event. (Surely, no one associated with the campaign would have dared to ask such a favor of Vince Lombardi.) In an impressive act of chutzpah, the organization even telegraphed Bob Gibson and Orlando Cepeda of the Cardinals the day before Game 7 of the World Series, which Gibson started and lost, imploring both players to "spare a few minutes to phone us collect on assisting Vice President Humphrey" and asking that they tour New York City with him, win or lose, three days later: "You can make a tremendous contribution to victory for human dignity."[14]

The rush for signatures prompted a *Wall Street Journal* reporter to mock-report endorsements from the only athletic figures left unsigned, a small school's assistant coach and a champion handball player. This wasn't far from the truth: one Humphrey campaign assistant sourly jotted down, after being hung up on, that the agent for golfers Sam Snead, Ken Venturi, and Tom Weiskopf was "a real SOB—said he had been contacted by Rockefeller, Nixon people—was so tired of the whole thing, would not pass on any info or suggest anyone." But reality soon outstripped satire. By the 1972 election, Nixon was hosting the first White House reception for drivers, and McGovern extolled the glories of motorcycling. Football players affiliated with the Humphrey and McGovern campaigns repeatedly visited tiny Bethune-Cookman College, a black church school in Florida and a prize in attracting youth and African American voters.

Such gestures quickly became a mandatory part of the political apparatus. A 1971 article described a panoply of organizations—Citizens, Dentists, Athletes for Nixon—as "standard equipment for presidential campaigns." These organizations had become so fully integrated into the electoral apparatus that they even became embroiled in scandal; Congress investigated charges that Nixon's people had pressured the Small Business Administration to lend $275,000 to Bennie McRae, a former Bears and Giants defensive back and co-chair of Athletes for Nixon in 1968 and 1972. "This is a White House case and the heat is on," the Richmond director instructed his subordinates.[15]

The End of the Dummy in Shoulder Pads

McGovern's campaign announced formation of an athletes' committee heavy on football players in April 1972. His father had played minor-league baseball, but the candidate described himself as "clumsy," like Nixon, and thus "particularly pleased by support from the playing field." The campaign had an oddly bifurcated character, at once glitzy and grassroots: McGovern boasted the "Mighty McGovern Art Players," an entourage of celebrities that included movie stars Shirley MacLaine and Warren Beatty. "Nearly everyone campaigning for McGovern was better-known than he was," MacLaine remembered. At the same time, in the words of youthful campaign manager Gary Hart, "the principle of a decentralized campaign organization" was McGovern's "unique contribution to insurgency politics." In Hart's telling, leadership and responsibility ideally flowed down from the national organization, "until every block in every neighborhood in every community had a responsible McGovern supporter."[16]

No one better captured this duality than Ray Schoenke, organizer of Athletes for McGovern. An academic All-American as a history major at SMU, Schoenke "came out of there a socialist" whose political leanings were deepened by his experiences with intolerance in Texas. (Getting in touch with his Hawaiian heritage in the islands had rendered him especially sensitive to racial prejudice.) After one political argument too many at a Cowboys' team party, he and his wife decided to hold their peace in the interest of harmony. But the assassinations of Martin Luther King and Robert Kennedy prodded him to get involved, at first with a church-run youth program in south Dallas and then more broadly in the community. "If you stood up," he learned, "things happened."[17]

So it hardly struck Schoenke as a big step when, as a member of the Redskins, he walked over to McGovern's office in the summer of 1971, without an appointment, and knocked on the door. "The city was pretty much open to you," he recalled. He was looking to throw his weight behind someone who opposed the war clearly and vigorously. Minutes later, he was encouraging McGovern to put together a group of athletes who would help present him as aggressive and authoritative. McGovern had won the Distinguished Flying Cross for piloting a B-24 bomber in World War II ("a man's airplane. . . . It always required, and sometimes demanded, almost superhuman strength to fly"), but popular opinion had already stereotyped the candidate as "the Pavlovian liberal," as his press secretary put it. Schoenke displayed an instinctive grasp of the athletic symbolism RFK had pioneered. "You were a war hero," he reminded McGovern, suggesting that the candidate get himself photographed alongside "some big defensive linemen," like the Chiefs' Buck Buchanan and George Seals, to accentuate his toughness.

Nixon's repeated invocation of football symbolism helping to cement the association of Republicanism and manliness, the next summer the far-right John Birch Society charged McGovern with shirking his duty. The charge was aired widely by the publisher of New Hampshire's conservative *Manchester Union Leader*, forcing McGovern to produce his record and refute the smear. (McGovern's campaign plane, *Dakota Queen II*, similarly prodded voters to remember the candidate's wartime heroics.) After approaching his teammates at training camp and handing around campaign literature, Schoenke obtained rosters from the league office and worked the phones every night after practice, calling every NFL player. Several hundred "were looking for an opportunity to get involved," including twenty Redskins teammates as well as seventeen Cowboys, some of them former teammates, "though not a lot of quarterbacks."[18]

A "total novice" at political organizing, Schoenke simply let fellow athletes meet McGovern and be swayed by the force of his conviction. Consistent with the campaign's emphasis on local autonomy, he received no directives about what players should say. "Speak from the heart," he instructed them. "Tell the people why you support him." These appearances positioned the players as simultaneously ordinary citizens and celebrities. Those who had grown up on farms talked to farmers in their own language; those who had visited Vietnam described the war from firsthand experience. The last thing Schoenke wanted was for any of them to be applauded merely for playing football: "The time when the jock was king is gone, when you just had to stand up and everybody'd swoon. Now you better have something to say, or they'll boo you right down." One report from the campaign trail noted approvingly that only one of those speaking on McGovern's behalf resorted to "metaphors of the gridiron." At the same time, the players accompanied their speeches with highlight films, suggesting that some part of their appeal still *did* lie in their day jobs.

Numerous Redskins spoke on the candidate's behalf throughout the Washington metropolitan area. "Our society seems to think athletes know only about underarm deodorants," one of them explained. "I did what I thought was right because I felt an obligation." "These guys aren't just props," Schoenke argued. "They are citizens with convictions." Schoenke himself hit the road everywhere east of the Mississippi, from New Hampshire down South, attending all of the early primaries until training camp forced him to scale back his commitment and prevented him from running for DNC delegate. But he helped kick off McGovern's efforts in Maryland, later delivering a speech extolling

Autographed photograph of George McGovern and Ray Schoenke on the campaign trail, 1972. McGovern thanked Schoenke, who "did so much to help in '72." (Courtesy Ray Schoenke)

"a man who will make changes," end the war, and fill the spiritual void left by King and Kennedy, then did more than his part by going door-to-door, helping with voter registration, auctioning off autographed footballs, and posing for Polaroids with kids for $1 a shot. He remained involved during the season: an AP photo showed him, teammate John Wilbur, and Lady Bird Johnson's former press secretary heading out in mid-October to prospect for votes in six southern states a mere four days before the Redskins played Dallas.[19]

Ray Schoenke was far from alone. The Chiefs' Ed Podolak put in what he estimated as 10,000 miles, "at significant sacrifice in time and money," on behalf of McGovern in Wisconsin, Iowa, Nebraska, California, and New York in the spring. After being invited to endorse the candidate, Podolak pored through his position papers—being particularly convinced by their call for cuts in defense spending and emphasis on domestic affairs—and then closed the deal after an hour-long conversation. That personal connection mattered: "I was raised on a family farm in Iowa," Podolak recalled, "and saw my father, who dearly loved the profession of farming, forced off the land into the city. Senator McGovern was the first and loudest voice to speak of the small farmer."

He canvassed house-to-house after training camp broke and learned that being a football player might get him in the door ("we seem to reach people who might not listen otherwise"), but only the substance of his positions would win converts. "We've done something about destroying the generalization of the dummy in shoulder pads," he said. By October he had spoken in twelve states, fielding questions about amnesty, welfare, and the war—"the major issue" in the campaign. Podolak did especially well in "bar areas and construction sites" because "nobody's gonna call him a sissy." He planned to speak every Monday until the election took place and predicted that, with the Super Bowl scheduled for just before the inauguration, the president-elect would do Nixon one better: "We're expecting him to call and give us a couple of plays to use in the game." For his part, if elected, McGovern pledged not to besiege coaches and quarterbacks with play designs.[20]

Journalists covering these stories frequently wondered how players balanced day jobs and political commitments. Schoenke just as frequently denied that his activism had incurred any penalties or in any way lessened his devotion to his sport. But he later admitted that noted Nixon man George Allen did not like what he was up to, questioning his loyalty at the end of the exhibition season. "I went apeshit," Schoenke remembered. Offensive-line coach Mike McCormack confronted him directly. "How dare you criticize the Commander in Chief?" McCormack demanded. "Last time I heard," Schoenke responded, "I was a citizen. I have that freedom." "No you don't," McCormack responded, then cut his playing time for the rest of the season.

Ironically, the experience ultimately brought Schoenke and Allen closer. Schoenke's demand for a no-cut contract for the next season, which Allen granted just before training camp opened, won the coach's respect, and he began to consult Schoenke about pregame speakers and team planning. After McGovern's crushing loss—"one of the dullest political football games ever played before a nationwide TV audience," one columnist called it—Schoenke recalled, teammates begged him, " 'please, don't tell anybody I was with you.' That was embarrassing. But I really believed in the man." His own political commitment did not slacken. He worked on Jimmy Carter's campaign in 1976, running Artists and Athletes for Carter, subsequently went into fundraising, and even ran for governor of Maryland in 1998. "Being youthful and naive and idealistic were good things," he says. "I pat myself on the back for doing it."[21]

Hubert Humphrey, who remained as besotted with athletes as was the president, began his campaign for the 1972 nomination with the same visual cues, this time launching his quest alongside and later being escorted by the Vikings' heralded "Purple People Eaters" defensive line, both bodyguards and cultural ambassadors to the black community. "Our purpose is to show our concern for the man we believe represents what this country is all about," their PR man insisted. "The color issue is not the big reason for being here."[22]

Nixon's team began thinking about the role athletes might play in his reelection campaign as early as November 1971, suggesting that those involved the last time out be honored with an official visit if they had not already been so. Many of them had registered the snub: two weeks later, Cy Laughter chided the president that "it has been brought to my attention by many of the athletes and celebrities who supported you in 1968 that they were not invited to the White House as you said they would be." An article early in the summer of 1972 in a government-insider magazine took note of McGovern's early lead of "at least 100 athletes," "folk heroes to much of the American public," twenty-five of whom were already out campaigning, as compared to the Republicans' "insensitive, ham-handed approach to the whole business." "Out of such little drops of water can come floods," a veteran political observer commented in a note to the president's soon-to-be-notorious Committee to Re-Elect. "I am sure this is simply unfounded rumor," the president's spokesman wrote in passing the note up the chain, but perhaps someone in the campaign should make sure that the article was inaccurate.

The president attempted to do his part by dabbling in playbooks. His first foray into public play-calling was a failed flanker reverse for the Redskins in the 1971 playoffs; in the 1972 Super Bowl, Nixon called Don Shula after midnight with the idea of a pass to Paul Warfield, the team's best receiver. "His only objective is to prevent the Dolphins from imposing their totalitarian type of football on the peace-loving Washington team," Art Buchwald joked. This too failed to come off. Redskins guard John Wilbur later smilingly noted that because Warfield was a fellow McGovernite, the president "was bound to end up a loser."[23]

By October, reporters counted 463 names in the "Nixon line-up," many of them previously Kennedy men, and only 146 for McGovern. The co–vice chairs of Democrats for Nixon prominently included Sam Huff, who had stumped for both Kennedys and run to the left of the incumbent in a West Virginia House race in 1970. He had been leaning Nixon's way anyhow—"if you're a

Hubert Humphrey with Alan Page and Carl Eller of the Vikings, 1972. (Courtesy Minnesota Historical Society)

man and stand by your convictions you can't be flip-flopping around," he said in dismissal of McGovern—but felt no need to make that support public; personal contact with the president ("he called me and McGovern didn't") got his name on the list. Unlike the Humphrey campaign, the Nixon campaign was not interested in athletes as proxies or political thinkers, slotting them into the "PR" rather than "substance" category. They should endorse the president, be photographed schmoozing with him, verify his regular-guy bona fides. Nixon gave Redskins coach George Allen a commemorative autographed photo above a list of those who had supported his reelection effort and the instructive caption, "Performing under pressure . . . the mark of a professional."[24]

It was almost a necessary corollary of the new politics that campaigns would broaden their appeal by moving into associated fields. Athletes expanded politicians' area of influence and extended their brand identities, lending the candidate a literally All-American quality. Professional football players, given their new cachet, were especially sought after. Nixon tended to use athletes as window dressing, as testimonials to his regular-guy affect. But the Humphrey and McGovern campaigns treated athletes as responsible democratic citizens whose opinions mattered. Though there are ample grounds to regard the growth of these auxiliaries as cynically as did Victor Gold, at least some of the time presidential campaigns treated athletes' endorsements as a valuable way to extend their reach beyond the usual orbits—and the players themselves discovered a refreshing opportunity to authentically express who they were and what they stood for. What seemed at first glance to be just another trivialization of political discourse also represented, sometimes even meaningfully articulated, the new politics to new audiences.

Like Coach Lombardi Says, You Should Shoot for the Top

If political candidates craved the credibility athletes provided, why not turn "the most respected of all celebrities" into candidates? "The national passion for jocks is the most commonly used PR vehicle going," Gold noted. The 1970 elections marked a watershed: Sam Huff threw his helmet in the ring in West Virginia, Jack Kemp in upstate New York, Bill McColl in California. Bart Starr was mooted as a candidate in Wisconsin. Later in the decade, John Baker, whose crushing tackle had produced Morris Berman's iconic 1964 photograph, won election as sheriff of Wake County, North Carolina by reprinting that image with the caption, "look what John Baker did to Y.A. Tittle. He's going to do the same thing to crime." "It may be that our writers will all have to become . . . expert[s] . . . in this previously foreign field," the publisher of *Sports Illustrated* predicted in December. Hunter S. Thompson made the connection on the campaign trail in 1972, discerning "not much difference in basic temperament between a good tight end and a successful politician."

More than one spectator thought football players' running for office was a terrible idea: "That's what happens when a guy gets hit in the head once too often," the *Los Angeles Times* caustically observed. "Kemp was a bum quarterback for the Chargers, so there is no reason why he shouldn't be a bum quarterback for the nation," an angry fan wrote *Sports Illustrated*. From a practical standpoint, though, football players made prototypical new politicians. The head of a broadcast advertising firm described the ideal candidate as "attractive, dynamic, have the look of a winner, be likeable, warm, and human"—precisely the skills necessary for the modern celebrity athlete. Skills nurtured on the playing field resonated now in a way they hadn't before—perhaps especially on the *football* field, which produced more politicians than all other sports combined. "What changes is which groups of celebrities turn to politics. . . . Today's system promotes expert persuaders," a political scientist argued in 1978. Or as Huff, who as middle linebacker had called signals for the Giants' defense, put the same point on the campaign trail, "I've been working on a committee of eleven men for a lot of years."[25]

Kemp spent more than three decades in Washington, serving as secretary of Housing and Urban Development during the George H. W. Bush administration and running for vice president in 1996 with Bob Dole. Huff's career began and ended within three months, after he lost the Democratic primary in West Virginia's First Congressional District. Both had served as endorsers and proxies on the campaign trail before running for office. Both knew firsthand about speaking with constituents and lining up backers. Both authentically incarnated notions of pro football as modern, forward-thinking, and dynamic that the NFL wanted to sell. And yet spinning football celebrity into electoral gold proved tricky. What differentiated the two was less skill or clarity of message than luck—the opponents each candidate faced, the national support each campaign enjoyed. In fact, the two share something much more fundamental: the glitter of their success in a heavily mediated sport meant that football players already came across as far from common men.

The Violent World made Huff a national figure, but he was already famous in West Virginia. Campaigning for Kennedy in 1960, he testified to the "great man's" "long interest in the laboring man and woman," joined Ted Kennedy at town halls and high schools, and campaigned extensively in the state's panhandle. In October, Huff became a founding member of Sportsmen for Kennedy. He remembered his experience warmly, saying "I'd like to think" they were good friends and that "ever since that experience . . . politics had always been in the back of my mind." He proudly displayed an oil painting depicting him standing at Kennedy's side in his home, an image re-created from a contemporary snapshot. In 1968, he did "a lot of quiet talking" for Bobby in New York and West Virginia and rode his funeral train.[26]

In the summer of 1969, West Virginia University history professor Wesley Bagby organized the Coalition for Alternatives to Senator Byrd, running an ad in the personals column of the *New Republic* blasting the incumbent as one of "Mississippi's three senators" and the state's "resident reactionary." Bagby phoned Huff in the fall and asked him to consider running in 1970. (In his autobiography, Byrd remembered Huff as "a challenger not to be ignored.") Huff welcomed the call: "Maybe I could do something to help fight poverty, bad government, and corrupt politicians." He told reporters that, "like Coach Lombardi says, you should shoot for the top" and considered the idea of a Senate run until voter surveys and advisors' guidance convinced him that Byrd "was simply too powerful" to challenge. In early February Huff announced his candidacy for West Virginia's First District instead. He referred to "the benefit of association" with all three Kennedy brothers over the previous decade and laid out a set of comprehensive reforms: aid to education and disabled workers; better standards for mine safety, care for senior citizens, and medical facilities; health insurance for all. As would Jack Kemp, Huff pointed out that pro football had endowed him with "the perspective to deal with the crucial need for cooperation and brotherhood between the races," though this seems to be the last time he mentioned this issue.[27]

He ran a typical, if not especially adept, new-politics campaign. David Hackett Associates, led by a former friend of Bobby Kennedy, advised him, perhaps not firmly enough—Huff "insisted on using" a "hopelessly saccharine, unconvincing" image on the cover of his brochure. Most of his events included a showing of *The Violent World*. Huff put 15,000 miles on his car and wore through two pairs of shoes. "Sam Huff 70," his uniform number, furnished an advertising theme, the number of his post-office box, and the last two digits of the campaign phone number. A journalist following him discovered a "very effective campaigner" with a taste for oddball constituents who "doesn't talk about football as much as you might think." At an early event featuring Ethel Kennedy and David Halberstam, he spoke feelingly of growing up "a dirty-faced kid" with "three dead cousins" who had perished in the mines. "If I hadn't played football, I probably would have been a miner, too," he added. The *Charleston Gazette*'s endorsement described his candidacy as "a fresh and invigorating breath of political air in a district that sorely needs it." The governor, a college friend, predicted that "Sam could surprise a lot of people."

But Huff developed neither a compelling argument for his candidacy nor much infrastructure. His ads simply encouraged voters to win "better government . . . better representation in Washington. . . . You might even help end the war in Vietnam." At an early rally, he hardly came off as a polished politician, admitting that "I've convinced myself I can do the job—I mean represent West Virginia in Congress. . . . After all, I was with the Giants eight years and in six of those eight we were in the championship game." Financial-disclosure forms revealed that he underwrote nearly one-third of his campaign himself. "It's costing a fortune," he complained.[28]

"If I was betting on Sam, I'd have to have three touchdowns," a local Democratic operative remarked the week before the election. Even the students studying American history at the local high school gave his opponent 75 percent of the vote. Actual returns were comparable. The incumbent won more than 36,000 votes to Huff's nearly 17,000 and every county in the district—even, woundingly, Huff's hometown. "A lot of those folks who vote never saw a football game," an influential local sportswriter observed. The biggest reason was Huff's second job. He had worked for the textile firm of J.P. Stevens since 1962, often showing up bruised at 41st and Broadway on Monday morning. "Hell, I need the money," he explained to surprised co-workers. The world's second-largest textile manufacturer, Stevens's ferocious "resistance to unionism," as highlighted in a special report in the *New York Times,* was "second to none." In congressional testimony, organizers accused "the most militantly anti-union company in the anti-union textile industry" of "sadistic, cruel, and inhuman tactics."[29]

Those ties destroyed any chance at victory. In the First District, "the union population and union money . . . can almost guarantee the election of the candidate of their choice," researchers from Ralph Nader's Congress Project found. Huff protested that he was every bit a union man: his father paid dues to the UMW for forty years, three of his cousins died in the mine disaster of 1968, and he had helped organize the NFL Players' Association ("it's really a union"). He even belonged to an AFL-CIO affiliate, the Screen Actors Guild. As for Stevens, "here I am, close to three unions, and they hint I'm a scab. . . . I was a salesman in an office building in New York." Unconvinced, the AFL-CIO endorsed Huff's opponent, Robert Mollohan, as did the United Steelworkers and International Association of Machinists; Mollohan's campaign garnered nearly as much in donations from labor alone as did Huff's entire organization.[30]

Football saved Sam Huff from the coal mine, brought him into the Kennedys' circle, made him a spokesman for a major corporation. It induced a reformist professor to consider him a viable challenger to West Virginia's most powerful politician. Football also made him the subject of mockery, a dilettante armed with goodwill and dubious athletic metaphors. It made Huff, despite his public reputation for toughness (no headline writer titling a campaign story could resist a "violent world" allusion), comparatively innocent in the ways of politics; he obviously expected a fairly contested race with, in essence, penalties for unstatesmanlike conduct. Five years later, he still fantasized about putting "one party on one side of the 50-yard line, the other party on the other side and let[ting] them fight like hell." The connections football had made to rich and influential people put him out of touch. "I had a heck of a time establishing myself as the son of a simple mine worker," he recalled. The voters knew him instead as "a rich guy trying to tell them how they should vote." Being a football star helped more than it hurt, but barely. Huff made a better proxy than an actual candidate.[31]

Similar faith in fair play, and reliance on lessons learned on the field, animated Jack Kemp's career from beginning to end. For Kemp football underscored the truths he already believed. It tutored the attentive in free-market economics: "Our government under law, much the same as the impartial football referee, should preserve the climate wherein people may freely compete." It proved that any field was open to the willing striver: teammate Ron Mix was "not born an all-pro lineman, [but] he made himself one." Some of the traits that made him a star quarterback helped him succeed politically, but others posed significant handicaps. And despite Kemp's faith in his natural political skill and exhausting work ethic, in many ways his campaign very much resembled Huff's in its rhetorical vagueness and initial stumbles. Crucial strokes of luck made all the difference.[32]

Signed by the Chargers after several disheartening years on NFL and Canadian Football League taxi squads, in 1960 Kemp met *San Diego Union* editor Herb Klein, a longtime Nixon aide who hired him as a youth-affairs columnist and smoothed his way into politics. Already plowing through the classical-liberal reading list percolating through the conservative intellectual sphere, Kemp amassed practical experience as well: as a Nixon booster at the start of his 1962 gubernatorial campaign; an intern in Ronald Reagan's office in the spring of 1967; staffer and campaigner for Nixon in 1968. The next year, as special assistant to RNC chair Rogers Morton, he continued his messenger-to-youth duties by visiting college campuses to "close the gap in communications." But his best years happened in the country's opposite corner. While leading the Bills to AFL titles in 1964 and 1965 (winning MVP in 1965), Kemp kept active: a 1966 article counted more than 1,200 speaking engagements over the previous four years at universities, law schools, and the Jaycee National Convention. One such speech, to the Niagara Falls Rotary Club in 1965, yoked "Football and the Free Speech Movement," which Kemp termed "a complete prostitution of free speech." But the environment proved far less politically congenial than had conservative San Diego. One observer noted that the crowd was "on him so hard" in an early season loss in 1967: Buffalo was "absolutely hostile to Kemp. . . . And it's not so much they object to his football as his politics."[33]

A "mature" yet "tough" negotiator uniquely solicitous of management, Kemp co-founded the AFL Players' Union in 1964 and served five terms as president, through 1969. He squirmed away from anything smacking of left politics, clarifying that "this is not a class struggle" and describing "a voluntary association of employees collectively banded together to better our working conditions" rather than a union. Influential San Diego sportswriter Jack Murphy lionized him as "no Eugene V. Debs in cleats." He accepted a no-strike pledge that the owners desired and supported merging the two leagues despite the cost to players' leverage, arguing that the resulting stability would improve everyone's bottom line. "I am not for a free market in sports franchises," he subsequently explained.

Two years later, as NFL players requested support from their AFL counterparts for a threatened walkout, Kemp reiterated that "we all have a responsibility to make sure that our demands are based on economics, not emotion" and then won his union a more generous pension agreement than NFL players enjoyed. He laughed that he was going to write a book called *Can a Republican Find Happiness in the Labor Movement?* The *Buffalo Evening News*' labor writer certainly believed Kemp had done so, celebrating him as "as shrewd and effective at the bargaining table as on the football field," in tune with modern workplace truths of flexible collaboration and common purpose rather than the "collision of implacable enemies" beloved of those stuck in "the dinosaur age"—so appealingly contemporary an image that his local representative, a Democrat, quickly had the article read into the *Congressional Record*.[34]

In March 1970, after months of speculation and several weeks of consultation in Washington, Kemp formally announced his candidacy for the Thirty-Ninth District. Sort of. "I expect next year to be serving as a U.S. congressman and not playing football," he told a crowd of about one hundred. "The times demand a person who can rise above the politics of the '60s and be more concerned with the next generation." Later that summer, Herb Klein, now White House communications director, revealed that Nixon "has taken a personal interest" in the campaign of "a rising national figure." Kemp was "a Congressman made to Richard Nixon's order," one journalist thought. An article on his campaign showed him conversing amiably with the president in the Oval Office. On election night, Nixon called yet another winning locker room, Kemp accepting congratulations at a headquarters festooned with envelopes reading "From the White House."[35]

"Machiavelli couldn't have come up with a better game plan," read the subhead for an exhaustive study of Kemp's campaign in *Sports Illustrated*, the best-informed treatment of the subject. According to the Federal Communications Commission, Kemp's House race was probably the nation's most expensive, with spending totaling nearly $70,000 between both sides. Kemp's campaign was just barely more ideological than Huff's, but his organization was far stronger. "It's our country, let's help it," read the red-white-and-blue cover of his campaign brochure.

At the outset, Campaign Management Services worried that, despite his huge advantage in name recognition—76 percent of the voters in his district already knew of him—Kemp's "impression of not wanting to press flesh" would hurt. "Quarterbacks are lazy," a staffer grumbled on a "particularly difficult day." On the day he declared, Kemp received a "private & confidential" thirty-two-point memo offering often brutal strategic counsel. "Get rid of that picture now being used in the newspapers," item #1 read. "It makes you look buck-toothed and jug-eared!" #11 predicted that his "somewhat high-pitched voice" might pose a problem, depending on whether it came from "natural nervousness or whether that is the way it is." Buttoned-down good looks might also undercut his credibility. Since he looked "too kiddish," remarked the creative director, campaign photos played up Kemp's "Kennedyish" wrinkles and airbrushed in stray hairs to make him seem approachable. He was coached to "talk in generalities; he should sound like he is saying something but say nothing at all." At the Republican Candidates' School, he was tutored in handshaking, dressing, and speechmaking, told to skim books by John Gardner for "really excellent quotes," and even handed a playbook called "How To Win" bursting with suggested advertisements, billboard designs, and scripts for commercials.[36]

Kemp enjoyed an immense bit of luck: his Democratic opposition was enterprisingly sabotaging itself, an especially encouraging sign since, despite a 25,000-voter plurality in registered Republicans, the district had gone Democratic in both 1966 and 1968. The incumbent decided to run for Senate, finished fourth, then tried to reenter the House race. After months of unproductive jockeying, he finally endorsed the party's candidate.

JACK KEMP'S STAKE IN THE FUTURE

This is Jack Kemp's family. The future of their generation is his most compelling reason to believe as he does about the issues which affect our country.
Jack Kemp's concern and commitment have earned him the 1970 New York State Jaycees' Distinguished Service Award, "Outstanding Citizen" honor from the Buffalo Evening News, national recognition from the Fellowship of Christian Athletes, and pro football's choice as the AFL player who has contributed the most to his community and country.

A COMMANDING MAN

No professional politician, Jack Kemp speaks out as a citizen who shares your concerns. You know where he stands. You can depend upon him to use his experience and knowledge as labor negotiator, businessman and active concerned citizen to represent your best interests. His integrity, his leadership qualities, and high principles are needed badly in public life.

VOTE JACK KEMP FOR CONGRESS NOVEMBER 3

KEMP FOR CONGRESS

It's our country, let's help it.

Brochure from Jack Kemp's first campaign for Congress, 1970. (Library of Congress)

Kemp's people took advantage of the break to soft-pedal his athletic background even while pointing out just how many famous people knew him because of that background. Photographs showed him smiling with Ford, Nixon ("accessibility to the President and Key Administration members" would amass pork for the district), the postmaster general, and NFL Players' Association head John Mackey. The Republican National Committee profile added shots with Klein, Health, Education, and Welfare Secretary Robert Finch, and Ronald Reagan. The "confident, determined leadership" he'd learned on the field, and that he'd been celebrating in print for nearly a decade, had taught Kemp perseverance. But he was moving on. "I'm not running as a football player," he told a college newspaper. "I would hardly run after having two lousy seasons. I would have run in 1966." His talk of small government and opportunity, and his comfort with the powerful, worked well on suburbanites, businessmen, and old-line Republicans, less so in the district's working-class outposts. "Football is what helps me with these people," he whispered before one awkward meeting, heavy on game anecdotes, with a group of machinists.[37]

On Election Day, Kemp won 52 percent of the vote, a margin of only six thousand, his closest call ever. "I'm very grateful to football," he rejoiced, "but this is something I've been dreaming about for a long time." Given the narrowness of his victory, and with political prognosticators forecasting that the wave of eighteen-year-olds eligible to vote in 1972 (as many as 54,000) could swamp him, the powers that be looked out for his future. Redistricting early that year specifically targeted to his needs moved him to a district that had not elected a Democrat since 1937, cutting out most black and Polish voters and freeing Kemp to appeal to his primarily suburban constituency, among whom he pulled down more than 70 percent of the vote against what a local paper mocked as "a string of obscure, subservient stiffs" in every one of the next seven elections. (His margin in 1972 was the largest of any Republican in New York.) His identity as a football player had not been important in the 1970 campaign and clearly was not sufficient to explain his victory—his opponent much more effectively damned Kemp as a Nixon yes-man, and Kemp built his appeal around his usual soaring celebrations of the American idea.[38]

"He's really come a long way from passing footballs to passing legislation," mused a teammate invited to his swearing-in. Kemp later admitted that "I was always a little defensive, self-conscious about being a pro football player among 400 lawyers." His earliest speeches reflected this self-consciousness: he told the American Electroplaters' Society that he wished they had outfitted him with a metal uniform before seguing into his main topic, waste disposal, with the boast that "I have been dumped more times than anyone in this room." Yet a resentful senior colleague called him unquestionably "the big star of the freshman class." Chosen as class president by fellow Republican freshmen, he was placed on the Education and Labor Committee and invited into the "exclusive, secretive" Chowder and Marching Club, "an incubator for future presidents" that Nixon had organized in his own first term. In the 1972 campaign, Kemp was one of three Representatives to make the roster of thirty-five "presidential surrogates" on the order of Ronald Reagan and Barry Goldwater who traveled the country at the behest of CREEP to spread the gospel of Nixon far and wide. At the end of the summer, he gave the "electrifying" speech seconding Agnew's renomination in Miami. Minority

Leader Gerald Ford drew on their shared background to commend his "loyal teamwork throughout the 92nd Congress."[39]

Kemp never quite escaped his past, for better and worse. Nor was he averse to trading on the personal and social benefits football conferred. Sympathetic recent biographers celebrate him as "a quarterback in mentality all his life," an identification on which other politicians agreed. He loaded autographed footballs in the trunk of his car to help smooth the way out of frequent speeding tickets and traded another set for rooms at and passes to the 1992 Republican convention, where he was being frozen out by George Bush's forces. His 1988 presidential campaign video leaned hard on this legacy, dissolving from announcement of Kemp's candidacy to photos of him in uniform, "a leader for his entire life," and a (factually inaccurate) recitation of the championships he'd won. First he was on the field, in a business suit, then he joined Ronald Reagan in contemplating a football. He continued to imbue the sport with ideological meaning: "our government is the other team—and it's winning." Four years later, Barry Goldwater, whom Kemp always credited for making him a conservative, encouraged him to try again with the promise that "a guy sitting out here in the desert . . . would like to run a little interference for you."

Quarterbacking taught him supply-side economics: "You have three seconds to get the ball, get back, and choose a receiver. . . . It's incentive. It's price theories, a reward-risk ratio. . . . If you don't learn them well enough, you are forced to go into politics." Too many taxes stifled investment, a lesson he drove home by imagining a perverse policy that incentivized parents to raise quarterbacks but did not similarly reward the raising of team owners, which would ultimately produce no football at all. In 1996, Bob Dole's campaign manager informed him that Kemp had joined the ticket by simply stating, "Quarterback's coming on board." Rhetorically, nothing had changed. "Football and taxes are the only two certainties of life on the Kemp plane," reported one journalist.[40]

"I think football players can make good politicians," Huff's teammate Dick Modzelewski, a Nixon man, argued. "They know how to reach the average man." But the opportunities football afforded Huff and Kemp, to different degrees celebrity football players running as celebrity football players, created a catch-22. The sport made them famous and won them influential friends. Yet those very connections diminished their common-man appeal. His membership in the Screen Actors Guild notwithstanding, unions deserted Huff en masse in West Virginia. "Most of what Sam has said is that West Virginia is a lousy state," one observer wrote, "but he also agrees that it is better to be rich than poor. That probably comes from the fact that he has been acquainted with the Kennedys."

Like Huff, Kemp belonged to the AFL-CIO because of his work as a broadcaster. But his natural constituency was affluent suburbanites, not working-class ethnics, and subtraction of such voters from his district helped him retain his seat. A 1974 profile tartly noted that Kemp still relied on his football career to bridge the gap with those "with whom he has little else in common": his "idea of labor experience is his role as cofounder of the AFL Players Association, which some feel is a long way from knowing about picket lines and the 40-hour work week."[41] That sons of a miner and a truck driver could hobnob with presidents and embark on political careers because of their athletic celebrity testifies to the resonance of professional football within the new politics. That neither Huff nor Kemp could fully transcend the limitations of that celebrity testifies to the new politics' limits. The field remained open for someone who could seize the cultural advantages pro football offered without being hindered by the costs.

7
Out of Their League

A professional athlete has a right to express his views publicly. When he writes on politics, race, drugs, war and other issues, he may not be an expert. But his views get a wide hearing.
—Bill Glass, evangelist and former defensive end[1]

"My super-star-athlete-revolutionary has yet to appear. The more I find out about professional sports, the more I get convinced that my dream is destined to be forever unfulfilled," radical *Liberation News Service* sports columnist Lefty Millman mourned in 1968. Just three years later, sportswriter Jack Mann rejoiced that "the free thinkers are infiltrating football, no matter what barriers of tradition the Woody Hayes mentality imposes."

Football players weren't just thinking freely. Many of them were writing books. Prodded by increasing controversy over Vietnam, the runaway popularity of former pitcher Jim Bouton's tell-all *Ball Four,* and mainstreaming of counterculture concerns and the counterculture dollar, publishers rushed exposés to bookstores. The market for books heralding the rise of professional football naturally produced a counterweight, a market for books revealing the underside of professional football. Johnny Sample's *Confessions of a Dirty Ballplayer* appeared in 1970, Chip Oliver's dropout memoir *High for the Game* and Bernie Parrish's scandal-mongering *They Call It a Game* in 1971. Their experiences drenched the splendid Pop abstraction that the league's promotional apparatus had made of the sport with sweat and blood. Dial Press's advertising campaigns for Sample and Parrish pointedly emphasized the disparity between their books and the NFL's version of the game. The press boasted that Sample provided unparalleled insight into the "brutal, mercenary world" of pro football "that you'll never see on your TV screen"; nine months later, Dial marketed Parrish's book as "far beyond any other yet written . . . a revelation to the millions of pro football fans who throng stadiums every fall." It positioned the book in classic muckraking terms as "an indictment of the pro football establishment: how it manipulates and protects its billion-dollar monopoly at the expense of the players and public." Jim Brown called it "the hardest-hitting sports book ever written," and the Literary Guild, Sports Illustrated Book Club, and Playboy Book Club offered it to subscribers.[2]

As the ad copy implies, the freethinkers came to conclusions about the NFL's role in American history that the league had little interest in promoting. Former Jet George Sauer, who read Camus and kept notes on the existential quality of playing, was troubled by a lineage of elitism and racism traceable to founding father Walter Camp's brother-in-law, social Darwinist William Graham Sumner: "the same powers that keep a football player pretty much locked in place throughout his whole career are the same kind of powers that would keep black people, disadvantaged minorities, Mexican Americans, and Indians locked in place. . . . It's not surprising to me that the power structure of football is going to wind up on the side of militarism and imperialism." Muckraking former Brown Parrish, in contrast, loved the sport's "rational, orderly, mathematical, and exciting" aspects while comprehensively documenting how owners hid their bottom lines from the public to sell the notion of the NFL as robustly capitalist yet so tenuously successful that the merest whisper of unionism might blow it over.

Watching football on mescaline blew Oliver's mind. The Raider linebacker met "face-to-beard" with Al Davis, announced he was tired of being regarded as a "slab of beef" playing "a silly game," and moved everything he owned into a vegetarian commune in Larkspur. "In pro football, I was only a machine," Oliver explained. "I don't want to be a machine." Joe Kapp, the "people's replacement" for Governor Ronald Reagan, brought 15,000 Central Valley farmworkers roaring to their feet by exhorting them to "fight the bastards!" Rick Sortun, who had worked in a bank and voted for Goldwater, went back to school. Angered by what he learned about Vietnam, he "began to tie together my earlier moral feelings with socialist analysis." Sortun joined SDS and sent Cardinal owner Stormy Bidwill a postcard decorated with a picture of Ho Chi Minh and the cheerful notice that "football as a professional sports activity will no longer take place and I hope that when the barricades are drawn you will be on the right side."[3]

Most alarmingly, there was Dave Meggyesy. When he graduated from college, "my political analysis was zero," but graduate classes directed his thinking toward the game's "reactionary" structure: "We live in a goddamn military camp, completely authoritarian." He paid for buses transporting demonstrators from St. Louis to a peace march in Washington, agitated against training-table grapes picked by non-union labor, and convinced thirty-seven teammates to sign a petition calling for American withdrawal from Vietnam. Eventually he quit football, grew his hair, and wrote his own book. He had so much trouble landing a mainstream publisher for *Out of Their League* that he had to resort to the editorial imprint of *Ramparts* magazine, yet editors quickly realized that they'd struck gold. An envious Hunter S. Thompson noted that he'd gotten a mere $1,000 for getting beaten up by the Hells Angels, but *Look* was paying Meggyesy something like $12,000 for two excerpts. A Book-of-the-Month-Club selection, his memoir sold out its first edition and went on to sell 650,000 copies in paperback after its release in late 1970. Meggyesy took direct aim at Nixon, charging that "it's no accident that the most repressive regime in our history is ruled by a football freak." He attacked the sport as the worst kind of catharsis, "Middle America's theater, Nixon's theater . . . laid out every Sunday" and felt no doubt about what the future held: "When the revolution comes, football is going to be obsolete."[4]

It is tempting to conclude from all of this protest, and awareness of this protest, and scattered journalistic support for this protest, that "in the professional game," as political journalist Michael Tomasky recalled three decades later with more hope than evidence, "matters were tilting very left." But that would overstate the matter. Vociferous attempts at refutation by journalists, players and coaches, the league itself, and even prominent politicians, suggest a more cautious accounting, as do responses from newly politicized Christian athletes who had recently concluded that their place was *in* the world as well as *of* it. Recalling *The Jungle,* about which Upton Sinclair famously remarked that he had aimed for the public's heart and hit its stomach, one reviewer predicted that *Out of Their League* would produce only minor reforms.

Yet that understates the book's effect. In retrospect, Michael Oriard is closer to the mark in noting that, for all of the dreams of radical transformation, Joe Namath's consumerist "rebellion" smoothed the game's path into an era of individualist self-indulgence: Namath transformed the sport "in ways that made it easier for the great American public to continue loving football after the convulsions of the 1960s. . . . What Namath finally stood for is 'doing your own thing,' a fundamental principle of American life in the 1970s . . . [He] made the NFL safe for a post-1960s world in which Vince Lombardi had lost relevance." But Meggyesy played a role here too by challenging the league to accommodate the post-1960s world. The lesson is not that football was "tilting left." Aside from sporadic gestures of support for the radicals, it wasn't. But nor was it that, as historians once posited about the decade, "it seemed like nothing happened." Rather, Namath provided an obvious model of selling a self and Meggyesy provided another. Both could appear on talk shows and campuses and bestseller lists, and both could become culture heroes of a sort.[5]

Just a Hippie and St. Louis Is Better Off without Him

Athletic autobiography, proletarian tract, and consciousness-raising at once, *Out of Their League* mixed genres in unexpected ways: while recounting his steady progress from high school through college and the NFL, and from there to growing recognition of his need to leave the game, Meggyesy recounted a fair amount of in-game action while simultaneously presenting a greatest-hits compendium of football critiques. When he went off to college on scholarship, "I was real gung-ho, believed in America the great, the capitalist ethic." Under-the-table payments at Syracuse ("most athletes are accustomed to being on the take"), steering of players to easy classes and discouragement of academic or political individualism, and the coaching staff's violent authoritarianism began to turn him off. But his consciousness was not yet where it should have been. Brainwashed, he "continued to play tough, hard-hitting, fanatical football. . . . It's like the fictional American soldier played by John Wayne who fights on with crippling, fatal wounds. In the Catch-22 world of football, as in war, this passes for reasonable behavior." Off the field, Wayne's politics loomed large, too. Meggyesy recalled Jim Ringo, the former Syracuse and Green Bay Packers center, teaching him to destroy an opponent's knee and then turning that lesson into a geopolitical drill: "The Commies are on one side of this ball and we're on the other. That's what this game is all about."[6]

Meggyesy entered the NFL "anxious to prove myself. . . . I finally had the chance to test myself against the very best." His first season rekindled his enthusiasm. But the NFL's decision to play its full slate immediately after the JFK assassination "began to disillusion me. . . . It would [later] be impossible for me not to see football as both a reflection and reinforcement of the worst things in American culture." He was stunned by rampant prescription-drug abuse, endemic racism ("even in its orgies, the Cardinals team was Jim Crow all the way"), political repression, and systemic dehumanization and brutalization not just of players but of fans—"the millions of Americans who watch football every weekend in something approaching a sexual frenzy." Offseason graduate work with a Marxist sociologist at Washington University "began to turn my head around." Team officials told him to "cool it" and warned that he was under FBI surveillance.

As his antiwar politics grew louder and his alienation from the game stronger, the chasm between his in-season and off-season cracked open; in training camp in 1968, he and Rick Sortun discussed the advisability of circulating a Eugene McCarthy petition before concluding that McCarthy was "merely a reformist." He spent more and more time on the West Coast, eventually fleeing there at the end of the 1969 season. "By the time I went home, I knew what had to be done. . . . It had taken a long time, but I had finally made the break. Now that football and the split personality it forced on me were part of the past, I knew I could get down to the real work—joining forces with those individuals and groups trying to change this society," he concluded. A year later, with the help of Jack Scott, he'd written a book. "Reading Meggyesy on politics is about as interesting and enlightening as reading the warranty on a refrigerator," thought the *Wall Street Journal*'s critic, predictably irritated by the author's countercultural stance. But he could not get the book out of his mind: it "is revealing, and revolting. . . . What he has seen is enough to deflate the image of football as nothing but good, clean all-American sport."[7]

Meggyesy invoked counterculture semiotics as well as the next dropout, his appearance tracing the archetypal trajectory for anyone renouncing the mainstream. The front and back of *Out of Their League* compress an entire moral arc into two photographs. On the front, long-haired and bearded and wearing jersey and shoulder pads, the author challenges the reader from the football field; on the back, having permanently stowed his athletic gear in a locker, he stares down at us in jeans, vest, and headband, his brow furrowed in concentration, pondering where his life goes from here. That visual package, with its explicit rejection of an entire worldview, provoked special resentment as a signal of all things effeminate, anti-American, and un-football. "He does his thing, as the vernacular goes, well," sneered a Milwaukee columnist. "His long tresses and luxuriant beard showed up frequently on television, and his soft, smooth voice could be heard on radio." The Associated Press story covering his retirement needed only one adjective to summarize Meggyesy's politics—"bearded."

The beard earned criticism from the left as well. Ira Berkow, who generally treated dissenting athletes with sympathy, observed snidely that the author "living in Oakland, is as hirsute as a bear, and is radically 'politicized.' . . . He seems to be overcompensating and accepting the clichés of the world of 'groovy' and 'right on.'" A pro-Meggyesy article began with the frank admission that, "I have to emphasize Meggyesy's long hair and whiskers, because they are his badge of protest and this woolly badge may influence some of my Wasp, Rotarian, Elk, and Uncle Tom friends to write off Meggyesy as a gadfly in society as we have known it." A largely positive *New York Times* review derided a photograph of Meggyesy at Esalen, the "bearded figure of the saint, contemplative . . . [which] intermingles camp and poignancy."[8]

Long hair on football players mattered a great deal. One journalist noted in 1970 that "the sports world . . . still seethes with controversy over a man's right to choose the length of his hair or the mode of his casual attire." For college and pro coaches, it marked the entering wedge of dissent. Notre Dame's Ara Parseghian ruled that "wearing a beard or a mustache gives empathy or sympathy to a movement that is certainly the direct opposite of what we strive for in college football." Similarly, Darrell Royal informed a hip interviewer that he "couldn't play football for me. . . . You might be a damn good player, but your sideburns go down a full inch below your earlobes and I've got a rule about that." Oriard observes that his "Stanford-grown beard—I was a graduate student from January through June" may have persuaded Chiefs coach Hank Stram to cut him in 1974. Stram imposed an automatic $500 fine for any player whose sideburns grew longer than the coach's, and he banned mustaches and goatees altogether. Every profile of Chip Oliver began with his hair and beard.[9]

Conservative critic William Bennett worried that what players like Meggyesy represented struck "a note which many are all too ready to hear." Indeed, people who didn't particularly care about football very much wanted to know Meggyesy's thought on a range of topics. His one-hour visit with a *Boston Globe* columnist stretched to six as the pair discussed Rollo May, Charles Reich, and R. D. Laing. Meggyesy received enthusiastic notices in *Business Week* and in the *New York Times Book Review,* from novelist and fellow Syracuse alum Richard Elman; in the daily paper, lead book critic Christopher Lehmann-Haupt

HEY! A JOCK WITH BALLS!

1958 Solon, Ohio
High School Senior

Making it through Springfield, Massachusetts, unscathed, Dave Meggyesy will soon be back in Berkeley turning on athletes to the Bay Area to their liberation.

It was in Springfield, where basketball was invented as a sport, that the hulking former professional football star Meggyesy was first confronted with threats by uptight athletes who didn't like his talk about jock liberation.

Meggyesy spoke February 2 at the college with Jack Scott, former UC Berkeley instructor and full-time director of Berkeley's Institute on the Study of Sport in Society. And it came off without incident.

It turned out to be just another speaking engagement on Meggyesy's lengthy tour of promoting his jock liberation philosophy and his recent book, "Out of My League: Why I Quit Pro Football," which is already in its third printing.

"We knew of threats of violence to us before arriving," noted Scott, who came ahead of Meggyesy back to the Bay Area, where he lives in a Jock Lib commune in Oakland.

"Athletes there were saying that we may not leave in one piece

if we came...and they were saying it openly. That's the first time that's happened, although I know that if we look our message very far into the South, there would probably be more than threats," he said.

However, as it turned out, over 2,500 students overflowed the Springfield auditorium, which has a capacity of 1,500.

"Dave spoke about Angela Davis. He talked about his abhorrence of the violence of football, but then he talked about the need for revolutionary violence," Scott reported. "That was met with a negative response from the students."

"I spoke on the changeover in the last two or three years in the attitudes of athletes," he went on. "Traditionally, athletes have been the most right-wing reactionaries on campus, but they have been going through some big changes, especially on campuses like Berkeley, Columbia and Kansas, and especially since the U.S. invasion of Cambodia last spring."

Scott is the author of the first revolutionary book about athletics, "Athletics for Athletes." His second book, "The Athletic Revolution" will be out in a month.

He also spoke of the need of athletes to organize into athletic unions in their schools.

Meggyesy's plans are to return to his Berkeley home soon and to become involved with the growing jock lib movement here.

Among the other new residents

of Berkeley is Chip Oliver, a former pro football star like Meggyesy, but with the Oakland Raiders, rather than the speaking circuit, had chosen the life of seclusion in a Mendocino County commune upon his exit from organized sports...but he is now planning a move to Berkeley.

Here he joins Meggyesy and Scott along with 1966 Olympic marathon runner Bob Dyros, former Kansas decathlon star Sam Goldberg and former Cal sprinter Randy Smythe, among others, who are fully involved in the movement.

Centered around the Oakland collective, Jock Lib in the Bay Area is in the process of organizing into a Woodstock Nation Athletic Association, that will compete on the same level with such oppressive and controlling athletic organizations as the Athens Club, or in southern California, the Los Angeles Striders.

"These clubs dominate the lives of the athletes in the area of track and field," a jock libber reported. "Our concept would be a club of freaks, who would be in a much freer atmosphere to compete."

Sam Goldberg, who was mauled and arrested when he disrupted halftime activities at the Cal-Stanford football game last Fall by running across the field waving a Viet Cong flag, prefers to be known as Sam Jim Thorpe Yippie, minister of sport to the Youth

International Party.

He says he is still in top condition, as he and quartermiler Smythe work out every day, and claims he will embellish his uniform with a Viet Cong flag when he runs under the banner of the Woodstock Nation club.

In addition to creating an athletic club as an outlet for the more proficient performers in the reestablishment sports, Jock Lib wants to get into organizing the world's frisbee players and women's basketball players.

"We want to start an East Bay Athletic Conspiracy," reported a Libber, "by getting all the frisbee players, freaks turned on to physical health, to organize into a political physical action thing." He said that people have been

getting it on together on Sunday afternoons on the athletic field.

"We get lots of young athletes who come to us interested in what we are about," he said. "We'll get them together with Scott or Meggyesy over a meal...a Jock a lot of people are being turned on."

He reports that the collective, which houses eight liberated jocks now, is "a revolutionary Holiday Inn," where jocks from all over the country come to make contact, rap down the scene, and crash.

However, with all that Jock Lib is getting into, it has yet to deal with the assertion of others in the Berkeley scene who insist that the only revolutionary liberation for men in this society is gay liberation.

—Nick Benton

1958 Starting Linebacker
St. Louis Cardinals

1970 FREE
Writing book and living at Berkeley

The *Berkeley Barb* profiles Dave Meggyesy, February 1971. (Courtesy *Berkeley Barb,* www.berkeleybarb.net)

considered Parrish and Oliver, and, in a separate piece, Meggyesy alongside two books on Vince Lombardi. "If your inclination is to yawn and turn away because you don't happen to be interested in football, then resist the temptation for a moment," he insisted. These books "can be read as a debate on certain profound values in the American culture."[10]

Footage of the first of his three appearances on the *Dick Cavett Show*, in August 1970, three months before the first excerpts of the book appeared, suggests the breadth of Meggyesy's appeal. Resplendent in jeans, tie-dyed purple T-shirt, and cowboy boots, he ambled out and sat between old-Hollywood royalty Gloria Swanson (who'd been famous so long that she'd played a has-been in *Sunset Boulevard* twenty years before) and Janis Joplin, who smoked Marlboros on-air and petted his muscles, murmuring, "my goodness!" Cavett asked why so many people were not looking forward to his book, after which the two discussed the damage football wrought in college and the pros, the misconception that all players were right-wing, even the euphony of coaches' names. (Lombardi, they agreed, resonated better than Ewbank.) Meggyesy declared his disinterest in playing again, and Joplin suggested that loving each other was better than hurting each other and that it was nicer to move into a commune, as Chip Oliver had decided, than to play linebacker. Swanson agreed. More broadly, Cavett wondered, "Are there any professional athletes who *aren't* writing a book this year?"

The specter of freethinkers' cultural capital haunted football for several years. At the end of 1971, *The Boston Globe* named Meggyesy one of the "Movers of the Year" for "speaking for a new type of athlete." Whether or not they had disdained Meggyesy (sometimes, *while* disdaining him), reviewers now complained when athletes' memoirs lacked some critical edge. Dick Butkus's recounting of a single week in the 1971 season "does seem a little out of touch," according to one reader. "After iconoclastic—if not hysterical—books by such as Dave Meggyesy, Bernie Parrish and Larry Merchant, *Stop-Action* is anticlimactic. . . . Most of Butkus' predecessors in the genre raised more basic questions, like what football does to a player's spirit, or whether there is an NFL blackball, or how come so many defensive secondaries are black." So angrily retrograde was the author's lack of political consciousness that "his editors missed a bet by not giving his book a more appropriate title. Say, The Wit and Wisdom of Archie Butkus." "On the field . . . there's no nigger or whitey," Butkus explained. "Everybody looks alike to me."

Pete Axthelm wrote in the summer of 1971 that Joe Namath bored him: Meggyesy, Oliver, and Sauer had shown that "free-thinking can mean much more than bragging about how much Scotch you drink or how often you score with the ladies. . . . Against the deeper concerns of Meggyesy and others, [Namath's] particular style of rebellion has grown pallid." Dolphin running backs Larry Csonka and Jim Kiick were not particularly known for their politics, though Csonka became notorious for surreptitiously flipping off the viewer on an August 1972 cover of *Sports Illustrated.* Even so, Csonka told *Sport* that Nixon "upsets me with his role as a superjock. . . . I don't identify with him, and I haven't met a player yet who does." The next year, the pair's rambunctious dual autobiography insulted the president's football acumen as "a big joke" and noted in passing that, as a consequence of his very public fandom, "the danger is that some people then think everything is right with football."[11]

Even if you weren't talking about Meggyesy, you had to talk about Meggyesy. Every columnist who mentioned "soul-searching linebackers" was alluding to him. Tom Beer's comic odyssey through the dregs of the AFL took time to distinguish his story from "the Bernie Parrishes and the Dave Meggyesys," all of whom "have made their points, many of them well taken." Beer's experience "wasn't fun, but I can look back on the experience without rancor now that it's over." "A Game of Violence," the first chapter of Paul Zimmerman's hugely influential *A Thinking Man's Guide to Pro Football,* fought Meggyesy's criticisms to a standstill. Neither Alex Kroll's *How to be a TV Quarterback* nor Hal Higdon's *Pro Football, USA,* both of which covered much the same territory before Meggyesy's book appeared, had felt any anxiety on this question. Kroll, a former offensive lineman for the Jets, merely explained that the "single most important fact of pro football [is that] the game is constructed on violence."

Zimmerman felt compelled to explore a variety of players' reactions to Meggyesy. He noted that many of them not only didn't but *wouldn't* read excerpts from *Out of Their League,* which hit them where they lived. Baltimore center Bill Curry felt "terribly threatened" because "it might show me things I was too stupid to see." Ultimately, Curry decided, he found contradictions in Meggyesy's arguments that gave him confidence, but the book "made me think." After running through a range of up-close-and-personal descriptions of violence ("I'm still alive, if only barely," Merlin Olsen admitted), Zimmerman, an influential journalist, fan, and even semi-pro player, found himself unable to wrestle a coherent meaning out of his evidence. "You are left wondering why they actually play the game," he thought, then added that players deeply resented being called violent.

Zimmerman kept grappling with Meggyesy on his own. Several years later, his book on Jets coach Weeb Ewbank's last season returned to *Out of Their League* for an authoritative perspective on the racial baggage Charley Winner, Ewbank's son-in-law and presumptive heir, would bring from St. Louis. Zimmerman thought that the club's black/white situation was "nothing that high-powered," though "low-key racial antagonisms bubbled beneath the surface."

Other famously hardline coaches admitted that he wasn't entirely wrong. "Proudly" wearing a flag pin, Vince Lombardi claimed that Meggyesy represented "an isolated case" who misunderstood the true relationship between games and reality: "There's a lot more violence outside of football than in it. What violence there is in football is controlled." On the other hand, he implicitly complimented Meggyesy's ability to nurture an individualism his peers simply couldn't handle: "Football players are used to discipline. . . . Most people shout that they want independence, but really most want to be told what to do." After disdaining violent protest in chilling terms ("I don't say shoot them . . . but so many other [young people] only care about destruction"), Lombardi agreed that youth were right to be riled up. Dallas coach Tom Landry, frequently mocked for his rigid standards and upright Christianity, worried that without football, "society would lose one of the great strongholds—paying the price. There's not much discipline left in this country." But he too recognized that "you can't change the atmosphere. . . . People need more freedom than they've ever had before. . . . I think our young people are more sensitive and not as materialistic as my generation was, and I don't think that's bad." Meggyesy's revolution never arrived, inside the game or out (though it should be noted that both he and Rick Sortun followed the classic proletarian-novel trajectory by becoming labor organizers). But he sparked, even demanded, argument, concession, sometimes agreement from football's defenders.[12]

Still, wider sampling reveals that voices like his were definitely in the minority. The football and journalistic establishments usually mocked or undercut the dropouts. *Sports Illustrated* sneeringly titled a generally fair-minded article on Chip Oliver "Wow, Like Let's Really Try to Win." The *Los Angeles Times* sardonically relished "a stroke of good fortune we probably don't really deserve. Imagine, having the meaning of life explained to us by a man so uniquely equipped to unravel it all." Wells Twombly, a reliable source of outrage on things countercultural, mourned that Meggyesy was undermining national morale: "Irreverence is a pox that affects everything. . . . Hardly a month goes by without some indignant jock publishing a book telling how crummy football really is. Few people actually sing the alma mater at homecoming games, let alone stand up when the band is playing it." An Idaho columnist wondered how "an otherwise bright young man" like Oliver suddenly decided that "wearing a beard and shaggy hair and associating with non-productive types could somehow be more rewarding than being a top line pro athlete." On the other hand, it was probably a good thing that Oliver quit, since the game had neither capacity nor tolerance for diversity: "It may have turned out to be quite an embarrassing venture into the NFL this year with 39 All-American types and 1 other guy who had such a far-out philosophy." According to one outraged Texas journalist, it was only a step or two from quitting football to setting up your sniper rifle above Dealey Plaza: "The real cause for alarm is those people who say to hell with ANY 'society,' I'm gonna do exactly what I want to do, whether it be breaking a window or getting a coach fired or assassinating a President. Killing someone is the most abominable, yet most absolute, form of individual freedom."[13]

In his handling of Meggyesy, the media-savvy Rozelle paid close attention to baseball commissioner Bowie Kuhn's counterproductive attempt to suppress *Ball Four*. A June 1970 column explicitly noted that the league "has been quietly investigating its handful of rebels in the last several days since two of them [Oliver and Meggyesy] retired to join the flower children." Happily, the columnist added, Meggyesy did not pose as dangerous a threat as did gambling, the investigators concluding that few would follow his lead. One author alleges that Rozelle issued a league-wide gag order forbidding response to *Out of Our League,* and indeed, at first NFL officials did not eagerly discuss the book. One article just after *Look* published the first excerpt in November refers to "the National Football League line . . . [not to] say anything that might help promote the sale of Mr. Meggyesy's book."[14]

But many insiders eventually responded to Meggyesy's allegations, which suggests that he had become so prominent that *not* responding would let him dominate the conversation. Rozelle began to discuss the book in wide-ranging interviews, including one with the Associated Press in January 1971. Rather than trying to suppress *Out of Their League,* he trotted out his own collection of role models, the first two Republican politicians, to refute Meggyesy. If players were "warped," he replied, "it has happened to a mighty fine group of people—including Dr. Bill McColl [a former Chicago Bear who earned a medical degree at the University of Chicago and later ran unsuccessfully for Congress three times] and Jack Kemp."[15]

Denouncing Dave Meggyesy became a cottage industry, whether or not the terms of the denunciation held together. Unsurprisingly, Johnny Unitas told him off, grousing from a golf tournament that "I just couldn't see myself putting up with these different types of people and the attitudes they have. I would have to be upset most of the time or fire half of them." (At this point in his career, the eternally crewcut Unitas "was from the age of Magellan," Steve Sabol recalled.) The ageless George Blanda remarked, "sure, pro football is violent, that's one of the nicest things about it," and decided that "you read Chip's book and Meggyesy's book and they're just telling kids to revolt against authority, that's all. . . . They aren't interested in winning." Blanda subsequently told his biographer that football was "a humanizing experience" but also that Meggyesy "wouldn't have lasted six seconds" at Bear Bryant's notoriously brutal late-40s training camps. Besides, he added, "what job isn't just a little dehumanizing?"

Some younger players dismissed these claims as well. Putative freethinkers like Marty Domres, a young quarterback whose libertine autobiography, *Bump and Run*, appeared months after Meggyesy's, dropped in the odd sneer at claims about rampant drug abuse and dehumanization. Notoriously iconoclastic Raiders like Jim Otto and Ben Davidson suddenly rushed to proclaim their love of the system. In his autobiography, Otto remembered Oliver as "the weirdest of all" the characters on the Raiders, "a victim of drugs." In a college lecture "billed as giving the majority view of NFL ball," Davidson admitted the existence of a "pharmaceutical problem" and the irritating persistence of curfews for adults in the NFL but primarily enumerated the benefits of a pro-football career: a short work year, excellent fringe benefits, meritocracy, and "lifelong friends all over the United States." Just-elected Jack Kemp took time out from his new career to present his customary defense of the American way, stressing that "pro football is not a competitive rat race where only the fittest survive. . . . We have accomplished much in this country in just a little less than 200 years. Why don't they stress the tangible results and not the utopia they want?" As Ira Berkow explained, "most professional athletes are locked into establishment thought. They are not idealists. . . . It is the System, and they are slaves to it."[16]

While players disagreed with Meggyesy's experience, coaches lined up to dismiss his right to speak—the same restriction Ray Schoenke would face for endorsing the wrong presidential candidate. "Never before in our society have quitters and losers been so glorified," USC coach John McKay grumbled. "If they want to wear bellbottoms, let 'em join the Navy," sneered Falcon coach Norm van Brocklin, a notorious fanatic for old-school grooming. Lions coach Joe Schmidt wanted the football players on his side when the revolution came. Wally Lemm, Meggyesy's first coach in St. Louis, dismissed him as "an agitator and disruptive force . . . just a hippie and St. Louis is better off without him."[17]

Speakers close to the president saw the same danger. In an article published in *Sports Illustrated* in the summer of 1971, Spiro Agnew lambasted Meggyesy, Oliver, and Sauer, whose "particular form of hand-wringing" did not surprise him in the least; they might have deluded themselves that they left the game for good reasons, but anyone considering the question honestly knew that they simply sought "openly to justify their quitting." Look at everyone who remained connected. Individualism, in sports or in politics, was a fad. Just as every young athlete should seize the chance to be molded by a Bear Bryant, so should youthful protestors reject "the virulent conceit of infallibility" and heed their elders' wisdom. To do otherwise was literally un-American: free enterprise found its fullest expression on the field, which distinguished success from failure with ruthless clarity.

The next January, at the Touchdown Club's annual banquet in Birmingham, Agnew joined Alabama coach Bear Bryant, Auburn coach Shug Jordan, and Governor George Wallace and delivered another assault on these traitors. Glorying in his membership in "the Ogre Club of the Utopian Leftist Establishment," he mocked "over-publicized drop-outs, fawned on by the media." Failures like Meggyesy had always afflicted American culture, but never before had "professional malcontents" exalted their weakness and lack of character. At least, he thought, airing their grievances revealed their "unremitting contempt, indeed a detestation of the values which the overwhelming majority of Americans hold dear." Had they been in charge of American forces at Valley Forge, they would have shrugged their shoulders and given up, and where would we be today? Fortunately, Agnew knew well that "we, as a Nation, are not going to shirk the challenge of greatness." As long as there was an America, competition would continue. "And we are going to run *to win*."[18]

Baltimore's Mike Curtis was a year younger than Meggyesy, but his *Keep Off My Turf* read very much like Agnew in shoulder pads. "There's too much anti-football sentiment in the air these days," he began, then warned, "Dave Meggyesy isn't going to like this." Curtis was, perhaps not coincidentally, a particular favorite of the vice president, a dedicated Colts fan who owned an autographed photograph of Curtis and sent him a crystal ashtray decorated with his own autograph and the vice-presidential seal as a wedding present. Sounding very much like Agnew, Curtis mocked the critics as "also-rans" "on the fringes of fame" and blamed "permissiveness or ultraliberalism or whatever terms you prefer" for unrest in this "age of the malcontents."

"Mike is conservative in nearly everything," one profile noted. "Politics, his wardrobe, his recreation, even his attitude toward young ladies." He resorted to red-baiting—"if it's good for your cause that makes it OK. That's their attitude. It was the attitude of Karl Marx"—before announcing that "nothing in the life of a pro football player today justifies a strike." Curtis practiced what he preached: Oriard notes that he "has the unfortunate distinction of being the first in a depressingly long line of NFL players willing to be scabs," which he did *twice,* proudly crossing picket lines in 1970 and 1974. Where Meggyesy diagnosed football as a pathology of violent, imperialist Amerika, Curtis celebrated the sport *because* it was "so much like the rest of American society," a "decent game, played by decent people, operated by decent people, and watched and enjoyed by decent people."[19]

Mike Curtis meant what he said. Teammates remembered him hitting full-force even in practice ("he couldn't help it," one recalled), and he carried out the threat in his book's title by cold-cocking an excited fan who ran onto the field and grabbed the ball in the fourth quarter of a Colts victory over the Dolphins in December 1971. Curtis later explained, "that fellow had no right on the field. I felt it was in line to make him aware of his wrongdoing." An article in 2009 described him as "still stewing" over the Colts' defeat in Super Bowl III.

All-American brutality was his brand, one that the Colts' ticket packages played up. In the fall of 1970 "Mike Curtis Enterprises" issued a brochure promoting its sole client to advertisers "as that special man who can appeal to anyone and help you sell products." A more brazenly commercial proposition than Stanford's simultaneous flacking for Jim Plunkett, the eight-page spread exhibited Curtis in a variety of costumes, including tuxedo and swimsuit; played up the disparity between his animalistic on-field conduct and his gentlemanliness everywhere else through laudatory quotations from Agnew and fellow players and comparisons to Paul Bunyan, Rock Hudson, and Jack the Ripper; and summed it all up with the tag line "a man's man, a woman's hero, and a young boy's idol and a little girl's dream." Later that fall, before filming his newest commercial, Curtis cheerfully recalled recent collisions with the bullish Csonka that "rattled my brain a few times," remarking that he felt fine, "as long as they don't mess up my hair." In his autobiography, he straight-forwardly noted that, when Agnew visited the locker room, "I wanted to ask the Vice-President if he uses the hair tonic mentioned in my commercials, but I decided I'd better show some sense of propriety." His patriotic snarl was clearly real, but also just as much good business as Dave Meggyesy's beard.[20]

Running with God

A more interesting response came from Christians who were beginning to inflect football with beliefs that often directly opposed radicals' aims. According to the 1975 book *Running with God,* the Christian athlete represented "a growing force in a world of organized sports threatened by commercialism and greed. Though a minority, their influence is felt far beyond their numbers." Although the Fellowship of Christian Athletes (FCA) was founded in 1954 and Athletes in Action, an offshoot of Campus Crusade for Christ, in 1966, open religion remained an unwelcome novelty in the mid-'60s locker room. One journalist commented that believers "are not too popular with other players or the writers because they are too eager to recruit members or talk too much in public about what they used to do before they saw the light."

But times were changing. Nixon's prayer with Rex Kern and Bud Wilkinson in mid-October 1970 marked the FCA's first chance to conduct a worship service inside the White House. Professional Athletes Outreach was founded in 1971, and Billy Graham became the first clergyman to serve as grand marshal of the Rose Bowl parade. Graham boasted to *Newsweek* that year that there were "probably more really committed Christians" in sports than in any other occupation in America. By 1973, twenty of the twenty-six NFL franchises included some sort of religious service as part of pregame preparation. Miami, especially proud of its ecumenical devotion, brought a minister, rabbi, and priest on the road and was so often delayed by extensive pregame devotions that the press corps bet on the sermon's length. One journalist chalked that new popularity up to the eclipse of the Lombardi ethic, implying that religious belief was now every bit as much a lifestyle choice as dissent: "In the 1960s—years of war and division—the athletic philosophy of winning-is-everything was in the ascendancy. . . . There is time now for godliness on the schedule." At least two players quit the game in this period to preach without attracting anywhere near the attention, or disdain, that Meggyesy did.[21]

The Knicks' iconoclastic Phil Jackson thought that football accorded all too well with the essential demands of fundamentalism: "There is no room for argument, for examination. This fits perfectly with the football mentality." This was sometimes true. Terry Bradshaw extolled the Steelers' pastor because "the Bible is so confusing, and this guy makes it so simple." Dolphin tackle Norm Evans's muscular-Christian memoir, *On God's Squad,* found spiritual truth in the right brand of obedience, what a later generation would call servant leadership: "It requires a goodly proportion of self-discipline to be a coachable person. You have to listen and then apply what you hear in order to give direction to your desire and dedication."

But Baptist minister Tom Skinner, who joined the Redskins in 1971 and led them in the first televised prayer session after their defeat of the Cowboys in the 1972 playoffs, preached something more like liberation theology. Though he expounded on a "Locker Room Jesus, the man with hair on His chest and sweat on His brow" and later officiated at George Allen's funeral, Skinner forcefully dissented "from any argument which says God sends troops to Asia, that God is a capitalist, that God is a militarist." Others challenged the premise that such divergent value systems could truly harmonize. Peter Gent argued that "I just don't think you can run a pro team and be a true Christian." The FCA's *Christian Athlete* published an article beseeching Christians to come up with "a whole new conception of sports . . . in the light of Jesus. . . . There is win, or lose, but no middle ground. Is it any wonder that Vietnam has become such an enigma?" The organization's communications director worried, "it's 'in' to get with pro athletes and have a chapel. It's so professionalized and organized, we've almost made it a part of the game."[22]

Former Browns defensive end Bill Glass had long experience in putting America's game to the Lord's purposes. A historian of religion and sport describes him as equal parts "pragmatic salesman" and "evangelical ideologue." He had been saved as a high-school junior and was one of a number of "football-playing ministerial students" to graduate from Baylor, at which minister/ sports announcer Jarrell McCracken had recorded "The Game of Life," an allegorical LP providing play-by-play for a football game between good and evil. Glass invented pregame chapel with the Lions in 1958 and preached to the Baptist World Congress inside Miami's Orange Bowl in 1965.

His extremely muscular Christianity did not have any truck with lily-livered pacifists. "The weak shouldn't play in the first place," he said. Sounding very much like Richard Nixon or Wallace Newman, he advised, "don't ever be a good loser. Be a bad loser. Good losers usually lose." Despite general resentment of open Christianity, he was popular with his teammates, Bernie Parrish finding him a fascinating "paradox, a fundamentalist preacher off the field but a lusty, physical man when the pressures of the moment called for it. . . . He was extremely uninhibited." Glass, who quit football a month after Meggyesy did to run his ministry full-time (he counted 10,000 saved in 1969 alone), was so unsettled by *Out of Their League* that he mailed a questionnaire about "moral habits and beliefs" to current NFL players to ascertain the book's accuracy. More than 250 responded. Many of the players drank and "chased broads," Glass reported, "but they are ashamed of it. That's the big difference."[23]

Glass's *Don't Blame the Game: An Answer to Super Star Swingers and a Look at What's Right with Sports,* graced with a foreword from Roger Staubach, represented the "decent majority." The famously iconoclastic journalist Jim Murray recognized that the book was "not shrill or name-calling or sensationalized. It's as low-key as a Supreme Court brief." Glass did not echo Nixon/Agnew rhetoric in the way Mike Curtis did, nor did he foreshadow contemporary brands of sports evangelism in arguing for a wider fundamentalist social agenda. Rather, Glass thought seriously about what Meggyesy, Sauer, Oliver, and Namath (all of whom he treated as equally threatening to professional football) had said, quoting and footnoting their remarks.

Though he claimed that "no one else in professional football . . . shares Meggyesy's view," an obvious falsehood, he willingly engaged in debate and conceded some of the dissidents' charges. While insisting that "there isn't any special treatment of the pros by draft boards," Glass admitted the existence of racial injustice ("even if a black athlete is treated fairly by the coaches, he still has to live in a prejudiced society") and the possibility that players might intentionally hurt one another. But he argued for a fundamentally different vision of what it meant to play the game than did Sauer or Meggyesy. Football itself was ethically and politically neutral, Glass thought; your choices, on and off the field, were what mattered. He had no interest in the notion of the game as symbolic war. "The differences are significant. Wars are political contests. Sports are not." From his perspective, Meggyesy's complaints about dehumanization of players paled next to larger evils: "Poverty, war, racism—these really do dehumanize." Glass challenged his readers not simply to dismiss Meggyesy, but to consider his arguments within a wider critique of contemporary America.[24]

Murray Kempton, whose extensive consideration of critical sports autobiographies in the *New York Review of Books* signaled intellectuals' interest in questions of sports and morality, argued that Meggyesy's real threat lay in his ability to fully conquer that portion of his consciousness that loved the sport: "The uneasiness that Meggyesy causes among football players who, even if not revolted by it, have attained detachment from the game as an institution is, I think, caused by his heroic effort to expel every trace of this ambivalence." That may have been his most difficult feat. Peter Gent admitted in the foreword to the thirtieth-anniversary edition of *North Dallas Forty* that "I felt more in one Sunday afternoon than I did later on in whole years." A bemused Ron Mix wrote that he vowed to quit after high school, yet eight years later here he was, selling "my body for another year." Jerry Kramer thought that the worst part was giving up the way of life: "I doubt I'll ever be so close again to a group of people." George Sauer and Chip Oliver both tried comebacks.[25]

And even Meggyesy could not banish the game's lure. In the fall of 1970, a San Francisco reporter saw him at a 49er game. For the next two decades, the standard Meggyesy sighting depicted him wistfully reconsidering an environment he had rejected—Syracuse, the NFL—dreaming of rejoining it while refusing to compromise the principles that drove him to depart. "Sports are great," he told a crowd at Appalachian State in 1974. "I'd still be playing football if I could play it under humane conditions." He worked for the players' union and even coached a season of football at Mt. Tamalpais High in Marin, emphasizing "the importance of participating as a team." "Football is, basically, a game," he explained. "And if you are not enjoying it then that's not the answer for you." But in the early '70s, his wholesale rejection of its political, emotional, and sartorial values, and the quixotic and often lonely battle he was willing to wage, struck observers as signaling worrisome things, both about football itself and a wider world in which no one could depend on bastions of American identity. If football players stopped playing the game, what next?[26]

The Namath Effect

Journalists of the early '70s often hailed Joe Namath as a revolutionary. "Is there a Joe Namath in the House? In the Senate? Out on the Streets, maybe?" wondered the *East Village Other* just after Super Bowl III. Marty Ralbovsky's exaltation of the "Namath effect" began with salutes by George Wallace and New York Mayor John Lindsay and never cooled down. Among the honorifics he bestowed on the quarterback, in addition to comparisons to Mick Jagger, Robert Redford, and JFK: "the bugler for Armageddon," "to sports what Frank Wills is to Watergate," and "the jockstrap equivalent of Jane Fonda." Meggyesy complained that the serialized portions of his book misled readers in search of similar thrills: "We made a mistake. . . . Sex and racism, sex and racism, that's not what the book's about." Bill Glass, of all people, agreed: "Some of what they say is true. But they aren't giving the whole picture, not by a long shot." Meggyesy's revolution did not take place, and young men continued to come out for football. The counterculture dollar, it turned out, could mute countercultural concerns.

But not entirely. Those counterculture dollars mattered. People took Dave Meggyesy seriously. In addition to *Cavett*, he appeared on *To Tell the Truth* and conversed with David Frost. An appearance at his alma mater in December 1970 turned into a civil-rights flashpoint between students and administration whose repercussions echoed for months. He booked speaking engagements and took part in symposia about "the Football Myth" at more than a hundred campuses while making his home in a Berkeley commune, "'a revolutionary Holiday Inn' where jocks from all over the country come to make contact, rap down the scene, and crash." His series on radical Berkeley radio station KPFA in the fall of 1971 took in "the athlete and radical consciousness," "dope in pro ball," and "the football mind," among other topics. Meggyesy tirelessly put out his message, telling a 1972 panel on "Sport in a Changing World" at the University of Wisconsin that the game provided "a perfect model of social control. If it wasn't for big-time football there would be revolution in the streets."

In 1972, he covered the Super Bowl, likening the game to bread and cir-cuses with a stench of fascist bloodlust. "Radicals should understand . . . how thousands of placid straight people can be driven into a frenzy of demented ecstasy," he thought. "I can just see soon they'll tire of marching bands and want some real action—hippies and cops fighting each other to the death." That fall, his hair "down to his breastbone," Meggyesy advocated for Proposition 19, legalizing marijuana in California. A year later, his beard shaved, he co-directed the Esalen Sports Center and at one seminar recalled seeing auras around other players that helped him anticipate their moves "in a kind of precognitive playing trance." He even cropped up during Jack Scott's brief run as Oberlin athletic director, where he was accused of driving out longtime faculty who refused to attend his "retraining" session. As late as 1974, the *New York Times* listed him on its roster of lecture-circuit "Supermouths" like Dick Gregory, Christine Jorgensen, and Uri Geller.[27]

Both Meggyesy and Namath grew adept at selling themselves to different audiences. They were part of a wave. "Madison Avenue is fast becoming a sportsman's paradise," one journalist wrote. The 1970s marked "the decade of the athlete in marketing," another magazine noticed, but the lessons were complicated. Inside the game or out, the notion that "the personal is political," first articulated in the feminist movement, keyed a developing sense that whatever self-exploration you undertook mattered in the larger culture—if it sold.

Though this hardly represented radical notions of transformation bruited about in, say, 1968, neither was it devoid of significance. Doing good could mean doing well, and telling your story required selling your story. Racial or political identity and honesty, as long as they were not too overt, mattered less than marketability. Before 1970, few African Americans, no matter their family-friendly appeal, had enjoyed much opportunity to advertise products aimed at white consumers. "How many black athletes have ever endorsed toothpaste?" an angry Harry Edwards demanded in 1969. "One wonders if it could really be true . . . that white buyers would rather fight than switch to a cigarette brand endorsed by a black," *Sports Illustrated* observed in 1968. Now O. J. Simpson, *Advertising Age*'s Star Presenter of the Year for 1977, represented Hertz, Dingo Boots, and Spot-Bilt athletic shoes, among many other product lines, because he tested as credible, persuasive, and merchandisable to male and female teenagers, a spokesman "without color . . . beyond any ethnic identification in his projection." Simpson carried "a certain flamboyance"; the equally accomplished Walter Payton did not. Mean Joe Greene's 1979 Coke ad became the stuff of legend.

The same balance held true for believers. Distressed by the primacy of sybarites like Joe Namath in advertising, the FCA attempted to expand its influence by urging its more photogenic members to get their faces on TV. This further diluted an already diluted spirit. "I have found among the golden boys a distressing theological superficiality," wrote one critic. "God is a *great* general manager. Jesus is a *terrific* coach. . . . That's about it." Bill Glass wrote that "this great Coach has never fumbled. . . . He always has won, and He always will win." Norm Evans predicted that nowadays Jesus would manifest as an unstoppable 6'6" defensive lineman who "would be a star in this league." One team executive described sports preachers as "guys who are really excited about football. The majority of the time the sermons are very athletic."

Presbyterian minister Billy Zeoli, whom a journalist twitted as the "most Valuable Preacher" in "Sportianity," climbed to the top of the mountain by mastering both trades. He got his start running Gospel Films in western Michigan before his staple sermon, "God's Game Plan," delivered at a Redskins prayer breakfast, moved Gerald Ford to commit himself to Christ. Zeoli preached to players before numerous Super Bowls, became Ford's spiritual counselor, and gifted him with a devotional message every Monday during his tenure as president. In a note to an advisor, Ford described Zeoli as "a very good friend of the family. I do, when he visits, pray with him." As reproduced in print, "God's Game Plan" anticipated the PowerPoint mantras of today, boiling Zeoli's guidance down to bullet points:

The closing chapter of this book is a message I have used with every football team to which I have spoken. It is the Gospel of Jesus Christ.
It is the Message that has
    transformed,
    changed,
    revitalized
The lives of every one of us in this book. . . .
Every football team always has a game plan. . . .
In His rule book for life, called
      the Bible
God presents His game plan in a very clear and expressive way.[28]

Surveys found that respect for particular endorsers did not matter. Consumers bought what the showy Namath was peddling without admiring or trusting him. As in politics, credible performance mattered. Mike Curtis's endorsement career never took off, but Rosey Grier sang "It's All Right to Cry" on the feminist special *Free to be You and Me* in 1972. "Authenticity," within a mainstream pushed by the counterculture to embrace wider conceptions of truth and honesty, could embrace self-indulgence, existential pain, radicalism, conservatism, black self-assertion, even the rudiments of the Moral Majority—a possibility equally open to Joe Namath, Chip Oliver, Dave Meggyesy, Mike Curtis, Johnny Sample, and Bill Glass. (The public wasn't yet ready to embrace every kind of football player; by coming out in 1975, Dave Kopay pushed beyond a boundary that no active NFL player has crossed.) Meister Brau Lite, scuttling along the bottom of the beer market, most effectively capitalized on this logic by rebranding itself as Miller Lite, then running commercials that simultaneously traded on and undercut icons of manliness, treating athletes, tough-guy actors, and authors who wrote about tough guys (the first spots featured Jets running back Matt Snell, movie heavy Sheldon Leonard, and hard-boiled novelist Mickey Spillane) as interchangeable. The subsequent sequence of ads lent low-calorie beer he-man cred, made celebrities of Bubba Smith and Dick Butkus (who beat out Sam Huff for the role), and won multiple Clio Awards. Miller Lite then completed the circle by becoming the official beer of the NFL.[29]

Meggyesy's second career as America's most celebrated ex-football player rendered both parts of the term equally significant and made him, in essence, the sport's first public intellectual. As did more centrist players who took part in campaigns and ran for office, Meggyesy and his cohorts created new ways of looking and talking inside football. Although NFL Films had usurped their right to tell their own stories, all of these players found newly resonant means to thrust themselves back into the public sphere and promote new notions of the meaning of playing and watching America's most popular sport. Meggyesy certainly didn't win, but he didn't quite lose. There were now many different ways to be a football hero, some of which did not require playing football at all.

8

Right Coach, Wrong Game

When they get to the bottom of Watergate,
they'll find a football coach.
—Indiana University basketball coach
Bobby Knight[1]

At the Houston Rotary Club's first annual Vince Lombardi Award dinner in 1971, Spiro Agnew made common cause with embattled coaches: "I doubt that many of us here tonight would be allowed to 'do our thing.' I have in mind the fact that in the New Left rankings of the people's enemies the institution known as the Football Coach ranks high in the top ten—not far behind the Joint Chiefs of Staff, General Motors, the CIA, the FBI, John Wayne, and yours truly." His speech had in fact been delayed for twenty minutes by several hundred demonstrators demanding an end to "suppression of dissent by our leaders" before the police hauled many of them off. Thirty-seven, including a *Houston Chronicle* reporter covering the protest, were arrested, many of them cut and bleeding. Troubled by this kind of upheaval, in late 1969 the American Football Coaches Association's trustees put "the problems of football coaches as they relate to militants and student groups" on next year's agenda.

The association's 1970 meeting, which drew more mainstream coverage than it ever had or ever would again, cemented the popular image of football coaches, irrespective of race and location, as authoritarian figureheads. At the main session, Florida A&M's Jake Gaither joked about kids today, to much laughter: "Every time I see you with that beard and long hair, I think of you as a sissy. Do you want your coach thinking of you as a homosexual?" Southern University's Al Taber remembered facing off against "a black power guy" who wondered why Taber did not let his players participate in demonstrations. "Because I believe in America too strongly," Taber replied. Two weeks after the meeting, the Nixon administration publicly confirmed that it had sounded out two of those present about their interest in heading up the Selective Service Administration.

To underline how crucial it was to hold the line, the special guest speaker, assistant commander of the Marines General Lew Walt, urged these "distinguished, influential and loyal Americans" to shoulder responsibility for "the future character and security of our nation" in the face of the "deterioration of order and discipline in some of our educational institutions." Walt, whom the 1971 CBS exposé *The Selling of the Pentagon* described as "for years . . . the Marine speaker most in demand," spent his days traveling the country to win hearts and minds to the Pentagon's point of view. He did so explicitly here by equating the Medal of Honor winner and the All-American, "team players" with the "belly power" to fulfill the drive to greatness. Woody Hayes, who had gone in-country four times in the previous three years, took the opportunity to introduce Vince Lombardi to Walt and convince Lombardi himself to visit Vietnam, an opportunity he was unable to seize because of illness.[2]

A few years later, Walt expanded on what he'd told the coaches, warning darkly of the threat of remorseless Soviet encroachment unless "plain Americans" got together and elected a Congress that spent less on butter and more on guns and was willing to remilitarize the nation "in a hurry." America was "on our own goal line, in the last quarter of the game, with the clock running out" because a fearful, weak-minded and internationalist Establishment forbade the country from "making any offensive plays at all."[3]

As the atmosphere surrounding this meeting suggests, coaches seemed to offer perfect candidates for the new politics. They cultivated an aura of authority, enjoyed national profiles generally independent of party identification, hobnobbed with prominent political and military figures, and often enjoyed a compliant local press prone to describing the team as "we" and defending the maestro from ignorant outsiders. Bear Bryant began one chapter of his 1974 autobiography by noting that he admitted to thinking about a political career: "If movie stars can make it, football coaches ought to be able to." He then displayed a fine instinct for bipartisan pandering by celebrating, over the course of a page and a half, his ties to three Kentucky governors, the Kennedys, George Wallace, Nixon, and Agnew.[4]

But surprisingly few coaches cut the political figure that supporters like Lew Walt hoped they would. Oklahoma's Bud Wilkinson failed to reach the Senate in 1964, as did his son Jay the House in 1970. Vince Lombardi, despite wide and bipartisan interest in the prospect of his candidacy, enjoyed the attention more than the compromises necessary for a political career.[5] George Allen campaigned actively for Richard Nixon and privately reassured Nixon of the rightness of his conduct, but expressed little public interest himself in anything that distracted from his single-minded pursuit of victory.

Lombardi, to some degree inaccurately, struck many as an overtly political figure; covertly, Allen *was* one. Yet both men spoke powerfully to and for tradition-minded Americans. Though neither coach was or became a politician, what matters is that supporters and opponents *thought of them in those terms.* The language and assumptions that surround coaches help us understand how Americans articulated concerns about work, power, and authority at a time when such personal questions had inevitable political resonances. And they also showed where this new political culture was heading, as coaches too became salesmen. The coach as management guru endorsed slogans and principles that turned common football metaphors to commercial use in ways that subsequently trickled into politics.

The Only Man in America Nixon Viscerally Respects

Football coaches often turned up in the popular press to issue quasi-fascist edicts on the diseased state of contemporary culture. "The bums eat the food our society produces, they wear the clothes our society produces and now they want to destroy our society," raged USC assistant Marv Goux. "Like pigs, they have no pride or discipline." So it made sense to prospect for quasi-Nixons in their ranks. There were obvious stylistic similarities. Murray Kempton waspishly observed that "one source of the disquiet Mr. Nixon arouses is his fondness for explaining things with charts, blackboards, and pointers, the materials we especially associate with losing football coaches."

Lombardi, a winning football coach, was only occasionally a political animal. He rarely addressed current controversies and had almost nothing to say about foreign policy. But toward the close of his time in Green Bay in 1968, he began to opine on the decline of all things in the contemporary world, giving a much-discussed speech decrying young people's idealization of freedom over order: "Everything has been done to strengthen the rights of the individual and at the same time weaken the rights of the judge, of the state and of all authority." Lombardi had actually been delivering "the Speech," as his son called it, since the early '60s, beginning with a hospital fundraiser, moving to business groups, and, as the decade wore on, adding new criticisms of student unrest that doubled its length.

Lombardi generally began "the Speech" by claiming that all he knew was football, which nonetheless offered lessons in courage, stamina, and coordination that could be usefully applied at the hospitals, Catholic charities, and large corporations that paid him to appear. Violence, he explained, required discipline, and sports like football required the best in everyone. They allowed no room for racial or class bigotry. Competition was essential to bring out the best in individuals and nations, as was recognition of inherent inequality: not all of us were cut out to be leaders. But leaders should never lord their power over the led; they should be humble, simple, Spartan, and embody a spirit of Christian love that demanded the very best of themselves and others. "Heart power is the strength of your company, of your organization, of America," he wrote. "Hate power is the weakness of the world."[6]

The Speech did not strike just one note politically—Lombardi's call for "sacrifice, self-denial, love, fearlessness, and humility" was less right-wing jeremiad against contemporary America than summoning of deeply Catholic virtues that in several aspects resonated with leftish spiritual aspirations. But conservatives loved what they heard. In the spring of 1969, at the FBI's Communion Breakfast, Lombardi's "inspiring speech wherein he decried the violent anarchism and lawlessness in our society . . . in which he referred in a most complimentary manner to the Bureau and the Director, was enthusiastically received," an internal FBI memorandum noted. When the NFL made all twenty-six coaches available to the media in the spring of 1970, Lombardi "siphoned off nearly all the reporters" in the room, all of them eager to solicit the "potential for controversy" that his remarks would surely kindle. After Lombardi entered the hospital that summer for treatment, J. Edgar Hoover sent an affectionate note wishing him good health and a speedy recovery.[7]

Various political fixers began to wonder whether or not he might want to contend for a different title. After the conversation with Richard Nixon in New Hampshire early in 1968 that revealed how well Nixon knew football, Hunter

S. Thompson gained the "powerful impression" that Lombardi was "the only man in America that [Nixon] viscerally respected." Nixon had had his campaign manager look into Lombardi as a possible vice president before discovering, to the party's chagrin, his admiration for the Kennedys. But Lombardi was a prototypical Reagan Democrat. Given his burgeoning distaste for the drift of America, he could well have strengthened the Nixon ticket in 1972 had he lived.

On the other side of the aisle, Bobby Kennedy asked Lombardi to "be my coach" four days after he announced his retirement from Green Bay in 1968, while a member of the Democratic National Committee lobbied eventual nominee Hubert Humphrey to explore the possibility of putting him on the ticket. A banner someone put up at "A Salute to Vince Lombardi Day" in August 1968 read simply, "Vince for President." A writer for the *Milwaukee Sentinel* described him as "not ruling out" a political role when addressing the Football Writers' Association, though all he committed to was "something to help my country." Three weeks later, the *Sporting News* added more of his remarks, to the effect that Americans were confusing "freedom with license" and that sympathy for the underprivileged was not limitless: "we must have sympathy for the doer, too. . . . Let us respect success."

Lombardi had the Redskins stage a flag celebration on the Sunday before the Mobilization in November 1969, explaining that "that's our answer to whatever they're doing." Heartened, Nixon sent Lombardi a note thanking him for "this most welcome show of patriotism . . . at a time when it can do the most good." But the coach teased the possibility of politics much more than he actually explored it; the external hunger for a Lombardiesque leader was stronger than any internal drive on his part. From all accounts, molding winning football teams utterly consumed him. Another newspaper took precisely the same observations he had made about the contemporary scene and headlined the story, "No Politics for Lombardi."[8]

To his legions of admirers, Lombardi embodied all manner of wonderfully traditional faiths: simplicity, honesty, trust, diligence, team spirit. His skirmishes with nosy reporters reflected an inner integrity that was in essence spiritual; one journalist called it his "Trappist-monk silence." "Each year, and probably more than once a year, I tell our team that, during the football season, there are only three things in which each man should be interested: 1) his family; 2) his religion; 3) the Green Bay Packers," he remarked in 1967. As with everything Lombardi said, he repeated this statement hundreds of times. Every drop of sweat, every ache his practices induced served a larger collective purpose, the unceasing pursuit of excellence. His ideal self-portrait, from *Run to Daylight!*, the 1963 as-told-to book chronicling a week in his life, portrayed him as meticulous craftsman, civic fixture, family man, educator, philosopher, psychologist: a sensitive soul doing what was necessary to win a violent game. Football is a sport "through which you find self expression," he said, and his job was simply to bring his players face-to-face with their fullest potential: "They call it coaching, but it is teaching."[9]

When his film career ended, Ronald Reagan spent a decade delivering a pro–free enterprise talk for GE in a successful effort to establish his credibility in a new line of work. Might the speech be pointing Lombardi in a similar direction? During his brief retirement, he issued a number of pronouncements that, depending on how you interpreted them, could read as moral injunction, corporate-speak, anguished complaint about contemporary society—or all three at once. Being Vince Lombardi suddenly became good business, old-line grit and drive being eminently salable. The version that many readers encountered, "What It Takes To Be Number One," published nationwide in magazines and newspapers, preached that "there is something in good men that really yearns for—needs—discipline and the harsh reality of head-to-head combat."

In 1968, Lombardi put this ethos into practice by starring in a short motivational film, *Second Effort*, in which he somewhat woodenly schools a sad-sack salesman in his trademark virtues. "You're the ball carrier," he teaches. "And I guess you could say that the ball is the product." When his son gently criticized his performance, Lombardi demanded acting tips.[10]

Lombardi's ideals quickly became marketable as a key to corporate achievement. *Sports Illustrated* dubbed him "America's leading Success Symbol and Dean of Champions." In 1971, a management consultant noted that CEOs of successful companies believed "in essence, the same thing" as Lombardi's fundamental dictum that "winning football games was a matter of getting inside the players." In 1972, seven former Packers took to the road with a film of their own, *The Habit of Winning*, that distilled Lombardi's teachings for commercial use. Ford, IBM, General Motors, and the Small Business Administration (SBA) all ordered copies, and the SBA showed the film in management-training courses it offered to small businessmen around the country. Jerry Kramer was a real-estate investor, Fuzzy Thurston and Max McGee restaurateurs, Jim Taylor a success in construction, Willie Davis a flourishing Schlitz distributor who had increased sales by a quarter-million cases in his first year alone. And they owed it all to their old coach. "It's a matter of dedication once you have decided where you want to go, and how to prepare yourself for it," Kramer said. Early the next year, a journalist pointed out that Wall Street personnel managers seeking candidates for sales positions had come to the same understanding and invariably preferred those who were resilient, aggressive, and team-oriented—"in short, those qualities that Vince Lombardi prized so dearly in football players."[11]

When Lombardi died in September 1970, honors poured in from all corners. In the first hours his body lay in repose, mourners included former Chief Justice Earl Warren, Pete Rozelle, the Italian ambassador, and ordinary people: policemen, janitors, nurses, priests, "young kids with footballs," even "some long-hairs in tee shirts, dungarees and sandals." The Olympic torch was lighted in Los Angeles and multiple TV networks immediately aired commemorative documentaries. The *Washington Post*'s Shirley Povich celebrated him as "football coach, lecturer, philosopher, tough guy, moralist and practicing patriot." Conducting a mass in his honor in St. Patrick's Cathedral on Fifth Avenue, Cardinal Terence Cooke, Roman Catholic Archbishop of New York, compared him to St. Paul, both men abounding in "the dynamic Christian spirit" necessary for "meeting the challenges of our day." Redskins wide receiver Charley Taylor mourned that "all the people whom I love and admired and gained so much from in my life aren't with us anymore": JFK, Martin Luther King, and now Lombardi. "I will never meet his peer," Jerry Kramer lamented at graveside. "The Lombardi legend will long shine among the glories of our state," the *Milwaukee Journal* prophesied.

Encomia arrived from across the political spectrum, often in strikingly similar terms: liberal Wisconsin Senator William Proxmire called Lombardi "a man of the discipline, dedication and self-sacrifice this country needs today," while Victor Gold lionized him in *National Review* as "a vintage American winner; in the autumns of indecision, a man to reassure us that our doleful intellectual compatriots are wrong. . . . His game will greatly miss his primitive virtues; his countrymen even more." In mourning, the nation recreated a kind of unity it could find nowhere else. Richard Nixon issued a statement commemorating Lombardi's "belief in fundamentals . . . his church, his home, his friends, and his family" and predicted that "he will always hold a commanding place in the memory of this Nation." The next summer, Nixon sat down with Frank Gifford to commemorate the coach.[12]

Richard Nixon honors Vince Lombardi, 1971. (Courtesy Richard M. Nixon Library)

Yet not everyone cheered during (or especially after) Lombardi's life. Distrust of—or more accurately, conspicuous disrespect for—his precepts marked one's ideological territory. By the time of his death, Lombardi's defenders sounded like an embattled minority, constantly pleading that the dominant impression omitted his most impressive qualities. To detractors, opposing him as human being, football coach, and citizen—and the "Lombardiist" ideology that he was accused of standing for—meant opposing mindless conformity, stupidly aggressive foreign policy, repression.

Stan Isaacs found Lombardi "overbearing, condescending, hypocritical. He demanded and got a sycophantic press." For Leonard Shecter, he was in essence an avatar of fascism: "A lifetime in athletics, most of the years spent commanding the soft, empty minds of young people, is nearly certainly bound to lead one down the labyrinths of authoritarianism to Lombardiism. . . . Patriotism, conformity, religion . . . these are the raw materials a coach demands. For after them, blank-eyed dedication to hard work, team spirit and the ignoring of painful injury come more easily." Shecter's assault on Lombardi, "The Toughest Man in Pro Football," published in *Esquire* in January 1968, was so scabrous that one reporter recalled Lombardi, purple with rage, demanding, "am I really like this?" when he read the piece. "Nothing pained him more deeply" than this impression, wrote another. Even his mother called to ask why he came across so badly. Years after his father's death, Vince Lombardi II was still complaining.

Shecter painted Lombardi as a grasping tyrant who indulged in petty authoritarianism he could exercise only in the Podunk town he dominated—"a sort of fiefdom," he called Green Bay, in which city residents and players obligingly parroted the Great Man's numerous aphorisms. In Shecter's sights, Lombardi came off as a homemade knockoff of every Latin American despot, strutting around "with his belly sucked in and his chest extended like a pigeon's," limitlessly contemptuous of those beneath him and copiously indulging his vanity; all he lacked were the statues.[13]

In the same way the conservative athlete or coach signaled his politics by denouncing Dave Meggyesy, the surest mark of the dissident athlete was to immediately declare one's opposition to Lombardi. He was the enemy in writings by Meggyesy, George Sauer, and Johnny Sample. Sauer observed that the "Vince Lombardi type of coach hollering at you to hate the other guy" typified football's ridiculous antihuman mentality. Meggyesy called him "a pint-sized Patton" and warned that if you glorified people like Lombardi, "you're gonna dig fascism when it comes down." This was an opinion Lombardi reciprocated in full: even as he lay dying in the summer of 1970, his wife heard him mutter, "Joe Namath! You're not bigger than football!" As if in sympathy, Nixon honored Namath as the only athlete on his enemies list.

His numerous sayings were mocked as guidelines for aspiring sheep, the middle-American inversion of Mao's Little Red Book. James Dickey's 1971 poem "For the Death of Vince Lombardi" mourned that Lombardi's philosophy wrung greatness from men, but at enormous human cost:

> Coach, don't you know that some of us were ruined
> For life? Everybody can't win. What of almost all
> Of us, Vince? We lost. And our greatest loss was that we could not survive
> Football.

An entire 1973 column rejoiced in growing rejection of the "winning-is-everything philosophy" throughout American culture, a trend that would promote healthier families, fuller and more enjoyable lives, and better character. James Michener devoted the closing chapter of his encyclopedic *Sports in America* to debating the "revulsion against overcompetitiveness" for which Lombardi most forcefully stood, linking it to everything from bribes to foreign agents to school violence to heart attacks.[14]

Some observers argued that this counter-narrative missed the point just as badly. After his death, Red Smith wrote that only wrestlers less resembled their public images than did Lombardi, to whom contemporary writers attributed "the least endearing characteristics of Attila the Hun and the Marquis de Sade." A documentary on closeted Redskins' receiver Jerry Smith pointed out that Lombardi had a gay brother and was notably protective of gay players' privacy. Tom Dowling, who observed Lombardi throughout the 1969 season, recounted an instance two months after the Stonewall riots in which an unnamed gay Redskin "had come up at a coach's meeting in a less than charitable fashion. Lombardi was reported to have winced and said that he had never felt so strongly about a player making the club . . . for he believed the man was a victim of prejudice." Other former players also remember Lombardi's Redskins as the most tolerant team in the league in this respect, and in 2014, his son remarked that Lombardi would have been the ideal coach for Michael Sam, then attempting to become the first openly gay NFL player.

From Emlen Tunnell onward, many observers noted his scrupulous, if utilitarian, fairness toward African American players as well. Former Packer Willie Davis recalled that he "did more to promote diversity than any other coach in the league." Lombardi arranged exhibition games to avoid southern segregation and assigned roommates in alphabetical order, explaining that "I don't feel that way [bigoted]. I'm very grateful for that, because, first of all, to feel that way is wrong, and second, it's good football." Reporters suddenly alerted to racial strife inside pro football by 1967 or so repeatedly described Lombardi's Packers as the league's most harmonious team. Nor did he simply mouth the-sky-is-falling platitudes; he told a reporter asking him about

Meggyesy's charges that "there should be a concern about pollution, about Vietnam, about Cambodia and about poverty; I'm concerned about that, too." He responded to Nixon's Honor America Day that "it's not 'my country right or wrong.' . . . When I was young I fought for liberty and innovation. It's always been the function of the young to do that."[15]

The always-iconoclastic Robert Lipsyte argued that there was really no such thing as "Lombardiism." The coach's most famous aphorism, "winning isn't everything, it's the only thing," was self-evident—in football, Lipsyte thought. To equate America with the Green Bay Packers, and the NFL with the planet Earth, absolutely was fascist. But Lombardi never actually drew those connections. Bart Starr remembered the phrase as "winning isn't everything, but making the effort to is." "There's a big difference," he added. The line was "not what my father was about, and that certainly wasn't his leadership model," his son wrote.

In fact, the aphorism for which Lombardi is best known probably originated with UCLA coach Red Sanders in the 1930s, from whom it migrated to a 1953 John Wayne football movie, *Trouble Along the Way*, that Lombardi may well have seen. More than anything, that line has nonetheless dogged his legacy and made him into the default Nixon proxy. In an entirely typical linkage, Ron Fimrite criticized Nixon for having "a sense of values" appropriate to "a true sports fan." And then followed the mandatory winning-isn't-everything citation, followed by the indictment of that slogan as the key to American racism and militarism: "Though the dissenters—poor people, Indochinese, Indians—may decry such a philosophy, we sports fans may take heart in the President's reaffirmed position on our side of the field." A social-psychology textbook published in the 1970s directly criticized Lombardi for fomenting an insidious anything-goes-if-you-win atmosphere that was poisoning American culture. Well aware of the cost of such connections, before he died Lombardi told Jerry Izenberg, "I wish to hell I'd never said the damn thing. . . . I sure as hell didn't mean for people to crush human values and morality."[16]

Reading the chronicle of his final season, one gets a sense that to some degree Lombardi played himself and that reporters understood that they also played their parts in continuing or challenging everyone else's criticisms of that character: a meta-narrative spiral about the coach in which many of those involved were aware of, yet invested in, the roles they were playing. "Now don't get excited, but I'm going to put on a little performance to get this one across," Lombardi whispered to a Redskins staffer at a league meeting, just before winning twenty-four of twenty-six votes. Tom Dowling's take on Lombardi suggested that only something akin to magic realism could truly capture the quality of his presence in Green Bay, where he had sunk deep into "the rich loam of small-town myth . . . even the detractors had to fall back on magnification." Lombardi's small hypocrisies and quiet kindnesses proved as endlessly fascinating to observers as his larger-than-life persona. An oral history published the year after his death burst with ruefully affectionate reminiscences from rival coaches, owners, players, and even Ethel Kennedy, who was drawn to Lombardi "because he was so much like Bobby." By the end of 1969, Lombardi had bellowed the Redskins to their first winning season since 1955. Cancer made it impossible for him to continue, and the next September he was dead.[17]

The Coach in the Gray Flannel Suit

After a one-season interregnum, George Allen led the Redskins almost to the mountaintop. While Lombardi brought literature to mind, Allen came straight out of 1950s sociology, an organization man whose instincts and interests were limited to doing his job with an essentially religious perfection of intent. His main contribution to the book of American quotations was "Every time you win, you're reborn; when you lose, you die a little." He told a prominent football writer that he would like to be remembered as someone who "want[ed] to win so bad I'd give a year off my life" and wrote that "the world belongs to those who give 110%." His ideal hire would be an unmarried young coach with about four years of experience who would work day and night, seven days a week, for no pay. "That guy," Allen said, "would be a picture of myself 26 years ago."

Though he fathered four children, "he just seemed so unhappy to be at home with us," Allen's daughter remembered, and he once instructed his twelve-year-old son to drive him to a game so he could squeeze in additional time with the playbook along the way. "Don't you realize who we're playing today?" he demanded of the highway patrolman who pulled him over. Allen sparked none of the guarded but authentic affection his predecessor did. He was unnerving, a creature of pure, grinding effort, "pale and sunken-chested . . . like a cheerleader or an academic dean . . . a guy who had written six books" (which in fact he had) living "a life of total monastic dedication," as his biographers described him. Michener thought his ethic "super-tense"; Robert

Lipsyte imagined him as Nixon's secret sharer. "Under questioning," wrote a journalist detailed to spend a week prying information from Allen, "he looks about as comfortable as a burglary suspect."[18]

Well before Nixon's complicity in his own third-rate burglary, the stylistic harmonies were telling. Allen had played college football, though he too rarely got into games, at a small school. Both men were noted for extraordinary devotion to hard work and robustly middle-American culinary tastes: the famously abstemious Allen drank nothing stronger than milk and subsisted on peanut-butter sandwiches. He even had an endorsement deal with a local dairy when he coached the Rams. It sponsored his pregame show and delivered gallons straight to his house. Occasionally, he indulged in vanilla ice cream, which allowed him to keep game-planning. "Chewing would take his mind away from football," his wife said. Even the notoriously unhip Nixon called Allen "the All-American square" with affectionate condescension.

Allen's and Nixon's darknesses aligned particularly neatly. Allen continually ran into trouble with what one Rams executive called "shady, little things." At his first job, at Morningside College in Sioux City, Iowa, some onlookers already perceived a "problem in following procedures." With the Rams, he used what amounted to a slush fund to pay a player outside the regular contract structure, and as Redskins coach, he traded the same draft choices to two different teams, incurring a $5,000 fine and a severe reprimand from Pete Rozelle. When his teenage son wandered away from the bench during a game and made repeated attempts to distract the Eagles' quarterback, Allen denied knowing him, telling the referee, "he must be one of those people they gave us as ball boys." Allen hired his own security operative, was implicated (though never formally charged) in a murky attempt to spy on the Cowboys, and was so secrecy-crazed that one columnist only somewhat jokingly surmised that he must hire assistants straight from the CIA. A sportscaster, remembering the strength of Allen's defenses, "always wondered if the Redskins had tapped their opponents' phones from upstairs."[19]

In a particularly Nixonian gesture, Allen repeatedly prevented the press from talking to his players. Dispatches from reporters covering Redskins' training camp often read as if smuggled out of a particularly repressive dictatorship. By his lights, "the first down is more important than the First Amendment," Shirley Povich quipped. In the fall of 1972, the question of whether Billy Kilmer or Sonny Jurgensen would start at quarterback provoked a brief war between coach and media. The *Post* assigned its lead political reporter, David

Broder, to indulge in a bit of Kremlinology after the last preseason game and predict that Kilmer would open the season under center. In November, Allen became incensed that Redskins beat reporters had revealed state secrets: Kilmer was not leading the first string in practice. He forced them to wait in the lobby until practice ended, then had them escorted down onto the field, where he slammed them for failing to support the team. "If we lose Sunday, it'll be your fault," he harangued the assembled media during a rain-soaked fifteen-minute lecture. "They're leaking Pentagon Papers around here and we can't get into the Redskins' locker room," one sportswriter lamented. The standoff was finally resolved a week later at a summit meeting between Allen, Ben Bradlee, and the *Post's* sports editor.

James Wechsler of the *New York Post* thought that in this case the coach was acting in the worst kind of presidential manner: "Plainly it is Allen's belief that the sportswriter's obligation is to 'the team,' that any diligent reporting of its internal affairs is a divisive intrusion giving aid to 'the enemy,' and that criticism of the coach is inherently destructive." He theorized that "one can almost hear Mr. Nixon offering him private reassurance that he has long endured similar irritation." Nixon actually *did* offer such assurances, instructing Allen not to confide in any of "those bastards," who would "shoot their grandmother for a story." Spiro Agnew, the period's most famous media critic, joined the chorus of executive support, reminding him to "tell them all to go to hell—you're the coach and they live off what you make in the way of news."[20]

Allen was Nixon's closest friend in the coaching fraternity. In his second job, coaching Whittier's team, he replaced Nixon's mentor, Chief Newman. The two became acquainted at a sports banquet in 1952, early in Allen's tenure, and began a consistent correspondence soon after. When getting his career started, Allen requested help from the vice president in finding work; after Nixon's defeat in 1960, he consoled him that both men had known the pain of loss: "As you know, the better team and better man does not always win. When plans are upset, and years of effort seem to go down the drain, it is difficult to smile. We also experienced this in 1960, on a fourth down pass, with seventeen seconds remaining, versus the Colts." Whether or not this comparison of a football game to a presidential election brought the former vice president comfort, Allen was offering consolation in the ways most congenial to him. He encouraged Nixon to remain "cheerful and hopeful," to go about his business with a smile and take his chances. And he offered assistance whenever and however Nixon needed it "—just say the word." He sent along clippings

George Allen and family present Nixon with the autographed game ball from the Pro Bowl. (Courtesy Richard M. Nixon Library)

and cartoons critical of the Kennedy administration when Nixon languished far from power and wired his apology for not being able to make a victory celebration in 1968 because more pressing matters intervened: "unable to attend tonight as we are getting ready for our big game with the Chicago Bears."

But early the next year Allen stopped by the White House to give the new president a gift, the autographed game ball from the Pro Bowl, adding that "I am so pleased" with his victory and that "we tried to help out all we could during the campaign." Several years later, Nixon pulled it out of his desk to show Allen's family. It was in perfect condition, Allen's daughter vividly recalled, "as if it was kept sealed in plastic at night, then taken out, every morning, to be reinflated and cleaned and shined."[21]

With always-scarce Redskins tickets suddenly, if possible, even more desirable after Allen's hiring, he offered the president free use of his twenty-three-person box. The offer extended to the rest of the administration: Henry Kissinger thanked Allen for the seats during a 1972 game against the Cardinals. Allen was so popular that *Washingtonian* magazine named him a "Washingtonian of the Year" for 1971 because his team's improved play "lifted our hopes and helped bring us together." If the president could not make the game, he stayed up late to hear the team play on the West Coast, went to Camp David, which got the Baltimore channel that carried Redskins games, or kept the phone line open when he was in Key West so he could listen to the play-by-play. He even scheduled travel around game telecasts, Dwight Chapin ordering an assistant to find out whether the team's playoff game against the 49ers would be shown nationally or just locally in December 1971 so he could plan the president's departure for Florida around it. This was the game in which Allen notoriously ran a play Nixon had supposedly designed, a flanker reverse. It lost thirteen yards.[22]

Allen dropped by the White House often enough that Nixon's special assistant in charge of visitors gave him his private phone number to arrange calls by the coach or his players. He sent the president numerous presents, including an inscribed copy of his 1970 book *Inside Football,* a copiously illustrated four-hundred-page tome whose microscopic attention to detail captured Allen's will to total knowledge of and authority over the game and his players. In it he presented instructions for everything from proper grooming ("all athletes should try to be neat") to somewhat ironic counsel about dealing with the press ("cooperate to the fullest extent. . . . Be honest, cooperative, and fair"). "I can readily see I have exciting reading in store!" Nixon responded.[23]

In turn, Nixon had so many notes of encouragement and sympathy hand-delivered to the Allen family home that they filled a shoebox. When Allen took the Redskins job, Nixon's top assistants, Bob Haldeman and John Ehrlichman, sat down with Etty Allen inside the White House to help her find a place to live in the Washington area. Nixon sent Allen golf balls, wired him congratulations on his multifarious trades, called the house frequently, invited him to a state dinner, and turned up at practice to rally the troops at a crucial point in Allen's first season, just after the team continued a losing streak with a loss to the division-leading Cowboys.

The president told the players that he had long ago promised Allen, "I won't be coming to a game till you need me," and now he was paying his friend back. He expounded on his belief in struggling through adversity (in an ironic reversal of his usual practice, he explained this concept to football players with an analogy from war), told the team that everyone in Washington was proud of them, and predicted that they would make the playoffs. Coincidentally or not, the Redskins won their final three games and did indeed make the post-

Nixon drops by Redskins' practice to rally the troops, November 1971. (Courtesy Richard M. Nixon library)

season. Allen and the president appeared in conversation in the photograph atop the Athletes for Nixon ad in 1972, Nixon looking on admiringly as Allen dispensed wisdom to the masses. In the wake of his overwhelming victory, Nixon wrote Allen that "it would be impossible for me to repay you adequately for all the work you did during the campaign."[24]

Allen never voted, because Election Day was a distraction in the middle of the season. Asked by *The Washingtonian* as Watergate stumbled to its end whether there were any heroes left in America, Allen nominated the Redskins' owner for his "perseverance." But Lipsyte was, in the most literal sense, correct: Allen secretly shared his opinions with the president. He invariably found Nixon's policies realistic, intelligent, and sure to accomplish their purpose. The more vociferous the opposition, the more strongly Allen commended these policies. Less than three weeks after Kent State, Nixon thanked Allen for his "encouragement for our country's goals in Southeast Asia," which "means a great deal to America's fighting men as well as to me."

Two years later, the president announced a hugely controversial escalation that protestors greeted with a blockade on the highway and a die-in at his campaign headquarters. Outside the headquarters, wounded veteran Ron Kovic declared himself "opposed to the insanity of President Nixon's putting the whole world in jeopardy with his lies." "What are you doing, Mr. Nixon?" pleaded a *Los Angeles Times* editorial. Registering the extent of public distress, Allen immediately sent the president a handwritten note on Redskins stationery: "I liked your decision and to hell with the second guessers. Warm regards." Nixon responded that "a demonstration of national unity" would make America's commitment clear, and that he regarded Allen's message as "an important part of this effort, and I am grateful for your willingness to speak out."

That fall, Nixon gave a "tumultuous" speech in Long Island pledging that America would end the war only if it could do so "with honor"; in the melee, one protestor was hit in the face, others dragged bodily off while the crowd gave what one horrified onlooker called "a sustained, sickening Nuremberg roar" and Nixon grinned—perhaps out of nervousness, perhaps approval. Allen loved the speech, and the gesture, telling him, "that was better than any of my trades."[25]

1972 was the best year of both men's lives. Nixon trounced McGovern in November, after which he called twice to make sure Allen actually came to the private victory party, and the Redskins made the Super Bowl. Allen decorated his office with photographs of himself with Nixon. Things went downhill after that, rather more quickly for the president than for his favorite coach. Given the depth of their personal and ideological sympathies (Allen's daughter called it a "basic paranoid philosophy"), naturally Allen considered Watergate just another obstacle for a winner to surmount. He repeatedly sent the president supportive notes over the summer of 1973, telling him that his course was right and his fight would be won. On the very day Nixon resigned, Allen spoke admiringly of "his courage to fight through this thing. . . . A lot of lesser individuals would have resigned a long time ago." As long as Nixon believed he had done his best, he should stay on. "That's the type of determination and leadership and doggedness you have to have in a president," Allen added.[26]

George Allen fortified the president with the knowledge that right-thinking Americans, winners, supported him, no matter how much his policies infuriated voters and editorialists. Not winning made life meaningless. "I can't think of a thing . . . money will buy that a loser could enjoy," he wrote near the conclusion of *Inside Football*. Allen dealt from the bottom of the deck, exchanged numerous gifts with the president and repeatedly visited the White House. In significant respects, his career and Richard Nixon's ran in parallel, and at the very least he sustained Nixon's determination to stay his ruinous course. As Lipsyte surmised, these two workaholic achievers shared an essential spiritual affinity.

And yet when it came time to explain Watergate, Allen's very colorlessness, his extreme personal and temperamental similarities to and sympathies with Nixon, made him redundant as an explanatory force. He was so exact a Nixon double that he was simply not compelling as a character on his own to dramatize trenchant cultural issues. Instead, the arrows pointed the other way, Nixon being repurposed to explain Allen. When he fled Washington in 1978 to return, briefly, to the Rams, shrouded in the same murky double-dealings and confusions about who'd promised what to whom, and when, with which he'd fled the Bears in the mid-'60s (as well as new allegations of expense-account padding and use of team staff to perform yard work at Allen's house), the *Washington Post* headlined its extensive plumbing of the process "The Final Plays," echoing *The Final Days,* Woodward and Bernstein's sequel to *All the President's Men*. "This wasn't a CIA or Watergate operation. It was a simple thing really," the Rams' owner clarified. Tom Dowling's lengthy investigation of Allen's firing in the *Washingtonian* continued the metaphor by pondering the identity of Deep Throat in this case for approximately one sentence before concluding that it "could not be more obvious" that it was Redskins' owner Edward Bennett Williams.[27]

Anyone reading the editorial pages in these years might be pardoned for believing that Vince Lombardi was somehow at the root of the scandal. Lombardi would doubtless have been horrified politically and morally to learn about that slogan decorating CREEP's secret planning room. Conservative columnist George Will was much closer to the mark when he predicted that "the Green Bay Packers syndrome . . . the religion of efficiency," would actually doom Nixon: "This Republican administration has a lot of unique characteristics, but conspicuous, believable competence isn't one among them." But instead Lombardi, a tireless champion of playing by the rules, became the default what's-wrong-with-us explanation. His outsized reputation and literary appeal made him feel relevant even four years after his passage from the world.

The connection proved irresistible. Bill Moyers mourned the deterioration from Grantland Rice's "how you played the game" maxim to Lombardi's.

Counterculture apostle Timothy Leary observed that "the influence of Vince Lombardi (win at any cost) on the American right-wing cannot be overestimated. It is no accident that Lombardi died in Washington," then rejoiced that such influences were on the wane: "Nixon will never recover from Watergate. Neither will the country. Competitive politics is dying. Vince Lombardi is a crewcut dinosaur. The secret is out." A journalistic assault on the "jock empire," published the year Nixon resigned, argued that "one of the worst things that has happened to sports and society in recent years is the adoption of the dictum, popularized by Vince Lombardi but hardly unique to him, that winning is everything. You see it everywhere. . . . Behind the Watergate affair is the thought that anything can be forgiven if you win."

Even after the fallout from the scandal had settled, this rhetorical link remained. Representative William Cohen of Maine remarked that the Watergate conspirators "forgot that winning isn't everything, not if it comes at the cost of foul play." "Maybe we might be a more compassionate people if we didn't dwell on victory at all costs, wouldn't hatch Watergates, or odd neuroses," Larry L. King hypothesized. In a postmortem on the scandal's effects, eminent historian Arthur Schlesinger remarked in 1975 that "the republic is closer on issue after issue to the McGovern of 1972 than to the Nixon of 1972. . . . Winning an election may not be the only thing."[28] A contemporary observer added that the White House needed "less Vince Lombardi and more Abraham Lincoln." What it actually needed was less George Allen.[29]

What It Takes to Be #1

Lombardi cut an entirely different figure than critics at the time understood. He was not a politician, despite the attempts of observers on both left and right to press him into that mold. He spoke for traditionalist Americans, but at times he also recognized that one could not simply close cultural fissures through harder work, more sweat, more commitment. And he did not actually believe that winning was everything. He authentically wanted to use his platform to condemn social dissolution even as he eagerly sold himself as *the* incarnation of "traditional values" at a time that such ideas seemed, at best, antiquated and at worst dangerously repressive. That combination most accurately renders him a transitional figure, a deeply troubled observer of society but also a purveyor of the first coaching brand who discovered that good morals and good business were not mutually exclusive.

In ways that no one at the time could have known enough to register, he foretold one political future. Oddly enough, Lombardi was accompanied in this venture by Chiefs' coach Hank Stram, in many ways his stylistic antithesis. In 1967, NFL Films' *They Call It Pro Football* had showcased the sideline gesticulations of the Eagles' Joe Kuharich as he bellowed, raved, and harangued the officials. "I never realized before that Kuharich is the biggest ham actor in pro football," a reviewer wrote. But Stram was "the first coach who really understood . . . that football was also entertainment," Steve Sabol said. Stram was so eager to promote the AFL before Super Bowl I that "he would have made commercials if we had done them," the head of league promotion recalled.

He missed his chance that time, but NFL Films made Stram the star of the show when the Chiefs returned to Super Bowl IV. (His opposite number, Minnesota's legendarily taciturn Bud Grant, gets less than ten seconds of screen time.) Stram later pretended that this was not the case, claiming that, "once the game started, I never gave it a second thought" and that he had later groaned "when I heard myself extemporize" and then wondered, "do I really have to have myself revealed in this manner?"

In fact, Stram openly regarded the arrangement as a business transaction. "The Mentor," he demanded, adorning himself with the third-person egotistical, "will agree to wear a microphone for the Super Bowl, but some coin of the realm is going to have to change hands." The Sabols shook their heads and paid, and the dapper coach rewarded the filmmakers with a jittery, riveting performance—he's the first person we see in the highlights and the first to speak, chattering endlessly, exhorting his team, working the referees. Most famously, his injunction to "keep matriculating that ball down the field," as well as ceaseless championing of the rarely used 65 Toss Power Trap, which went for the Chiefs' first touchdown, made him a new NFL Films ideal. His players had no idea what was going on: running back Mike Garrett remembered him as "unusually animated" during the game, and quarterback Len Dawson was surprised by how frequently Stram called him over to tell him what play to run. In different ways, both coaches pioneered the notion of selling their modes of guidance.[30]

These notions of coach-as-model-businessman (a notion that became political in the president-as-CEO candidacies of Ross Perot, Mitt Romney, and Donald Trump, among others) later became commonplace. In 1993, *Harvard Business Review* ran its first interview with a football coach, celebrating Bill Walsh's "businesslike approach to maximizing the potential of players and

MAKING FOOTBALL POLITICAL

coaches." The article described him as a "turnaround CEO" who argued, "the old bludgeon approach is leaving football the same way it is leaving business." In response, a professor who studied both business management and football protested, "right coach, wrong game." He found that "U.S. male managers, especially those over 50, in senior positions, with long tenure," constantly offered Lombardi-style drilling and execution as a metaphor for their jobs, a problem because that vision of the sport fostered rigid, hierarchical "industrial-era designs" appropriate to the Taylorized factory floor of seventy years before. Today's postindustrial workplace demanded individual creativity, initiative, and leverage, traits that Walsh endorsed but football did not: "Corporate America needs fewer football teams but more Bill Walshes."

Over the next decade, corporate America got both. *Harvard Business Review* published an article by Bill Parcells in 2000 and one on the Browns' organizational effectiveness in 2005. Individual coaches, too, peddled leadership elixirs. In 2001, Vince Lombardi Jr. further advanced his father's brand with *What It Takes to Be #1: Vince Lombardi on Leadership,* followed the next year by Donald Phillips's *Run to Win: Vince Lombardi on Coaching and Leadership.* In a book-length hagiography of Bill Belichick in 2005, renowned journalist David Halberstam argued that Belichick's exacting, self-effacing precision offered a model of management that people like George W. Bush *should* emulate: "He is a leader without the swagger, selfishness, and pomposity that so many men in business, politics, and sports embrace as an entitlement."

Urban Meyer, Pete Carroll, and Nick Saban, who boasted ten national titles and a Super Bowl win among them, built highly commercial brands around the skills that underpinned their teams' on-field dominance. Tony Dungy's empire of personal/moral/spiritual advice was ratified first by, as his Web site notes, the fact that he "led the Indianapolis Colts to Super Bowl victory." Their PowerPoint-ready panaceas "hold true for the president of Ford Motor Company and for the cashier at a local Wal-Mart," as Saban promised. Meyer's "Performance Pathway" and 10-80-10 Principle, which he referred to "when I talk to corporate groups or business leaders," and Carroll's "Win Forever philosophy" drilled you in how to take your earning power as far as you could push it. "How good do you want to be?" Saban demanded.[31]

These sorts of lessons are all around us now. Biographies of coaches celebrate them as innovators, leaders, disrupters equipped with the keys to success—a similarity only amplified by the flood of data analytics across the sports and business worlds. In 2011, professor and strategist Roger Martin's study *Fixing the Game,* published by the *HBR* Press and blurbed by the unlikely pair of former Federal Reserve chair Paul Volcker and former NFL commissioner Paul Tagliabue, brought things full circle. Martin described the NFL as not "a perfect metaphor for business, [but] . . . a highly instructive one," then explored the lessons furnished by the NFL's devotion to fan experience, its organizational clarity, and its ceaseless willingness to tweak its product to maintain the quality of competition among teams: "In part, we can learn from the NFL just what to do." Martin began with an epigraph that read, "We would accomplish many more things if we did not think of them as impossible." The author was, perhaps inevitably, Vince Lombardi.[32]

EPILOGUE
Hollywood Ending

That's one for the Gipper.
—Alleged dedication by right halfback Jack
Chevigny after scoring Notre Dame's first
touchdown against Army, 1928[1]

The clock ran out on the Nixon administration during a football game. In a pleasing bit of literary symmetry, a federal jury announced guilty verdicts for Attorney General John Mitchell, Chief of Staff H. R. Haldeman, and domestic advisor John Ehrlichman, the major players in the Watergate cover-up, during the 1975 Rose Bowl, which Ohio State's Woody Hayes, the president's friend, supporter, and favorite college coach, was in the process of losing. The Ford administration was even more appearance-conscious than its predecessor; Ford's earliest hires included a personal photographer, a new press secretary, and a chief speechwriter, supplemented within a month by a professional gag-writer and a television advisor.

A former center at the University of Michigan, Ford preferred football analogies that involved effective line play. "I only wish that I could take the entire United States into the locker room at halftime. . . . We have lost yards against the line drives of inflation and the end runs of energy shortages," he exhorted listeners. "The hall was silent" at this sally, *Newsweek* reported. But football did him far more harm than good. The dumb-jock stigma encapsulated by Lyndon Johnson's barbed joke that he was "a nice fellow who spent too much time playing football without a helmet" (to which White House reporters later appended the retort, "he can't even play president without a

helmet") so tainted subsequent perceptions of Ford's tenure, and by extension seemed to explain the country's prevailing lack of direction, that former
staffers interviewed for an oral history thirty years later remained uniformly
angry about that perception.[2]

It mattered very much to Nixon that his football acumen be respected.
For Ford, such allusions came naturally. Neither president managed to create
a lasting political language. But the lesson was not that Kennedy/Lombardi
politics were useless; it was that they awaited a more adroit practitioner. Ronald
Reagan was that person, the most adept political actor this country has yet
produced. He picked and chose idiosyncratically from among the languages that
contended in the '70s, rejecting the ambivalent and complicated versions of the
sport put forward by the NFL and the more informed, though very different,
visions of Nixon and Dave Meggyesy. If anything, his vision echoed the "rag
days" nostalgia that arose in the early '70s in opposition to the league's cultivation of spectacle. "I have been involved in a love affair with football that began
as far back as my memory goes," Reagan told the National Football Foundation
upon receiving its Gold Medal in 1971. "There is a mystic something about
football. . . . It's typical of the American personality, and I, for one, think there's
something very important in America that would be lost if those psychiatrists
had their way, and we ever lost our emotional attachment to this game."

Knowledge lost out to myth, or what Reagan called "emotional attachment." Genially uninterested in rooting for particular teams, Reagan was free
to enlist football in the American political imaginary because he approached
it as he approached everything—as an array of symbols and anecdotes to be
deployed for emotive effect. Associations and connotations mattered, not
accuracy or facts. So if he could underpin a public image of sincerity and
integrity through scripted lines depicting a mythologized version of a real
person, he would and did.[3]

A success in every form of media that transformed twentieth-century
America, Reagan made especially expert use of television to put across his
agenda. Television was just then making it easier to convey these kinds of
messages. In 1977 *Monday Night Football* impresario and ABC Sports head
Roone Arledge took over ABC News, sending "shock waves" through the network business. "Sports and news have a common challenge, dealing as they
do with the transmission of events," the network's president explained when
announcing the change. "No one does that kind of television better." Perfectly
distilling recent developments in American political culture, Arledge imported

vividness and immediacy to the news beat, bringing viewers up-close-and-personal with politicians "the same way I personalize sports figures."

In a neat piece of circularity, Arledge had originally adopted the technique from political conventions, at which networks had introduced hand-held cameras to get viewers onto the floor. In a now-famous 1960 memo laying out his vision of transformed NCAA-football coverage, he promised that "we will have cameras mounted in jeeps, on mike booms, in risers or helicopters, or anything necessary to get the complete story." He'd honed these techniques in the Olympics: "We routinely run documentary profiles of the athletes. The next morning, Americans know not only what people like Olga Korbut and Dorothy Hamill look like but where they come from and, to at least some extent, what kind of people they are." Sports had merely been the vehicle for telling stories. Now these innovations, perfected on *Monday Night Football,* revolutionized the world of "straight" news.[4]

Onlookers greeted this announcement with horror—one reporter considered the appointment "the single biggest insult that management could inflict upon the news department"—but from Arledge's perspective, sports were harder to cover than politics. "People expect you, if you're a news reporter, to come in and find the truth and present that truth. If you're in sports, they expect your reportage to be that of a cheerleader." He thought he was truly fulfilling TV's democratic mandate, finding a way that "the average person can get involved in the issues which have become much more subtle in recent years.... I wanted to make ABC News smarter, not dumber." His real challenge was the inverse of what his detractors presumed: surveys repeatedly showed that television viewers did not want to see anything too intellectual, much less foreign or difficult.

On *World News Tonight,* Arledge pursued his vision by allowing his anchors to editorialize, as he had with Cosell, even splitting the narrative responsibilities among all three, just as he had in the *Monday Night Football* booth. In an even deeper stylistic carryover, the hit program *Nightline,* which began in the fall of 1979, revolutionized late-night programming with its deployment of the tools Arledge had amassed over the previous decade. Driving music, exciting slogans and graphics, coverage relayed from anywhere via satellite, mini-dramas told via carefully edited highlights, expert analysis: all of these could just as well tell stories of geopolitical entanglement as Saints vs. Patriots. The show began with coverage of the Iran hostage crisis and quickly matured into a defining institution.[5]

Nightline's stories, painting an America so lacking in manly force that it was humiliated by a ninety-eight-pound weakling country few citizens could point out on a map, particularly suited Reagan's image. Football played a central role in that image's construction. Though Reagan was no Gerald Ford on the field, neither was he Richard Nixon. He made it as far as the Eureka College varsity, for which he played guard, on a partial scholarship. Yet what helped sell him as a bearer of reassuring American masculine tradition were not his own modest achievements on the field but a movie in which he *played* a football player, appearing in four scenes comprising about eight minutes of screen time before his character died. Reagan campaigned passionately for the role of George Gipp in the 1940 film *Knute Rockne, All American*—"no one could have wanted to play it more than I did," he recalled. When Warner Brothers executives decided he was too small for the part, the actor sped home and dug up his college yearbook to prove he'd actually played the game.

Before filming began, Reagan told a group of Notre Dame alumni that he had idolized Gipp as a child and spoke with him several times while working as a radio announcer. Considering that Reagan was nine when Gipp died, this is highly unlikely, to say the least. The movie whitewashed the life of a dissipated gambler, pool shark, and layabout who never uttered the remark for which history remembers him. Gipp's most famous line, a deathbed injunction to Rockne to inspire some future Notre Dame squad to "win one for the Gipper," was in this respect a perfectly Reaganite statement, something in which the president wanted badly to believe irrespective of its actual truth. Rockne himself furnished an especially apposite figure for Reagan. Former Horseman Jim Crowley described his old coach's locker-room rousers, not without affection, as "blatant lies." Rockne's former associate wrote a book praising this *Salesman from the Sidelines*, who, despite his pretenses to "high-minded" advocacy for amateur sport, "became his own merchandise" by endorsing Wilson football equipment, Studebaker cars, and Barbasol shave cream and delivering syndicated lectures and columns. At his height, Rockne took home more each year from endorsement deals than Studebaker's president earned in salary. The plane in whose crash he died was en route to Hollywood, where he planned to sign a $50,000 contract with Universal Pictures to play a football coach. It would be hard to imagine a more fitting predecessor for Reagan to lionize.[6]

Delivering one line by a character who was fictional in nearly every sense of the word made Reagan's film career, winning him roles in the studio's A films. That inspiring speech then became an emblem for his political career from start to finish, a *Newsweek* reporter asking Reagan's advisors how they planned to "win one for the Gipper" in 1966 and the *New York Times* invoking it repeatedly upon his death in 2004.

Michael Rogin's discussion of Reagan's mythographic appeal argues that "in Reagan's film-mediated history the son (George Gipp) produced the father (Ronald Reagan)." That process took time: initial uses of the term, which were sporadic, spotlighted the superficiality of an electorate that could elect an actor. "The movie actor who played George Gipp in *Knute Rockne—All American* . . . is favored to win the Republican nomination for governor. It could happen only in the Golden State," marveled one widely circulated editorial. In January 1966, before the campaign got underway, humor columnist Russell Baker mockingly misremembered Gipp as a figure of frivolity: "I watched Gipp sit through an entire week of old Ronald Reagan movies without a whimper. . . . Why did Max [*sic*] Gipp do it? . . . Because he believed in something. He believed in old Ronald Reagan movies." Around the same time, Madison's liberal *Capital Times* worried that Washington would become a "Hollywood dumping ground": "Half the voters of California will think they are voting for the late George Gipp." Campaign banners exhorted the candidate to "Win This One for the Gipper," but the whole mythology was "laughable now," thought a *Los Angeles Times* sportswriter. "Ideology aside, I see the man's victory as a blow for what made this country great—sports," argued the *San Francisco Chronicle*.[7]

In the early 1970s, Gipp began to overtake Reagan. Gipp now struck observers as an attractive fantasy, a relic of surety and commitment discarded without reason or reflection and thus all too emblematic of what was wrong today. A public-television special on the athletic revolt in early 1971 dramatized changing times by cutting from Reagan-as-Gipp kicking a ball out of Notre Dame's stadium to the ball's landing in the arms of Dave Meggyesy, "beard and all." Imagining a conversation between conservative coaches Tom Landry and George Allen, journalist Tom Dowling had Allen ask, "no pre-game slogans? Do you actually mean to say you let them go out there and play football?" "It's a rotten shame," Landry replies. "They just won't do it for the Gipper anymore." Allen, for his part, does not even know how to spell the name. Radicals chortled that the movie furnished the first evidence of Reagan's attacks on the university system.

Adrift in such iconoclasm, one sportswriter wrote yearningly that "there are no heroes, only anti-heroes. Where are you, Gipper, now that we need you? Is it true that you are alive and well and living in Sacramento . . . in the governor's mansion? Good grief." This more knowing version of the question Simon & Garfunkel had famously posed in "Mrs. Robinson," "where have you gone, Joe DiMaggio?" offers fascinating internal contradictions. An actor-politician's most famous role, which the writer admits was only a role, nonetheless somehow captures authentic popular yearning for a brand of straightforward heroism that we should agree to believe in, whether or not it is real. A decade later, another columnist agreed that fantasy outdid reality: a generation that learned about football through this "romanticized bit of make-belief [*sic*] might have been a lot better off than the generation that sees Joe Namath's pantyhose."[8]

Even so, it took another decade for the Gipper to resonate politically in the way Reagan wanted. Journalists covering the 1976 campaign used the term far less frequently, and much less affectionately, than in 1980. Frank Sinatra ridiculed Reagan and Ford as "the Gipper and the Tripper" onstage, and a song written by reporters on the campaign bus parodied Reagan's prospects to the tune of the Notre Dame victory march: "Whether the state be great or small/ Reagan's the one who'll lose overall/Ford is stuck with victory/But Ron hits the old stone wall." The Gipper was more joke than resonant cultural symbol.

In the interim, Reagan downplayed the apocalyptic rhetoric that made him a convention sensation in 1976, sketching a renewed, reinvigorated America grounded in romantic memories of his experiences as a youth. Suddenly Reagan-as-Gipp seemed an appealing composite of reality and myth. The 1980 campaign, in which he ran on the themes of "leadership, restoration, and rebirth," was suffused with enough affectionate mentions of the Gipper to suggest that George Gipp had risen from the grave for one last run. Fans urged him to win one for the Gipper along the campaign trail; opponents demanded a better choice than "an incompetent incumbent or the Gipper." One reporter concluded that Reagan was still playing his greatest role: "The halting, tearful tones" in which he uttered his most famous line on screen "are the same tones he uses in his stump speech today." The candidate returned to a pep rally at his alma mater and accepted a ceremonial football jersey from his old coach, which he donned without mussing his hair, then gave a speech. The Reagan-Bush committee gave the term official sanction, running an ad in the Notre Dame/Navy game program the weekend before the election that posed Reagan-as-Gipp above a photograph of candidate Reagan, along with the slogans "Win One for The Gipper!" and "Reagan For President."[9]

The Reagan-Bush Committee encourages Notre Dame fans to win one for the Gipper, November 1980.

His victory in November suggested that many voters shared Reagan's affection for these fictions. He brought traditional rhetoric roaring back, and with it the sentimental visions of football, gender, and the nation it championed, "the mythic America most of us inhabit in our hearts"—Grantland Rice's America, not Dave Meggyesy's. "I don't even know if we will ever be able to identify and prove what each man learns from football so that we can list it and hang it on a wall like a diploma or like a license for the practice of a profession," he had concluded his speech to the National Football Foundation. "I do know that down through the years I've somehow placed my faith in men of the sports world and seldom has that faith ever been betrayed." In February, the new president awarded his first exclusive interview to *Inside Sports*, telling interviewer Mark Shields that playing football had given him a "particular sense of accomplishment" and "a kind of inner confidence," as well as an opportunity to stand up for racial equality.[10]

At Notre Dame's commencement in May 1981, his first appearance outside Washington after John Hinckley's assassination attempt nearly took his life, Reagan reasserted himself by returning to Gipp. The ceremony repeatedly conflated the two: Pat O'Brien, who played Rockne in the film, met Reagan there; Rev. Theodore Hesburgh, the school's president, "welcome[d] the Gipper at long last back to get his degree" and subsequently sent honorary certificates of membership in the honorary Monogram Club to both Reagan and Gipp. "That one [Gipp's] will be particularly treasured," Reagan responded. Here we see Rogin's argument in its truest form: Reagan built his speech around the notion of winning one for the Gipper and even invented new melodramatic turns in the story. The Rockne movie, he asserted, "says something about America": "It's only a game," but "there will come times in the lives of all us when we'll be faced with causes bigger than ourselves, and they won't be on a playing field." The Founding Fathers "rose to such selfless heights." So too the graduates faced a world rife with challenges. Communism was on the march, and the federal government had grown too powerful as well, its "prohibitive taxes and burdensome regulations" strangling innovation and freedom itself. The youth and strength of the next generation were crucial, especially if coupled with respect for what people like George Gipp incarnated, "the time-tested values upon which civilization was built."[11]

Reagan invoked this image to rally support for his tax cuts, another relic of the culture of the 1920s, giving "a locker room speech that would make Knute Rockne proud," one senator gushed. Conservative columnists were especially taken with the power of Gipp, Pat Buchanan posing the rhetorical question, "Who would win that head-to-head between [House Speaker] Tip [O'Neill] and The Gipper?" By the mid-'80s, one biographer remarked, "Ronald Reagan had practically become George Gipp." After a shaky performance in his first debate with Walter Mondale in 1984, Gipp incarnated Reagan's best self, "assured, alert." Which one would show up for the next debate, a columnist wondered, the Gipper or the Geezer? Reagan himself told a correspondent in 1986 that Gipp "has remained very much a part of my life." When he came back to Notre

Athletic prowess remained central to Reagan's image as president. Here he mimes throwing a pass in the Oval Office, March 1982. (Courtesy Reagan Library)

Dame in 1988 to dedicate a Knute Rockne postage stamp, he tossed a "perfect pass" to Heisman winner Tim Brown. "Never in our wildest dreams did we ever think that George Gipp would be president of the United States," said the athletic director. As he left the stage, Reagan summoned the ghost once again, his exit speech at the 1988 Republican National Convention pressing George Bush "make it one more" for the Gipper.[12]

It wasn't what the NFL's essay contest had envisioned, but in many ways these repeated, and knowing, conflations of image and reality derived directly from the mass-mediated vision that the league had been promoting. The Gipper was more than a nickname: it stood for a whole way of seeing the world. A movie character, fictionalized from the start, had come to stand in for reality and stand for essential American truths that had less to do with college or professional football than with what "football" in the abstract had been sold as incarnating. Football captured "exactly the ethos Reagan embodied," enthused conservative columnist Jeffrey Hart. "All the values are the same. America is still the shining city on a hill, America the beautiful. Honesty, decency, and courage still pay."[13] David Boss's books promoted pro football as "the game of our time" for the 1970s, and Reagan made clear that that notion, collectively ratified across the wider culture over the next decade, would still serve as a resonant symbol in American politics, through the '80s and beyond.

Notes

Introduction

1. *Washington Post* (March 23, 1969): 51.

2. Roger Kahn, "Football's Taking Over," in *Best American Sports Stories 1961*, ed. Irving T. Marsh and Edward Ehre (New York: E.P. Dutton, 1961), 118, 121, 122; George Preston Marshall, "Baseball Isn't Our National Sport," *Saturday Evening Post* (December 9, 1961): 10, 14; "Vinnie, Vidi, Vici," *Time* (December 21, 1962): cover, 58; Herbert Warren Wind, "Packerland," *New Yorker* (December 8, 1962): 226; Stephen Mahoney, "Pro Football's Profit Explosion," *Fortune* (November 1964): 155; Champ Clark, "The Mystique of Pro Football," *Time* (November 9, 1970): 42; Marshall McLuhan, *Understanding Media: The Extensions of Man* (Cambridge, Mass.: MIT Press, 1994 [1964]), 239, 240; Ira Berkow, "Odyssey of Meggyesy," *Colorado Springs Gazette Telegraph* (December 2, 1970): 2-C; Lefty Millman, "If the Umpires Have Balls, They'll Strike," *Liberation News Service* #125 (December 12, 1968): 17; "President's 'Honor Starr' Affair Didn't Hurt Badger GOP Candidates," *Sheboygan Press* (October 19, 1970): 8.

3. Dave Brady, "Harris Survey for NFL Finds People Like Football Best," *Washington Post* (January 23, 1972): B2; Michael MacCambridge, *America's Game: The Epic Story of How Pro Football Captured a Nation* (New York: Random House, 2004), 212, 492–93; Kenneth Denlinger, "Football Power Sells Products," *San Francisco Chronicle* (October 6, 1972): 56; Mary McGrory, "Deliver Us from Football," *Chicago Tribune* (October 13, 1975): A4.

4. Denlinger, "Football Power Sells Products."

5. J. Kirk Sale, "The Man to Watch Is . . . the Middle Linebacker," *New York Times Magazine* (December 10, 1967); William Phillips, "A Season in the Stands," *Commentary* (July 1, 1969); Rex Lardner, "The 'In' Game," *New York Times Book Review* (October 25, 1970): 33; Gary Hart, *Right from the Start: A Chronicle of the McGovern Campaign* (New York: Quadrangle, 1973), 41.

6. Memo from Mary to David Parker, September 1972; folder Football January 1, 1971–December 20, 1972, Box 5, White House Central Files: Recreation—Sports; Chuck Benedict to Richard Nixon, April 14, 1964; folder, Chuck Benedict, Box 2, Wilderness Years: Series I: Sub-Series A: Correspondence, 1963–1965; Letter, Chuck Benedict to H. R. Haldeman, August 9, 1972, folder Football January 1, 1971–December 20, 1972, Box 5, White House Central Files: Recreation—Sports; all in Richard Nixon Papers, Richard M. Nixon Presidential Library and Museum, Yorba Linda, Calif.; Larry Merchant, . . . *and Every Day You Take Another Bite* (Garden City, N.Y.: Doubleday, 1971), 31; Mike Curtis with Bill Gilbert, *Keep Off My Turf* (Philadelphia: J.B. Lippincott, 1972), 15; "Kill 'em," *Berkeley Tribe* (January 8–15, 1971): 17; "Out of Their League," *Bragg Briefs* (April 1971): 4; Mike Rush, "Greenbriar and the Super Bowl," *The Rag* (January 24, 1972): 8; Paul Zimmerman, *The Last Season of Weeb Ewbank* (New York: Farrar, Straus, and Giroux, 1974), 189.

7. "Freak Football," *The Rag* (August 14, 1969), 4; Paul Kaplan, "McGovern Won't Coach," *Washington Star* (September 1, 1972): E4.

Chapter 1. No Football Fans, Just Football Intellectuals

1. *Esquire* (October 1965): 71.

2. Bob Barnett and Bob Carroll, "Black Hats in a Golden Age," *The Coffin Corner* 15, 4 (1993); "Savagery on Sunday," *Life* (October 24, 1955): 133–37; Frank Litsky, "Bucko Kilroy, 86, N.F.L. Star and Executive, Dies," *New York Times* (July, 12, 2007); Dan Daly, "The 'Savagery on Sunday' Trial," *Pro Football Daily* (August 24, 2014), http://profootballdaly .com/scan-experiment/; "Fans Riot, Fight Cops; 49ers Beat Colts in Final," *San Francisco Examiner* (December 15, 1958): 1; "Fans Fight Cops, Bring Riot Call After 49er Win," *San Francisco Chronicle* (December 15, 1958): 1, 2.

3. "Rookies in the Line-Up," *Time* (December 1, 1967): 66; Burling Lowrey, "Boooooo," *The Washingtonian* (March 1971): 85. The pioneering collagist Richard Hamilton celebrated Pop as "a consumer product absorbed by the total population but created for it by the mass entertainment machine, which uses the intellectual as an essential part of its technique. The results are highly personalized and sophisticated." Richard Hamilton, "Popular Culture and Personal Responsibility (1960)," in *Theories and Documents of Contemporary Art: A Sourcebook of Artists' Writings*, ed. Kristine Stiles and Peter Howard Selz (Berkeley: University of California Press, 1996), 298.

4. Michael Oriard, *King Football: Sport and Spectacle in the Golden Age of Radio and Newsreels, Movies and Magazines, the Weekly and the Daily Press* (Chapel Hill: University of North Carolina Press, 2001), 219–21; Tony Barnhart, "Rough Play in the 1950s," *The Coffin Corner* 9, 8 (1987); John Sayle Watterson, *College Football: History, Spectacle, Controversy* (Baltimore: Johns Hopkins University Press, 2002), 219–41, 293–99; Miles Jackson, "College Football Has Become a Losing Business," *Fortune* (December 1962), reprinted in *Sport, Culture, and Society: A Reader on the Sociology of Sport,* ed. John Loy and Gerald Kenyon (London: Macmillan, 1981), 234.

5. Arthur Daley, "Pros and Cons of Pro Football," *New York Times Magazine* (November 20, 1955): 17; Paul O'Neil, "The Giant Defense Is Triumph of Mind," *Life* (December 5,

1960): 122; Allen Barra, *Big Play: Barra on Football* (Washington, D.C.: Potomac Books, 2004), 101–2; Richard Crepeau, *NFL Football: A History of America's New National Pastime* (Champaign: University of Illinois Press, 2014), 55, 56; "A Man's Game," *Time* (November 30, 1959).

6. William Barry Furlong, "Wise Old Men of Pro Football," *New York Times Magazine* (November 20, 1960): 34; Bobby Layne as told to Murray Olderman, "This Is No Game for Kids," *Saturday Evening Post* (November 14, 1959): 98; "Battle of Pros—Violence Under Control," *Life* (October 14, 1966): 78; Perian Conerly, *Backseat Quarterback* (Jackson: University of Mississippi Press, 2003), xiii.

7. Felix von Moschzisker, "Take Me Out of the Ball Game," *Life* (March 5, 1971): 14; Alexander Wolff, "The NFL's Jackie Robinson," *Sports Illustrated* (October 12, 2009): 60–71; Frank Gifford and Harry Waters, *The Whole Ten Yards* (New York: Random House, 1993), 81–82; Don Weiss with Chuck Day, *The Making of the Super Bowl: The Inside Story of the World's Greatest Sporting Event* (Chicago: Contemporary Books, 2003), 311; Leonard Shecter, *The Jocks* (Indianapolis: Bobbs-Merrill, 1969), 47; Peter Gent, *North Dallas Forty* (Toronto: Sport Classic Books, 2003), 197.

8. Michael MacCambridge, *America's Game: The Epic Story of How Pro Football Captured a Nation* (New York: Random House, 2004), 157–59; Michael Lerner, "Respectable Bigotry," in *The White Majority: Between Poverty and Affluence,* ed. Louise Kapp Howe (New York: Random House, 1970), 201; Michael Novak, *Unmeltable Ethnics: Politics and Culture in American Life* (New Brunswick, N.J.: Transaction Publishers, 1996), 179; Paul Hood, "'No One Enjoyed It Except the Fans,'" *National Observer* (January 25, 1971): 12.

9. Michael Oriard, *Brand NFL: Making and Selling America's Favorite Sport* (Chapel Hill: University of North Carolina Press, 2010), 3; MacCambridge, *America's Game,* 289–90; John Lardner, "S.2545 and the War," *Newsweek* (February 8, 1960): 93; John Fortunato, "Pete Rozelle: Developing and Communicating the Sports Brand," *International Journal of Sport Communication* 1 (2008): 362, 364; Jerry Izenberg, *Rozelle: A Biography* (Lincoln: University of Nebraska Press, 2014), 60; Travis Vogan, *Keepers of the Flame: NFL Films and the Rise of Sports Media* (Urbana: University of Illinois Press, 2014), 195n32.

10. Robert Lyons, *On Any Given Sunday: A Life of Bert Bell* (Philadelphia: Temple University Press, 2009), 258; Harvey Frommer, *When It Was Just a Game: Remembering the First Super Bowl* (Lanham, Md.: Taylor Trade Publishing, 2015), 27, 135; Jeff Davis, *Rozelle: Czar of the NFL* (New York: McGraw-Hill, 2007), 124–28; Tom Callahan, *The GM: The Inside Story of a Dream Job and the Nightmares That Go with It* (New York: Crown, 2007), 261; Gerald Eskenazi, *Gang Green: An Irreverent Look behind the Scenes* (New York: Simon & Schuster, 1998), 147; Roger L. Martin, *Fixing the Game: Bubbles, Crashes, and What Capitalism Can Learn from the NFL* (Boston: Harvard Business Review Press, 2011), 133, 135, 136.

11. Vogan, *Keepers of the Flame,* 44; David Harris, *The League: The Rise and Decline of the NFL* (New York: Bantam, 1986), 4–5, 16 ; Izenberg, *Rozelle: A Biography,* 51, 57, 59, 60, 206; Weiss, *The Making of the Super Bowl,* 15; Charles Ross, *Mavericks, Money, and Men: The AFL, Black Players, and the Evolution of Modern Football* (Philadelphia: Temple University Press, 2016), 16.

12. Melvin Durslag, "After New Orleans, What?" *TV Guide* (January 10, 1970): 13; Bob

Curran, *The Violence Game* (New York: Macmillan, 1966), vii; Joe Flaherty, "Can the Mets Survive Respectability?" *New York* (May 27, 1968): 44; Jerry Izenberg, *The Rivals* (New York: Holt, Rinehart and Winston, 1968), 130; Frederick Exley, *A Fan's Notes* (New York: Vintage, 1988), 2; Hunter S. Thompson, *The Great Shark Hunt: Strange Tales from a Strange Time* (New York: Summit Books, 1979), 75; Stephen Norwood, "The Dallas-Washington Football Rivalry," in *Rivals: Legendary Matchups That Made Sports History* (Fayetteville: University of Arkansas Press, 2010), 278; Barry Tarshis, "Can Ex-Athletes Make It On Wall Street?" *New York* (January 8, 1973): 28.

13. William Phillips, "A Season in the Stands," *Commentary* (July 1, 1969); Thomas Edwards, "The Sporting Gripe," *Partisan Review* 28, 3 (1971): 334; Rex Lardner, "The 'In' Game," *New York Times Book Review* (October 25, 1970): 33.

14. Thomas Morgan, "The Wham in Pro Football," *Esquire* (November 1959): 102, 97; Richard Schickel, "On Pro Football," *Commentary* (January 1969): 66, 68; Phillips, "A Season in the Stands."

15. James Toback, *Jim: The Author's Self-Centered Memoir on the Great Jim Brown* (Garden City, N.Y.: Doubleday, 1971), 5–6; Schickel, "On Pro Football," 68; Kevin Sheets, "Is Percy Houghton Alive?" *The Spectator* (November 5, 1968): 17; Champ Clark, "The Mystique of Pro Football," *Time* (November 9, 1970).

16. Edwards, "The Sporting Gripe," 330–36.

17. David Israel, "How Important Is the NFL Role in U.S. History?" *Washington Star* (October 1, 1975): E1, E4; e-mail from Eric Miller, March 20, 2015.

18. Don DeLillo, *End Zone* (New York: Penguin, 1972), 111–12.

19. MacCambridge, *America's Game,* 288–89; "David Boss," *USA Today Sports Images,* https://www.usatodaysportsimages.com/photographers/David_Boss; Thomas Frank, *The Conquest of Cool* (Chicago: University of Chicago Press, 1997), 9; Robert MacNeil, *The People Machine: The Influence of Television on American Politics* (New York: Harper & Row, 1968), 210; Richard McCarthy, *Elections for Sale* (Boston: Houghton Mifflin, 1972), 85.

20. *The First Fifty Years: A Celebration of the National Football League in its Fifty-Sixth Season* (New York: Ridge Press/Benjamin Company, 1975); Douglas Looney, "Football Books Star in the Yule Bowl," *National Observer* (December 15, 1973): 12.

21. Tex Maule, *The Game,* revised ed. (New York: Random House, 1967), 238, 3.

22. *The First Fifty Years,* 23–24.

23. *The First Fifty Years,* 23, 133, 25–26, 55, 228, 240, 119; Gale Sayers with Al Silverman, *I Am Third* (New York: Viking Press, 1970), 74.

24. *The Pro Football Experience,* designed and edited by David Boss (New York: Harry N. Abrams, 1973), 27, 28, 29; Looney, "Football Books Star in the Yule Bowl."

25. *The Pro Football Experience,* 30, 88, 188, 224.

Chapter 2. Search and Destroy

1. *Life* (December 5, 1960), 113.

2. Mary Anne Watson, *The Expanding Vista: American Television in the Kennedy Years* (Durham, N.C.: Duke University Press, 1994), 136; Martin Mayer, "How Good Is TV at Its

Best?" *Harper's* (August 1960): 84; Burton Benjamin, "TV Documentarian's Dream in a Challenging World," *Variety* (January 4, 1961): 91; Bert Burns, "The Changing Techniques for TV Documentaries," *National Observer* (December 17, 1962): 18; "The Twentieth Century," *Archive of American Television*, http://www.emmytvlegends.org/interviews /shows/twentieth-century-the.

3. Tom Callahan, *Johnny U: The Life & Times of Johnny Unitas* (New York: Crown Publishers, 2006), 172–73; "From Dale Barton's Keyboard," *Carroll Times Daily Herald* (December 30, 1958): 2; Jack Gould, "TV's Eye on the Ball," *New York Times* (December 20, 1959): X17; Roone Arledge, *Roone: A Memoir* (New York: HarperCollins, 2003), 30; Phil Patton, *Razzle-Dazzle: The Curious Marriage of Television and Professional Football* (New York: Dial Press, 1984), 42; Jonathan Rand, *The Year That Changed the Game: The Memorable Months That Shaped Pro Football* (Washington, D.C.: Potomac Books, 2008), xv, 19, 143; Michael MacCambridge, *Lamar Hunt: A Life in Sports* (Kansas City: Andrews & McMeel, 2012), 84; Michael Oriard, *Brand NFL: Making & Selling America's Favorite Sport* (Chapel Hill: University of North Carolina Press, 2010), 3.

4. "As We See It," *TV Guide* (January 19, 1957): inside front cover; *Government and the Sports Business,* ed. Roger Noll (Washington, D.C.: Brookings Institution, 1974), 321; Melvin Durslag, "Look Ma—No Teeth," *TV Guide* (December 10, 1960): 23; Gould, "TV's Eye on the Ball"; Charles Ross, *Mavericks, Money, and Men: The AFL, Black Players, and the Evolution of Modern Football* (Philadelphia: Temple University Press, 2016), 39; *The New York Times at the Super Bowl,* ed. Leonard Koppett (New York: Quadrangle, 1974), 35–36.

5. "'The Twentieth Century' Schedule, October 30 Through December 25, 1960," Folder 4, Schedules, 1957–1963, Box 14; CBS press release, "Introducing Radio Station H-U-F-F," October 14, 1960; Folder 5, *The Violent World of Sam Huff,* Box 3; Burton Benjamin Papers, Wisconsin Historical Society, Madison, Wis.; *The Violent World of Sam Huff,* https://www .youtube.com/watch?v=9jxd4ONwp1Q; Burton Benjamin, "Sam Huff's World: Another Look Back," *New York Times* (February 7, 1982): S2; Travis Vogan, *Keepers of the Flame: NFL Films and the Rise of Sports Media* (Champaign: University of Illinois Press, 2014), 136; Dan Daly and Bob O'Donnell, *The Pro Football Chronicle* (New York: Macmillan, 1990), 173.

6. Arthur Daley, "No Need for the Cops," *New York Times* (November 25, 1960): 36; "Pro Football's Really Violent: 'Huff' Test Proves It For Sure," *Lima News* (October 24, 1960): 18; John P. Shanley, "Inside Pro Football," *New York Times* (October 31, 1960): 55; review in *Variety* (November 2, 1960): 27; Jack McKinney, "When Chuck Bednarik Knocked Out Frank Gifford," originally published in *Philadelphia Daily News* (November 20, 1960), http://www .philly.com/philly/sports/eagles/When_Chuck_Bednarik_knocked_out_Frank_Gifford .html; "The Growling Giants," *Newsweek* (October 31, 1960): 86.

7. *The Violent World of Sam Huff;* "'Twentieth Century' Style Football Player," *Broadcasting* (October 24, 1960): 94; Michael Harrington, *The Other America* (New York: Simon & Schuster, 1997), 45; Sam Huff with Kristine Setting Clark, *Controlled Violence: On the Field and in the Booth* (Chicago: Triumph Books, 2011); Chuck Landon, "He Played as Hard as He Grew Up," *Charleston Daily Mail* (July 5, 1999): 1B.

8. Paul O'Neil, "The Giant Defense Is Triumph of Mind," *Life* (December 5, 1960): 127; Perian Conerly, *Backseat Quarterback* (Jackson: University of Mississippi Press, 2003), 58.

9. Thomas Morgan, "The Wham in Pro Football," *Esquire* (November 1959): 99; Stan Walker to Bill Smith, n.d. [mid-October 1960], Folder 5, Box 3, Benjamin Papers; Murray Olderman, "Between You'n'Me," *Altoona Mirror* (October 20, 1960): 73; Huff with Clark, *Controlled Violence;* Benjamin, "Sam Huff's World: Another Look Back"; Frank Gifford and Harry Waters, *The Whole Ten Yards* (New York: Random House, 1993), 115–16.

10. Shanley, "Inside Pro Football"; Sid Ziff, "Packers Pan Huff," *Los Angeles Times* (January 9, 1963): B3; Sam Huff with Leonard Shapiro, *Tough Stuff: The Man in the Middle* (New York: Macmillan, 1989), 117, 76; Bob Curran, *Pro Football's Rag Days* (Englewood Cliffs, N.J., Prentice-Hall: 1970), 97–98; Bernie Parrish, *They Call It a Game* (New York: Dell, 1971), 123; Jack Mann, "Letters 'n' Lip from the Fans," *Washington Daily News* (August 3, 1971): 43; Arthur Daley, "Farewell to Sam," *New York Times* (December 27, 1967): 32; Dave Kindred, "Huff's Election to Hall Proves His Play Wasn't Just for Show," *Washington Post* (January 28, 1982): D1, D6; Joe Kapp, "A Misfit Who Lives to Win," *Sports Illustrated* (July 27, 1970); Milton Gross, "Giants' Sam Huff: A Vengeful Man," *San Francisco Chronicle* (December 30, 1962): 19; Mike Curtis with Bill Gilbert, *Keep Off My Turf* (Philadelphia: J.B. Lippincott, 1972), 106; Cooper Rollow, "Tarkenton is Funny, Frank, and Revealing," *Chicago Tribune* (October 24, 1976): 3:2. As late as 1988, a review of Huff's autobiography echoed his critics' claim that he "played middle linebacker . . . [with] more hot-dogging, showboating, piling on and late hitting than insight." Joan Ryan, "Dee-Fense!" *New York Times* (October 30, 1988): A20.

11. Olderman, "Between You'n'Me"; McKinney, "When Chuck Bednarik Knocked Out Frank Gifford"; Greg Bedard, "John Zimmerman's Bednarik-Gifford Photo," *The MMQB* (May 20, 2014), http://mmqb.si.com/2014/05/20/nfl-history-in-95-objects-photo-chuck-bednarik-frank-gifford/; Bruce Lowitt and Gary Shelton, "Crunch Time: Hitting Is Still the Name of the Game in the NFL," *St. Petersburg Times* (January 24, 1991): 4C; Michael Shapiro, "Fallen Giant," *Smithsonian Magazine* (February 2007), http://www.smithsonianmag.com/people-places/fallen-giant-144796136/?page=1&no-ist; Y. A. Tittle with Kristine Setting Clark, *Nothing Comes Easy: My Life in Football* (Chicago: Triumph Books, 2009), 199–200.

12. Lewis Nichols, "In and Out of Books," *New York Times* (December 25, 1966): B8; Scott Sherman, "In His League," *The Nation* (February 24, 2009), http://www.powells.com/review/2009_02_24.html; George Plimpton, *Paper Lion* (New York: Pocket Books, 1966), 39, 151.

13. Plimpton, *Paper Lion,* 72, 152.

14. "The Violent Face of Pro Football," *Sports Illustrated* (October 24, 1960): 26; "Fans Go Ga-Ga Over Pro Football," 113.

15. MacCambridge, *America's Game,* 182–83, 286–87; Vogan, *Keepers of the Flame,* 22, 7–10, 15, 17, 110–11; Tom Brody, "C.B. DeMille of the Pros," *Sports Illustrated* (November 20, 1967); Joe Posnanski, "How NFL Films Transformed Football," *Sports Illustrated* (February 3, 2010), http://www.si.com/more-sports/2010/02/03/sabol; "New Film Highlights Pro Football Plays," *Banking* (December 1966): 70; Melvin Durslag, "They Sell Everything But the Goal Posts," *TV Guide* (November 1, 1969): 6–8; "Everything But the Live Action," *Broadcasting* (August 24, 1970): 40; *Vietnam Chronicles: The Abrams Tapes, 1968–1972,* ed.

Lewis Sorley (Lubbock: Texas Tech University Press, 2004), 689; "People in Sports," *Washington Star* (November 8, 1971): C5. The numbers differ according to who is presenting them. The NFL Films site claims that Sabol bid $5,000 for these rights, though Steve Sabol repeatedly uses the $3,000 figure in the films.

16. Vogan, *Keepers of the Flame*, 18, 23–24, 51, 65, 123; Jerry Izenberg, *Rozelle: A Biography* (Lincoln: University of Nebraska Press, 2014), 209; Ben Yagoda, "Not So Instant Replay," *New York Times Magazine* (December 14, 1986): 68.

17. *Pro Football's Longest Day, NFL Films: Legends of Autumn, Vol. I: In the Beginning* (NFL Films, 2006); Rich Cohen, "They Taught America to Watch Football," *The Atlantic* (October 2012), http://www.theatlantic.com/magazine/archive/2012/10/they-taught-america-to -watch-football/309083/2/. For comparison, see "1958 NFL Championship Game," *YouTube*, https://www.youtube.com/watch?v=tHbBQleOfWw; Mark Yost, *Tailgating, Sacks, and Salary Caps: How the NFL Became the Most Successful Sports League in History* (Chicago: Kaplan Publishing, 2006), 91–92.

18. Vogan, *Keepers of the Flame*, 19, 187, 127; Thomas Danyluk, "Steve Sabol—President, NFL Films, July 16, 1998," *The Coffin Corner* 23, 1 (2001); Sid Ziff, "'NFL in Action'—A Film Classic," *Los Angeles Times* (March 23, 1967): B3; Cohen, "They Taught America to Watch Football"; "Our History Is Our Mission, and More," *NFL Films: About*, http://www.nflfilms .com/about.html.

19. *They Call It Pro Football, NFL Films: Legends of Autumn, Vol. I: In The Beginning* (NFL Films, 2006).

20. Or, to be accurate, that the Sabols had hired away from the AFL, where they'd admired it in a championship-game shot by Ernie Ernst. Both Sabols discuss the technical difficulties of getting this particular shot in *Sundays with Soul, Legends of Autumn, Vol. II: The Men Who Played the Game* (NFL Films, 2007).

21. Posnanski, "How NFL Films Transformed Football"; Joseph Alsop, "Major Results Produced by Our Vietnam Fighters," *Los Angeles Times* (September 27, 1966): A6; Robert Lipsyte, "From Draft to Desert Storm," *New York Times* (April 19, 1991): B12; "Tonight's Top TV Shows," *Chanute Tribune* (March 21, 1967): 4.

22. Lipsyte, "From Draft to Desert Storm"; David Harris, *The League: The Rise and Decline of the NFL* (New York: Bantam, 1986), 5; Ziff, "'NFL in Action'"; Vogan, *Keepers of the Flame*.

Chapter 3. The NFL's Role in American History

1. *New York* (November 3, 1975): 41–44.

2. *Federal Club v. National League*, https://casetext.com/case/federal-club-v-national -league; *Flood v. Kuhn*, 407 U.S. 258 (1972), https://supreme.justia.com/cases/federal /us/407/258/case.html; Gerald Gems, *For Pride, Profit, and Patriarchy: Football and the Incorporation of American Cultural Values* (Lanham, Md.: Scarecrow Press, 2000), 98–99; Michael MacCambridge, *America's Game: The Epic Story of How Pro Football Captured a Nation* (New York: Random House, 2004), 290, 286; Craig R. Coenen, *From Sandlots to the Super Bowl: The National Football League, 1920–1967* (Knoxville: University of Tennessee Press, 2005), 101–2; FDR to Rep. John McCormack, June 1, 1942, President's Personal File 1787,

FDR Papers, Franklin D. Roosevelt Presidential Library, Hyde Park, N.Y.; Matthew Algeo, *Last Team Standing: How the Steelers and the Eagles—the "Steagles"—Saved Pro Football During World War II* (Chicago: Chicago Review Press, 2013), 22.

3. Randy Roberts and Ed Krzemienski, *Rising Tide: Bear Bryant, Joe Namath & Dixie's Last Quarter* (New York: Twelve, 2013), 169; Tricia Jenkins, "When We Cheer for Our Team, Do We Have to Cheer for America, Too?" *Washington Post* (January 31, 2013); Don Weiss and Chuck Day, *The Making of the Super Bowl: The Inside Story of the World's Greatest Sporting Event* (Chicago: Contemporary Books, 2003), 195; Stephen Norwood, "The Dallas-Washington Football Rivalry," in *Rivals: Legendary Matchups that Made Sports History,* ed. David Wiggins and Pierre Rodgers (Fayetteville: University of Arkansas Press, 2010), 268; Letter from Elmer Laanczos, October 10, 1966, Box 294, Emanuel Celler Papers, Manuscript Division, Library of Congress, Washington, D.C.

4. Hedrick Smith, *Power Game: How Washington Works* (New York: Random House, 1988), 117; Mary McGrory, "Deliver Us from Football," *Chicago Tribune* (October 13, 1975): A4; Glenn Dickey, "Allen's Dedication Is a Little Frightening," *San Francisco Chronicle* (September 19, 1973): 66; "Kissinger's Advice," *Time* (October 31, 1969): 10; Thomas Meehan, "Cruise Director on the Titanic," *New York Times Magazine* (January 2, 1972): 22; Burling Lowery, "Booooooo," *The Washingtonian* (March 1971): 61; Frank Turaj, "The Redskins: Booooooo," *The Washingtonian* (December 1973): 131, 133.

5. "Oral History Transcript: Lawrence O'Brien, Interview 17, December 17, 1986," http://www.discoverlbj.org/item/oh-obrienl-19861217–17–92–28, 5–6; George Will, "Fumbling the NFL Draft," *Washington Post* (January 3, 1975): A25.

6. Andy Barr, "NFL Kicks in Big for GOP," *Pittsburgh Post-Gazette* (September 19, 2009); Sébastien Arcand, Stéphane Éthier, and Joseph Facal, "'Gentlemen, We Will Chase Perfection': The Extraordinary Success of the National Football League," *International Journal of Case Studies in Management* (March 2016): 1; Roger L. Martin, *Fixing the Game: Bubbles, Crashes, and What Capitalism Can Learn from the NFL* (Boston: Harvard Business Review Press, 2011), 72; S. M. Oliva, "Abolish the NFL Draft," *Reason* (April 23, 2013).

7. Chris Willis, *The Man Who Built the National Football League: Joe F. Carr* (Lanham, Md.: Scarecrow Press, 2010), 343; "Pro Gridders Strive to Equalize Strength," *Hanover Evening Sun* (February 10, 1936): 3; "Player Plan Is Adopted," *New York Times* (February 10, 1936): 24; Algeo, *Last Team Standing,* 184; Mark Yost, *Tailgating, Sacks, and Salary Caps: How the NFL Became the Most Successful Sports League in History* (Chicago: Kaplan Publishing, 2006), 54, 55.

8. *Government and the Sports Business,* ed. Roger Noll (Washington, D.C.: Brookings Institution, 1974), 290, 306; Jonathan Rand, *The Year That Changed the Game: The Memorable Months That Shaped Pro Football* (Washington, D.C.: Potomac Books, 2008), 190; Albert Hunt, "TV & Sports: Network Money Brings New Riches but Also Begins Changing Games," *Wall Street Journal* (April 22, 1966): 1; chart of both leagues' radio-TV deals, *Broadcasting* (August 28, 1961): 40; Bob Curran, *The $400,000 Quarterback, or: The League That Came in from the Cold* (New York: Macmillan, 1965), 247.

9. Dave Dixon, *The Saints, the Superdome, and the Scandal* (Gretna, La.: Pelican Publishing, 2008), 65–69; *Hearings Before the Antitrust Subcommittee of the Committee on the Judiciary,*

House of Representatives, 89th Congress, Second Session, on S. 3817 (Washington, D.C.: Government Printing Office, 1966), 117; Matthew Mitten and Aaron Hernandez, "The Sports Broadcasting Act of 1961," 751, https://law.onu.edu/sites/default/files/745%20-%20Mitten .pdf; "Foss Appeals for Strong Americanism," *Huron Daily Plainsman* (May 22, 1950): 8; 15 U.S. Code § 1291 https://www.law.cornell.edu/uscode/text/15/1291.

10. *Hearings Before the Antitrust Subcommittee*, 52; Yost, *Tailgating, Sacks, and Salary Caps*, 67–68, 73–74; Arthur Daley, "Trick Play," *New York Times* (October 23, 1966): S2.

11. MacCambridge, *America's Game*, 229; Morris Siegel, "Celler Is Tougher than Green Bay," *Washington Star* (October 14, 1966): A17; Letter from Harry Kuhr, October 19, 1966; Letter from W. S. Doxey, October 19, 1966; both in Box 294, Celler Papers; *Hearings Before the Antitrust Subcommittee*, 26, 29, 34, 38–42; Statement by Robert Kastenmeier, October 18, 1966; Legislative Files, 1961–1970, Box 133, Folder 37, Robert Kastenmeier Papers, Wisconsin Historical Society, Madison, Wis.; Dave Brady, "Rozelle, Thwarted at Hearings, Gloomy Over Merger of Pros," *Washington Post* (October 7, 1966): E1.

12. James Olson, *Stuart Symington: A Life* (Columbia: University of Missouri Press, 2003), 410; Lamar Hunt to Stuart Symington, October 8, 1965; Stuart Symington to Lamar Hunt, November 6, 1965; Lamar Hunt to Stuart Symington, July 29, 1966; all in Alphabetical Correspondence Series, Folder 4989; Stuart Symington to Emanuel Celler, July 22, 1966, Folder 4944; Stuart Symington Papers, Missouri Historical Society, Columbia; Letter from Sen. Stuart Symington, September 28, 1966; Letter from Norman Hecht, September 13, 1966; Letter from Felix Goldman, September 10, 1966; Letter from Ronald Houtman, October 11, 1966, all in Box 294, Celler Papers.

13. Lewis Atchison, "Draft Is Vital to Grid Merger," *Washington Star* (October 13, 1966): D4; *Government and the Sports Business*, 200; Bernie Parrish, *They Call It a Game* (New York: Dial Press, 1971), 224, 124; Dave Brady, "Kemp Says Players Back Merger," *Washington Post* (October 23, 1966): C4; telegrams in Folder 15, Box 56, Hale Boggs and Lindy Boggs Papers, Manuscript Collection 1000, Louisiana Research Collection, Howard-Tilton Memorial Library, Tulane University, New Orleans; *Hearings Before the Antitrust Subcommittee*, 70.

14. "Oral History Transcript: Lawrence O'Brien," 5; *Hearings Before the Antitrust Subcommittee*, 101, 102; Michael Martin, "New Orleans Becomes a Big League City: The NFL-AFL Merger and the Creation of the New Orleans Saints," in James Vlasich, *Horsehide, Pigskin, Oval Tracks and Apple Pie* (Jefferson, N.C.: McFarland, 2006), 123; Hale Boggs to David Kleck, September 20, 1966; David Dixon to Hale Boggs, June 15, 1966; David Dixon to Hale Boggs, August 3, 1966; Hale Boggs to Pete Rozelle, April 28, 1966; Folder 15, Box 56, Boggs Papers; William Wallace, "Congressional Approval of Pro Football Merger Hastens Expansion Plans," *New York Times* (October 22, 1966): 34.

15. "Merger Provision Clears Congress," *Washington Star* (October 21, 1966): C1; Jerry Izenberg, *Rozelle: A Biography* (Lincoln: University of Nebraska Press, 2014), 148; David Dixon to Pete Rozelle, Folder 5, Box 1259; Folder 15, Box 56; Boggs Papers.

16. Dennis Deninger, *Sports on Television: The How and Why Behind What You See* (New York: Routledge, 2012), 44–45; "NFL Blackout Rule: Richard Nixon Hated It," *Denver Post* (July 7, 2013); *The New York Times at the Super Bowl*, ed. Leonard Koppett (New York: Quadrangle, 1974), 203; Thomas Foley, "Congress Votes to Lift Some Blackouts on TV,"

New York Times (September 14, 1973): D1; Nicholas von Hoffman, "The NFL's Broken Play: Congress Unifies the Fans," *Washington Post* (September 17, 1973): B1.

17. Dick Young, "Young Ideas," *New York Daily News* (October 13, 1966); clipping in Folder 5, Box 1259, Boggs Papers; Jerry Izenberg, "Return of the Body-Snatchers," *Pittsburgh Press* (January 27, 1971): 61; Will, "Fumbling the NFL Draft."

18. Mike Curtis with Bill Gilbert, *Keep Off My Turf* (Philadelphia: J.B. Lippincott, 1972), 131; Spiro Agnew, *Frankly Speaking: A Collection of Ordinary Speeches* (Washington, D.C.: Public Affairs Press, 1970), 18–20, 46–47, 64, 67; "Agnew, Warner Man of Year, Heaps Praise on Allen, Shula," *Washington Post* (May 4, 1973): D6; Spiro Agnew with John Underwood, "Not Infected with the Conceit of Infallibility," *Sports Illustrated* (June 21, 1971): 62, 66–67, 68; Lamar Hunt to Stuart Symington, August 2, 1973; Hunt to Symington, October 29, 1973; Symington to Hunt, November 1, 1973; all in Folder TV, Football, 1973, Box 313, Symington Papers.

19. Jack Kemp, preface to Yost, *Tailgating, Sacks, and Salary Caps*, vi; *Pro Sports: Should Government Intervene?* (Round Table at the American Enterprise Institute, February 22, 1977): 12; Rosabeth Moss Kanter, "Four Winning Lessons from the Super Bowl," *Harvard Business Review* (January 31, 2011).

20. Ron Fimrite, "Playing the Money Game," *San Francisco Chronicle* (July 27, 1970): 41. It's not until recently, in books like Stefan Fatsis's 2008 *A Few Seconds of Panic*, that journalists have taken seriously the notion of players as workers and the locker room as a workplace. "The game itself is a fun, thrilling, scary, addictive turn-on: Sunday!" Fatsis writes. "The rest of the job is a largely joyless, stultifying, demoralizing, infantilizing, breakdown-inducing drag" (310). His presiding authority is less Hemingway than Barbara Ehrenreich: in his telling, Bronco camp becomes a postindustrial workplace beset by endless PowerPoint presentations and corporate-speak, with players highly skilled but insecure contractors scraping by as best they can in an economy ravaged by scarce opportunity and harsh, ceaseless competition; even the successful recognize all too clearly that they are only a serious injury or two from the scrap heap.

21. Michael Lomax, "The Quest for Freedom: The NFLPA's Attempt to Abolish the NFL Reserve System," *Football Studies* (2004): 70–107; Michael Oriard, *Brand NFL: Making and Selling America's Favorite Sport* (Chapel Hill: University of North Carolina Press, 2010), 79–89; Leonard Koppett, "Press Secretary's Secretary," *Sporting News* (March 11, 1972): 4; Red Smith, "The Strike Seen from Capitol Hill," *New York Times* (August 21, 1974): 47; Jefferson Cowie, "'Vigorously Left, Right, and Center': The Crosscurrents of Working-Class America in the 1970s," in Beth Bailey and David Farber, *America in the Seventies* (Lawrence: University Press of Kansas, 2004), 102; Milton Richman, "People Indicate in Letters Concerning NFL Strike: Players Are Wrong and Owners Are Right," *Defiance Crescent-News* (July 19, 1974): 16; Izenberg, *Rozelle*, 184.

22. Oriard, *Brand NFL*, 80–88; Parrish, *They Call It a Game*, 133–39; William Barry Furlong, "Ploys Will Be Ploys, But Enough's Enough," *Washington Post* (July 11, 1974): D1, D4.

23. Walter Byers, "A Personal Viewpoint . . . Lessons in Learning," *NCAA News* (July 1970): 2; "Student-Athletes Will Visit Vietnam," *NCAA News* (June 1970): 1, 2; "Vietnam Tour Builds Morale," *NCAA News* (October 1, 1970): 2.

24. *Survey of Broadcast Journalism 1970–1971: A State of Siege,* ed. Marvin Barrett (New York: Grosset & Dunlap, 1971), 152, 160–62, 159; James Westheider, *Fighting in Vietnam: The Experiences of the U.S. Soldier* (Mechanicsburg, Pa.: Stackpole Books, 2011), 94; Meredith Lair, *Armed with Abundance: Consumerism & Soldiering in the Vietnam War* (Chapel Hill: University of North Carolina Press, 2011), 127–31; Christian Appy, *Patriots: The Vietnam War Remembered from All Sides* (New York: Penguin Books, 2004), 211.

25. Entertainment Evaluation, July 4, 1970; Memorandum from Staff Entertainment Director to Director of Special Services Agency (Provisional), HQ, USARV, July 22, 1970, Box 20; Memorandum for Director of Special Services Agency (Provisional), HQ, USARV, January 20, 1971; Entertainment Evaluation, December 28, 1970, Box 24; USO files, Record Group 472: Records of the U.S. Forces in Southeast Asia, 1950–1976, National Archives, College Park, Md.; "Athletes Go to Vietnam for Holidays," *NCAA News* (December 15, 1970): 1, 2.

26. Art Rosenbaum, "A Quarterback's Near Miss," *San Francisco Chronicle* (July 29, 1970): 56; Jim Plunkett and Dave Newhouse, *The Jim Plunkett Story* (New York: Arbor House, 1981), 65; Neil Amdur, "Football Future Called Clouded," *New York Times* (August 18, 1970): 41; Larry DiNardo, "Instant Replay in Reverse," *Purdue–Notre Dame Program* (September 26, 1970), 5, 8.

27. Terry Shields, "'The Worst Thing' Stops DiNardo," *Notre Dame Observer* (November 19, 1970): 7; Jerry Kirshenbaum, "The Greening of the Fighting Irish," *Sports Illustrated* (December 14, 1970); William Lunch and Peter Sperlich, "American Public Opinion and the War in Vietnam," *Western Political Quarterly* (March 1979): 25; Penny Lewis, *Hardhats, Hippies, and Hawks: The Vietnam Antiwar Movement as Myth and Memory* (Ithaca, N.Y.: Cornell University Press, 2013), 50; Marty Ralbovsky, "Time the Academy Did Some Bending," *Naples Daily News* (November 26, 1970): 9B.

28. Frank Gifford and Harry Waters, *The Whole Ten Yards* (New York: Random House, 1993), 229; *USO Annual Report,* 1971, 12; *USO Annual Report,* 1972, 10; both in Sabrina Frizzell Collection, Virtual Vietnam Archive, Texas Tech University, Lubbock; Murray Kempton, "Jock-Sniffing," *New York Review of Books* (February 11, 1971); Press Release, January 1969, Folder USO Tour—Pro Football Unit 1—January 25, 1969, USARV; Memo by Capt. David Thorpe, Escort Officer, to Special Services Officer, HQS, USARV, February 17, 1969; Box 9, USO Papers; Hal Boyle, "Da Nang Press Center Has No Telephone," *Park City Daily News* (May 7, 1965).

29. This was equally true of major-league baseball, in which few top players actually served despite the league's vociferous avowal of its central role in promulgating Americanism. Robert Elias, *The Empire Strikes Out: How Baseball Sold American Foreign Policy and Promoted the American Way Abroad* (New York: New Press, 2010), 201–2.

30. "USO," NFL.com (April 7, 2013), http://www.nfl.com/news/story/09000d5d82389235/printable/uso; "Football and America: The Vietnam War," Pro Football Hall of Fame, http://www.profootballhof.com/history/general/war/vietnam/page3.aspx; Algeo, *Last Team Standing,* xv, 29; Tony Barnhart, "The 40s: NFL Goes to War," *The Coffin Corner* 9, 8 (1987); "Bald Case in Point: Pro Football's Magical Immunity," *Life* (December 9, 1966): 44–47; Myra MacPherson, *Long Time Passing: Vietnam and the Haunted Generation* (Bloomington:

Indiana University Press, 1984), 144; Mitchell Hall, *Crossroads: American Popular Culture and the Vietnam War* (Lanham, Md.: Rowman & Littlefield, 2005), 107; Lawrence Baskir and William Strauss, *Chance and Circumstance: The Draft, the War, and the Vietnam Generation* (New York: Random House, 1978), 48–49; "Sergeant Accused of Taking Bribe to Let AFL Player Beat Draft," *New York Times* (December 3, 1965): B1; Raymond Anderson, "Jet Back's Beat-Draft 'Bribe' Traps Sergeant," *New York Times* (December 3, 1965): 1; "Nab 2d in Military: Say Bribe Sought," *Pacific Stars and Stripes* (December 7, 1965): 23; "3 Indicted in Case of Jets Rookie," *Middletown Times Herald Record* (February 16, 1966): 63.

31. "Probe of Pro Athletes' Draft 'Immunity' Asked," *Los Angeles Times* (December 8, 1966): C1; B. Drummond Ayres, "Reserves Told to Enlist Men as Names Come Up," *New York Times* (December 23, 1966): 11; "360 Pros Reported Exempt from Draft," *New York Times* (April 8, 1967): S23; Dave Brady, "Only Three Redskin Players 1-A in Draft, Survey Reveals," *Washington Post* (April 23, 1967): D4; Jerry Baulch, "Draft Status May Be Cleared by June," *Oshkosh Daily Northwestern* (May 26, 1967): 5.

32. "Card QB Johnson Called for 2-Year Hitch with Army," *Los Angeles Times* (August 12, 1967): A1, A5; Dave Brady, "Giant Kicker Has No Kicks Coming?" *Washington Post* (September 2, 1967): D3; Louis Harris, "Present Draft Believed Unfair," *Los Angeles Times* (June 19, 1967): A5; Rocky Bleier with Terry O'Neil, *Fighting Back* (New York: Stein and Day, 1975), 67–70; Arthur J. Rooney Jr. with Roy McHugh, *Ruanaidh: The Story of Art Rooney and His Clan* (Pittsburgh: Art Rooney Jr., 2008), 325; Jack Mann, " 'Ya Can't Argue With Ali's (What's That?) Sincerity," *Washington Daily News* (January 12, 1971): 42.

33. Ironically, that mission had provided a lesser-known sequel to NBC's notorious November 1968 *Heidi* game. On December 22, when CBS cut away from the last 2 ½ minutes of the first half of the Western Conference final between the Colts and Vikings for a broadcast from 140,000 miles in space, more than two thousand "irate football lovers" jammed the switchboard with complaints. "TV Switch Sends Fans Into Orbit," *Los Angeles Times* (December 23, 1968): C1; "Shades of 'Heidi'! Astronauts Eclipse Title Game on TV," *New York Times* (December 23, 1968): 54.

34. Oriard, *Brand NFL*, 22–23; Ira Berkow, "Once Again, It's the Star-Spangled Super Bowl," *New York Times* (January 27, 1991): S6; "Super Bowl Entertainment," http://www.nfl.com/superbowl/history/entertainment; Harvey Frommer, *When It Was Just a Game: Remembering the First Super Bowl* (Lanham, Md.: Taylor, 2015), 163, 203; Dave Anderson, *Countdown to Super Bowl* (New York: Random House, 1969), 194; Travis Vogan, *Keepers of the Flame: NFL Films and the Rise of Sports Media* (Urbana: University of Illinois Press, 2014), 176; William Taaffe, "Footage That Can Go to Your Head," *Sports Illustrated* (September 5, 1984): 85; George Solomon, "Could Gowdy and Cosell Have Saved the Moonshot?" *Washington Daily News* (February 10, 1971): 63; *The New York Times at the Super Bowl*, 327.

35. Austin Murphy, "It's . . . Halftime," http://www.si.com/longform/halftime/; "Scalpers Soaked As Rains Pass," *New York Times* (January 12, 1970): 52; Marty Ralbovsky, *Super Bowl: Of Men, Myths and Moments* (New York: Hawthorn Books, 1971), 125–26, 132, 143; "As We See It," *TV Guide* (February 21, 1970): 1; Harvey Stone, "Thanks?" *The Rag* (November 25, 1968); 7; Sandy Padwe, "Sports and Politics Must Be Separate—At Least SOME Politics, That Is," *Philadelphia Inquirer* (December 14, 1971): 35; Jerry Izenberg, *How Many Miles to*

Camelot? (New York: Holt, Rinehart and Winston, 1972), 185; Ronald A. Smith, *Play-by-Play: Radio, Television, and Big-Time College Sport* (Baltimore: Johns Hopkins, University Press, 2001), 132; Izenberg, "Return of the Body-Snatchers"; Thompson quoted in Kiki Levathes, "Rolling Stone Voice Predicts Mad Future," *Washington Star* (December 14, 1971): B1.

36. Dan Jenkins, *Semi-Tough* (New York: Atheneum, 1984), 191–92; Michael Roberts, *Fans!: How We Go Crazy Over Sports* (Washington, D.C.: New Republic, 1976), xv.

37. Ron Fimrite, "A Time to Honor the King," *San Francisco Chronicle* (August 6, 1970): 49; court records discussed in Daly and Bob O'Donnell, *The Pro Football Chronicle* (New York: Macmillan, 1990), 14, reveal that the Bears actually turned a profit exceeding $21,000 that year.

38. *The First Fifty Years: A Celebration of the National Football League in Its Fifty-Sixth Season* (New York: Ridge Press/Benjamin, 1975), 30.

39. Bob Curran, *Pro Football's Rag Days* (Englewood Cliffs, N.J.: Prentice-Hall, 1969), 2; Gerald Eskenazi, *There Were Giants in Those Days* (New York: Grosset & Dunlap, 1976), 3; Myron Cope, *The Game That Was* (New York: World Publishing, 1970), 5,4, 11, 58, 127, 151; Murray Greenberg, *Passing Game: Benny Friedman and the Transformation of Football* (New York: PublicAffairs, 2008), 276; Coenen, *From Sandlots to the Super Bowl*, 97; Gifford, *The Whole Ten Yards*, 214; "Farmington Honors All-Pro Sam Huff," *Raleigh Register* (December 30, 1959): 9; Victor Gold, *I Don't Need You When I'm Right: The Confessions of a Washington PR Man* (New York: Morrow, 1975), 82–84; Richard Parker, "Stevens Uses a Real Linebacker to Back Its Line," *Broadcasting* (July 5, 1965): 18.

40. Mary McGrory, "Deliver Us from Football," *Chicago Tribune* (October 13, 1975): A4; John Warner, letter to George Allen, March 13, 1975, ARBA, General Office Records, Box 65, General Correspondence Folder, NACP; Memo and Brief Sheet from Carlos C. Campbell, AIP, Deputy Assistant Administrator, Resource Development, to William Butler, May 28, 1975, ARBA, Programs, States, and Communities Division, Records of Nationally Recognized Programs, 1972–1977, Box 261, National Football League Bicentennial Program, NACP, Records Group 452, National Archives Building, College Park, Md.

41. Brief Sheet, Box 261, Programs, States, and Communities, Records of Nationally Recognized Programs, NACP; John Warner to Pete Rozelle, ARBA, Day Files, Box 78, Chron. John W. Warner, June 1975, ARBA Records.

42. Byron Rosen, "NFL Enters Bicentennial Act with Shoulder Emblem, Essay," *Washington Post* (August 5, 1975): D3; the image depicted ran in the *Los Angeles Times* (October 3, 1975): I2; "Football and the Bicentennial," *Wall Street Journal* (October 13, 1975): 8.

43. "NFL Fumbles with Essay Contest," *Southern Illinoisian* (October 16, 1975): 4; Russell Baker, "Superhistory," *New York Times* (October 19, 1975): 234; C. C. Johnson Spink, "Delusions of Grandeur," *Sporting News* (December 6, 1975): 14; Furman Bisher, "Dynasties Are Vulnerable," *Sporting News* (January 31, 1976): 2; "The NFL's Role in American History (Somebody's Gotta Be Kidding)"; Steve Harvey, "Reviewing Lowlights of Football Season," *Los Angeles Times* (December 30, 1975): D2; Roz Liston, "Bicentennial Looking Like 'Buycentennial,'" *Wisconsin State Journal* (December 8, 1975): 5. Despite the quantity of mockery it faced, the NFL wasn't ready to let this question go: the official program for Super Bowl XXVI in 1992 contained an essay by Eugene McCarthy on Johnny Blood that began, once more, with the essay prompt and Henry Steele Commager's dismissal of that

prompt. McCarthy observed that a critic might say the same thing of other significant art forms. "The influence of football, like that of poetry, is not obvious or superficial or broadly social, but subtle and personal." Eugene McCarthy, "He Was of a Different Kind," in *The NFL Super Bowl Companion,* ed. John Wiebusch (Chicago: Triumph Books, 2002), 82.

44. "Virginia Girl Takes Top Prize for Football Essay," *New York Times* (January 18, 1976): 164; Jaime Aron, *Dallas Cowboys: The Complete Illustrated History* (Minneapolis: MBI Publishing, 2010), 91.

Chapter 4. The Kennedy/Lombardi School

1. Walter Rugaber, "The End of Secrecy: A Spook Is Seen on Camera," *New York Times* (May 20, 1973): 207.

2. "Football and the Bicentennial," *Wall Street Journal* (October 13, 1975): 8; Tom Goff, "Reagan Watches Rams; Holds San Diego Rally," *Los Angeles Times* (October 29, 1970): 29; "Dr. Leary to Tell Political Plans," *Los Angeles Times* (September 21, 1969): 26A; Dick Friendlich, "Rod Sherman Receives a Call," *San Francisco Chronicle* (December 28, 1970): 43; Jeannie Morris, "Pro Football Players Take Political Sides," *Dubuque Telegraph-Herald* (October 8, 1972): 30.

3. Mary McGrory, "Deliver Us from Football," *Chicago Tribune* (October 13, 1975): A4; Pat Ryan, "The Making of a Quarterback 1970," *Sports Illustrated* (December 7, 1970); Michael Mewshaw, "Gent," *Texas Observer* (November 30, 1973): 16; Jerry Izenberg, *How Many Miles to Camelot?: The All-American Sports Myth* (New York: Holt, Rinehart, and Winston, 1972), 147, 148.

4. George Solomon, *The Team Nobody Wanted: The Washington Redskins* (Chicago: Henry Regnery, 1973), 52; Leonard Shecter, *The Jocks* (Indianapolis: Bobbs-Merrill, 1969), 268; Dave Kindred, "Gentler Times," *Washington Post* (March 31, 1979): D1, D4.

5. Arlen Large, "Stars on the Stump: More Celebrities Try to Capitalize on Fame by Entering Politics," *Wall Street Journal* (May 4, 1970): 1, 20; Jules Abels, *The Degeneration of Our Presidential Election: A History and Analysis of an American Institution in Trouble* (New York: Macmillan, 1968), 51; Victor Gold, *I Don't Need You When I'm Right: The Confessions of a Washington PR Man* (New York: William Morrow, 1975), 212; *Survey of Broadcast Journalism 1970–1971: A State of Siege,* ed. Marvin Barrett (New York: Grosset & Dunlap, 1971), 50; Shelby Coffey III, "Political Consultants: Their Tentacles Grow and Grow," *Washington Post* (November 1, 1970): 9, 10; David Ricci, *The Transformation of American Politics: The New Washington and the Rise of Think Tanks* (New Haven, Conn.: Yale University Press, 1994), 111.

6. This was not merely a figure of speech. Ronald Reagan's PR agency for California's 1966 gubernatorial election had previously worked for the liberal Nelson Rockefeller; Pat Brown's agency represented Barry Goldwater in 1964.

7. Victor Gold, "Agnew Agonistes," *Newsweek* (September 24, 1973): 22; "Shepherd to the Wordsmith," *Time* (October 18, 1971): 107; Victor Gold, *PR as in President: A Pro Looks at Press Agents, Media, & the 1976 Candidates* (Garden City, N.Y.: Doubleday, 1977), 67, 56, 141, 199; Jerry Bruno and Jeff Greenfield, *The Advance Man* (New York: William Morrow, 1971), 58.

8. Thomas Fleming, "Selling the Product Named Hubert Humphrey," *New York Times Magazine* (October 13, 1968): 139; David Lee Rosenbloom, *The Election Men: Professional Campaign Managers and American Democracy* (New York: Quadrangle Books, 1973), 132, 131; Larry Sabato, *The Rise of Political Consultants: New Ways of Winning Elections* (New York: Basic Books, 1981), 18; Stephen Hess, "A Memo to the Ervin Committee," in Robert Agranoff, *The New Style in Election Campaigns,* 2d ed. (Boston: Holbrook Press, 1976), 425; Ike Balbus, "Politics as Sports: The Ascendency of the Sports Metaphor in America," *Monthly Review* (March 1975): 26; Edwin Newman, *Strictly Speaking: Will America Be the Death of English?* (New York: Bobbs-Merrill, 1974), 149.

9. *The Political Image Merchants: Strategies for the Seventies,* ed. Ray Hiebert, Robert Jones, John d'Arc Lorenz, and Ernest Lotito (Washington, D.C.: Acropolis Books, 1975), 102–3; Sabato, *The Rise of Political Consultants,* 161; Fran Tarkenton as told to Brock Yates, *Broken Patterns: The Education of a Quarterback* (New York: Simon & Schuster, 1971), 7; Sally Quinn, "The Old Political Football, Well Tossed," *Washington Post* (July 13, 1971): B7.

10. J. M. Perry, *The New Politics: The Expanding Technology of Political Manipulation* (New York: Potter, 1968); Gene Wyckoff, *The Image Candidate* (New York: Macmillan, 1968); Joseph Napolitan, *The Election Game and How to Win It* (Garden City, N. Y.: Doubleday, 1972).

11. Richard Harwood, "Television Shaping the New Politics," *Washington Post* (March 29, 1970): 1; Joe McGinniss, *The Selling of the President, 1968* (New York: Trident Press, 1969), 115; "The Selling of the Candidates 1970," *Newsweek* (October 19, 1970): 34, 35, 37, 38; "Report/Professional Managers, Consultants Play Major Roles in 1970 Political Races," *National Journal* (September 26, 1970): 2083; Rosenbloom, *The Election Men,* 12, 139; *The Political Image Merchants,* 25.

12. "Jim Plunkett: Stanford's Heisman Trophy Nominee," *Los Angeles Times* (October 24, 1970): 12A; "Archie Who," https://www.youtube.com/watch?v=6cDsNxjbVLI; Art Rosenbaum, "The Overmodest Campaigner," *San Francisco Chronicle* (September 14, 1970): 48; "Stanford," *Sports Illustrated* (September 14, 1970): 74; Art Rosenbaum, "One Vote for Plunkett," *San Francisco Chronicle* (November 17, 1970): 50; Jim Plunkett and Dave Newhouse, *The Jim Plunkett Story* (New York: Arbor House, 1981), 79; *Stanford University's Heisman Trophy Nominee* (Stanford Athletics, 1970), 3; Phil Finch, "Sports Flacks: Image for Sale," *San Francisco Sunday Examiner & Chronicle* (January 24, 1971): C5; Bob Murphy, Heisman Trophy Announcement, November 24, 1970; Ted Miller, "Where Have All the Heisman Trophy Promotions Gone?" *ESPN.com* (August 14, 2015), http://espn.go.com /college-football/story/_/id/13426041/heisman-trophy-promotions-taking-less-meaning -college-football; Melvin Durslag, "The Heisman Trophy," *TV Guide* (November 13, 1971): 53–54; "Here Are the Facts! Heisman Trophy Campaign Cost $319," *Los Angeles Times* (April 17, 1971): E3; Frank Dolson, "Heisman Trophy an Over-Inflated Joke," *Philadelphia Inquirer* (December 2, 1971): 30.

13. Martin Nolan, "The Re-Selling of the President," *The Atlantic* (November 1972): 79–81; Neil Hickey, "'Make News, Not Commercials,'" *TV Guide* (May 27, 1972): 8; Herbert Alexander, *Financing the 1972 Election* (Lexington, Mass.: Lexington Books, 1976), 78, 245–48; James Wooten, "Unexpected 'Preview' Provides a Jolt to a Hitherto Predictable

Convention," *New York Times* (August 23, 1972): 26; Gold, *PR as in President,* 6, 8; *The Political Image Merchants,* 32; *Campaign '72: The Managers Speak,* ed. Ernest May and Janet Fraser (Cambridge, Mass.: Harvard University Press, 1973), 186, 172, 196, 49, 234; "Podium Design Shouts Dignity," *Milwaukee Journal* (August 21, 1972): 10; Ripon Society, *Jaws of Victory: The Game-Plan Politics of 1972, The Crisis of the Republican Party, and the Future of the Constitution* (Boston: Little, Brown, 1972), 3, 4.

14. Wells Twombly, "Maximum Leader," *San Francisco Sunday Examiner and Chronicle* (January 17, 1971): C3; Ron Fimrite, "Maybe They Shouldn't Play," *San Francisco Chronicle* (August 4, 1970): 39.

15. James Reston, "Sports and Politics in America," *New York Times* (September 12, 1969): 42; Balbus, "Politics as Sports," 27, 33; George Will, "Saying What You Mean," *Washington Post* (October 4, 1974): A23; Leonard Koppett, "Lesson of Watergate in Sports World," *Sporting News* (July 7, 1973): 6; Glenn Dickey, *The Jock Empire: Its Rise and Deservéd Fall* (Radnor, Pa.: Chilton, 1974), v.

16. Kenneth Denlinger, "Politics and Sport Are United in Goal," *Washington Post* (September 12, 1976): F1, F6; Joseph Lelyveld, "The Selling of a Candidate," *New York Times* (March 28, 1976): 189; Paul Weaver, "Captives of Melodrama," *New York Times Magazine* (August 29, 1976): 48, 55.

17. Joseph Finnigan, "Nothing Is Cheap These Days," *TV Guide* (December 12, 1970): 42; John Schulian, "TD Club: A Black-Tie Smoker," *Washington Post* (January 19, 1976): D8; Myron Cope, "Who's the Broad in Pro Football's Huddle?" *True* (December 1968): 43; Dan Jenkins, "Another Nightmare for the Year Ahead," *Sports Illustrated* (September 14, 1970): 46; Louis Kampf, "A Course on Spectator Sports," *College English* (April 1977): 839; "The Politics of Football & Other War Games," *Ain't I a Woman* (October 30, 1970): 16.

18. Jack Kemp, "Black and White," in John Wiebusch, *The NFL Super Bowl Companion: Personal Reflections on America's Favorite Game* (Chicago: Triumph Books, 2002), 176–79; Thompson quoted in Kiki Levathes, "Rolling Stone Voice Predicts Mad Future," *Washington Star* (December 14, 1971): B1.

19. Leonard Koppett, "Only Winning Counts," *New York Times* (November 5, 1967); Anne Jenkins, "Football—The All-American Sport," *Great Speckled Bird* (December 27, 1971): 24; Paul Gardner, *Nice Guys Finish Last: Sport and American Life* (New York: Universe Books, 1974), 123; George Carlin, "Football or Baseball," https://www.youtube.com/watch?v=qmXacL0Uny0; Ron Powers, "Women's Lib Target: Monday Football," *San Francisco Chronicle* (August 2, 1970): C5; Jack Mann, "Implementing the Coach's Offensive Game Plan," *Washington Daily News* (March 25, 1971): 78; Jay Weiner, "The Uncapping of Coach Richard," *Berkeley Barb* (July 20–26, 1973): 2.

20. Michael Novak, *The Joy of Sports,* revised ed. (Lanham, Md.: Rowman & Littlefield, 1993), 267; Michael Novak, *Unmeltable Ethnics: Politics and Culture in American Life* (New Brunswick, N.J.: Transaction Publishers, 1996), 180; William Bennett, "In Defense of Sports," *Commentary* (February 1976); Morton Kondracke and Fred Barnes, *Jack Kemp: The Bleeding-Heart Conservative Who Changed America* (New York: Sentinel, 2015), 103; Robert Lipsyte, "God's Quarterback," *New York Times* (November 9, 1967): 66.

21. Herbert Klein, *Making It Perfectly Clear* (Garden City, N.Y.: Doubleday, 1980), viii;

James Naughton, "Whisperjet: 'I'm an Ordinary Man,'" *New York Times* (December 27, 1970): 31.

22. Jim Benagh, *Making It to #1: How College Football and Basketball Teams Get There* (New York: Dodd, Mead, 1976), 254; George Will, "The Wrath of Woody Hayes," *Washington Post* (November 19, 1974): A19.

23. Interview with Rich Zitrin, October 22, 2015; Jerry Izenberg, *The Jerry Izenberg Collection* (Dallas; Taylor Publishing, 1989), 42, xiii; Jerry Izenberg, "Through My Eyes," *Newark Star-Ledger* (November 5, 2006).

24. W. Joseph Campbell, *Getting It Wrong: Ten of the Greatest Misreported Stories in American Journalism* (Berkeley: University of California Press, 2010), ch. 7; Red Smith, foreword to Ira Berkow, *Beyond the Dream: Occasional Heroes of Sports* (New York: Athenaeum, 1975), ix–x; Robert Lipsyte, *SportsWorld: An American Dreamland* (New York: Quadrangle, 1975), 282; for sample Sports Focus stories, see Marty Ralbovsky, "Is it Exploited in Athletics?: Our National Anthem," *Sunday San Francisco Examiner & Chronicle* (November 15, 1970): C7 or Ira Berkow, "Looking Beyond the Lance Rentzel Case," *Sunday San Francisco Examiner & Chronicle* (December 20, 1970): C5; Pete Schwab, "They Go Bananas at Ohio State," *San Francisco Examiner* (January 1, 1971): 59; Thompson, *Fear and Loathing in America: The Brutal Odyssey of an Outlaw Journalist 1968–1976* (New York: Simon & Schuster, 2000), 451; "The Further Confessions of a Sports Editor," *Washingtonian* (October 1971): 16; Burling Lowrey, "You Can't Tell the Sportswriters without a Program," *Washingtonian* (October 1972): 150.

25. Burling Lowrey, "Booooooo," *Washingtonian* (March 1971): 61; Tom Quinn, "United They Stand," *Washington Daily News* (August 26, 1971): 75; Tom Dowling, "Inside Report," *Washington Star* (November 7, 1971): B2; Kiki Levathes, "Sex and the Athlete: Taboos Explored," *Washington Star* (November 14, 1971): C8; Leonard Shecter, "Johnny Sample: 'I'll Break Them in Half If I Have To,'" *Sport* (January 1967): 75; James Bylin, "The Radical Idea of Democracy in Football," *Wall Street Journal* (November 20, 1972): 20. Mann's columns on ecology ran in the *Washington Daily News*, July 7–9, 1971. The Kiki Levathes series ran in the *Star* December 13–17, 1971.

26. Joseph Kraft, "Daley and Police Have a Point in Claiming Press Is Biased," *Washington Post* (September 3, 1968): A11; Glenn Dickey, "World Series: Just Like Second Coming," *San Francisco Chronicle* (October 24, 1972): 46; Glenn Dickey, "When Sport Ceases to Be Fun," *San Francisco Chronicle* (October 30, 1972): 50; Hal Lebovitz, "Is 'Sportswriter' a Dirty Word?" *Cleveland Plain Dealer* (December 3, 1970): 2F; Jack Mann, "The Thinking Fan's Guide to Sport Writers," *Washington Daily News* (February 4, 1971): 66; Jack Mann, "They Watch Out for Bass When He Puts the Pads On," *Washington Daily News* (July 26, 1971): 55; Ira Berkow, *Full Swing: Hits, Runs, and Errors in a Writer's Life* (Chicago: Ivan R. Dee, 2006), 116.

27. Letter from John Pyne, *Washington Post* (June 20, 1972): A19; Mann, "They Watch Out for Bass"; Jack Mann, "Of Fans and Sophistry, Relevance and Writers," *Washington Daily News* (August 6, 1971): 75; Jack Mann, "Unfortunately, the Silent Majority's Serious Again," *Washington Daily News* (August 9, 1971): 54; Dave McKenna, "Fanfare for the Uncommon Man," *Washington City Paper* (March 17, 2000); Alex Belth, "The Elements of Style," *Bronx*

Banter (June 7, 2011), http://www.bronxbanterblog.com/2011/06/07/the-yellow-pages
-you-could-look-it-up/; Alex Belth, "Mann, Oh Mann," *Bronx Banter* (June 15, 2011), http://
www.bronxbanterblog.com/2011/06/15/mann-oh-mann-2/; Kenneth Denlinger, "Please,
the Mann Has Something to Say," *Washington Post* (August 12, 1971): C1.

28. Jack Mann, *The Decline and Fall of the New York Yankees* (New York: Simon & Schuster,
1967), 49; Randall Poe, "The Writing of Sports," *Esquire* (October 1974): 175; Shecter
quoted in Alex Belth, "The Flower of America," *Bronx Banter* (July 1, 2013), http://www
.bronxbanterblog.com/2013/07/01/bgs-the-flower-of-america/; Sean Deveney, *Fun City:
John Lindsay, Joe Namath, and How Sports Saved New York in the 1960s* (New York: Sports
Publishing, 2015), 75.

29. Edwin Pope, "Super-ficials Call the Plays for Those Who Come to Super," *Miami Herald*
(January 14, 1967): D1; Izenberg, *The Rivals,* 105, 17, 133; *The New York Times at the Super
Bowl,* ed. Leonard Koppett (New York: Quadrangle, 1974), 35, 79.

30. *The New York Times at the Super Bowl,* 285, 330, 331; Marty Ralbovsky, *Super Bowl:
Of Men, Myths, and Moments* (New York: Hawthorne, 1971), xiii, xiv; Michael Roberts,
Fans! How We Go Crazy Over Sports (Washington, D.C.: New Republic, 1976), xiv; Robert
Lipsyte, "It's Only a Game?" *New York Times* (January 16, 1971): 20; Wells Twombly, "Silly
Putty," *San Francisco Examiner* (January 18, 1971): 49; Memo from David Parker to Pat
Buchanan, October 2, 1972; folder Football 1/1/72, Box 5, White House Central Files:
Recreation—Sports; Richard Nixon Presidential Library and Museum, Yorba Linda, Calif.

31. *The New York Times at the Super Bowl,* 311; Roger Angell, "Super," *The New Yorker*
(February 11, 1974): 43, 44, 60, 68.

32. Hunter S. Thompson, "Fear and Loathing at the Super Bowl," *Rolling Stone* (February 13, 1973); Hunter S. Thompson, "Fear and Loathing at the Super Bowl," *Rolling Stone*
(February 28, 1974); Al Stump, "'Super Bowl' or 'Super Bore'?" *TV Guide* (January 12, 1974):
13; review of Leonard Koppett, ed., *The New York Times at the Super Bowl, Library Journal*
(March 1, 1975): 498.

33. Paul Hendrickson, "The Super Bowl and the Boys in the Box," *National Observer*
(January 31, 1976): 1, 15; "As We See It," *TV Guide* (February 7, 1976): A-4.

34. David Shaw, *Journalism Today: A Changing Press for a Changing America* (New York:
Harper's College Press, 1977), 149, 158; Lowrey, "You Can't Tell the Sportswriters," 151;
Letter from Jack Scott, "19th Hole: The Readers Take Over," *Sports Illustrated* (December
21, 1970): 112; Howard McMillen, "Portrait of a Candidate—in the Age of Television," *TV
Guide* (January 18, 1975): 3; Agranoff, *The New Style in Election Campaigns,* 358.

Chapter 5. A Real Coup with the Sports Fans

1. *Berkeley Barb* (January 24–30, 1969): 4.

2. Robert Coughlan, "Success Story of a Vice President," *Life* (December 14, 1953): 151;
Kathleen Hall Jamieson, *Packaging the Presidency: A History and Criticism of Presidential
Campaign Advertising* (New York: Oxford University Press, 1984), 154; "As Bill Leiser Sees
It," *San Francisco Chronicle* (August 19, 1959); folder 8/14/59—Football Writers' Association
of America—All Star Game; Box 112; Pre-Presidential Papers, Appearances, 1948–1962;

Richard Nixon Papers, Richard M. Nixon Presidential Library and Museum, Yorba Linda, Calif.; Richard Nixon, *In the Arena* (New York: Simon & Schuster, 1990), 104.

3. Michael Oriard, *Bowled Over: Big-Time College Football from the Sixties to the BCS Era* (Chapel Hill: University of North Carolina Press, 2009), 30; Murray Ross, "Football Red and Baseball Green: The Heroics and Bucolics of American Sport," *Chicago Review* (January–February 1971): 38; Richard Nixon, *RN: The Memoirs of Richard Nixon* (New York: Grosset & Dunlap, 1978), 541; Art Buchwald, "Games Presidents Play," *Los Angeles Times* (January 9, 1972): H1; David Greenberg, *Nixon's Shadow* (New York: W.W. Norton, 2003), xxvii.

4. Bruce Mazlish, "Toward a Psychohistorical Inquiry: The 'Real' Richard Nixon," *Journal of Interdisciplinary History* (Autumn 1970): 67; David Abrahamsen, *Nixon vs. Nixon: An Emotional Tragedy* (New York: Farrar, Straus, and Giroux, 1977), 93–97; Richard Dougherty, *Goodbye, Mr. Christian: A Personal Account of McGovern's Rise and Fall* (Garden City, N.Y.: Doubleday, 1973), 145–46; Philip Roth, *Our Gang* (New York: Bantam, 1971), 24–25.

5. Hunter S. Thompson, *The Great Shark Hunt* (New York: Summit Books, 1979), 190, 191; Dick Schaap, "Will Richard Nixon Trip Over Himself Again on His Way to Victory?" *New York* (June 10, 1968): 26; Stewart Alsop, "Nixon and the Square Majority: Is the Fox a Lion?" *Atlantic* (February 1972); James Reston, "Washington: Why Mr. Nixon Goes to the Football Games," *New York Times* (December 7, 1969): 10; Frank Walsh to John Whitaker, May 25, 1968; Campaign 1968 Collection, Nixon Papers.

6. Iwan Morgan, "Nixon Biographies," in *A Companion to Richard Nixon,* ed. Melvin Small (Malden, Mass.: Wiley-Blackwell, 2011), 7; Robert Mason, "Political Realignment," in *A Companion to Richard Nixon,* ed. Melvin Small (Chichester, U.K.: Wiley-Blackwell, 2011), 266; Robert Mason, *Richard Nixon and the Quest for a New Majority* (Chapel Hill: University of North Carolina Press, 2004), 96–99, 41.

7. The phrase is Walter Dean Burnham's, quoted in Joel Silbey, Allan G. Bogue, and William H. Flanigan, Introduction to Part One, *The History of American Electoral Behavior* (Princeton, N.J.: Princeton University Press, 1978), 34; Joseph Kraft, "Daley and Police Have a Point in Claiming Press Is Biased," *Washington Post* (September 3, 1968): A11; "Revolt of the Middle Class," *U.S. News and World Report* (November 24, 1969): 56, 53; Pete Hamill, "The Revolt of the White Lower Middle Class," *New York* (April 14, 1969).

8. The standard account holds that as Haggard's band passed a sign pointing to Muskogee as it toured the Southwest, someone on the bus mused that nobody there smoked pot—while passing around a joint. Or that Haggard heard evangelist Garner Ted Armstrong preaching *The World Tomorrow* on the radio, noted a line about small southern colleges' failure to erupt, and added the line about football. Haggard further muddied the waters by counting "about 18 different meanings in that song" and telling interviewers that "barefooted bums" would probably resent how accurately it portrayed them: "What do they have to offer humanity?" David Cantwell, *Merle Haggard: The Running Kind* (Austin: University of Texas Press, 2013), 145–58.

9. Richard Lemon, *The Troubled American* (New York: Simon & Schuster, 1970), 13, 28, 101, 147; Champ Clark, "The Mystique of Pro Football," *Time* (November 9, 1970); Arthur Schlesinger, "The Amazing Success Story of 'Spiro Who?'" *New York Times Book Review* (June 26, 1970).

10. Harry Dent to Dwight Chapin and Bob Haldeman, October 6, 1969; folder Football 10/1/1969, Box 5, White House Central Files: Recreation—Sports; Nixon Papers; Roy Reed, "In the South, Football Is a Religio-Social Pastime," *New York Times* (October 6, 1969): 34; Harry Dent, *The Prodigal South Returns to Power* (New York: John Wiley & Sons, 1978), 6; Joseph Crespino, *Strom Thurmond's America* (New York: Hill & Wang, 2012), 148, 231, 232; Art Buchwald, "Yeah, Team, Fight for Good Old You-Know-Who!" *Los Angeles Times* (September 23, 1969): A7; Leah Wright Rigueur, *The Loneliness of the Black Republican* (Princeton, N.J.: Princeton University Press, 2015), 165.

11. C. J. Schexnayder, "The Big Shootout: The Documentary of the 1969 Texas-Arkansas Game," *SB Nation* (April 9, 2013), http://www.footballstudyhall.com/college-football-history/2013/4/9/4202864/the-big-shootout-the-documentary-of-the-1969-texas-vs-arkansas-game; Memorandum from H. S. Wagner to James Josendale, December 4, 1969; folder Fayetteville, Arkansas, to attend the football game between the University of Texas and the University of Arkansas 12/6/1969, Box 32, White House Central Files: Subject Files: Trips; Nixon Papers.

12. Memorandum for John Ehrlichman, Dwight Chapin, et al., December 5, 1969; Telegram from Earl (Red) Blaik to Richard Nixon, December 9, 1969; both in folder Football 10/1/1969, Box 5, White House Central Files: Recreation—Sports; Nixon Papers; Terry Frei, *Horns, Hogs & Nixon Coming: Texas v. Arkansas in Dixie's Last Stand* (New York: Simon & Schuster, 2002), 247; "Remarks During a Television Interview in Fayetteville, Arkansas. December 6, 1969," *Public Papers of the Presidents of the United States: Richard M. Nixon, 1969* (Washington, D.C.: Government Printing Office, 1971), 996–98; H. R. Haldeman, *The Haldeman Diaries* (New York: G. P. Putnam, 1994), 113.

13. Telegram from Raymond Shafer to Richard Nixon, December 5, 1969; Telegram from Norbert Tiemann to Richard Nixon, December 6, 1969; Memorandum for John Ehrlichman from J. Bruce Whelihan, December 6, 1969; all in folder Football 10/1/1969, Box 5, White House Central Files: Recreation—Sports; Nixon Papers; John Brutzman, "Fans' Fury Forces Presidential Punt," *Centre Daily Times* (December 6, 1969): 1; Shirley Povich, "A Plaque on Both Your Houses," *Washington Post* (December 9, 1969): D1.

14. Letter from John Riener to Richard Nixon, December 5, 1969; Letter from J. W. Lindsey to Richard Nixon, December 8, 1969; Letter from Patriotic Citizens of Central Pennsylvania to Richard Nixon, December 10, 1969; Letter from Charles Kalinoski to Richard Nixon, December 7, 1969; Note from E. R. Thorpe to Ron Ziegler, December 6, 1969; all in folder Football 10/1/1969, Box 5, White House Central Files: Recreation—Sports; Nixon Papers; Neil Amdur, "Survey Indicates Athletic Programs Face Demanding Test in Fall," *New York Times* (May 24, 1970): S5; Joe Paterno, Penn State commencement speech, June 16, 1973, https://pennstatermag.files.wordpress.com/2012/01/paterno1973commencementspeech.pdf.

15. Jack Patterson, "Bucks Borrow Michigan Play," *Akron Beacon Journal* (November 22, 1970): B3; Memo from Ann Morgan to Patrick Buchanan, January 6, 1971; memo from Patrick Buchanan to H. R. Haldeman, January 6, 1971; Letter from Ray Price to Bruce Kehrli, January 7, 1971; folder Football 1/1/1971, Box 5, White House Central Files: Recreation—Sports; Nixon Papers.

16. Charles DeBenedetti, *An American Ordeal: The Antiwar Movement of the Vietnam Era* (Syracuse, N.Y.: Syracuse University Press, 1990), 248; Tom Wells, *The War Within: America's Battle Over Vietnam* (Berkeley: University of California Press, 1994), 352, 354, 372; Melvin Small, *Covering Dissent: The Media and the Anti-Vietnam War Movement* (New Brunswick, N.J.: Rutgers University Press, 1994), 93, 95, 96, 98; "Mr. Nixon in Trouble," *Newsweek* (October 13, 1969): 30.

17. Wells, *The War Within*, 375–77; Small, *Covering Dissent*, 104–5.

18. Herbert Klein, *Making It Perfectly Clear* (Garden City, N.Y.: Doubleday, 1980), 107; Memo from Herbert Klein to Richard Nixon, October 8, 1969; folder Football 10/1/1969, Box 5, White House Central Files: Recreation—Sports; Nixon Papers; *Miami News* (October 6, 1969): 1; *Miami Herald* (October 5, 1969): 2.

19. Wells, *The War Within*, 382–83, 385, 387; Memo from Alexander Butterfield to Dwight Chapin, November 19, 1969; Memo from Hugh Sloan to Haldeman, November 26, 1969; both in folder Football 10/1/1969, Box 5, White House Central Files: Recreation—Sports; Nixon Papers; the photograph appears in *Princeton Alumni Weekly* (November 25, 1969): 13; Henry Kissinger, *White House Years* (New York: Simon & Schuster, 2011), 337.

20. Small, *Covering Dissent*, 114, 116–26; Haldeman, *Haldeman Diaries*, 108; Murray Marder, "White House: A Display of Normality," *Washington Post* (November 16, 1969): A1, A18; "Secluded Nixon Talks Football," *San Francisco Sunday Examiner & Chronicle* (November 16, 1969): A19; Raymond Price, *With Nixon* (New York: Viking Press, 1977), 157; President Richard Nixon's Daily Diary, November 15, 1969, http://www.nixonlibrary.gov/virtual library/documents/PDD/1969/017%20November%201–15%201969.pdf; Dan Jenkins, "Ohio State: Alone at the Top," in *Woody Hayes: The Man & His Dynasty*, ed. Mike Bynum (Birmingham: Gridiron Football Properties, 1991), 72; Art Buchwald, "How Ball Bounces Worth a TV Look," *Washington Post* (November 20, 1969): A21; Tom Dowling, *Coach: A Season with Lombardi* (New York: W.W. Norton, 1970), 244, 250–51; Dave Brady, "Jerry Smith Admits He Bombed As Soldier," *Washington Post* (November 21, 1969): D1.

21. "No," *Washington Post* (November 18, 1969): A22; Walter Hickel, *Who Owns America?* (Englewood Cliffs, N.J.: Prentice-Hall, 1971), 227–28; Dan Rottenberg, "Richard M. Nixon Dead at 84; U.S. President in Early War Years," *The Washingtonian* (December 1970): 16; Thomas Edwards, "The Sporting Gripe," *Partisan Review* 28, 3 (1971): 331; Art Buchwald, "Who Said, 'Why Can't Timahoe Be More Like Checkers?'" *Washington Post* (March 31, 1974): L1. Daniel Ellsberg recalled that, whenever he gave speeches about this moment in time, "everybody remembers the football game. It was very effective." Clara Bingham, *Witness to the Revolution* (New York: Random House, 2017), 200.

22. Mason, "Political Realignment," 254; Mason, *Richard Nixon and the Quest for a New Majority*, 50, 46; Wright Rigueur, *The Loneliness of the Black Republican*, 169.

23. Geoffrey Kabaservice, *Rule and Ruin: The Downfall of Moderation and the Destruction of the Republican Party, from Eisenhower to the Tea Party* (New York: Oxford University Press, 2012), 296, 302–5.

24. Melvin Small, *At the Water's Edge: American Politics and the Vietnam War* (Chicago: Ivan R. Dee, 2005), 160; Stephen Ambrose, *Nixon: The Triumph of a Politician* (New York: Simon & Schuster, 1987), 392; Nixon, *RN*, 200; Wells, *The War Within*, 459; R. W. Apple,

"Nixon Guides Republicans on Senate Races, Recruiting a Slate Aimed at Gaining Control of Chamber," *New York Times* (April 6, 1970): 12; "At the Campaign Kickoff—Strategies of Both Parties," *U.S. News and World Report* (September 14, 1970): 19.

25. Robert Lipsyte, "Changing Seasons," *New York Times* (August 10, 1970): 41; Memorandum for Dwight Chapin, August 10, 1970; Memo from Dwight Chapin to Hugh Sloan, August 26, 1970; Memo from Bud Wilkinson to Hugh Sloan, September 9, 1970; Letter, Roger Ailes to Dwight Chapin, August 27, 1970; Memo from Harry Dent to Dwight Chapin, October 6, 1970; all in folder Football 10/1/69, Box 5; White House Central Files: Subject Files: Recreation—Sports: Football; Nixon Papers; John Carmody, "You Can't Take the Football Out of Wilkinson," *Washington Post* (October 25, 1970).

26. All scheduling and travel information taken from the President's Daily Diary. Memo from Herb Klein to the President, December 7, 1970, folder Football 10/1/69; Memo from Ronald Walker to H. R. Haldeman, January 4, 1971, folder Football 1/1/71–12/20/72; Nixon Papers.

27. Letter, James McCain to Bob Dole, June 24, 1970; Memo from Dwight Chapin to Hugh Sloan, August 3, 1970; Memo from Dwight Chapin to Murray Chotiner, August 21, 1970; telephone call, August 28, 1970; folder Manhattan, Kansas-Kansas State University, Ahearn Fieldhouse 9/16/1970; Box 43; White House Central Files: Subject Files: Trips; Nixon Papers.

28. "Nixon: The Pursuit of Peace and Politics," *Time* (September 28, 1970): 6; Ernest V. Murphy IIII, "University Readies for Nixon Visit," *Kansas State Collegian* (September 14, 1970): 1; Mike Moffet, "KSU Meets Nixon on 'Black Wednesday,'" *Daily Kansan* (September 16, 1970): 12; Rusty Monhollon, *"This Is America?": The Sixties in Lawrence, Kansas* (New York: Palgrave, 2002), 182; Joel Rhodes, *The Voice of Violence: Performative Violence as Protest in the Vietnam Era* (Westport, Ct.: Greenwood Publishing Group, 2001), 62–72; Tom Blackburn, "'Cow Town' Expresses Soft Spoken Dissent," *Kansas State Collegian* (November 12, 1969): 5; Ed Taylor, "Research Indicates Warm Nixon Reception," *Kansas State Collegian* (September 15, 1970): 3.

29. Ralph Gage, "Manhattan or Manhatten—Purple Pride Shows," *Lawrence Daily Journal-World* (September 17, 1970): 1; Photograph of banner in *Daily Kansan* (September 17, 1970): 1; Richard Nixon: "Address in the Alfred M. Landon Lecture Series at Kansas State University," September 16, 1970. Online by Gerhard Peters and John T. Woolley, *The American Presidency Project*, http://www.presidency.ucsb.edu/ws/?pid=2663.

30. Sandy Padwe, "Big-Time College Football Is on the Skids," *Look* (September 22, 1970): 69; Glen Iversen, "Vince Gibson's Reign: A Long Walk Over Water," *Kansas State Collegian* (October 3, 1969): 2A; "Big Eight Places Kansas, Kansas State on Probation," *Joplin Globe* (October 8, 1970): C1.

31. Nixon, "Address in the Alfred M. Landon Lecture Series"; Spiro Agnew, *The Real Spiro Agnew: Commonsense Quotations of a Household Word* (Gretna, La.: Pelican Publishing, 1970), 49.

32. "Roaring Throng Hears Nixon," *Kansas State Collegian* (September 17, 1970): 1; "Nixon: The Pursuit of Peace and Politics"; Dick Haines, "The Day the President Came . . .," *K-Stater* (October 1970): 5; Ray Morgan, "Roar of Nixon Support Drowns Shouts of Protest," *Kansas*

City Times (September 17, 1970): 1A, 12A, "Reactions Surface After Nixon Leaves," *Kansas State Collegian* (September 17, 1970): 1.

33. "Nixon's Kansas Visit," *Lawrence Journal-World* (September 17, 1970): 4; Robert Wuthnow, *Red State Religion: Faith and Politics in America's Heartland* (Princeton, N.J.: Princeton University Press, 2012), 250; Thurston Clarke, *The Last Campaign: Robert F. Kennedy and 82 Days That Inspired America* (New York: Macmillan, 2008), 47; Sandy Flickner, "We Were Used—Exactly as Planned," *Kansas State Collegian* (September 17, 1970): 4; Frank "Klorox" Cleveland, "Country Dick Wins Game," *Kansas State Collegian* (September 18, 1970): 4.

34. Ron Fimrite, "First a Winning Season, Then to the Barricades," *San Francisco Chronicle* (September 17, 1970): 66; "A Pep Rally in Kansas," *Kansas State Collegian* (September 21, 1970): 2; "Making the Most of the President's Visit," *Oberlin Herald* (September 24, 1970); "Cup Runneth Over," *Larned Daily Tiller & Toiler* (September 21, 1970); "President Welcome," *Liberal Southwest Daily Times* (September 21, 1970); all in James C. Carey papers, Box 6, Folder 1, Morse Department of Special Collections, Kansas State University Libraries; Haldeman, *Haldeman Diaries*, 193, 194; Ambrose, *Nixon: The Triumph of a Politician,* 377; Letter from James McCain to Richard Nixon, September 22, 1970; folder Manhattan, Kansas-Kansas State University, Ahearn Fieldhouse 9/16/1970; Box 43; White House Central Files: Subject Files: Trips; Nixon Papers; Sally Brownlee, "Congratulatory Messages Pour In," *Kansas State Collegian* (September 28, 1970): 3.

35. John Osborne, *The Second Year of the Nixon Watch* (New York: Liveright, 1971), 163; "Nixon's Last-Minute Push for a Republican Victory," *U.S. News and World Report* (November 2, 1970): 20.

36. "Nixon News 'Overwhelms' Starr," *Appleton Post-Crescent* (October 13, 1970): B12; James McCulla, "6,000 Cheer Starr, Nixon," *Milwaukee Journal* (October 18, 1970): 22; "Remarks at a Testimonial Reception in Honor of Green Bay Packers Quarterback Bart Starr," *Public Papers of the Presidents of the United States: Richard M. Nixon, 1970* (Washington, D.C.: Government Printing Office, 1971), 873; Frank Church, "President Lauds Starr," *Appleton Post-Crescent* (October 18, 1970): 1; Gordon Randolph, "Nixon Plugs State Ticket," *Milwaukee Journal* (October 18, 1970): 1; Belman Morin, "Nixon Mixes Plays for Gains," *Portsmouth Times* (February 21, 1968): 30.

37. "Statement on the Death of Football Coach Vincent T. Lombardi. September 3, 1970," "Toast of the President at a Dinner Honoring Labor Leaders. September 7, 1970," *Public Papers of the Presidents: Richard M. Nixon, 1970,* 699, 698, 711; Jules Witcover, "Nixon Campaigning Like a Head Coach," *Los Angeles Times* (October 26, 1970): 19; Jules Witcover, *White Knight: The Rise of Spiro Agnew* (New York: Random House, 1972), 359; Russell Baker, "The Democrat in the White House," *New York Times* (October 27, 1970): 45; Jules Witcover, *Very Strange Bedfellows: The Short and Unhappy Marriage of Richard Nixon and Spiro Agnew* (New York: PublicAffairs, 2007), 114; Art Buchwald, "Political Football Has Already Started," *Lawrence Journal-World* (September 17, 1970): 4.

38. "Famous Rex," photograph in *Ohio State Lantern* (October 20, 1970): 9; "Woody Hayes Joins Appeal for Victory," *Bryan Times* (October 20, 1970): 1, 2; "Remarks in the Ohio State House, Columbus, Ohio. October 19, 1970," *Public Papers of the Presidents of the United States: Richard M. Nixon, 1970,* 878; Haldeman, *Haldeman Diaries,* 202–4; "Surprise

Visit Stuns Students," *Ohio State Lantern* (October 20, 1970): 1; Carroll Kilpatrick, "Nixon Says It's Time to Draw Line," *Washington Post* (October 20, 1970): A4.

39. "Remarks in the Ohio State House, Columbus, Ohio. October 19, 1970," 881.

40. In 1968, both sides bought two minutes on NFL football on CBS, and Nixon bought twenty-eight on regional NFL broadcasts as well; Humphrey purchased three minutes on NBC's AFL broadcasts. Joseph Napolitan, *The Election Game and How to Win It* (Garden City, N.Y.: Doubleday, 1972), 57–58, 59.

41. Small, *At the Water's Edge,* 161; "Remarks About the 1970 Elections. November 1, 1970," *Public Papers of the Presidents of the United States: Richard M. Nixon, 1970,* 1063–64; Jeb Stuart Magruder, *An American Life: One Man's Road to Watergate* (New York: Athenaeum, 1974), 129; Shirley Povich, "This Morning . . .," *Washington Post* (November 1, 1970): C1; Kiki Levathes, "The Lingering Guest and Why He Stays," *Washington Star* (December 15, 1971): E1; Don Oberdorfer, "Both Parties Plan TV Ads at Halftime," *Washington Post* (October 30, 1970): A11; Art Buchwald, "Nixon Thrown for a Loss as He Mixes Football, Politics," *Los Angeles Times* (November 8, 1970): E7.

42. Witcover, *White Knight,* 355, 393; *Survey of Broadcast Journalism 1970–1971: A State of Siege,* ed. Marvin Barrett (New York: Grosset & Dunlap, 1971), 50; "The Nation: A Campaign Retrospective," *Ripon Forum* (December 1970): 3, 4; Buchwald, "Nixon Thrown for a Loss"; Haldeman, *Haldeman Diaries,* 207; Mason, *Richard Nixon and the Quest for a New Majority,* 110–12; Tom Wicker, "Not Quite a Field Goal," *New York Times* (November 10, 1970): 47.

43. John Egerton, *The Americanization of Dixie: The Southernization of America* (New York: Harper's Magazine Press, 1974), 179; Dominic Sandbrook, *Mad as Hell: The Crisis of the 1970s and the Rise of the Populist Right* (New York: Knopf, 2011), 58–59; William Safire, *Before the Fall: An Inside View of the pre-Watergate White House* (Garden City, N.Y.: Doubleday, 1975), 561–62; Ruy Teixeira and Alan Abramowitz, "The Decline of the White Working Class and the Rise of a Mass Upper Middle Class," Brookings Institution Working Paper (April 2008), https://www.brookings.edu/wp-content/uploads/2016/06/04_demographics_teixeira.pdf. Nixon won 52 percent of the Catholic vote in 1972.

44. Wright Rigueur, *The Loneliness of the Black Republican,* 163, 190, 193; Memo from Dwight Chapin to H. R. Haldeman, September 29, 1972; Robert Brown, Schedule Proposal, September 14, 1972; all in folder Football 1/1/72, Nixon Papers; Victor Gold, *I Don't Need You When I'm Right: The Confessions of a Washington PR Man* (New York: Morrow, 1975), 150; Letter to Ronald Reagan, July 21, 1972, Magruder files, Nixon Papers; Memorandum from Stanley Scott, August 10, 1972; Box 18, folder Presidential Meetings, 1971–1975 (1), Stanley Scott Papers, Gerald R. Ford Presidential Library and Museum, Ann Arbor, Mich.; Dean Kotlowski, *Nixon's Civil Rights: Politics, Principle, and Policy* (Cambridge, Mass.: Harvard University Press, 2002), 184; "Black Stars for Nixon Denounced," *Washington Post* (October 18, 1972): A15; "Did They Have the Right—Analyzing the Blacks Who Endorsed Nixon," *Black Business Digest* (January 1973): 34–38.

45. Wright Rigueur, *The Loneliness of the Black Republican,* 193; Alsop, "Nixon and the Square Majority"; Robert Lipsyte, "Of Sports, Comebacks, and Nixon," *New York Times* (May 1, 1994): S11.

Chapter 6. I Really Believed in the Man

1. The item ran in the *Charleston Gazette* (August 10, 1972): 8A, just after announcement of Huff's membership in Democrats for Nixon.

2. Victor Gold, *I Don't Need You When I'm Right: The Confessions of a Washington PR Man* (New York: Morrow, 1975), 149; Robert Walters, "John Wilbur: Pro McGovern," *Washington Star* (June 4, 1972): C8; Frank Mankiewicz Oral History interview, RFK #5, October 2, 1969, http://www.jfklibrary.org/Asset-Viewer/Archives/RFKOH-FM-05.aspx, 71; Robert Lipsyte, "The Teammates," *New York Times* (June 8, 1968): 34; Memo from Cy Laughter to Bud Wilkinson, April 10, 1969; Laughter files, Richard Nixon Papers, Richard M. Nixon Presidential Library and Museum, Yorba Linda, Calif.; Kenneth Denlinger, "Candidates Woo Athletes," *Washington Post* (October 14, 1972): C3; Athletes for Nixon brochure, Campaign 1968 Files, Nixon Papers.

3. Thurston Clarke, *The Last Campaign: Robert F. Kennedy and 82 Days that Inspired America* (New York: Macmillan, 2008), 29, 272–73; Frank Gifford and Harry Waters, *The Whole Ten Yards* (New York: Random House, 1993), 263; Evan Thomas, *Robert Kennedy: His Life* (New York: Simon & Schuster, 2013), 180–81; Rafer Johnson, Oral History Interview, May 13, 1969, 31, 32, John F. Kennedy Papers, John F. Kennedy Presidential Library and Museum, Boston, Mass.; Peter Schweizer and Rochelle Schweizer, *The Bushes: Portrait of a Dynasty* (New York: Doubleday, 2004), 497.

4. Gloster Current, "Why Nixon Lost the Negro Vote," *Crisis* (January 1961): 8.

5. Letter from Cy Laughter, October 18, 1960; letter from Cy Laughter, October 24, 1960; both in Drown Collection; letter from Frank Walsh to John Whitaker, May 25, 1968; 1968 campaign files; Athletes for Nixon brochure; Athletes Who Have Joined With Dick Nixon; both in Campaign 1968 collection; Nixon Papers; "Athletes for Nixon Group Organized," *Washington Post* (July 13, 1968): A2; Gold, *I Don't Need You When I'm Right*, 149; Richard Nixon: "Address Accepting the Presidential Nomination at the Republican National Convention in Miami Beach, Florida," August 8, 1968. Online by Gerhard Peters and John T. Woolley, *The American Presidency Project,* http://www.presidency.ucsb.edu/ws/?pid=25968.

6. Lewis Gould, *1968: The Election That Changed America* (Chicago: Ivan R. Dee, 2010), 81; Dominic Sandbrook, *Eugene McCarthy: The Rise and Fall of Postwar American Liberalism* (New York: Knopf, 2004), 192; Robert Lipsyte, "The Line-Ups," *New York Times* (August 5, 1968): 51; Michael A. Cohen, *American Maelstrom: The 1968 Election and the Politics of Division* (New York: Oxford University Press, 2016), 54, 151, 154; "Committee of Athletes for McCarthy Is Formed," July 18, 1968, 1968 Presidential Campaign, National Files, Box 28, Eugene McCarthy Papers, Elmer L. Andersen Library, University of Minnesota, Minneapolis.

7. Lipsyte, "The Teammates"; Memo from Jim Fowler to David Rosenbloom, March 29, 1968; RFK Campaign Files, 1968; JFK Library; Johnson Oral History Interview, 45; Rosey Grier, *Rosey, an Autobiography: The Gentle Giant* (Tulsa, Okla.: Honor Books, 1986), 196–99, 201, 206, 239.

8. Press Release, October 13, 1968; memo for Julie Cahn from Hubert Humphrey, May 2, 1968; memo for Bob Short from Hubert Humphrey, July 9, 1968; memo from Julie Cahn to Mel Klein, July 17, 1968; all in 1968 Presidential Campaign Files, Series 2: Citizens for

Humphrey: Sports; Hubert H. Humphrey Papers, Minnesota Historical Society; Douglas Hartmann, *Race, Culture, and the Revolt of the Black Athlete: The 1968 Olympic Protests and Their Aftermath* (Chicago: University of Chicago Press, 2003), 137; Carl Solberg, *Hubert Humphrey: A Biography* (New York: W.W. Norton, 1984), 38, 68–69; Edgar Berman, *Hubert: The Triumph and Tragedy of the Humphrey I Knew* (New York: G.P. Putnam's Sons, 1979), 85.

9. Memo from Bob Short for Hubert Humphrey, July 11, 1968; memo from Win Griffith to John Stewart, July 22, 1968; Julius Cahn to Joseph Shosid, August 20, 1968; Humphrey Papers; Simeon Booker, "How Candidates Battle for Black Votes," *Jet* (July 25, 1968): 15; Harry Edwards, *The Revolt of the Black Athlete* (New York: Free Press, 1969), photo insert.

10. Rob Parker to Wayne Phillips, May 29, 1968; memo from Julius Cahn to Hubert Humphrey, June 7, 1968; "Athletes for Rockefeller," n.d.; memo from Roger Waldman to Julius Cahn, July 9, 1968; memo from John Waxman, August 1, 1968; telegram to Bill Burgish, June 21, 1968; Lloyd Jordan to Robert Short, August 16, 1968; Bill Lewis to Robert Short, August 13, 1968; Humphrey Papers.

11. Night Wire to David "Sonny" Werblin, May 18, 1968; telegram from Robert Short, July 9, 1968; telegram from Robert Short, August 8, 1968; Julius Cahn to Rafer Johnson, September 17, 1968; Humphrey Papers.

12. Report on Sports, August 6, 1968; Gerald Phipps to Mel Kline, July 22, 1968; Michael Goodman to Mel Klein, August 15, 1968; Humphrey Papers; Mark Kram, "This Man Fired Flipper," *Sports Illustrated* (December 15, 1969); Bob Oates, "How to Succeed in NFL," *Los Angeles Times* (January 14, 1972): F1, F7; Robert Herron, "What Is Joe Robbie's Real Game?" *Biography News* (October 1974): 1189.

13. Telegram from Larry Doby; telegram from Lance Alworth, John Hadl, and Speedy Duncan; telegram from Len Dawson; Memo from Julius Cahn to Jack Harris, August 5, 1968; Memo from Ted Rodgers to Julie Cahn, August 2, 1968; Ted Rodgers to Mrs. John McGee, August 29, 1968; Humphrey Papers.

14. Letter from Robert Short, July 29, 1968; handwritten notes, August 1968; Jack Harris to Phil Bengtson, August 19, 1968; telegrams from Citizens from Humphrey-Muskie to Bob Gibson and Orlando Cepeda, October 9, 1968; Humphrey Papers.

15. Gordon Weil, "Politicians' Scramble for Support Exhausts Supply of Celebrities," *Wall Street Journal* (August 1, 1968): 1; Call Log, 8/1–2/1968, Humphrey Papers; Gordon Martin, "Motor Sports Fans—In an Election Year," *San Francisco Chronicle* (November 7, 1972): 48; "President Re-Election Office Open," *Sarasota Journal* (July 2, 1971): 11-A; Tom Huth, "Black Church School in Florida Is Political Stalking Ground," *Washington Post* (March 14, 1972): A2; "SBA Mismanagement Charges," *CQ Almanac 1973,* http://library .cqpress.com/cqalmanac/document.php?id=cqal73–1228208; "Blacks' Role in Watergate Comes Under Investigation," *Jet* (December 13, 1973): 28–29; "House Unit Told of Nudge on SBA Loan," *Los Angeles Times* (November 27, 1973): 2.

16. Christopher Lydon, "Celebrities Rally Behind McGovern," *New York Times* (April 2, 1972): 28; Shirley MacLaine, *You Can Get There From Here* (New York: Norton, 1975), 64; Gary Hart, *Right From the Start: A Chronicle of the McGovern Campaign* (New York: Quadrangle, 1973), 19, 183.

17. Interview with Ray Schoenke, April 21, 2016.

18. Richard Dougherty, *Goodbye, Mr. Christian: A Personal Account of McGovern's Rise and Fall* (Garden City, N.Y.: Doubleday, 1973), 58; Stephen Ambrose, *The Wild Blue: The Men and Boys Who Flew the B-24s Over Germany* (New York: Simon & Schuster, 2001), 77; "McGovern Produces War Record," *Washington Post* (June 18, 1972): A23; Schoenke interview; Walters, "John Wilbur: Pro McGovern"; "Dallas Cowboys Join Washington Redskins in Athletes for McGovern," Press Release, October 30, 1972, George McGovern Papers, Seeley G. Mudd Manuscript Library, Princeton University, Princeton, N.J.

19. Schoenke interview; Kenneth Turan, "Ray Schoenke: Busy Being Involved," *Washington Post* (May 21, 1972): C4; Lydon, "Celebrities Rally Behind McGovern"; George Solomon, "Brundige: 'Frog' Turned Tiger," *Washington Post* (November 8, 1972): C3; Ira Berkow, "Redskins' Lineman Shows Courage of His Convictions," *Hendersonville Times-News* (November 1, 1972): 13; John Carmody, "'Grassroots' Fair for McGovern," *Washington Post* (June 12, 1972): B2; "A Families for McGovern Picnic," *Washington Star* (June 9, 1972): E4; Bill Grady, "Rally Speaker Urges 'Stand Up for McGovern,'" *Frederick News* (April 18, 1972): A1; "Heading South," *Aiken Standard* (October 19, 1972): 3A.

20. Charlie Smith, "Chiefs' Stars Help George Do It," *Beaver County Times* (July 12, 1972): D2; Jeannie Morris, "Pro Football Players Take Political Sides," *Dubuque Telegraph-Herald* (October 8, 1972): 30; Barry Dunnegan, "Podolak Speaks for McGovern," *Oskaloosa Daily Herald* (October 17, 1972): 1; Lydon, "Celebrities Rally Behind McGovern"; "Ed Stumping Makes Store Edgy," *Lawrence Journal-World* (October 17, 1972): 11; Bill Richardson, "Podolak on McGovern's Team," *Kansas City Times* (July 19, 1972): 37; Denlinger, "Candidates Woo Athletes"; Paul Kaplan, "McGovern Won't Coach," *Washington Star* (September 1, 1972): E4.

21. Art Buchwald, "Halftime at the Ballot Bowl," *Los Angeles Times* (October 1, 1972): E3; Amy Argetsinger, "Against Long Odds, Ex-Redskin Is Ready to Challenge Glendening," *Washington Post* (January 19, 1998); Dave McKenna, "Political Football," *Washington City Paper* (June 26, 1998); Schoenke interview.

22. Sam Lacy, "Politicians and Their Priorities," *Baltimore Afro-American* (January 18, 1972): 15; Saul Kohler, "Vikings 'Front 4' Joins Humphrey," *Lincoln Sunday Journal & Star* (January 16, 1972): 10A.

23. Memo from Herbert Klein to H. R. Haldeman, November 10, 1971; memo from Jeb Magruder to John Mitchell, April 21, 1972; CREEP Files; letter from Cy Laughter to Richard Nixon, November 22, 1971; Nixon Papers; "Athletes for McGovern," *Government Executive* (July 1972): 11; Ron Ziegler to Jeb Magruder, August 1, 1972; CREEP: Magruder; Nixon Papers; Art Buchwald, "Deee-fense! Deee-fense!" *Washington Post* (January 7, 1973): K1; Walters, "John Wilbur: Pro McGovern."

24. Denlinger, "Candidates Woo Athletes"; "Announcing: Democrats for Nixon," *San Francisco Chronicle* (August 16, 1972): 14; "Sam Huff Deserts for Nixon," *Weirton Daily Times* (August 28, 1972): 4; Martin Nolan, "The Re-Selling of the President," *The Atlantic* (November 1972): 79; Sandy Padwe, "George Allen: Early Bird Who Gets the Win," *Los Angeles Times* (December 24, 1972): C1, C7.

25. Gold, *I Don't Need You When I'm Right*, 82, 123; Bucky Harris, "How to Go Into Politics," *Morgantown Sunday Dominion-Post* (March 1, 1970): 6-D; Bill Utterback, "Former Steeler

Baker Still the Enforcer," *The Coffin Corner* 11, 1 (1989); J. Richard Munro, "Letter from the Publisher," *Sports Illustrated* (December 7, 1970); Hunter S. Thompson, *Fear and Loathing on the Campaign Trail '72* (New York: Simon & Schuster, 2012), 68; Charles Maher, "A Matter of Opinion," *Los Angeles Times* (March 28, 1970): C2; letter from Larry Moskowitz, *Sports Illustrated* (December 21, 1970): 112; Jay Weitzner, president of the Broadcast Placement Company, quoted in *The Political Image Merchants: Strategies for the Seventies,* ed. Ray Hiebert, Robert Jones, John d'Arc Lorenz, and Ernest Lotito (Washington, D.C.: Acropolis Books, 1975), 102–3; "Alumni in Politics," *The Coffin Corner* 5,5 (1983); Stephen Hess, *The Presidential Campaign: an Essay* (Washington, D.C.: Brookings Institution Press, 1988), 106.

26. James Dent, "The Gazetteer," *Charleston Gazette* (June 10, 1968): 19; "Kennedy Raps Religious Issue, Asserts Primary Getting 'Mean,'" *Fairmont Times* (April 19, 1960), http://www.wvculture.org/history/1960presidentialcampaign/newspapers/19600419fairmont times.html; Sam Huff with Leonard Shapiro, *Tough Stuff* (New York: Macmillan, 1989), 214; "Humphrey Will Speak Today," *Fairmont Times-West Virginian* (April 21, 1960), http://www.wvculture.org/history/1960presidentialcampaign/newspapers/19600421fairmont timeswestvirginian.html; "Smith and Cousins on Dinner Program," *Fairmont Times* (April 23, 1960), http://www.wvculture.org/history/1960presidentialcampaign/newspapers/1960 0423fairmonttimes.html; Sportsmen for Kennedy, October 29, 1960, http://www.jfklibrary.org/Asset-Viewer/Archives/JFKCAMP1960–1034–008.aspx; Huff, *Tough Stuff*, 216; M. M. Flatley, "Huff's Friends Rally Around Political Game," *Fairmont Times* (March 31, 1970): 2; Russell Baker, "Observer: On the Southbound Train," *New York Times* (June 11, 1968): 46.

27. "Liberal Demos Want to Unseat Jackson, Byrd," *Lewiston Daily Sun* (August 1, 1969): 13; Herbert Rogers, "Chance of Shooting Down Byrd Slim, Worth Try," *Charleston Gazette* (July 26, 1969): 5; Wesley M. Bagby, "Senator Robert Byrd's Shift to the Right," *Morgantown Dominion-News* (September 9, 1969): 4; Huff, *Tough Stuff*, 213–14, 216; "WVU Professor Confirms Group Encouraging Huff," *Charleston Daily Mail* (January 24, 1970): 10; Steve Guback, "Vision of Senate Dances in Sam's Head While Awaiting Signal from Vince," *Washington Star* (January 21, 1970): B13; "Sam Huff to Decide Which Office to Seek," *Bluefield Daily Telegraph* (February 3, 1970): 8; Mike Whiteford, "Huff Thinks He Can Help West Virginia," *Fairmont Times* (February 9, 1970): 1, 2; "Sam Huff Seeks Congress Post," *Gadsden Times* (February 10, 1970): 8.

28. Robert Byrd, *Child of the Appalachian Coalfields* (Morgantown: University of West Virginia Press, 2005), 275–80; ad in *Weirton Daily Times* (April 22, 1970): 22; Herb Little, "Byrd Enhances Winning Record," *Charleston Daily Mail* (May 15, 1970): 2; Stubby Currence, "Locker-Room Smell," *Bluefield Daily Telegraph* (April 26, 1970): 1; Don Marsh, "It's Much Tougher to Be Huff, the Politician," *Charleston Gazette* (May 9, 1970): 9; Shelby Coffey III, "Political Consultants: Their Tentacles Grow and Grow," *Washington Post* (November 1, 1970): 9, 10; ad from Sam Huff for Congress, *Fairmont Times* (May 12, 1970): 2; Sally Quinn, "Political Yardage," *Washington Post* (March 23, 1970): B3; Bob Mellace, "From One Who Won," *Charleston Daily Mail* (February 27, 1970): 6.

29. Marsh, "It's Much Tougher"; "Bob Mollohan, Byrd Win Easily at Mannington," *Fairmont Times* (May 12, 1970): 14; ad from Sam Huff for Congress, *Fairmont Times* (May 12, 1970): 2; "Mollohan Had Total of 36,225," *Fairmont Times* (May 14, 1970): 2; A. L. Hard-

man, "Huff Doing Public Relations Work," *Charleston Gazette* (January 12, 1959): 8; Huff, *Tough Stuff*, 137–38; William Wallace, "Warp-and-Woof World of Sam Huff," *New York Times* (May 15, 1964); Walter Rugaber, "Union Drive at Stevens Has Wide Import for South," *New York Times* (August 19, 1967): 13; James Gross, *Broken Promise: The Subversion of U.S. Labor Relations* (Philadelphia: Temple University Press, 2010), 177–81; Jeremy Brecher, *Strike!* (Boston: South End Press, 1997), 256.

30. Christopher Finch and Robert Fellmeth, "Robert H. Mollohan," in *Ralph Nader Congress Project: Citizens Look at Congress* (Washington, D.C.: Grossman Publishers, 1972), 1, 2, 4, 6; Marsh, "It's Much Tougher"; "USW Head Criticizes Sam Huff," *Weirton Daily Times* (April 29, 1970): 18; "Congressman Robert Mollohan Gets First District COPE 'O.K.,'" *West Virginia AFL-CIO Observer* (March 1970): 4; "Bob Mollohan Runs Through Sam Huff," *The Machinist* (May 7, 1970): 1.

31. Dick Wright, "U.S. Work Helps Keep DND Architects Busy," *Washington Star* (September 20, 1975): E9; Cooper Rollow, "Football's Huff Not Violent, Just Worldly Now," *Chicago Tribune* (June 12, 1971): 2:3.

32. Jack Kemp, "Freedom Is Goal When Playing 'Game,'" *San Diego Union* (August 17, 1963): A15; Jack Kemp, "U.S. Liberty, Greatness Were Earned," *San Diego Union* (July 6, 1963): A13.

33. Jack Murphy, "Speaking of Kemp, Drysdale, Wills and Assorted Subjects," *San Diego Union* (September 13, 1962): A17; Gene Roswell, "The QB Takes a Stand," *New York Post* (May 26, 1967): 87; "Jack Kemp Big Name More Ways Than One," undated clipping, Box 380, Folder: Scrapbooks, Vol. 5, 1965, December 24; 1970, March 6–1976, February 25, Jack Kemp Papers, Manuscript Division, Library of Congress, Washington, D.C.; "Quarterback Tells Rotarians Competition Pro Football Key," *Niagara Falls Gazette* (April 6, 1965); all in 1970 Profile, Box 201, Folder Political File, Campaigns, Congressional 1970, Kemp Papers.

34. "AFL's Not Party to Any Squabble," *San Diego Union Evening Tribune* (July 14, 1968); "AFL Won't Back Strike, Kemp Says," *Los Angeles Times* (July 9, 1968); both in Box 380, Folder: Scrapbooks, Vol. 6, 1968, June 28–1969, July 6, Kemp Papers; Jack Murphy, "A Conservative Gets Into Labor and Gives a Solid Performance," *San Diego Union* (May 17, 1968): C1; *Pro Sports: Should Government Intervene?* (Roundtable at American Enterprise Institute, February 22, 1977), 40; "NFL Draft, Contracts Defended," *Washington Post* (February 9, 1971): D2; Ed Kelly, "Jack Kemp's Quarterbacking Excels at Bargaining Table, Too," *Buffalo Evening News* (January 11, 1969), Folder Scrapbooks, Vol. 5, Kemp Papers; the article appeared in the *Congressional Record* for January 16, 1969.

35. "Buffalo Bills Quarterback to Enter Politics," *Ogdensburg Journal* (March 24, 1970): 9; Jack Murphy, "No Place for Republican Q-B," *San Diego Union* (September 21, 1967): C-1; Transcript of Press Conference, March 23, 1970, Kemp Papers; Pat Ryan, "The Making of a Quarterback 1970," *Sports Illustrated* (December 7, 1970): 83.

36. "15 Biggest Spenders Lost in House Races in the State," *New York Times* (June 20, 1971): 36; "Broadcast Spending: No Election Guarantee," *Congressional Quarterly* (July 30, 1971): 1625–27; memo for Jack Kemp, March 23, 1970; "It's Our Country" brochure; both in Campaign Files 1970, Kemp Papers; Ryan, "The Making of a Quarterback"; Paul Parsons, "Rookies Learn Politics at Candidates' School," *Boca Raton News* (October 26, 1980): 17A.

37. Kemp campaign leaflet; "Profile of Jack Kemp"; both in Campaign Files 1970, Kemp papers; "An Interview: Jack Kemp," *The Griffin* (September 23, 1970): 6; Ryan, "The Making of a Quarterback 1970."

38. "Jack Kemp Wins Seat in House," *Adirondack Daily Enterprise* (November 4, 1970): 1; Warren Weaver, "Youth Vote Role in State Weighed," *New York Times* (September 26, 1971): 72; James Clarity, "An Incumbent's Friend: Ethnic and Racial Considerations Called Factors in Drawing of Lines," *New York Times* (March 20, 1972): 46; "Tough Local Opponent Has Jack Un-Kemp-Ed," *Schenectady Gazette* (July 5, 1986): 25.

39. Peter Andrews, "Kemp Takes Oath; Offers Proposals," *Buffalo Courier-Express* (January 22, 1971); Box 362, Folder: Speeches, Statements, and Writings 1971, January–March, Kemp Papers; Proposed Speech Before the American Electroplaters' Society, June 14, 1971; Box 362, Folder: Speeches, Statements, and Writings 1971, June–July, Kemp Papers; Richard Madden, "In Congress, You Can't Tell Players with a Scorecard," *New York Times* (October 25, 1971): 34; Alan Otten, "Politics and People," *Wall Street Journal* (November 18, 1971): 22; Dale van Atta, *With Honor: Melvin Laird in War, Peace, and Politics* (Madison: University of Wisconsin Press, 2008), 31; note from Richard Nixon to Jack Kemp, May, 1, 1972, Box 380, Folder: Scrapbooks, Vol. 8, 1972, April 13–ca. 1975, Kemp Papers; Lou Cannon, "35 'Stand-Ins' Campaign for Nixon's Re-Election," *Washington Post* (September 1, 1972): A6; Max Frankel, "Nixon Asks Support for a 'New Majority' After Agnew Is Renamed as Running Mate," *New York Times* (August 24, 1972): 46; Peter Andrews, "Kemp Electrifies Convention Crowd," *Buffalo Courier-Express* (n.d.); Gerald Ford to Jack Kemp, October 26, 1972; Box 153, Folder: Congressional Press, Chronological File, 1972, July–August, Kemp Papers.

40. Morton Kondracke and Fred Barnes, *Jack Kemp: The Bleeding-Heart Conservative Who Changed America* (New York: Sentinel, 2015), 4, 125, 249, 264; Jack Kemp, *An American Renaissance: A Strategy for the 1980's* (New York: Harper & Row, 1979), 2, 33, 34; "Remarks Prepared for Delivery by the Hon. Jack Kemp (R-N.Y.) Before the Members of the Economic Club of New York, December 4, 1978," Folder Kemp, Representative Jack (R-N.Y.), Reagan 1980 Campaign, Ronald Reagan Papers, Ronald Reagan Presidential Library and Museum, Simi Valley, Calif.; Sidney Blumenthal, "Kemp's Fast Forward: A Campaign Video for the '88 Candidacy," *Washington Post* (July 29, 1987); Barry Goldwater to Jack Kemp, August 29, 1992, Series I, Sub-series A, Box 10, Folder 10: Jack Kemp, Barry Goldwater Papers, Archives and Special Collections, Arizona State University Libraries, Tempe, Ariz.; Michael Lewis, *Trail Fever* (New York: Knopf, 1997), 245.

41. Steve Guback, "Little Mo Prefers Football," *Washington Star* (April 3, 1970): B11; Currence, "Locker-Room Smell"; Nancy Pliszka, "Jack Kemp Is a Team Player," *Buffalo New Times* (March 24, 1974): 6, Box 153, Folder: Congressional Press, Chronological File, 1974, January–March, Kemp Papers.

Chapter 7. Out of Their League

1. Bill Glass and William Pinson Jr., *Don't Blame the Game: An Answer to Super Star Swingers and a Look at What's Right with Sports* (Waco, Tex.: Word, 1972), 9.

2. Lefty Millman, "Free Speech in Sports?" *Liberation News Service* #122 (November 27,

1968): 27; Jack Mann, "Football's Decorum Has Come a Long Way, Baby," *Washington Daily News* (January 14, 1971): 62; Paul Zimmerman, "They Call It a Game," *New York Times Book Review* (September 26, 1971): 44; advertisement for *They Call It a Game, New York Times* (September 23, 1971): 58; "Advance Galley Information for *Confessions of a Dirty Ballplayer*," (July 1970), Series I, Box 3, Folder 27; "Advance Galley Information for *They Call It a Game*," (June, 1971), Series I, Box 4, Folder 27; Dial Press Records, Yale Collection of American Literature, Beinecke Rare Book and Manuscript Library, New Haven, Conn.

3. Bernie Parrish, *They Call It a Game* (New York: Dial Press, 1971), xiv, 35–36, 72, 79, 81; Jack Scott, "Sports," *Ramparts* 12 (December 1971): 67; "A Raiders Dropout: 'It's a Silly Game,'" *Oakland Tribune* (May 10, 1970): 1; Blaine Newnham, "The Linebacker at the Mustard Seed," *Oakland Tribune* (May 10, 1970): 39; Milton Richman, "Chip Oliver Says He Now Feels Liberated," *Columbus (Nebr.) Telegram* (May 12, 1970): 17; Al Stump, "Joe Kapp: Football's Fury On and Off the Field," *True* (September 1970): 52; Roger Rapoport, "Pro Football's Dropouts," in *The Best of Sport, 1946–1971*, ed. Al Silverman (New York: Viking Press, 1971), 582, 590; "An Interview with Two Cardinals," *The Fire Next Time* (August 1969): 16–17.

4. David Remnick, "Still on the Outside," *Sports Illustrated* (October 5, 1987); Hunter S. Thompson, *Fear and Loathing in America: The Brutal Odyssey of an Outlaw Journalist 1968–1976* (New York: Simon & Schuster, 2000), 367; Book-of-the-Month Club advertisement, *Washington Post* (May 2, 1971): 9; "An Interview with Two Cardinals"; *The Dick Cavett Show*: Rock Icons, August 3, 1970; Rapoport, "Pro Football's Dropouts."

5. Michael Tomasky, "North Malice Forty: What the Republicanization of Testosterone Means for the Democrats," *American Prospect* 16 (January 2005): 34; Kenneth Turan, "Football Flip-Flop," *Washington Post* (January 11, 1971): B4; Michael Oriard, *Brand NFL: Making and Selling America's Favorite Sport* (Chapel Hill: University of North Carolina Press, 2007), 53.

6. Dave Meggyesy, *Out of Their League* (Berkeley, Calif.: Ramparts Press, 1970), 43, 78, 83, 46–47.

7. Meggyesy, *Out of Their League*, 106, 143, 145, 146, 201, 257; "An Interview with Two Cardinals"; Michael Gartner, "A View from Behind the Football," *Wall Street Journal* (January 19, 1971): 16.

8. Chuck Johnson, "Knock, Knock, Who's There? Meggyesy," *Milwaukee Journal* (February 16, 1971): 2: 14; "Revolution Will Doom Football," *Los Angeles Times* (May 23, 1970): D1; Ira Berkow, "Odyssey of Meggyesy," *Colorado Springs Gazette-Telegraph* (December 2, 1970): 2-C; David Condon, "In the Wake of the News," *Chicago Tribune* (January 24, 1971): 2:3.

9. Will Grimsley, "Mod Revolution in Sports Losing Battles, But Not the War—Yet!" *Joplin Globe* (November 22, 1970): 5B; Michael Oriard, *Bowled Over: Big-Time College Football from the Sixties to the BCS Era* (Chapel Hill: University of North Carolina Press, 2009), 16; James Toback, "Longhorns and Longhairs," *Harper's* (November 1970): 72.

10. William Bennett, "In Defense of Sports," *Commentary* (July 1976); Richard Elman, "Out of Their League," *New York Times Book Review* (January 31, 1971): 20; Christopher Lehmann-Haupt, "Is Pro Football Bad for Us?" *New York Times* (January 11, 1971): 29.

11. Nathan Cobb, "Lifestyle, 1971 . . ." *Boston Globe* (December 26, 1971): A3; Michael Olmert, "In 'Stop-Action,' The Bears' Dick Butkus May Have Taken His Title Too Seriously," *Sports Illustrated* (October 16, 1972); Dick Butkus and Robert W. Billings, *Stop-Action* (New York: E.P. Dutton, 1972), 63; Pete Axthelm, "The Third Annual Permanent Retirement of Joe Namath," *New York* (July 19, 1971): 49; Larry Merchant, . . . *and Every Day You Take Another Bite* (Garden City, N.Y.: Doubleday, 1971), 37, 38; Larry Csonka and Jim Kiick with Dave Anderson, *Always on the Run* (New York: Random House, 1973), 199.

12. Ron Fimrite, "The True Jock," *San Francisco Chronicle* (September 23, 1970): 64; Tom Beer with George Kimball, *Sunday's Fools: Stomped, Tromped, Kicked, and Chewed in the NFL* (Boston: Houghton Mifflin, 1974), vii; Paul Zimmerman, *A Thinking Man's Guide to Pro Football* (New York: Warner Paperback Library, 1971), 13–22; Alex Kroll, *How to Be a TV Quarterback* (Hartford, Conn.: Travelers Insurance, 1964), 8–9; Hal Higdon, *Pro Football, USA* (New York: G.P. Putnam's Sons, 1968); Paul Zimmerman, *The Last Season of Weeb Ewbank* (New York: Farrar, Straus, and Giroux, 1974), 61, 62; Milton Richman, "Vince Lombardi Considered a 'Traditionalist,'" *Ogden Standard-Examiner* (May 27, 1970): 8C; "Cards Lose Second to Football Dropout," *Morgantown Dominion-Post* (May 31, 1970): 3-D.

13. Blaine Newnham, "Wow, Like Let's Really Try to Win," *Sports Illustrated* (October 12, 1970); Charles Maher, "Is Football Inhuman?" *Los Angeles Times* (October 10, 1970): C2; Wells Twombly, "Leahy Battles Back," *Sporting News* (December 4, 1971): 31; Joe Richmond, "Bleacher Notes," *Idaho State Journal* (May 26, 1970): C2; Michael Grant, "Athletic Revolt Coming?" *Abilene Reporter-News* (July 15, 1970): 9A.

14. Herschel Nissenson, "Old Ben's Career Never Has Shown Brighter," *Syracuse Post-Standard* (November 10, 1970): 19. Andrew Cooper's *Playing in the Zone* (Boston: Shambhala, 1998) claims that Rozelle "issued a league-wide gag order on the book" (27). Neither Jeff Davis's *Rozelle: Czar of the NFL* (New York: McGraw-Hill, 2008) nor John Fortunato's *Commissioner: The Legacy of Pete Rozelle* (Lanham, Md.: Taylor Trade, 2006) mentions Meggyesy.

15. Bob Oates, "Pro-Football's Flower Children," *Los Angeles Times* (June 5, 1970): F1; "Rozelle Foresees NFL Expansion in Next Decade," *Syracuse Herald-Journal* (January 10, 1971): 53.

16. Ed Schoenfeld, "Unitas Blasts Apathetic Rookies," *Oakland Tribune* (February 9, 1971): 32; Tom Callahan, *Johnny U: The Life and Times of Johnny Unitas* (New York: Crown, 2006), 235; George Blanda, "That Impossible Season," *Sports Illustrated* (August 2, 1971); Jim Otto with Dave Newhouse, *Jim Otto: The Pain of Glory* (New York: Skyhorse Publishing, 2012); Earl Gustkey, "Answering the Critics. Raiders' Ben Davidson: 'Lucky to Be in Football,'" *Los Angeles Times* (April 3, 1972): D1, D9; Wells Twombly, *Blanda: Alive and Kicking* (Los Angeles: Nash Publishing, 1972), 289, 290, 291, 293; Bob Addie, "Introducing an Old Bill," *Washington Post* (February 19, 1971): D2; Ira Berkow, "Was Camus the Lombardi of 'Athletic Revolt'?" *Kingsport News* (September 29, 1971): 14.

17. Ira Berkow, "Football Quitters Turn Coaches Off," *Nashua Telegraph* (June 4, 1970): 17; John Hall, "Militants & Muscles," *Los Angeles Times* (May 29, 1970): E3; Tex Maule, *The Pro Season* (Garden City, N.Y.: Doubleday, 1970), 215; "Lemm Raps Meggyesy Story for 'Distortions,'" *Los Angeles Times* (November 26, 1970): E9.

18. Spiro Agnew with John Underwood, "Not Infected with the Conceit of Infallibility,"

Sports Illustrated (June 21, 1971): 62, 66–67, 68; Transcript, Address by the Vice President of the United States, Touchdown Club of Birmingham, January 18, 1972; Series 3: Vice President of the United States; Subseries 3.7: Public Statements, Spiro T. Agnew Papers, Special Collections, University of Maryland Libraries, College Park, Md.

19. Mike Curtis with Bill Gilbert, *Keep Off My Turf* (Philadelphia: J.B. Lippincott, 1972), 9, 13, 154, 33, 14, 34–35, 66, 124, 128, 137, 148, 138, 179; Tom Fox, "When You Call Mike Curtis an Animal, Smile," *Sport* (November 1969): 94; Oriard, *Brand NFL*, 58, 67, 68.

20. Neil Offen, *God Save the Players: The Funny, Crazy, Sometimes Violent World of Sports Fans* (Chicago: Playboy Press, 1974), 202; Stephen H. Norwood, *Real Football: Conversations on America's Game* (Jackson: University Press of Mississippi, 2004), 370; Brad Schultz, *The NFL, Year One* (Washington, D.C.: Potomac Books, 2013), 270n.14; "People," *Sports Illustrated* (September 7, 1970); John Steadman, "Colts Boast a Bearcat Defender: Mike Curtis," *Sporting News* (December 26, 1970): 7; William Gildea, "Colts' Curtis Sells Special Product," *Washington Post* (August 6, 1970): F2; "Big Mike Curtis Earns AP Honors for Miami Contest," *Colorado Springs Gazette* (November 5, 1970): 6D; Curtis, *Keep Off My Turf,* 96.

21. James Hefley, *Running with God: The New Christian Athletes* (New York: Avon Books, 1975), 14; Bob Curran, *The Violence Game* (New York: Macmillan, 1966), 141; William Baker, *Playing with God: Religion and Modern Sport* (Cambridge, Mass.: Harvard University Press, 2007), 201–2; Shirl James Hoffman, *Good Game: Christianity and the Culture of Sports* (Waco, Tex.: Baylor University Press, 2010), 137–38; Frank Deford, "Reaching for the Stars," *Sports Illustrated* (May 3, 1976); Douglas Looney, "You'll Find the Pros at Prayer," *National Observer* (January 13, 1973): 14; George Solomon, "NFL Teams Strive to Have God on Their Side," *Washington Post* (November 14, 1973): D6; Mike Roberts, "Religion and the NFL: Call It the Theology of Perspiration," *Washington Star* (November 6, 1974): C1, C7.

22. Deford, "Reaching for the Stars"; Norm Evans, *On God's Squad* (Carol Stream, Ill.: Creation House, 1971), 190; Michael Couture, "Evans on Dolphins and 'God's Squad,'" *Boca Raton News* (October 31, 1971): 11A; Mike Roberts, "A Chaplain's Delight," *Washington Star* (November 7, 1974): D6; William Willoughby, "The Redskins: Jesus in the Locker Room," *Washington Star* (January 13, 1973): A8; Randall Balmer, *Encyclopedia of Evangelism* (Louisville, Ky.: Westminster John Knox Press, 2002), 630; Mike Roberts, "Religion and the NFL: Reconciling Christianity and Violence," *Washington Star* (November 8, 1974): D1; Jerry Pyle, "Sports and War," *The Christian Athlete* (January 1972): 5, 7; "Interview with Gary Warner and Skip Stogsdill," *Wittenberg Door* (April–May 1975): 18.

23. James Baker, "Are You Blocking for Me, Jesus?" *Christian Century* (November 5, 1975): 1000; Baker, *Playing with God,* 203–4; "60 Years of Word," *Baylor Magazine* (Winter 2011–2012); Deford, "Reaching for the Stars"; Glass and Pinson, *Don't Blame the Game,* 27; Hoffman, *Good Game,* 134–35; Parrish, *They Call It a Game,* 43, 44; "Glass Plans Year-Round Church Work," *Washington Post* (June 8, 1969): 47; Hubert Mizell, "Glass Speaks Up for 'Decent Majority,'" *Syracuse Post-Standard* (December 14, 1972): 15.

24. Glass and Pinson, *Don't Blame the Game,* 55, 44, 54, 74, 19; Jim Murray, "New Voice Speaks Up," *Los Angeles Times* (December 20, 1972): B1; Milton Richman, "Bill Glass Big Enough to Take on 'Swing Set,'" *Ogden Standard-Examiner* (December 20, 1972): 5-C; Oriard, *Brand NFL,* 24.

25. Murray Kempton, "Jock-Sniffing," *New York Review of Books* (February 11, 1971); Andy Barall, "Remembering Pete Gent, Who Wrote 'North Dallas Forty,'" *New York Times* (October 2, 2011); Ron Mix, "I Swore I Would Quit Football," *Sports Illustrated* (September 16, 1963).

26. Jerry Kramer, *Farewell to Football,* ed. Dick Schaap (Cleveland: World Publishing, 1969), 7; Ron Fimrite, "The Mystic Linebackers," *San Francisco Chronicle* (October 5, 1970): 56; Tom White, "Brodie, Meggyesy Debate on Sport Ends in Draw," *Kingsport News* (October 2, 1974): 8B; "Football," *Tamalpais High 1981 Yearbook,* 174; "New Football Coach," *Tam News* (June 3, 1980): 4. For sample Meggyesy sightings, see Remnick, "Still on the Outside"; Mike Littwin, "Meggyesy Back in a Game He Hated," *Milwaukee Journal* (January 28, 1981), 14; Steve Hummer, "Meggyesy Is Happy to be Back in Their League," *Palm Beach Post* (September 30, 1981): D1, 4; "Meggyesy, a Critic, Is Back in Football," *New York Times* (September 1, 1980), C10.

27. D. A. Latmer, "Morrality Play," *East Village Other* (January 17, 1969): 27; Martin Ralbovsky, *The Namath Effect* (Englewood Cliffs, N.J.: Prentice-Hall, 1976), 10, 15, 25, 66; Kenneth Turan, "Meggyesy Writes, and People Read," *Washington Post* (January 24, 1971): D4; Glass and Pinson, *Don't Blame the Game,* 76; Douglas Kneeland, "Talk Isn't Cheap: The Lecture Circuit Is Big Business," *New York Times* (December 16, 1971): 37, 52; Mike Lucas, "Football Is Ritualistic Street Brawl—Meggyesy," *Madison Capital Times* (April 28, 1972): 29; Nick Benton, "Finally! A Jock with Balls!" *Berkeley Barb* (February 12–18, 1971): 6; Dave Meggyesy on Sports/Produced by Patrick Mayer, http://pacificaradioarchives.org/recording/bc077401–13?nns=Football; Tim Elcombe, "Reformist America: 'The Oberlin Experiment'—The Limits of Jack Scott's 'Athletic Revolution' in Post-1960s America," *International Journal of the History of Sport* (November 2005): 1068; John Jekabson, "Football Fascists," *Berkeley Barb* (January 14–20, 1972): 11; Maitland Zane, "A Linebacker for Grass," *San Francisco Chronicle* (October 14, 1972): 6; Michael Murphy, "News from Esalen," *Esalen Catalog* (October–December 1974): 4; James Lincoln Collier, "Live Lectures," *New York Times Magazine* (March 3, 1974): 58.

28. Melissa Ludtke, "Big Scorers in the Ad Game," *Sports Illustrated* (November 7, 1977): 60; Harry Edwards, *Revolt of the Black Athlete* (New York: Free Press, 1969), 23; Jack Olsen, *The Black Athlete: A Shameful Story* (New York: Time-Life Books, 1968), 185; Louis Haugh, "O.J. Tops Year's Star Presenters," *Advertising Age* (June 20, 1977): 1, 82; Frank Deford, *Lite Reading* (New York: Penguin, 1984), 21; Baker, "Are You Blocking for Me, Jesus?", 999; Roberts, "A Chaplain's Delight"; Bill Glass, *Get in the Game* (Waco, Tex.: Word Books, 1965), 150; Randall Balmer, *God in the White House: A History* (New York: HarperOne, 2008), 69–72; Alex Taylor, "There's a Reverend Billy in the White House Again, But It's Zeoli, Not Graham," *People* (April 28, 1975); Ford's annotation of memorandum for Bob Hartmann from Jack Hushen, September 27, 1974, Ford Library, https://www.fordlibrarymuseum.gov/library/document/0011/1683501.pdf; *Supergoal: Great Football Pros on the Game of Life,* with Billy Zeoli (Old Tappan, N.J.: Fleming H. Revell, 1972), 17, 118–19.

29. Niles Howard, "Playing the Endorsement Game," *Dun's Review* (August 1977): 45, 46; Deford, *Lite Reading,* 87–88, 41.

Chapter 8. Right Coach, Wrong Game

1. Ray Kennedy, "427: A Case in Point," *Sports Illustrated* (June 10, 1974).

2. John Coyne, *The Impudent Snobs: Agnew vs. the Intellectual Establishment* (New Rochelle, N.Y.: Arlington House, 1972), 445, 447; "Spiro and Sports," *San Francisco Examiner* (January 22, 1971): 51; "About Us," *Rotary Lombardi Awards,* http://www.rotarylombardiaward .org/index.php/about-us; "37 Are Jailed Here for Agnew Demonstration," *Houston Chronicle* (January 22, 1971): 1, 2; David Zang, *Sports Wars: Athletes in the Age of Aquarius* (Fayetteville: University of Arkansas Press, 2001), 135; Neil Amdur, *The Fifth Down: Democracy and the Football Revolution* (New York: Coward, McCann, and Geoghegan, 1971), 29–31, 120; "Minutes of Trustees Meeting," *Proceedings of the Forty-Seventh Annual Meeting of the American Football Coaches Association* (January 1970): 71, 70, 53, 55, 57; "New Draft Head Picked by Nixon," *Daily Pennsylvanian* (January 29, 1970): 1; Transcript of *The Selling of the Pentagon, Survey of Broadcast Journalism 1970–1971: A State of Siege,* ed. Marvin Barrett (New York: Grosset & Dunlap, 1971), 155.

3. General Lewis Walt, USMC (Ret.), *The Eleventh Hour* (Ottawa, Ill.: Caroline House, 1979), 2, 18, 19, 53, 41, 49.

4. Paul Bryant with John Underwood, *Bear: The Hard Life and Good Times of Alabama's Coach Bryant* (Boston: Little, Brown, 1974), ch. 34.

5. Ironically, in view of the fervor surrounding a potential Lombardi candidacy, his son served a term in Minnesota's state legislature in the early 1970s. George F. Allen served in the Virginia House of Delegates and for one term as senator.

6. John Hall, "Militants and Muscles," *Los Angeles Times* (May 29, 1970): E3; Murray Kempton, "Jock-Sniffing," *New York Review of Books* (February 11, 1971); Robert Lipsyte, "Ralph Houk for President," *New York Times* (October 7, 1968): 61; Vince Lombardi Jr., *What It Takes to be #1: Vince Lombardi on Leadership* (New York: McGraw-Hill, 2001), 32–43.

7. Memo from J. J. McDermott to N. P. Callahan, May 5, 1969, https://vault.fbi.gov /vincent-thomas-lombardi/vincent-thomas-lombardi-part-02-of-02/view; Note, J. Edgar Hoover to Vince Lombardi, June 25, 1970, https://vault.fbi.gov/vincent-thomas-lombardi /vincent-thomas-lombardi-part-01-of-02/view; Dave Brady, "Exponents of 'Violent World' Put on Defensive," *Washington Post* (May 26, 1970): D3.

8. Hunter S. Thompson, *Fear and Loathing in America: The Brutal Odyssey of an Outlaw Journalist 1968–1976* (New York: Simon & Schuster, 2000), 404; Bud Lea, "Vince Eyes Possible Role in Politics," *Milwaukee Sentinel* (August 3, 1968): 2: 3; David Maraniss, *When Pride Still Mattered: A Life of Vince Lombardi* (New York: Simon & Schuster, 1999), 445–47; Terry Bledsoe, "Vince in Politics? Some Guess Yes," *Sporting News* (August 24, 1968): 23; Tom Dowling, *Coach: A Season with Lombardi* (New York: W.W. Norton, 1970), 225; Richard Nixon to Vince Lombardi, November 14, 1969, folder Football 10/1/69, Nixon Papers; "No Politics for Lombardi," *Palm Beach Post* (August 8, 1968): 36.

9. Vincent Lombardi and W. C. Heinz, "A Game for Madmen," *Look* (September 5, 1967): 86; Jerry Izenberg, *Rozelle: A Biography* (Lincoln: University of Nebraska Press, 2014), 127; Vince Lombardi with W. C. Heinz, *Run to Daylight!* (Englewood Cliffs, N.J.: Prentice-Hall, 1963), 82, 109.

10. *Second Effort* is still available for $249 on DVD from the Dartnell Corporation. The blurb begins, "nothing represents America better than football."

11. Paul Hencke, "Honest Injun, Fans, I'm Going to Change," *Washingtonian* (February 1969): 67; Bob Greene, "Selling Isn't Everything," *Chicago Tribune* (January 22, 1997); William Johnson, "Arararararargh!" *Sports Illustrated* (March 3, 1969); "Marketing Memo," *Journal of Marketing* (October 1971): 7; Dick Friendlich, "The Lombardi Credo in Business," *San Francisco Chronicle* (October 17, 1972): 49; Charles Maher, "A Winning Habit," *Los Angeles Times* (May 19, 1972): E1, E8; Barry Tarshis, "Can Ex-Athletes Make It On Wall Street?" *New York* (January 8, 1973): 29–30.

12. "Warren: Lombardi Had Character Nation Needs," *Des Moines Register* (September 5, 1970): 1-S; "Torch Is Lit, More Tributes to Vince," *Milwaukee Journal* (September 4, 1970): 2:15; "Coach Lombardi," *Milwaukee Journal* (September 3, 1970): 24; "Rozelle: Youth Will Miss Vince," *Milwaukee Journal* (September 3, 1970): 2:20; Dave Brady, "Dignitaries, Common Fans Jam Final Lombardi Rites," *Des Moines Register* (September 8, 1970): 3-S; Victor Gold, "VTL: An American for All Seasons," *National Review* (September 22, 1970); "Statement on the Death of Football Coach Vincent T. Lombardi. September 3, 1970," *Public Papers of the Presidents: Richard M. Nixon, 1970* (Washington, D.C.: Government Printing Office, 1971), 698.

13. Bryan Curtis, "No Chattering in the Press Box," *Grantland* (May 2, 2012); Stan Isaacs, *Ten Moments That Shook the Sports World: One Sportswriter's Eyewitness Accounts of the Most Incredible Sporting Events of the Last Fifty Years* (New York: Skyhorse, 2008), 3; Leonard Shecter, *The Jocks* (Indianapolis: Bobbs-Merrill, 1969), 109; Leonard Shecter, "The Toughest Man in Football," *Esquire* (January 1968): 140, 145; Cooper Rollow, "The Lombardi I Knew . . .," *Chicago Tribune* (September 4, 1970): 3:1; *Lombardi,* ed. John Wiebusch (Chicago: Triumph Books, 1971), 94; Dowling, *Coach: A Season with Lombardi,* 59.

14. Michael Oriard, *Brand NFL: Making & Selling America's Favorite Sport* (Chapel Hill: University of North Carolina Press, 2010), 28–29; John Jekabson, "Football Fascists," *Berkeley Barb* (January 14–20, 1972): 11; James Dickey, *The Whole Motion: Collected Poems, 1945–1992* (Middletown, Conn.: Wesleyan University Press, 1992), 391; Douglas Looney, "Has Our Attitude Toward Competition Changed?" *Traverse City Record-Eagle* (July 23, 1973): 7; James Michener, *Sports in America* (New York: Random House, 1976), 519, 522.

15. Red Smith, "Lombardi's Ogre Image Not True Picture," *Milwaukee Journal* (September 3, 1970): 2:21; "A Football Life: Jerry Smith—Living a Double Life," http://www.nfl.com/videos/washington-redskins/0ap2000000316200/A-Football-Life-Jerry-Smith-Living-a-double-life; Dowling, *Coach: A Season with Lombardi,* 49, 22, 315; Eileen Shim, "What It Was Like to Be Gay in the NFL in the '70s—And Fall for Your Teammate," *Mic.com,* http://mic.com/articles/79807/what-it-was-like-to-be-gay-in-the-nfl-in-the-70s-and-fall-for-your-teammate (January 23, 2014); Jim Corbett, "Vince Lombardi Might Have Been Perfect Coach for Michael Sam," *USA Today* (February 11, 2014), https://www.usatoday.com/story/sports/nfl/draft/2014/02/11/vince-lombardi-michael-sam-gay-acceptance/5395467/#; Harvey Frommer, *When It Was Just a Game: Remembering the First Super Bowl* (Lanham, Md.: Taylor, 2015), 59; Milton Richman, "Vince Lombardi Considered a 'Traditionalist,'" *Ogden Standard-Examiner* (May 27, 1970): 8C.

16. Robert Lipsyte, *SportsWorld: An American Dreamland* (New York: Quadrangle, 1975), 3, 26, 7, xii, 39, 57; Larry Merchant, . . . *And Every Day You Take Another Bite* (New York: Dell, 1971), 65; Lombardi, *What It Takes to Be #1,* 227; Brooks Clark, "What'd I Say? Vince Lombardi Felt His Famous Quote About Winning Was Misinterpreted," *Sports Illustrated* (November 28, 1994); Ron Fimrite, "First a Winning Season, Then to the Barricades," *San Francisco Chronicle* (September 17, 1970): 66; Steven Overman, "'Winning Isn't Everything. It's the Only Thing': The Origin, Attributions and Influence of a Famous Football Quote," *Football Studies* (October 1999): 77–99; Michael O'Brien, *Vince: A Personal Biography of Vince Lombardi* (New York: Morrow, 1987), 378–82.

17. Dowling, *Coach: A Season with Lombardi,* 16; *Lombardi,* 41, 99, 197.

18. Robert Lipsyte, "Nixon's Favorite Coach Says, 'When You Lose, You Die a Little,'" *New York Times* (September 16, 1973): 94; George Allen with Joe Marshall, "A Hundred Percent Is Not Enough," *Sports Illustrated* (July 9, 1973): 76; William Gildea and Kenneth Turan, *The Future Is Now: George Allen, Pro Football's Most Controversial Coach* (Boston: Houghton Mifflin, 1972), 2, 37; Jennifer Allen, *Fifth Quarter: The Scrimmage of a Football Coach's Daughter* (New York: Random House, 2000), 12, 41. Michener, *Sports in America,* 522; Charles Maher, "A Week with George Allen: The Ram Coach: A Man for One Season," *Los Angeles Times* (October 11, 1967): B1.

19. Gildea and Turan, *The Future Is Now,* 37, 31, 32, 171, 55, 111, 194–95, 193; James Robenalt, *January 1973: Watergate, Roe v. Wade, Vietnam, and the Month That Changed America Forever* (Chicago: Chicago Review Press, 2015), 15; Leonard Shapiro and Nancy Scannell, "The Final Plays," *Washington Post Magazine* (April 16, 1978): 20; Tom Danyluk, *The Super '70s: Memories from Pro Football's Greatest Era* (Chicago: Mad Uke Publishing, 2005), 251.

20. George Solomon, "Allen's Ban on Writers Hardly a Big-League Move," *Washington Daily News* (August 31, 1971): 42; Shirley Povich, "Reporters Occupy Top Spot on Allen's Enemies List," *Washington Post* (November 18, 1973): D1; David Broder, "Tie's Aftermath Finds Kilmer on Top," *Washington Post* (September 10, 1972): C3; Jeannie Morris, "Sonny Days Again in Allen's Washington," *San Francisco Chronicle* (October 14, 1972): 44; George Solomon, *The Team Nobody Wanted: The Washington Redskins* (Chicago: Henry Regnery, 1973), 52, 89–93; Don Fulsom, *Nixon's Darkest Secrets: The Inside Story of America's Most Troubled President* (New York: St. Martin's Griffin, 2012), 217; Allen *Fifth Quarter,* 118.

21. George Allen to Richard Nixon, March 27, 1961; folder, Allen, George H.; Box 27, Pre-Presidential Papers: General Correspondence: Allen, Bewley—Allen, R. S.; George Allen to Richard Nixon, May 29, 1962; folder, Allen, George; Box I, Wilderness Years: Series I: Correspondence: Sub-series A: Alphabetical 1963–1965; wire from George Allen to Richard Nixon, December 5, 1968; note for Dwight Chapin, February 13, 1969; both in folder A, box 9; White House Central Files: Alphabetical Name Files; all in Richard Nixon Papers, Richard M. Nixon Presidential Library and Museum, Yorba Linda, Calif.; Allen, *Fifth Quarter,* 150.

22. In 1994, former Redskins assistant and later Buffalo coach Marv Levy revealed that Allen had drawn up the play, hoping its success would make the President "look very sage." His willingness to run it in such an important situation (the Redskins were on the 49er eight-yard-line and did not score on the drive, in a game they lost 24–20) testifies to the close spiritual affinities between the two. John Sayle Watterson, *The Games Presidents*

Play: Sports and the Presidency (Baltimore: Johns Hopkins University Press, 2006), 237. This wasn't Nixon's first venture into unsuccessful play-calling. In 1958, he suggested that Redskins' defensive end Gene Brito, his favorite player, take a turn on offense so he could catch a pass. Brito forgot to turn around, and the throw hit him in the back. Bruce Nash and Allan Zullo, *The Football Hall of Shame* (New York: Simon & Schuster, 1991), 127.

23. Gildea and Turan, *The Future Is Now,* 261; Note from Henry Kissinger to George Allen, October 4, 1972; Memo from Dwight Chapin to Stephen Bull, December 16, 1971; note from David Parker to George Allen, June 30, 1971; note from John Davies to George Allen, January 27, 1971; Richard Nixon to George Allen, November 25, 1970; folder A, box 9; White House Central Files: Alphabetical Name Files; Nixon Papers; "The Washingtonians of the Year," *The Washingtonian* (January 1972): 36; George Allen, *Inside Football: Fundamentals, Strategy, and Tactics for Winning* (Boston: Allyn and Bacon, 1970), 288, 376.

24. Allen, *Fifth Quarter,* 100; "Remarks to Members of the Washington Redskins Professional Football Team During a Practice Session at Redskins Park," November 23, 1971, *Public Papers of the Presidents: Richard M. Nixon* (Washington, D.C.: Government Printing Office, 1972), 1134–37; Richard Nixon to George Allen, November 22, 1972; folder A, box 9; White House Central Files: Alphabetical Name Files; Nixon Papers.

25. Amy Gordon, "Are There Any Heroes Left?" *The Washingtonian* (February 1974): 63–64; Richard Nixon to George Allen, May 21, 1970; note from George Allen to Richard Nixon, May 10, 1972; note from Richard Nixon to George Allen, May 15, 1972; wire from George Allen to Richard Nixon, October 26, 1972; all in folder A, box 5; White House Special Files: President's Personal Files; Nixon Papers; John Kendall, "War Protests Flare on Southland Cities," *Los Angeles Times* (May 9, 1972): 3; "What Are You Doing, Mr. Nixon?" *Los Angeles Times* (May 9, 1972): D6; Jules Witcover, "Nixon Pledges 'Full Prosperity Without War,' Strong Defense," *Los Angeles Times* (October 24, 1972): A1, A19; Timothy Crouse, *The Boys on the Bus: Riding with the Campaign Press Corps* (New York: Random House, 1972), 288.

26. Allen, *Fifth Quarter,* 97; Sandy Padwe, "George Allen: Early Bird Who Gets the Win," *Los Angeles Times* (December 24, 1972): C1, C7; Steve Guback, "Allen Stands Firmly Behind the President," *Washington Star-News* (August 8, 1974): D-3.

27. Confronted with these allegations, an enraged Allen sputtered that "many of them worked for us of their own free will. Sometimes we paid them." Shapiro and Scannell, "The Final Plays," 22, 44; Tom Dowling, "Saint Ed and the Dragon," *The Washingtonian* (June 1978): 60.

28. For connoisseurs of cycles-of-history theories, it's worth noting that this trend was short-lived. *Time* dubbed the 1978 midterms "the Vince Lombardi election. . . . Behind the ideas of the triumphant candidates burns the apparent conviction that the world cannot go on without them." Hugh Sidey, "Winning Was the Only Thing," *Time* (November 20, 1978): 40.

29. Allen, *Inside Football,* 408; Michael O'Brien, "In Search of Vince Lombardi: A Historian's Memoir," *Wisconsin Magazine of History* (Autumn 1987): 23; George Will, "Competence and the GOP," *Washington Post* (September 16, 1973): C6; John O'Connor, "No Back Talk from the Press, Please," *New York Times* (November 11, 1973): 161; Timothy Leary, "The Day I Was Busted by G. Gordon Liddy," *Ramparts* (December 1973): 47; Glenn Dickey, *The Jock*

Empire: Its Rise and Deservéd Fall (Radnor, Pa.: Chilton, 1974), 45; Larry L. King, "Coming of Age in the Locker Room," *Texas Monthly* (September 1974): 98; Arthur Schlesinger, "The Power of Positive Losing," *New York Times* (June 22 1975): 62; "Watergate Lesson Helps, Cohen Tells Jaycees," *Bangor Daily News* (February 24, 1975): 13; O'Brien, *Vince,* 378–82; Michener, *Sports in America,* 471.

30. Sean Lahman, *The Pro Football Abstract: A Hardcore Fan's Guide to All-Time Player Rankings* (Guilford, Conn.: Lyons Press, 2008), 265–66; "Hank Stram—Steve Sabol," *YouTube,* https://www.youtube.com/watch?v=YVEQnRy5Ttw; Jeff Miller, *Going Long: The Wild 10-Year Saga of the American Football League in the Words of Those Who Lived It* (Chicago: Contemporary Books, 2003), 347; Frommer, *When It Was Just a Game,* 71, 116; *America's Game: The 1969 Kansas City Chiefs* (NFL Films, 2003); *1970 Super Bowl Highlights* (NFL Films, 2003); Hank Stram with Lou Sahadi, *They're Playing My Game* (New York: Morrow, 1986), 168, 179.

31. Richard Rapaport, "To Build a Winning Team: An Interview with Head Coach Bill Walsh," *Harvard Business Review* (January–February 1993): 112; Robert Keidel, "The Trouble with Football," *Harvard Business Review* (May–June 1993): 175–78; David Halberstam, *The Education of a Coach* (New York: Hyperion, 2005), 270; "Tony Dungy," http://www.coachdungy.com/bio/; Nick Saban with Brian Curtis, *How Good Do You Want to Be?: A Champion's Tips on How to Lead and Succeed at Work and in Life* (New York: Ballantine Books, 2005), xvii, 22; Urban Meyer with Wayne Coffey, *Above the Line: Lessons in Leadership and Life from a Championship Season* (New York: New York, Penguin, 2015), 65, 161; Pete Carroll with Yogi Roth, *Win Forever: Live, Work, and Play Like a Champion* (New York: Portfolio, 2010), 84.

32. Roger L. Martin, *Fixing the Game: Bubbles, Crashes, and What Capitalism Can Learn from the NFL* (Boston: Harvard Business Review Press, 2011), 14, 217, 1.

Epilogue

1. Knute Rockne, *The Autobiography of Knute K. Rockne* (Indianapolis: Bobbs-Merrill, 1931), quoted in Murray Sperber, *Shake Down the Thunder: The Creation of Notre Dame Football* (New York: Henry Holt, 1993), 284.

2. Art Buchwald, "The Rose Bowl, Watergate, the Big Enchilada and Co.," *Washington Post* (January 7, 1975): B1; Victor Gold, *PR as in President: A Pro Looks at Press Agents, Media, and the 1976 Candidates* (Garden City, N.Y.: Doubleday, 1977), 7, 35, 130; "Republicans: The Early Birds," *Newsweek* (February 25, 1974): 30; Walter LaFeber, *The American Century: A History of the United States Since 1941* (Armonk, N.Y.: M.E. Sharpe, 2013), 219; see, in particular, the interviews with Dick Cheney and Donald Rumsfeld, *Gerald R. Ford Oral History Project,* http://geraldrfordfoundation.org/centennial/oralhistory/.

3. Ronald Reagan, "Speech at National Football Foundation," December 7, 1971, http://www.footballfoundation.org/News/NewsDetail/tabid/567/Article/52183football-played-a-formative-role-in-president-reagans-life.aspx.

4. Sam Merrill, "A Candid Conversation with Roone Arledge, Broadcasting Visionary," http://playboysfw.kinja.com/a-candid-conversation-with-roone-arledge-sports-broadc-1511880255 (originally in *Playboy,* October 1976); Leonard Goldenson, *Beating the*

Odds: The Untold Story Behind the Rise of ABC (New York: Charles Scribner's Sons, 1991), 186, 392; Marc Gunther, *The House That Roone Built* (Boston: Little, Brown, 1994), 18.

5. Gary Messinger, *The Battle for the Mind: War and Peace in the Era of Mass Communication* (Amherst: University of Massachusetts Press, 2011), 187–88; Robert Scheer, "Crisis in TV News: Show-Biz Invasion," *Los Angeles Times* (May 29, 1977): 1, 3; Les Brown, "Arledge Will Head ABC News; Disclaims Theatrical Flourishes," *New York Times* (May 3, 1977): 81; Sander Vanocur, "ABC News Sports a New Chief," *Washington Post* (May 3, 1977): B9; Lee Margulies, "ABC-TV Offensive: Commitment to Improve News," *Los Angeles Times* (May 12, 1977): G16; Gunther, *The House That Roone Built,* 28; Roone Arledge, *Roone: A Memoir* (New York: HarperCollins, 2003), 162–63.

6. Ronald Reagan, "Address at Commencement Exercises at the University of Notre Dame. May 17, 1981," http://www.reagan.utexas.edu/archives/speeches/1981/51781a.htm; Ray Didinger and Glen Macnow, *The Ultimate Book of Sports Movies: Featuring the 100 Greatest Sports Films of All Time* (Philadelphia: Running Press, 2009), 123–25; Jonathan Chait, "Notre Dame Never Fumbles the Myth," *Los Angeles Times* (September 24, 2006); H. W. Brands, *Reagan: The Life* (New York: Doubleday, 2015), 41; Stephen Vaughn, *Ronald Reagan in Hollywood: Movies and Politics* (New York: Cambridge University Press, 1994), 84; Murray Sperber, *Shake Down the Thunder,* 474, 281, 232–40.

7. Michael Rogin, *Ronald Reagan the Movie: and Other Episodes in Political Demonology* (Berkeley: University of California Press, 1988), 16; Matthew Dallek, *The Right Moment: Ronald Reagan's First Victory and the Decisive Turning Point in American Politics* (New York: Oxford University Press, 2004), 123; Russell Baker, "Bleary Is the Football TViewers," *San Francisco Chronicle* (January 5, 1966): 54; "Is Washington to Become Hollywood Dumping Ground," *Capital Times* (January 12, 1966): 44; John Hall, "One for the Gipper," *Los Angeles Times* (October 29, 1966): A3; "California Chooses," *Daily Sikeston Standard* (June 7, 1966): 2; Ron Fimrite, "Our Governor, the Gipper," *San Francisco Chronicle* (November 11, 1966): 53.

8. Phil Finch, "A Special: 'Take Me Out to the Ball Game,'" *San Francisco Sunday Examiner & Chronicle* (March 14, 1971): C9; Tom Dowling, "One 'P' or Two?" *Washington Star* (November 21, 1971): C2; Peter Heincken, "Ronnie's Shadowy Half-Life Overexposed!" *Berkeley Barb* (November 13–19, 1970): 9; Wells Twombly, "An Expose to End All Exposes," *Sporting News* (October 9, 1971): 10; Jim Kornkven, "Win One for the Gipper," *Kenosha News* (January 20, 1981): 33.

9. Donald Baker, "Stigma of Washington Felt in Neb. Campaign," *Washington Post* (May 10, 1976): A3; David Broder, "Jimmy Carter: Back on the Track," *Washington Post* (March 14, 1976): C7; Dominic Sandbrook, *Mad as Hell: The Crisis of the 1970s and the Rise of the Populist Right* (New York: Knopf, 2011), 383; "Let's Not 'Win One for the Gipper,'" *New York Times* (March 31, 1980): A22; T. R. Reid, "The Stages Change, The Man Doesn't," *Washington Post* (July 13, 1980): E1; Red Smith, "Too Much Notre Dame," *New York Times* (November 3, 1980): C7; Navy/Notre Dame game program (November 1, 1980): 20.

10. Lou Cannon, "The Man: An Optimism for Future, Rooted in Past," *Washington Post* (January 20, 1981): Z1; Reagan, "Speech at National Football Foundation"; Mark Shields, "President Reagan's Wide World of Sports," *Inside Sports* (March 1981): 26.

11. "Reagan Makes Nostalgic Return to Notre Dame," *Joplin Globe* (May 18, 1981): 1; "Grad Speaker Thanks Hesburgh for Gipp Award," *Notre Dame Observer* (August 22, 1981): 14; Reagan, "Address at Commencement Exercises."

12. Ira Allen, "Reaction to Reagan's Speech to Joint Session of Congress Follows General Party Lines," *Cumberland News* (May 1, 1981): 6; Patrick Buchanan, "Tax Cuts' Success Terrifies the Liberals," *Eureka Times-Standard* (May 28, 1981): 4; Richard Reeves, *President Reagan: The Triumph of Imagination* (New York: Simon & Schuster, 2005), 58; Sandy Grady, "Reagan: The Gipper or Geezer?" *Boca Raton News* (October 19, 1984): 6A; *Ronald Reagan: A Life in Letters* (New York: Free Press, 2003), 130; "Reagan Relives 'the Gipper' Days," *Spartanburg Herald-Journal* (March 10, 1988): A6; "Reagan's Farewell: 'Make It One More for the Gipper,'" *Observer-Reporter* (August 16, 1988): 1.

13. Jeffrey Hart, "Reagan Embodies 'the Gipper,'" *Kentucky New Era* (March 14, 1986): 4A.

Bibliography

Manuscript and Archival Sources

American Revolution Bicentennial Administration Records, National Archives, College Park, Md.

Barry Goldwater Papers, Archives and Special Collections, Arizona State University Libraries, Tempe, Ariz.

Burton Benjamin Papers, 1957–1966, Wisconsin Historical Society, Madison, Wis.

Dial Press Records, Yale Collection of American Literature, Beinecke Rare Book and Manuscript Library, New Haven, Conn.

Emanuel Celler Papers, Manuscript Division, Library of Congress, Washington, D.C.

Eugene McCarthy Papers, Elmer L. Andersen Library, University of Minnesota, Minneapolis, Minn.

Franklin D. Roosevelt Papers, Franklin D. Roosevelt Presidential Library, Hyde Park, N.Y.

George McGovern Papers, Seeley G. Mudd Manuscript Library, Princeton University, Princeton, N.J.

Gerald R. Ford Papers, Gerald R. Ford Presidential Library and Museum, Ann Arbor, Mich.

Hale and Lindy Boggs Papers, Manuscripts Collection 1000, Louisiana Research Collection, Howard-Tilton Memorial Library, Tulane University, New Orleans, La.

Henry Woessner Papers, Syracuse University Archives, Syracuse University, Syracuse. N.Y.

Herbert G. Klein Papers, Special Collections, USC Libraries, Los Angeles, Calif.

Hubert H. Humphrey Papers, Minnesota Historical Society, St. Paul, Minn.

Ira Berkow Papers, American Jewish Historical Society, New York, N.Y.

Jack Kemp Papers, Manuscript Division, Library of Congress, Washington, D.C.

James C. Carey Papers, Morse Department of Special Collections, Kansas State University Libraries, Manhattan, Kan.

Bibliography

John F. Kennedy Papers, John F. Kennedy Presidential Library and Museum, Boston, Mass.

Nelson A. Rockefeller Papers, Rockefeller Archive Center, Sleepy Hollow, N.Y.

Penn State Special Collections Library, University Park, Pa.

Richard Nixon Papers, Richard M. Nixon Presidential Library and Museum, Yorba Linda, Calif.

Robert Fitch Papers, Richard M. Nixon Presidential Library and Museum, Yorba Linda, Calif.

Robert Kastenmeier Papers, Wisconsin Historical Society, Madison, Wis.

Robert F. Kennedy Papers, John F. Kennedy Presidential Library and Museum, Boston, Mass.

Ronald Reagan Papers, Ronald Reagan Presidential Library and Museum, Simi Valley, Calif.

Spiro T. Agnew Papers, Special Collections, University of Maryland, College Park, Md.

Stanford University Athletic Archives, Palo Alto, Calif.

Stanley Scott Papers, Gerald R. Ford Presidential Library and Museum, Ann Arbor, Mich.

Syracuse University Archives, Syracuse University Libraries, Syracuse, N.Y.

United Service Organization Records, Records of the U.S. Forces in Southeast Asia, 1950–1976, National Archives, College Park, Md.

Virtual Vietnam Archive, Texas Tech University, Lubbock, Tex.

W. Stuart Symington Papers, State Historical Society of Missouri, Columbia, Mo.

West Virginia and Regional History Center, Morgantown, W.Va.

Woody Hayes Papers, The Ohio State University Archives, Columbus, Ohio.

Interviews

Tom Dowling, June 30, 2015.

Anna Leider, January 28, 2015.

Jerry Lewis, March 19, 2015.

Ray Schoenke, April 21, 2016.

George Solomon, October 16, 2015.

Richard Zitrin email, August 12, 2015; phone conversation, October 22, 2015.

Selected Articles

"A Man's Game." *Time* (November 30, 1959).

Aaron, Daniel. "Nixon as Literary Artifact." *Raritan* (Fall 1995).

Agnew, Spiro, with John Underwood. "Not Infected with the Conceit of Infallibility." *Sports Illustrated* (June 21, 1971): 62, 66–67, 68.

Allen, George, with Joe Marshall. "A Hundred Percent Is Not Enough." *Sports Illustrated* (July 9, 1973): 76.

Alsop, Stewart. "Nixon and the Square Majority: Is the Fox a Lion?" *Atlantic* (February 1972).

Amdur, Neil. "Football Future Called Clouded." *New York Times* (August 18, 1970): 41.

"An Interview with Two Cardinals." *The Fire Next Time* (August 1969): 16–17.

Bibliography

Anderson, Dave. "Undercover Agents Cover the Spread." *New York Times* (November 16, 1969): S2.

Angell, Roger. "Super." *New Yorker* (February 11, 1974).

"Announcing: Democrats for Nixon." *San Francisco Chronicle* (August 16, 1972): 14.

Apple, R. W. "Nixon Guides Republicans on Senate Races, Recruiting a Slate Aimed at Gaining Control of Chamber." *New York Times* (April 6, 1970): 12.

Arcand, Sébastien, Stéphane Éthier, and Joseph Facal. "'Gentlemen, We Will Chase Perfection': The Extraordinary Success of the National Football League." *International Journal of Case Studies in Management* (March 2016).

"As We See It." *TV Guide* (January 19, 1957): inside front cover.

"As We See It." *TV Guide* (February 7, 1976): A-4.

"At the Campaign Kickoff—Strategies of Both Parties." *US News and World Report* (September 14, 1970): 19.

Atchison, Lewis. "Draft Is Vital to Grid Merger." *Washington Star* (October 13, 1966): D4.

"Athletes for McGovern." *Government Executive* (July 1972): 11.

Axthelm, Pete. "The Third Annual Permanent Retirement of Joe Namath." *New York* (July 19, 1971).

Baker, James. "Are You Blocking for Me, Jesus?" *Christian Century* (November 5, 1975).

Baker, Russell. "Superhistory." *New York Times* (October 19, 1975): 234.

Balbus, Ike. "Politics as Sports: The Ascendency of the Sports Metaphor in America." *Monthly Review* (March 1975).

"Bald Case in Point: Pro Football's Magical Immunity." *Life* (December 9, 1966): 44–47.

Belth, Alex. "The Elements of Style." *Bronx Banter* (June 7, 2011).

———. "The Flower of America." *Bronx Banter* (July 1, 2013).

———. "Mann, Oh Mann." *Bronx Banter* (June 15, 2011).

Benjamin, Burton. "Sam Huff's World: Another Look Back." *New York Times* (February 7, 1982): S2.

———. "TV Documentarian's Dream in a Challenging World." *Variety* (January 4, 1961): 91.

Bennett, William. "In Defense of Sports." *Commentary* (February 1976).

Benton, Nick. "Finally! A Jock with Balls!" *Berkeley Barb* (February 12–18, 1971): 6.

Berkow, Ira. "Football Quitters Turn Coaches Off." *Nashua Telegraph* (June 4, 1970): 17.

———. "Odyssey of Meggyesy." *Colorado Springs Gazette-Telegraph* (December 2, 1970): 2-C.

———. "Redskins' Lineman Shows Courage of His Convictions." *Hendersonville Times-News* (November 1, 1972): 13.

———. "Was Camus the Lombardi of 'Athletic Revolt'?" *Kingsport News* (September 29, 1971): 14.

Blanda, George. "That Impossible Season." *Sports Illustrated* (August 2, 1971).

Bledsoe, David. "Vince in Politics? Some Guess Yes." *Sporting News* (August 24, 1968): 23.

Blumenthal, Sidney. "Kemp's Fast Forward: A Campaign Video for the '88 Candidacy." *Washington Post* (July 29, 1987).

Brady, Dave. "Draft Threatens Redskins." *Washington Post* (February 28, 1966): D3.

———. "Exponents of 'Violent World' Put on Defensive." *Washington Post* (May 26, 1970): D3.

———. "Giant Kicker Has No Kicks Coming?" *Washington Post* (September 2, 1967): D3.

———. "Harris Survey for NFL Finds People Like Football Best." *Washington Post* (January 23, 1972): B2.

———. "Rozelle, Thwarted at Hearings, Gloomy Over Merger of Pros." *Washington Post* (October 7, 1966): E1.

Brody, Tom. "C. B. DeMille of the Pros," *Sports Illustrated* (November 20, 1967).

Brown, Les. "Arledge Will Head ABC News; Disclaims Theatrical Flourishes." *New York Times* (May 3, 1977): 81.

Buchwald, Art. "Games Presidents Play." *Los Angeles Times* (January 9, 1972): H1.

———. "The Rose Bowl, Watergate, the Big Enchilada and Co." *Washington Post* (January 7, 1975): B1.

Buckley, William F. "Reflections on the Phenomenon." *Esquire* (October 1974).

Byers, Walter. "A Personal Viewpoint . . . Lessons in Learning." *NCAA News* (July 1970): 2.

Candaele, Kelly, and Peter Dreier. "Where Are the Jocks for Justice?" *The Nation* (June 28, 2004).

Cannon, Lou. "The Man: An Optimism for Future, Rooted in Past." *Washington Post* (January 20, 1981): Z1.

Clark, Champ. "The Mystique of Pro Football." *Time* (November 9, 1970): 42.

"Coach Lombardi." *Milwaukee Journal* (September 3, 1970): 24.

Cobb, Nathan. "Lifestyle, 1971 . . ." *Boston Globe* (December 26, 1971): A3.

Coffey, Shelby, III. "Political Consultants: Their Tentacles Grow and Grow." *Washington Post* (November 1, 1970): 9, 10.

Cohen, Rich. "They Taught America to Watch Football." *Atlantic* (October 2012).

Cope, Myron. "Who's the Broad in Pro Football's Huddle?" *True* (December 1968): 43.

Coughlan, Robert. "Success Story of a Vice President." *Life* (December 14, 1953): 151.

Curtis, Bryan. "No Chattering in the Press Box," *Grantland* (May 2, 2012).

Deford, Frank. "Reaching for the Stars." *Sports Illustrated* (May 3, 1976).

Denlinger, Kenneth. "Candidates Woo Athletes." *Washington Post* (October 14, 1972): C3.

———. "Football Power Sells Products." *San Francisco Chronicle* (October 6, 1972): 56.

DiNardo, Larry. "Instant Replay in Reverse." *Purdue-Notre Dame Program* (September 26, 1970), 5, 8.

Dowling, Tom. "The Great Sportscaster." *Washington Star* (November 28, 1971): B2.

———. "Spiro and Sports." *Washington Star* (January 20, 1972): D1.

———. "Sporting Thoughts Aboard a Merry-Go-Round." *Washington Star* (September 14, 1971): B1.

Durslag, Melvin. "After New Orleans, What?" *TV Guide* (January 10, 1970): 13.

———. "The Heisman Trophy." *TV Guide* (November 13, 1971): 53–54.

———. "Look Ma—No Teeth." *TV Guide* (December 10, 1960): 23.

———. "They Sell Everything But the Goal Posts." *TV Guide* (November 1, 1969): 6–8.

Edwards, Thomas. "The Sporting Gripe." *Partisan Review* 28, 3 (1971).

Elcombe, Tim. "Reformist America: 'The Oberlin Experiment'—The Limits of Jack Scott's 'Athletic Revolution' in Post-1960s America." *International Journal of the History of Sport* (November 2005).

Elman, Richard. "Out of Their League." *New York Times Book Review* (January 31, 1971): 20.

"Fans Go Ga-Ga Over Pro Football." *Life* (December 5, 1960).

Fimrite, Ron. "First a Winning Season, Then to the Barricades." *San Francisco Chronicle* (September 17, 1970): 66.

———. "The Mystic Linebackers." *San Francisco Chronicle* (October 5, 1970): 56.

———. "Our Governor, the Gipper." *San Francisco Chronicle* (November 11, 1966): 53.

Finch, Christopher, and Robert Fellmeth. "Robert H. Mollohan." In *Ralph Nader Congress Project: Citizens Look at Congress* (Washington, D.C.: Grossman Publishers, 1972).

Finch, Phil. "Sports Flacks: Image for Sale." *San Francisco Sunday Examiner & Chronicle* (January 24, 1971): C5.

Fleming, Thomas. "Selling the Product Named Hubert Humphrey." *New York Times Magazine* (October 13, 1968): 139.

"Football and the Bicentennial." *Wall Street Journal* (October 13, 1975): 8.

Fortunato, John. "Pete Rozelle: Developing and Communicating the Sports Brand." *International Journal of Sport Communication* (2008).

Fox, Tom. "The Lombardi Credo in Business." *San Francisco Chronicle* (October 17, 1972): 49.

———. "Rod Sherman Receives a Call." *San Francisco Chronicle* (December 28, 1970): 43.

———. "When You Call Mike Curtis an Animal, Smile." *Sport* (November 1969).

"From Dale Barton's Keyboard." *Carroll Times Daily Herald* (December 30, 1958): 2.

Furlong, William Barry. "Ploys Will Be Ploys, But Enough's Enough." *Washington Post* (July 11, 1974): D1, D4.

Gartner, Michael. "A View from Behind the Football." *Wall Street Journal* (January 19, 1971): 16.

Gold, Victor. "VTL: An American for All Seasons." *National Review* (September 22, 1970).

Gould, Jack. "TV's Eye on the Ball." *New York Times* (December 20, 1959): X17.

Grady, Sandy. "Reagan: The Gipper or Geezer?" *Boca Raton News* (October 19, 1984): 6A.

Graham, Otto. "Football Is Getting Too Vicious." *Sports Illustrated* (October 11, 1954): 26–30.

Grant, Michael. "Athletic Revolt Coming?" *Abilene Reporter-News* (July 15, 1970): 9A.

Grimsley, Will. "Mod Revolution in Sports Losing Battles, But Not the War—Yet!" *Joplin Globe* (November 22, 1970): 5B.

"The Growling Giants." *Newsweek* (October 31, 1960): 86.

Guback, Steve. "Allen Stands Firmly Behind the President." *Washington Star-News* (August 8, 1974): D-3.

———. "Vision of Senate Dances in Sam's Head While Awaiting Signal from Vince." *Washington Star* (January 21, 1970): B13.

Gustkey, Earl. "Answering the Critics. Raiders' Ben Davidson: 'Lucky to be in Football.'" *Los Angeles Times* (April 3, 1972): D1, D9.

Hall, John. "Militants and Muscles." *Los Angeles Times* (May 29, 1970): E3.

Hamill, Pete. "The Revolt of the White Lower Middle Class." *New York* (April 14, 1969).

Harris, Bucky. "How to Go into Politics." *Morgantown Sunday Dominion-Post* (March 1, 1970): 6-D.

Harris, Louis. "Present Draft Believed Unfair." *Los Angeles Times* (June 19, 1967): A5.

Harwood, Richard. "Television Shaping the New Politics." *Washington Post* (March 29, 1970): 1.

Haugh, Louis. "O.J. Tops Year's Star Presenters." *Advertising Age* (June 20, 1977): 1, 82.

Heinz, W. C. "Boss of the Behemoths." *Saturday Evening Post* (December 3, 1955): 72.

Hendrickson, Paul. "The Super Bowl and the Boys in the Box." *National Observer* (January 31, 1976): 1, 15.

Howard, Niles. "Playing the Endorsement Game." *Dun's Review* (August 1977): 45, 46.

Isaacs, Stan. "ABC's Lineup: America's Best Comedians?" *Tucson Daily Citizen* (December 1, 1971): 35.

Israel, David. "How Important Is the NFL Role in U.S. History?" *Washington Star* (October 1, 1975): E1, E4.

"Is Washington to Become Hollywood Dumping Ground?" *Capital Times* (January 12, 1966): 44.

Izenberg, Jerry. "Return of the Body-Snatchers." *Pittsburgh Press* (January 27, 1971): 61.
———. "Through My Eyes." *Newark Star-Ledger* (November 5, 2006).

Jekabson, John. "Football Fascists." *Berkeley Barb* (January 14–20, 1972): 11.

Jenkins, Anne. "Football—The All-American Sport." *Great Speckled Bird* (December 27, 1971): 24.

Jenkins, Dan. "Another Nightmare for the Year Ahead." *Sports Illustrated* (September 14, 1970): 46.

Kahn, Roger. "Football's Taking Over." In *Best American Sports Stories 1961,* ed. Irving T. Marsh and Edward Ehre (New York: E.P. Dutton, 1961).

Kanter, Rosabeth Moss. "Four Winning Lessons from the Super Bowl." *Harvard Business Review* (January 31, 2011).

Kemp, Jack. "Freedom Is Goal When Playing 'Game.'" *San Diego Union* (August 17, 1963): A15.
———. "U.S. Liberty, Greatness Were Earned." *San Diego Union* (July 6, 1963): A13.

Kempton, Murray. "Jock-Sniffing." *New York Review of Books* (February 11, 1971).

"Kill 'Em." *Berkeley Tribe* (January 8–15, 1971): 17.

Kindred, Dave. "Huff's Election to Hall Proves His Play Wasn't Just for Show." *Washington Post* (January 28, 1982): D1, D6.

Kirshenbaum, Jerry. "The Greening of the Fighting Irish." *Sports Illustrated* (December 14, 1970).

Koppett, Leonard. "Lesson of Watergate in Sports World." *Sporting News* (July 7, 1973): 6.
———. "Only Winning Counts." *New York Times Book Review* (November 5, 1967): 116.

Koster, Rich. "Sheepdog to the Pros." *Chicago Tribune* (May 3, 1970): J1–3.

Kraft, Joseph. "Daley and Police Have a Point in Claiming Press Is Biased." *Washington Post* (September 3, 1968): A11.

Landphair, Theodore. "Radicals at the Fifty-Yard Line?" *National Observer* (September 14, 1970): 14.

Lardner, John. "S.2545 and the War." *Newsweek* (February 8, 1960): 93.

Lardner, Rex. "The 'In' Game." *New York Times Book Review* (October 25, 1970): 33.

Large, Arlen. "Stars on the Stump: More Celebrities Try to Capitalize on Fame by Entering Politics." *Wall Street Journal* (May 4, 1970): 1, 20.

Lea, Bud. "Vince Eyes Possible Role in Politics." *Milwaukee Sentinel* (August 3, 1968): 2:3.

Leary, Timothy. "The Day I Was Busted by G. Gordon Liddy." *Ramparts* (December 1973): 47.

Lebovitz, Hal. "Is 'Sportswriter' a Dirty Word?" *Cleveland Plain Dealer* (December 3, 1970): 2F.

Leeward, Alan. "The Riot." *The Rag* (December 8, 1969): 1.

Lehmann-Haupt, Christopher. "Is Pro Football Bad for Us?" *New York Times* (January 11, 1971): 29.

———. "The Trouble with Football." *New York Times* (September 23, 1971): 59.

Levathes, Kiki. "Rolling Stone Voice Predicts Mad Future." *Washington Star* (December 14, 1971): B1.

———. "Sex and the Athlete: Taboos Explored." *Washington Star* (November 14, 1971): C8.

Lipsyte, Robert. "From Draft to Desert Storm." *New York Times* (April 19, 1991): B12.

———. "Nixon's Favorite Coach Says, 'When You Lose, You Die a Little.'" *New York Times* (September 16, 1973): 94.

———. "Of Sports, Comebacks, and Nixon." *New York Times* (May 1, 1994): S11.

———. "Sports Books: The Best of All Seasons." *Mother Jones* (July 1976): 61.

———. "The Teammates." *New York Times* (June 8, 1968): 34.

Liston, Roz. "Bicentennial Looking Like 'Buycentennial.'" *Wisconsin State Journal* (December 8, 1975): 5.

Lomax, Michael. "The Quest for Freedom: The NFLPA's Attempt to Abolish the NFL Reserve System." *Football Studies* (2004): 70–107.

Lombardi, Vince, and W. C. Heinz. "A Game for Madmen." *Look* (September 5, 1967): 86.

Looney, Douglas. "Football Books Star in the Yule Bowl." *National Observer* (December 15, 1973): 12.

———. "Has Our Attitude Toward Competition Changed?" *Traverse City Record-Eagle* (July 23, 1973): 7.

———. "You'll Find the Pros at Prayer." *National Observer* (January 13, 1973): 14.

Ludtke, Melissa. "Big Scorers in the Ad Game." *Sports Illustrated* (November 7, 1977): 60.

Lydon, Christopher. "Celebrities Rally Behind McGovern." *New York Times* (April 2, 1972): 28.

Madden, Richard. "In Congress, You Can't Tell Players with a Scorecard." *New York Times* (October 25, 1971): 34.

Mann, Jack. "Football's Decorum Has Come a Long Way, Baby." *Washington Daily News* (January 14, 1971): 62.

———. "Implementing the Coach's Offensive Game Plan." *Washington Daily News* (March 25, 1971): 78.

———. "Letters 'n' Lip from the Fans." *Washington Daily News* (August 3, 1971): 43.

———. "Of Fans and Sophistry, Relevance and Writers." *Washington Daily News* (August 6, 1971): 75.

————. "The Thinking Fan's Guide to Sport Writers." *Washington Daily News* (February 4, 1971): 66.

————. "Unfortunately, the Silent Majority's Serious Again." *Washington Daily News* (August 9, 1971): 54.

————. "'Ya Can't Argue With Ali's (What's That?) Sincerity." *Washington Daily News* (January 12, 1971): 42.

Marsh, Don. "It's Much Tougher to be Huff, the Politician." *Charleston Gazette* (May 9, 1970): 9.

Mayer, Martin. "How Good Is TV at Its Best?" *Harper's* (August 1960): 82–86.

Mazlish, Bruce. "Toward a Psychohistorical Inquiry: The 'Real' Richard Nixon," *Journal of Interdisciplinary History* (Autumn 1970).

McGrory, Mary. "Deliver Us from Football." *Chicago Tribune* (October 13, 1975): A4.

McMurtry, John. "Kill 'Em! Crush 'Em! Eat 'Em Raw." *Maclean's* (October 1971).

Mewshaw, Michael. "Gent." *Texas Observer* (November 30, 1973): 16.

Millman, Lefty. "Free Speech in Sports?" *Liberation News Service* #122 (November 27, 1968): 27.

————. "If the Umpires Have Balls, They'll Strike." *Liberation News Service* #125 (December 12, 1968): 17.

Mix, Ron. "I Swore I Would Quit Football." *Sports Illustrated* (September 16, 1963).

Mizell, Herbert. "Glass Speaks Up for 'Decent Majority.'" *Syracuse Post-Standard* (December 14, 1972): 15.

Moffet, Mike. "KSU Meets Nixon on 'Black Wednesday.'" *Daily Kansan* (September 16, 1970): 12.

Morgan, Thomas. "The American War Game." *Esquire* (October 1965).

————. "The Wham in Pro Football." *Esquire* (November 1959).

Morris, Jeannie. "Pro Football Players Take Political Sides." *Dubuque Telegraph-Herald* (October 8, 1972): 30.

Murphy, Austin. "It's . . . Halftime." http://www.si.com/longform/halftime/.

Murphy, Jack. "No Place for Republican Q-B." *San Diego Union* (September 21, 1967): C-1.

Murphy, Michael. "News from Esalen." *Esalen Catalog* (October–December 1974): 4.

Murray, Jim. "New Voice Speaks Up." *Los Angeles Times* (December 20, 1972): B1.

————. "Rx for a Nightmare." *Los Angeles Times* (April 29, 1976): 10.

Newnham, Blaine. "The Linebacker at the Mustard Seed." *Oakland Tribune* (May 10, 1970): 39.

————. "Wow, Like Let's Really Try to Win." *Sports Illustrated* (October 12, 1970).

"NFL Blackout Rule: Richard Nixon Hated It." *Denver Post* (July 7, 2013).

"The NFL's Role in American History (Somebody's Gotta Be Kidding)." *New York* (November 3, 1975): 41–44.

"Nixon: The Pursuit of Peace and Politics." *Time* (September 28, 1970): 6.

Oates, Bob. "Pro-Football's Flower Children." *Los Angeles Times* (June 5, 1970): F1.

Oliva, S. M. "Abolish the NFL Draft." *Reason* (April 23, 2013).

O'Neil, Paul. "The Giant Defense Is Triumph of Mind." *Life* (December 5, 1960).

Overman, Steven. "'Winning Isn't Everything. It's the Only Thing': The Origin, Attributions and Influence of a Famous Football Quote." *Football Studies* (October 1999): 77–99.

Padwe, Sandy. "Big-Time College Football Is on the Skids." *Look* (September 22, 1970).

———. "Sports and Politics Must Be Separate—At Least SOME Politics, That Is." *Philadelphia Inquirer* (December 14, 1971): 35.

Phillips, William. "A Season in the Stands." *Commentary* (July 1, 1969).

Poe, Randall. "The Writing of Sports." *Esquire* (October 1974).

Pope, Edwin. "Super-ficials Call the Plays for Those Who Come to Super." *Miami Herald* (January 14, 1967): D1.

Posnanski, Joe. "How NFL Films Transformed Football." *Sports Illustrated* (February 3, 2010).

Povich, Shirley. "Reporters Occupy Top Spot on Allen's Enemies List." *Washington Post* (November 18, 1973): D1.

Prato, Lou. "Who'll Be the First Black Coach in Pro Football?" *Sport* (May 1975).

"Probe of Pro Athletes' Draft 'Immunity' Asked." *Los Angeles Times* (December 8, 1966): C1.

Pyle, Jerry. "Sports and War." *The Christian Athlete* (January 1972): 5, 7.

Quinn, Sally. "The Old Political Football, Well Tossed." *Washington Post* (July 13, 1971): B1.

Ralbovsky, Marty. "Time the Academy Did Some Bending." *Naples Daily News* (November 26, 1970): 9B.

Rapaport, Richard. "To Build a Winning Team: An Interview with Head Coach Bill Walsh." *Harvard Business Review* (January–February 1993).

Reed, Roy. "In the South, Football Is a Religio-Social Pastime." *New York Times* (October 6, 1969): 34.

Reid, T. R. "The Stages Change, The Man Doesn't." *Washington Post* (July 13, 1980): E1.

Remnick, David. "Still on the Outside." *Sports Illustrated* (October 5, 1987).

Reston, James. "Washington: Why Mr. Nixon Goes to the Football Games." *New York Times* (December 7, 1969): 10.

Richardson, Bill. "Podolak on McGovern's Team." *Kansas City Times* (July 19, 1972): 37.

Richman, Milton. "Bill Glass Big Enough to Take on 'Swing Set.'" *Ogden Standard-Examiner* (December 20, 1972): 5-C.

———. "Vince Lombardi Considered a 'Traditionalist.'" *Ogden Standard-Examiner* (May 27, 1970): 8C.

Roberts, Mike. "Religion and the NFL: A Chaplain's Delight." *Washington Star* (November 07, 1974): D6.

———. "Religion and the NFL: Call It the Theology of Perspiration." *Washington Star* (November 6, 1974): C1, C7.

———. "Religion and the NFL: Reconciling Christianity and Violence." *Washington Star* (November 8, 1974): D1.

Rosen, Byron. "NFL Enters Bicentennial Act with Shoulder Emblem, Essay." *Washington Post* (August 5, 1975): D3.

Roswell, Gene. "The QB Takes a Stand." *New York Post* (May 26, 1967): 87.

Rudeen, Kenneth. "Sportsman of the Year." *Sports Illustrated* (January 6, 1964).

Ryan, Pat. "The Making of a Quarterback 1970." *Sports Illustrated* (December 7, 1970).

Sachare, Alex. "Many Athletes Taking Action in Support of Student Strike." *Columbia Daily Spectator* (May 6, 1970): 8.

"Sam Huff Seeks Congress Post." *Gadsden Times* (February 10, 1970): 8.

"Savagery on Sunday." *Life* (October 24, 1955): 133–37.

Schickel, Richard. "On Pro Football." *Commentary* (January 1969).

Schlesinger, Arthur. "The Amazing Success Story of 'Spiro *Who?*'" *New York Times Book Review* (June 26, 1970).

Scott, Jack. "Sports." *Ramparts* (December 1971): 67.

"The Selling of the Candidates 1970." *Newsweek* (October 19, 1970).

Shecter, Leonard. "Johnny Sample: 'I'll Break Them in Half If I Have To.'" *Sport* (January 1967): 75.

———. "The Toughest Man in Football." *Esquire* (January 1968).

Sheed, Wilfrid. "The Good Word: Unnecessary Roughness." *New York Times Book Review* (November 7, 1971): 2.

Shields, Terry. "'The Worst Thing' Stops DiNardo." *Notre Dame Observer* (November 19, 1970): 7.

Siegel, Morris. "Celler Is Tougher than Green Bay." *Washington Star* (October 14, 1966): A17.

Smith, Maureen. "New Orleans, New Football League, and New Attitudes: The American Football League All-Star Game Boycott, January 1965." In *Sports and the Racial Divide: African American and Latino Experience in an Era of Change,* ed. Michael Lomax and Kenneth Shropshire (Jackson: University Press of Mississippi, 2008), 3–22.

Smith, Red. "Lombardi's Ogre Image Not True Picture." *Milwaukee Journal* (September 3, 1970): 2:21.

Solomon, George. "NFL Teams Strive to Have God on Their Side." *Washington Post* (November 14, 1973): D6.

"The Souring of George Sauer." *Intellectual Digest* (December 1971).

"Spiro and Sports." *San Francisco Examiner* (January 22, 1971): 51.

"Student-Athletes Will Visit Vietnam." *NCAA News* (June 1970): 1, 2.

Stump, Al. "Joe Kapp: Football's Fury On and Off the Field." *True* (September 1970): 52.

———. "'Super Bowl' or 'Super Bore'?" *TV Guide* (January 12, 1974): 13.

Taaffe, William. "Footage That Can Go to Your Head." *Sports Illustrated* (September 5, 1984): 85.

Thompson, Hunter S. "Fear and Loathing at the Super Bowl." *Rolling Stone* (February 13, 1973).

———. "Fear and Loathing at the Super Bowl." *Rolling Stone* (February 28, 1974).

"360 Pros Reported Exempt from Draft." *New York Times* (April 8, 1967): S23.

Toback, James. "Longhorns and Longhairs." *Harper's* (November 1970).

Tomasky, Michael. "North Malice Forty: What the Republicanization of Testosterone Means for the Democrats." *American Prospect* (January 2005).

"Too Much Notre Dame." *New York Times* (November 3, 1980): C7.

Treadwell, Sandy. "Not Such a Bad Scene After All." *Sports Illustrated* (September 28, 1970).

Turan, Kenneth. "Meggyesy Writes, and People Read." *Washington Post* (January 24, 1971): D4.

Twombly, Wells. "An Exposé to End All Exposés." *Sporting News* (October 9, 1971): 10.

———. "Silly Putty." *San Francisco Examiner* (January 18, 1971): 49.

"Vietnam Tour Builds Morale." *NCAA News* (October 1, 1970): 2.

"The Violent Face of Pro Football." *Sports Illustrated* (October 24, 1960): 26.

"Virginia Girl Takes Top Prize for Football Essay." *New York Times* (January 18, 1976): 164.

von Hoffman, Nicholas. "The NFL's Broken Play: Congress Unifies the Fans." *Washington Post* (September 17, 1973): B1.

von Moschzisker, Felix. "Take Me Out of the Ball Game." *Life* (March 5, 1971): 14.

Wakefield, Dan. "In Defense of the Fullback." *Dissent* (Summer 1957): 311–14.

Walters, Robert. "John Wilbur: Pro McGovern." *Washington Star* (June 4, 1972): C8.

"The Washingtonians of the Year." *The Washingtonian* (January 1972): 36.

Weaver, Paul. "Captives of Melodrama." *New York Times Magazine* (August 29, 1976): 48, 55.

Weil, Gordon. "Politicians' Scramble for Support Exhausts Supply of Celebrities." *Wall Street Journal* (August 1, 1968): 1.

Whiteford, Mike. "Huff Thinks He Can Help West Virginia." *Fairmont Times* (February 9, 1970): 1, 2.

Wicker, Tom. "America Was Radicalized." *New York Times Magazine* (August 24, 1969): 94.

———. "Not Quite a Field Goal." *New York Times* (November 10, 1970).

Wiggins, David. "'The Future of College Athletics Is at Stake': Racial Turmoil on Three Predominantly White College Campuses, 1968–1972." *Journal of Sport History* (Winter 1988): 304–33.

Will, George. "Competence and the GOP." *Washington Post* (September 16, 1973): C6.

———. "The Wrath of Woody Hayes." *Washington Post* (November 19, 1974): A19.

Willoughby, William. "The Redskins: Jesus in the Locker Room." *Washington Star* (January 13, 1973): A8.

Witcover, Jules. "Nixon Campaigning Like a Head Coach." *Los Angeles Times* (October 26, 1970): 19.

Yagoda, Ben. "Not So Instant Replay." *New York Times Magazine* (December 14, 1986): 68.

Yardley, Jonathan. "Babe Ruth Still in His Heaven." *New Republic* (December 18, 1971).

Ziff, Sid. "'NFL in Action'—A Film Classic." *Los Angeles Times* (March 23, 1967): B3.

Zimmerman, Paul. "They Call It a Game." *New York Times Book Review* (September 26, 1971): 44.

Books

Abrahamsen, David. *Nixon vs. Nixon: An Emotional Tragedy* (New York: Farrar, Straus, and Giroux, 1977).

Agnew, Spiro. *The Real Spiro Agnew: Commonsense Quotations of a Household Word* (Gretna, La.: Pelican Publishing, 1970).

Albright, Joseph. *What Makes Spiro Run: The Life and Times of Spiro Agnew* (New York: Dodd, Mead, 1972).

Algeo, Matthew. *Last Team Standing: How the Steelers and the Eagles—the "Steagles"—Saved Pro Football During World War II* (Chicago: Chicago Review Press, 2013).

Allen, George. *Inside Football: Fundamentals, Strategy, and Tactics for Winning* (Boston: Allyn and Bacon, 1970).

Allen, Jennifer. *Fifth Quarter: The Scrimmage of a Football Coach's Daughter* (New York: Random House, 2000).

Ambrose, Stephen. *Nixon: The Triumph of a Politician* (New York: Simon & Schuster, 1987).

Amdur, Neil. *The Fifth Down: Democracy and the Football Revolution* (New York: Coward, McCann, and Geoghegan, 1971).

Anderson, Dave. *Countdown to Super Bowl* (New York: Random House, 1969).

Arledge, Roone. *Roone: A Memoir* (New York: HarperCollins, 2003).

Bailey, Beth, and David Farber. *America in the Seventies* (Lawrence: University Press of Kansas, 2004).

Baker, William. *Playing with God: Religion and Modern Sport* (Cambridge, Mass.: Harvard University Press, 2007).

Barra, Allen. *Big Play: Barra on Football* (Washington, D.C.: Potomac Books, 2004).

Barrett, Marvin, ed. *Survey of Broadcast Journalism 1970–1971: A State of Siege* (New York: Grosset & Dunlap, 1971).

Baskir, Lawrence, and William Strauss. *Chance and Circumstance: The Draft, the War, and the Vietnam Generation* (New York: Random House, 1978).

Beer, Tom, with George Kimball. *Sunday's Fools: Stomped, Tromped, Kicked, and Chewed in the NFL* (Boston: Houghton Mifflin, 1974).

Berkow, Ira. *Beyond the Dream: Occasional Heroes of Sports* (New York: Athenaeum, 1975).
———. *Full Swing: Hits, Runs, and Errors in a Writer's Life* (Chicago: Ivan R. Dee, 2006).

Bleier, Rocky, with Terry O'Neil. *Fighting Back* (New York: Stein and Day, 1975).

Boss, David, ed. *The Pro Football Experience* (New York: Harry N. Abrams, 1973).

Brondfield, Jerry. *Woody Hayes and the 100-Yard War* (New York: Random House, 1974).

Brown, Jimmy, with Myron Cope. *Off My Chest* (Garden City, N.Y.: Doubleday, 1964).

Brown, Larry, with William Gildea. *I'll Always Get Up* (New York: Simon & Schuster, 1973).

Bruno, Jerry, and Jeff Greenfield. *The Advance Man* (New York: William Morrow, 1971).

Butkus, Dick, and Robert W. Billings. *Stop-Action* (New York: E.P. Dutton, 1972).

Bynum, Mike, ed. *Woody Hayes: The Man and His Dynasty* (Birmingham: Gridiron Football Properties, 1991).

Callahan, Tom. *The GM: The Inside Story of a Dream Job and the Nightmares That Go with It* (New York: Crown, 2007).
———. *Johnny U: The Life and Times of Johnny Unitas* (New York: Crown Publishers, 2006).

Chudacoff, Howard. *Changing the Playbook: How Power, Profit, and Politics Transformed College Sports* (Urbana: University of Illinois Press, 2015).

Clarke, Thurston. *The Last Campaign: Robert F. Kennedy and 82 Days That Inspired America* (New York: Macmillan, 2008).

Coenen, Craig. *From Sandlots to the Super Bowl: The National Football League, 1920–1967* (Knoxville: University of Tennessee Press, 2005).

Conerly, Perian. *Backseat Quarterback* (Jackson: University Press of Mississippi, 2003).

Coover, Robert. *Whatever Happened to Gloomy Gus of the Chicago Bears?* (New York: Collier Books, 1987).

Cope, Myron. *The Game That Was* (New York: World Publishing, 1970).

Coyne, John. *The Impudent Snobs: Agnew vs. the Intellectual Establishment* (New Rochelle, N.Y.: Arlington House, 1972).

Crepeau, Richard. *NFL Football: A History of America's New National Pastime* (Champaign: University of Illinois Press, 2014).

Crouse, Timothy. *The Boys on the Bus: Riding with the Campaign Press Corps* (New York: Random House, 1972).

Csonka, Larry, and Jim Kiick, with Dave Anderson. *Always on the Run* (New York: Random House, 1973).

Curran, Bob. *The $400,000 Quarterback, or: The League That Came in from the Cold* (New York: Macmillan, 1965).

———. *Pro Football's Rag Days* (Englewood Cliffs, N.J.: Prentice-Hall, 1970).

———. *The Violence Game* (New York: Macmillan, 1966).

Curtis, Mike, with Bill Gilbert. *Keep Off My Turf* (Philadelphia: J.B. Lippincott, 1972).

Daly, Dan, and Bob O'Donnell. *The Pro Football Chronicle* (New York: Macmillan, 1990).

Davis, Jeff. *Rozelle: Czar of the NFL* (New York: McGraw-Hill, 2007).

DeBenedetti, Charles. *An American Ordeal: The Antiwar Movement of the Vietnam Era* (Syracuse, N.Y.: Syracuse University Press, 1990).

Deford, Frank. *Lite Reading* (New York: Penguin, 1984).

DeLillo, Don. *End Zone* (New York: Penguin, 1972).

Demas, Lane. *Integrating the Gridiron: Black Civil Rights and American College Football* (New Brunswick, N.J.: Rutgers University Press, 2010).

Deveney, Sean. *Fun City: John Lindsay, Joe Namath, and How Sports Saved New York in the 1960s* (New York: Sports Publishing, 2015).

Dickey, Glenn. *The Jock Empire: Its Rise and Deservéd Fall* (Radnor, Pa.: Chilton, 1974).

Domres, Marty, and Robert Smith. *Bump and Run: The Days and Nights of a Rookie Quarterback* (New York: Bantam, 1971).

Dougherty, Richard. *Goodbye, Mr. Christian: A Personal Account of McGovern's Rise and Fall* (Garden City, N.Y.: Doubleday, 1973).

Dowling, Tom. *Coach: A Season with Lombardi* (New York: W.W. Norton, 1970).

Easterbrook, Gregg. *The King of Sports: Why Football Must Be Reformed* (New York: St. Martin's, 2014).

Edwards, Harry. *The Revolt of the Black Athlete* (New York: Free Press, 1969).

Egerton, John. *The Americanization of Dixie: The Southernization of America* (New York: Harper's Magazine Press, 1974).

Ehrlichman, John. *Witness to Power: The Nixon Years* (New York: Simon and Schuster, 1982).

Elias, Robert. *The Empire Strikes Out: How Baseball Sold U.S. Foreign Policy and Promoted the American Way Abroad* (New York: New Press, 2010).

Eskenazi, Gerald. *There Were Giants in Those Days* (New York: Grosset & Dunlap, 1976).

Evans, Norm. *On God's Squad* (Carol Stream, Ill.: Creation House, 1971).

Fatsis, Stefan. *A Few Seconds of Panic* (New York: Penguin, 2008).

The First Fifty Years: A Celebration of the National Football League in Its Fifty-Sixth Season (New York: Ridge Press/Benjamin, 1975).

Frei, Terry. *Horns, Hogs, and Nixon Coming: Texas v. Arkansas in Dixie's Last Stand* (New York: Simon & Schuster, 2002).

Frommer, Harvey. *When It Was Just a Game: Remembering the First Super Bowl* (Lanham, Md.: Taylor, 2015).

Gardner, Paul. *Nice Guys Finish Last: Sport and American Life* (New York: Universe Books, 1974).

Gartner, Michael. *Ted Williams, Sam the Genius, and Other Sports Stories from the Wall Street Journal* (Princeton, N.J.: Dow Jones Books, 1970).

Gent, Peter. *North Dallas Forty* (Toronto: Sport Classic Books, 2003).

Gifford, Frank, and Harry Waters. *The Whole Ten Yards* (New York: Random House, 1993).

Gildea, William, and Kenneth Turan. *The Future Is Now: George Allen, Pro Football's Most Controversial Coach* (Boston: Houghton Mifflin, 1972).

Glass, Bill. *Get in the Game* (Waco, Tex.: Word Books, 1965).

Glass, Bill, and William Pinson Jr. *Don't Blame the Game: An Answer to Super Star Swingers and a Look at What's Right with Sports* (Waco, Tex.: Word Books, 1972).

Gold, Victor. *I Don't Need You When I'm Right: The Confessions of a Washington PR Man* (New York: Morrow, 1975).

———. *PR as in President: A Pro Looks at Press Agents, Media, and the 1976 Candidates* (Garden City, N.Y.: Doubleday, 1977).

Goldenson, Leonard. *Beating the Odds: The Untold Story Behind the Rise of ABC* (New York: Charles Scribner's Sons, 1991).

Greenberg, David. *Nixon's Shadow: The History of an Image* (New York: W.W. Norton, 2003).

Grier, Rosey. *Rosey, an Autobiography: The Gentle Giant* (Tulsa, Okla.: Honor Books, 1986).

Gunther, Marc. *The House That Roone Built* (Boston: Little, Brown, 1994).

Halberstam, David. *The Education of a Coach* (New York: Hyperion, 2005).

Haldeman, H. R. *The Haldeman Diaries* (New York: G.P. Putnam, 1994).

Harrington, Michael. *The Other America* (New York: Simon & Schuster, 1997).

Harris, David. *The League: The Rise and Decline of the NFL* (New York: Bantam, 1986).

Hart, Gary. *Right from the Start: A Chronicle of the McGovern Campaign* (New York: Quadrangle, 1973).

Hayes, W. Woodrow. *You Win with PEOPLE!* (Columbus, Ohio: Typographic Printing, 1973).

Hearings Before the Antitrust Subcommittee of the Committee on the Judiciary, House of Representatives, 89th Congress, Second Session, on S. 3817 (Washington, D.C.: Government Printing Office, 1966).

Hefley, James. *Running with God: The New Christian Athletes* (New York: Avon Books, 1975).

Hiebert, Ray, Robert Jones, John d'Arc Lorenz, and Ernest Lotito, ed. *The Political Image Merchants: Strategies for the Seventies* (Washington, D.C.: Acropolis Books, 1975).

Hoffman, Shirl James. *Good Game: Christianity and the Culture of Sports* (Waco, Tex.: Baylor University Press, 2010).

Huff, Sam, with Kristine Setting Clark. *Controlled Violence: On the Field and in the Booth* (Chicago: Triumph Books, 2011).

Huff, Sam, with Leonard Shapiro. *Tough Stuff* (New York: Macmillan, 1989).

Isaacs, Neil. *Jock Culture, U.S.A.* (New York: Norton, 1978).

Isaacs, Stan. *Jim Brown: The Golden Year 1964* (Englewood Cliffs, N.J.: Prentice-Hall, 1970).

Izenberg, Jerry. *How Many Miles to Camelot?* (New York: Holt, Rinehart and Winston, 1972).

———. *The Jerry Izenberg Collection* (Dallas: Taylor Publishing, 1989).

———. *The Rivals* (New York: Holt, Rinehart and Winston, 1968).

———. *Rozelle: A Biography* (Lincoln: University of Nebraska Press, 2014).

Jenkins, Dan. *Semi-Tough* (New York: Atheneum, 1984).

Kabaservice, Geoffrey. *Rule and Ruin: The Downfall of Moderation and the Destruction of the Republican Party, from Eisenhower to the Tea Party* (New York: Oxford University Press, 2012).

Kemp, Jack. *An American Renaissance: A Strategy for the 1980s* (New York: Harper & Row, 1979).

Klein, Dave. *The Football Mystique* (New York: Signet, 1978).

Klein, Herbert. *Making It Perfectly Clear* (Garden City, N.Y.: Doubleday, 1980).

Kondracke, Morton, and Fred Barnes, *Jack Kemp: The Bleeding-Heart Conservative Who Changed America* (New York: Sentinel, 2015).

Koppett, Leonard. *The Rise and Fall of the Press Box* (Toronto: Sport Media Publishing, 2003).

Koppett, Leonard, ed. *The New York Times at the Super Bowl* (New York: Quadrangle, 1974).

Lair, Meredith. *Armed with Abundance: Consumerism and Soldiering in the Vietnam War* (Chapel Hill: University of North Carolina Press, 2011).

Lasch, Christopher. *The Culture of Narcissism* (New York: W.W. Norton, 1991).

Lemon, Richard. *The Troubled American* (New York: Simon & Schuster, 1970).

Lipsyte, Robert. *SportsWorld: An American Dreamland* (New York: Quadrangle, 1975).

Lombardi, Vince, with W. C. Heinz. *Run to Daylight!* (Englewood Cliffs, N.J.: Prentice-Hall, 1963).

Lombardi, Vince, Jr. *What It Takes to Be #1: Vince Lombardi on Leadership* (New York: McGraw-Hill, 2001).

Lombardo, John. *A Fire to Win: The Life and Times of Woody Hayes* (New York: Thomas Dunne, 2005).

Lyons, Robert. *On Any Given Sunday: A Life of Bert Bell* (Philadelphia: Temple University Press, 2009).

MacCambridge, Michael. *America's Game: The Epic Story of How Pro Football Captured a Nation* (New York: Random House, 2004).

———. *The Franchise: A History of Sports Illustrated Magazine* (New York: Hyperion, 1997).

———. *Lamar Hunt: A Life in Sports* (Kansas City, Mo.: Andrews & McMeel, 2012).

MacNeil, Robert. *The People Machine: The Influence of Television on American Politics* (New York: Harper & Row, 1968).

Mandell, Arnold. *The Nightmare Season* (New York: Random House, 1976).

Mann, Jack. *The Decline and Fall of the New York Yankees* (New York: Simon & Schuster, 1967).

Maraniss, David. *When Pride Still Mattered: A Life of Vince Lombardi* (New York: Simon & Schuster, 1999).

Martin, Roger L. *Fixing the Game: Bubbles, Crashes, and What Capitalism Can Learn from the NFL* (Boston: Harvard Business Review Press, 2011).

Mason, Robert. *Richard Nixon and the Quest for a New Majority* (Chapel Hill: University of North Carolina Press, 2004).

Maule, Tex. *The Game,* revised ed. (New York: Random House, 1967).

———. *The Pro Season* (Garden City, N.Y.: Doubleday, 1970).

May, Ernest, and Janet Fraser, ed. *Campaign '72: The Managers Speak.* (Cambridge, Mass.: Harvard University Press, 1973).

McCarthy, Richard. *Elections for Sale* (Boston: Houghton Mifflin, 1972).

McGinniss, Joe. *The Selling of the President, 1968* (New York: Trident Press, 1969).

Meggyesy, Dave. *Out of Their League* (Berkeley, Calif.: Ramparts Press, 1970).

Merchant, Larry. *. . . and Every Day You Take Another Bite* (Garden City, N.Y.: Doubleday, 1971).

———. *The National Football Lottery* (New York: Holt, Rinehart, and Winston, 1973).

Michener, James. *Sports in America* (New York: Random House, 1976).

Miller, Jeff. *Going Long: The Wild 10-Year Saga of the American Football League in the Words of Those Who Lived It* (Chicago: Contemporary Books, 2003).

Namath, Joe Willie, and Dick Schaap. *I Can't Wait Until Tomorrow . . . 'Cause I Get Better-Looking Every Day* (New York: Random House, 1969).

Napolitan, Joseph. *The Election Game and How to Win It* (Garden City, N.Y.: Doubleday, 1972).

Nixon, Richard. *In the Arena* (New York: Simon & Schuster, 2013).

———. *RN: The Memoirs of Richard Nixon* (New York: Grosset & Dunlap, 1978).

Novak, Michael. *The Joy of Sports,* revised ed. (Lanham, Md.: Rowman & Littlefield, 1993).

———. *Unmeltable Ethnics: Politics and Culture in American Life* (New Brunswick, N.J.: Transaction Publishers, 1996).

O'Brien, Michael. *Vince: A Personal Biography of Vince Lombardi* (New York: Morrow, 1987).

Offen, Neil. *God Save the Players: The Funny, Crazy, Sometimes Violent World of Sports Fans* (Chicago: Playboy Press, 1974).

Olsen, Jack. *The Black Athlete: A Shameful Story* (New York: Time-Life Books, 1968).

Oriard, Michael. *Bowled Over: Big-Time College Football from the Sixties to the BCS Era* (Chapel Hill: University of North Carolina Press, 2009).

———. *Brand NFL: Making and Selling America's Favorite Sport* (Chapel Hill: University of North Carolina Press, 2010).

———. *King Football: Sport and Spectacle in the Golden Age of Radio and Newsreels, Movies and Magazines, the Weekly and the Daily Press* (Chapel Hill: University of North Carolina Press, 2001)

Osborne, John. *The Second Year of the Nixon Watch* (New York: Liveright, 1971).

Otto, Jim, with Dave Newhouse. *Jim Otto: The Pain of Glory* (New York: Skyhorse Publishing, 2012).

Parrish, Bernie. *They Call It a Game* (New York: Dell, 1971).

Patton, Phil. *Razzle-Dazzle: The Curious Marriage of Television and Professional Football* (New York: Dial Press, 1984).

Peterson, Robert W. *Pigskin: The Early Years of Pro Football* (New York: Oxford University Press, 1997).

Plimpton, George. *Paper Lion* (New York: Pocket Books, 1966).

Plunkett, Jim, and Dave Newhouse. *The Jim Plunkett Story* (New York: Arbor House, 1981).

Pro Sports: Should Government Intervene? (Roundtable at American Enterprise Institute, February 22, 1977).

Proceedings of the Forty-Seventh Annual Meeting of the American Football Coaches Association (January 1970).

Proceedings of the Forty-Eighth Annual Meeting of the American Football Coaches Association (January 1971).

Public Papers of the Presidents of the United States: Richard M. Nixon, 1969–1974.

Public Papers of the Presidents of the United States: Gerald R. Ford, 1974–1976.

Ralbovsky, Marty. *The Namath Effect* (Englewood Cliffs, N.J.: Prentice-Hall, 1976).

———. *Super Bowl: Of Men, Myths, and Moments* (New York: Hawthorne, 1971).

Rand, Jonathan. *The Year That Changed the Game: The Memorable Months That Shaped Pro Football* (Washington, D.C.: Potomac Books, 2008).

Reagan, Ronald. *Ronald Reagan: A Life in Letters* (New York: Free Press, 2003).

Reeves, Richard. *President Reagan: The Triumph of Imagination* (New York: Simon & Schuster, 2005).

Ripon Society. *Jaws of Victory: The Game-Plan Politics of 1972, the Crisis of the Republican Party, and the Future of the Constitution* (Boston: Little, Brown, 1972).

Roberts, Michael. *Fans! How We Go Crazy Over Sports* (Washington, D.C.: New Republic, 1976).

Roberts, Randy, and Ed Krzemienski. *Rising Tide: Bear Bryant, Joe Namath, and Dixie's Last Quarter* (New York: Twelve, 2013).

Rogin, Michael. *Ronald Reagan the Movie: And Other Episodes in Political Demonology* (Berkeley: University of California Press, 1988).

Rosenbloom, David Lee. *The Election Men: Professional Campaign Managers and American Democracy* (New York: Quadrangle Books, 1973).

Ross, Charles. *Mavericks, Money, and Men: The AFL, Black Players, and the Evolution of Modern Football* (Philadelphia: Temple University Press, 2016).

———. *Outside the Lines: African Americans and the Integration of the National Football League* (New York: New York University Press, 1999).

Roth, Philip. *Our Gang* (New York: Bantam, 1971).

Ryczek, William. *Crash of the Titans: The Early Years of the New York Jets and the AFL* (Jefferson, N.C.: McFarland, 2009).

Sabato, Larry. *The Rise of Political Consultants: New Ways of Winning Elections* (New York: Basic Books, 1981).

Safire, William. *Before the Fall: An Inside View of the pre-Watergate White House* (Garden City, N.Y.: Doubleday, 1975).

Sample, Johnny, with Fred J. Hamilton and Sonny Schwartz. *Confessions of a Dirty Ballplayer* (New York: Dial Press, 1970).

Sandbrook, Dominic. *Mad as Hell: The Crisis of the 1970s and the Rise of the Populist Right* (New York: Knopf, 2011).

Sayers, Gale, with Al Silverman. *I Am Third* (New York: Viking Press, 1970).

Scott, Jack. *The Athletic Revolution* (New York: Free Press, 1971).

Shaw, David. *Journalism Today: A Changing Press for a Changing America* (New York: Harper's College Press, 1977).

Shecter, Leonard. *The Jocks* (Indianapolis: Bobbs-Merrill, 1969).

Silverman, Al, ed. *The Best of Sport, 1946–1971* (New York: Viking Press, 1971).

Simpson, O. J., with Pete Axthelm, *O.J.: The Education of a Rich Rookie* (New York: Macmillan, 1970).

Small, Melvin. *At the Water's Edge: American Politics and the Vietnam War* (Chicago: Ivan R. Dee, 2005).

———. *Covering Dissent: The Media and the Anti-Vietnam War Movement* (New Brunswick, N.J.: Rutgers University Press, 1994).

Solberg, Carl. *Hubert Humphrey: A Biography* (New York: W.W. Norton, 1984).

Small, Melvin, ed. *A Companion to Richard Nixon* (Malden, Mass.: Wiley-Blackwell, 2011).

Sperber, Murray. *Shake Down the Thunder: The Creation of Notre Dame Football* (New York: Henry Holt, 1993).

Stiles, Kristine, and Peter Howard Selz, eds. *Theories and Documents of Contemporary Art: A Sourcebook of Artists' Writings* (Berkeley: University of California Press, 1996).

Stram, Hank, with Lou Sahadi. *They're Playing My Game* (New York: Morrow, 1986).

Tarkenton, Fran, as told to Jack Olsen. *Better Scramble than Lose* (New York: Four Winds Press, 1969).

Tarkenton, Fran, and Jim Klobuchar. *Tarkenton* (New York: Harper & Row, 1976).

Tarkenton, Fran, as told to Brock Yates. *Broken Patterns: The Education of a Quarterback* (New York: Simon & Schuster, 1971).

Tatum, Jack, with Bill Kushner. *They Call Me Assassin* (New York: Everest House, 1979).

Telander, Rick. *The Hundred-Yard Lie: The Corruption of College Football and What We Can Do to Stop It* (New York: Simon & Schuster, 1989).

Thompson, Hunter S. *Fear and Loathing in America: The Brutal Odyssey of an Outlaw Journalist 1968–1976* (New York: Simon & Schuster, 2000).

———. *Fear and Loathing on the Campaign Trail '72* (New York: Simon & Schuster, 2012).

———. *The Great Shark Hunt: Strange Tales from a Strange Time* (New York: Summit Books, 1979).

Toback, James. *Jim: The Author's Self-Centered Memoir on the Great Jim Brown* (Garden City, N.Y.: Doubleday, 1971).

Tunnell, Emlen, with Bill Gleason. *Footsteps of a Giant* (Garden City, N.Y.: Doubleday, 1966).

Twombly, Wells. *Blanda: Alive and Kicking* (Los Angeles: Nash Publishing, 1972).

Underwood, John. *The Death of an American Game: The Crisis in Football* (Boston: Little, Brown, 1979).

Vare, Robert. *Buckeye: A Study of Coach Woody Hayes and the Ohio State Football Machine* (New York: Harper's Magazine Press, 1974).

Vaughn, Stephen. *Ronald Reagan in Hollywood: Movies and Politics* (New York: Cambridge University Press, 1994).

Vogan, Travis. *Keepers of the Flame: NFL Films and the Rise of Sports Media* (Urbana: University of Illinois Press, 2014).

Wakefield, Dan. *New York in the Fifties* (Boston: Houghton Mifflin, 1992).

Walt, Gen. Lewis. *The Eleventh Hour* (Ottawa, Ill.: Caroline House, 1979).

Watterson, John Sayle. *College Football: History, Spectacle, Controversy* (Baltimore: Johns Hopkins University Press, 2002).

———. *The Games Presidents Play: Sports and the Presidency* (Baltimore: Johns Hopkins University Press, 2006).

Weiss, Don, with Chuck Day. *The Making of the Super Bowl: The Inside Story of the World's Greatest Sporting Event* (Chicago: Contemporary Books, 2003).

Wells, Tom. *The War Within: America's Battle Over Vietnam* (Berkeley: University of California Press, 1994).

Wiebusch, John, ed. *Lombardi* (Chicago: Triumph Books, 1971).

———. *The NFL Super Bowl Companion: Personal Reflections on America's Favorite Game.* (Chicago: Triumph Books, 2002).

Witcover, Jules. *White Knight: The Rise of Spiro Agnew* (New York: Random House, 1972).

Woodward, Stanley. *Sports Page* (New York: Simon and Schuster, 1949).

Wright Rigueur, Leah. *The Loneliness of the Black Republican* (Princeton, N.J.: Princeton University Press, 2015).

Yost, Mark. *Tailgating, Sacks, and Salary Caps: How the NFL Became the Most Successful Sports League in History* (Chicago: Kaplan Publishing, 2006).

Zang, David. *SportsWars: Athletes in the Age of Aquarius* (Fayetteville: University of Arkansas Press, 2001).

Zeoli, Billy. *Supergoal: Great Football Pros on the Game of Life* (Old Tappan, N.J.: Fleming H. Revell, 1972).

Zimmerman, Paul. *The Last Season of Weeb Ewbank* (New York: Farrar, Straus, and Giroux, 1974).

———. *A Thinking Man's Guide to Pro Football* (New York: Warner Paperback Library, 1971).

Zirin, Dave. *What's My Name, Fool? Sports and Resistance in the United States* (Chicago: Haymarket Books, 2005).

Index

celebrity of, 14, 149; endorsements by, 7, 77, 146–47; and unions, 151, 157–58; in Vietnam, 69; *The Violent World of Sam Huff*, 30, 32–38, 77

Humphrey, Hubert, 137–41, 146, *147*

Hunt, Lamar, 31, 58, 59–60, 64

ideology, 6, 157, 188–90, 198. *See also* conservatism/conservatives; liberalism/liberals; radicalism/radicals

imagery: in *Knute Rockne, All American*, 8; of Reagan as the Gipper, 213–14; Republican use of, 4; of violence, 41, 94

imperialism, 160, 172

individualism: in business, 202; and collectivization, 59, 63–64, 81; in films, 50–51; in player radicalism, 161–62, 168; as un-American, 171

inequality/inequities, 56–57, 184

Inside Football (Allen), 196, 198–99

Instant Replay (Kramer), 95

intellectual appreciation of football, 12, 13–19, 20–23, 32–33, 52, 176

In the Arena (Nixon), 108

Isaacs, Stan, 189

Ivy League, 117–18

Izenberg, Jerry, 16–19, 63, 74–75, 86, 98, 102–3

Jackson, Phil, 174

Jenkins, Dan, 94; *Semi-Tough*, 75

Jocks, The (Shecter), 86

John Birch Society, 143

Johnson, Lyndon, 205–6

Johnson, Rafer, 134, 136–37

Kahn, Roger, 1, 27–28

Kaine, Elinor, 94

Kalsu, Bob, 71

Kansas State University, 122–25

Kapp, Joe, 4, 38, 160

Kastenmeier, Robert, 59

Keep Off My Turf (Curtis), 171–72

Kemp, Jack: on the AFL/NFL merger, 60; on collectivization, 63, 64; congressional campaign of, 106, 153–57, *155*; endorsement by, 7; on football and

American values, 170; "Football and the Free Speech Movement," 152–53; on football as capitalism, 97; as a player-politician, 86, 149, 152–53; and players' unions, 153, 158; on racial equality, 95

Kempton, Murray, 176, 183

Kennedy, John F., 54

Kennedy, Robert F., 133, 136–37, 185

Kennedy family, 134–35

Kensil, Jim, 17–18

Kent State, 86–87, 120

Kilroy, Bucko, 11

Kindred, Dave, 86

King, Larry L., 200

Kissinger, Henry, 55

Klein, Herb, 97, 116–17, 130, 152, 153–54

Knute Rockne, All American, 8, 208–13

Koppett, Leonard, 93, 95, 103–4

Kraft, Joseph, 100, 111

Kramer, Jerry, 176, 186–87; *Instant Replay*, 95

Kuharich, Joe, 201

Kuhn v. Flood, 54

Laird, Melvin, 42

Landry, Tom, 168

language of football, 51, 88, 92–93, 183, 206

Lasch, Christopher: *The Culture of Narcissism*, 22

Layne, Bobby, 14

"League Think," 18

Leary, Timothy, 5, 85

legislators, 53–54, 55–56, 59–60

Levathes, Kiki: "Sports and the Intellectual," 100

liberalism/liberals, 4–5, 6, 26, 95–97, 98–102, 172

Liberation News Service, 2, 159

Lipsyte, Robert, 48, 98–99, 100, 103, 120, 132, 191; *Sportsworld: An American Dreamland*, 86

Lombardi, Vince: aphorisms of, 190–92, 203; as a businessman, 200, 202, 203; ideals of, 183–84, 186–87, 188–91; memorial honors for, 187–88, *188*; on player radicals, 168; as a political figure,

National Guard, 71–72
nationalism, 94
National Unity Week, 117
Nedzi, Lucien, 71–72
Nelson, Mariah Burton, 94
New Breed, The (NFL Films), 49–50
Newman, Edwin, 88
Newman, Wallace, 110, 123–24, 126, 135, 175
new politics: campaign consultants in, 87–93; candidates in, 94, 147–50; celebrities in, 8, 88, 158; coaches in, 88, 182–83
New York Times, 14, 93, 112
NFL (National Football League): as an American institution, 78–81; branding of, 2–3, 16–17; legislators and, 53–54, 55–56; merger of with the AFL, 6–7, 18–19, 55, 57–62, 63–64; and nostalgia, 76–77; political exploitation by, 73–75; promotions of, 2–3, 12, 33, 55–56, 81; publications of, 6, 12–13, 23–28; public relations in popularity of, 13–19; and Vietnam, 66–73; violence and intellectualism in, 20–23
NFL Creative Services Division, 12–13; *First 50 Years*, 24–28; *More Than a Game*, 26; *Pro Football Experience*, 27
NFL Films: aesthetics in, 41, 42, 47, 51, 221n20; Apollo 11 film by, 73–74; comedy in, 43; development and messaging of, 40–43; narration in, 43, 44–45, 46–48; *The New Breed*, 49–50; *Pro Football's Longest Day*, 44–45, 45, 48–49; "Rebel with a Cause," 50; Super Bowl IV film, 201; *They Call It Pro Football*, 45–49, 49, 51–52, 201; *This is the NFL*, 42
NFL Properties, 18
Nixon, Richard: and Allen, 183, 192–99, 195; *In the Arena*, 108; athlete endorsements of, 135, 146–47, 148; in blackout legislation, 62–63; college visits by, 113–15, 119–30; election of, 6; on football as second vocation, 92; on football's popularity, 2; football symbolism invoked by, 143; and Kemp, 153–54; and Lombardi, 184–85, 187–88, 188, 191; Meggyesy on, 161; in

NFL marketing, 3; in parodies, 96; as playcaller, 146, 251–52n22; and political protests, 115–19; praying with players, 173; at Redskins practice, 196, 197; and Sayers, 131; Southern strategy of, 130–32; and Starr, 126–27, 127; and the Super Bowl, 103; televised addresses by, 89; use of football by, 7, 86, 108–10, 111–15, 132; Watergate, 93, 198–200, 205
Nixon administration, 4, 7, 108–9, 119–20, 205
Noll, Chuck, 11
North Dallas Forty (Gent), 15
nostalgia, 76–77
Novak, Michael, 16, 96

O'Brien, Lawrence, 55, 61–62
Ohio State University, 128
"Okie from Muskogee" (Haggard), 111–12, 233n8
Oliver, Chip, 169, 170; *High for the Game*, 159–60
On God's Squad (Evans), 174
Orange Bowl, 1971, 117
Oriard, Michael, 13, 161–62, 164
Otto, Jim, 170
Our Gang (Roth), 109
Out of Their League (Meggyesy), 161, 162–63, 175–76, 246n14
owners, 59–60, 63, 66, 139–40

Packard, Vance: *The Hidden Persuaders*, 87
Page, Alan, 147
Paper Lion (Plimpton), 35, 39–40
parity, competitive, 56–66
parodies, 23, 41, 75, 96
Parrish, Bernie, 66, 166, 175; *They Call It a Game*, 37, 66, 159–60
Parseghian, Ara, 164
partisanship, 73, 74–75, 124
patriotism, 21, 55–56, 73–75, 81, 103–4
performance: by athletes, 13–14, 36–38; in elections, 89; by Lombardi, 186, 191–92; in NFL Films, 45–46, 201
personality, American, 206
Phillips, Donald: *Run to Win: Vince Lombardi on Coaching and Leadership*, 202

JESSE BERRETT earned a PhD in History at the University of California, Berkeley. He has worked as a rock critic, television columnist, and book reviewer. He teaches history at University High School in San Francisco.

SPORT AND SOCIETY

A Sporting Time: New York City and the Rise of Modern Athletics, 1820–70
  Melvin L. Adelman
Sandlot Seasons: Sport in Black Pittsburgh   *Rob Ruck*
West Ham United: The Making of a Football Club   *Charles Korr*
Beyond the Ring: The Role of Boxing in American Society   *Jeffrey T. Sammons*
John L. Sullivan and His America   *Michael T. Isenberg*
Television and National Sport: The United States and Britain   *Joan M. Chandler*
The Creation of American Team Sports: Baseball and Cricket, 1838–72   *George B. Kirsch*
City Games: The Evolution of American Urban Society and the Rise of Sports
  Steven A. Riess
The Brawn Drain: Foreign Student-Athletes in American Universities   *John Bale*
The Business of Professional Sports   *Edited by Paul D. Staudohar and James A. Mangan*
Fritz Pollard: Pioneer in Racial Advancement   *John M. Carroll*
A View from the Bench: The Story of an Ordinary Player on a Big-Time Football Team
  (*formerly* Go Big Red! The Story of a Nebraska Football Player)   *George Mills*
Sport and Exercise Science: Essays in the History of Sports Medicine   *Edited by*
  Jack W. Berryman and Roberta J. Park
Minor League Baseball and Local Economic Development   *Arthur T. Johnson*
Harry Hooper: An American Baseball Life   *Paul J. Zingg*
Cowgirls of the Rodeo: Pioneer Professional Athletes   *Mary Lou LeCompte*
Sandow the Magnificent: Eugen Sandow and the Beginnings of Bodybuilding
  David Chapman
Big-Time Football at Harvard, 1905: The Diary of Coach Bill Reid   *Edited by*
  Ronald A. Smith
Leftist Theories of Sport: A Critique and Reconstruction   *William J. Morgan*
Babe: The Life and Legend of Babe Didrikson Zaharias   *Susan E. Cayleff*
Stagg's University: The Rise, Decline, and Fall of Big-Time Football at Chicago
  Robin Lester
Muhammad Ali, the People's Champ   *Edited by Elliott J. Gorn*
People of Prowess: Sport, Leisure, and Labor in Early Anglo-America   *Nancy L. Struna*
The New American Sport History: Recent Approaches and Perspectives   *Edited by*
  S. W. Pope
Making the Team: The Cultural Work of Baseball Fiction   *Timothy Morris*
Making the American Team: Sport, Culture, and the Olympic Experience   *Mark Dyreson*
Viva Baseball! Latin Major Leaguers and Their Special Hunger   *Samuel O. Regalado*
Touching Base: Professional Baseball and American Culture in the Progressive Era
  (rev. ed.)   *Steven A. Riess*
Red Grange and the Rise of Modern Football   *John M. Carroll*
Golf and the American Country Club   *Richard J. Moss*
Extra Innings: Writing on Baseball   *Richard Peterson*
Global Games   *Maarten Van Bottenburg*
The Sporting World of the Modern South   *Edited by Patrick B. Miller*
Female Gladiators: Gender, Law, and Contact Sport in America   *Sarah K. Fields*

The University of Illinois Press
is a founding member of the
Association of American University Presses.

University of Illinois Press
1325 South Oak Street
Champaign, IL 61820-6903
www.press.uillinois.edu